The Southern Federalists, 1800–1816

The Southern Federalists 1800–1816

James H. Broussard

Louisiana State University Press

Baton Rouge and London

Manufactured in the United States of America

Design: Dwight Agner
Typeface: VIP Aster
Composition: LSU Press
Printing: Thomson-Shore, Inc.
Binding: John H. Dekker & Sons, Inc.

Chapters 15 and 20 appeared in slightly different versions in the *North Carolina Historical Review*, Winter, 1978, and the *Journal of Southern History*, February, 1977, respectively, and are reprinted by permission.

LIBRARY OF CONGRESS CATALOGING IN PUBLICATION DATA

Broussard, James H , 1941–
The Southern Federalists, 1800–1816.

Bibliography: p.
Includes index.
1. Southern States—Politics and government—1775–1865.
2. Federal Party. Southern States. 3. United States—Politics and government—1789–1815. I. Title.
F213.B76 320.9'75'03 78–2374
ISBN 0–8071–0288–1

To My Mother and Father

CONTENTS

Preface xi

Part One **Southern Federalists and the New Nation**

1 / The South in 1800 3
2 / The Election of 1800 16
3 / Facing the New Order 32

Part Two **Southern Federalists in National Politics: The Decline, 1801–1807**

4 / Defending Federalist Men and Measures, 1801–1807 43
5 / Attacking the Jeffersonian Program, 1801–1807 56
6 / Southern Federalists and Foreign Affairs, 1801–1807 68
7 / The Decline of Southern Federalism, 1801–1807 80

Part Three **Southern Federalists in National Politics: The Revival, 1808–1816**

8 / The Embargo Election, 1808 95
9 / Federalists and Domestic Affairs, 1807–1812 110
10 / Federalists and the Drift Toward War, 1809–1812 121
11 / The Election of 1812 139
12 / The Semiloyal Opposition, 1812–1815 154
13 / What Became of the Southern Federalists? 174

Part Four **The Southern Federalists in State Politics**

14 / The Virginia Federalists 199
15 / The North Carolina Federalists 215
16 / The South Carolina Federalists 235
17 / The Georgia Federalists 247
18 / Federalist Party Organization in the South 257
19 / The Southern Federalist Press 277
20 / Federalists in the Southern Legislatures 292

Part Five **Federalists and Southern Society**

21 / Federalism, Democracy, and Slavery 307
22 / Southern Federalists and Education 321
23 / Federalists and Banking 332
24 / Federalists and Southern Economic Development 350

Part Six **Who Were the Southern Federalist Voters?**

25 / Past Political Divisions and Party Affiliation 363
26 / Economic Status and Party Affiliation 375
27 / Demographic Patterns and Party Affiliation 388

Maps Showing Party Alignment by County 405
Bibliography 409
Index 429

TABLES

1 / Voting Behavior of Southern Congressmen, 1790–1797 11
2 / Results of Southern Congressional Elections, 1800–1807 86
3 / Votes of Southern Federalists on Nationalist Measures in Congress, 1815–1818 188
4 / Relation of Federalist Strength, 1800–1816 and Whig Strength, 1836–1848 195
5 / South Carolina Assembly Roll Call Votes on Wider Suffrage 243
6 / Age of Southern Federalist Leaders, 1800–1815 275
7 / Southern Federalist Newspapers, 1800–1816 281
8 / The Southern Party Press, 1800–1816 283
9 / Approximate Party Strength in Southern Legislatures, 1800–1816 294
10 / Level of Party Unity in South Atlantic Legislatures, 1800–1815: Indexes of Cohesion on Important Roll Calls in Lower Houses in Selected Years 300
11 / Legislative Votes on Bills Restricting Slaves and Free Negroes 319
12 / North Carolina Legislative Votes on the Antiuniversity Bill 325
13 / Comparison of Federalist Party Strength, 1800–1816, and Vote on the Constitution, 1788–1790 367
14 / Federalist Strength, 1800–1816, and Per Capita Wealth 385
15 / Testing the Generational Theory Against the 1810 Census 391
16 / Median Percentage Change in White Population, 1800–1820, for Federalist and Republican Counties 392
17 / Religion and Party Affiliation: Distribution of Church Accommodations (1850 Census) in Federalist and Republican Counties 396
18 / Division of Population in Federalist and Republican Counties According to National Origin, 1790 400

PREFACE

AMERICANS invented the first modern political parties. Although the machinery was not perfected until the Age of Jackson, the preceding generation built the working models. Because the first party system, which was created in the 1790s and matured after 1800, was the beginning of a new political age in world history, it has been increasingly studied of late. Sound monographs now exist for both the Federalist and Republican parties in many states; and excellent general studies cover the ideological origins of parties, the growth of Republican organization, and the beginnings of southern Federalism. However, the only general works dealing with the Federalist party after its national defeat in 1800 are concerned almost entirely with northern Federalists.

The greatest single gap in our knowledge of the first party system concerns the Federalist party in that half of the nation south of the Potomac. Even after a southern-dominated Republican party seized the national government in 1800, a sizable minority of southerners continued to support the Federalist cause through a decade and a half of unrelieved defeat. Who were these voters and what induced them to behave in this way? How much did the southern Federalists resemble their northern brethren in their reactions to the new Jeffersonian age? Aside from national questions, what was the role of Federalists in southern state and local issues? How well was the party organized on the hustings, in the press, and within the legislatures? How influential were its leaders in southern social and economic development? What became of southern Federalist leaders and voters after their party disappeared?

This book is directed toward answering such questions. It deals with the South Atlantic states: Virginia, the Carolinas, and Georgia. Maryland and Delaware, though slave states, are excluded both because they were more "middle" than "southern" states in many ways and because they have already been studied by capable scholars. The Southwest—Tennessee, Kentucky, and the territories—has been omitted because, except for a few individuals, there was no Federalist party there. In general this study ends in 1816, but there is some attention to the process by which Federalists later changed their views and entered the second party system in the 1820s.

This study first began when, as a graduate student, I found that there was no existing general work on the Federalist party below the Potomac. In the years since, I have had the help of many people. Robert H. Woody guided the work through the dissertation stage and gave it further attention thereafter, and John Alden also made valuable suggestions for improvements in style and interpretation. Richard P. McCormick, John A. Munroe, Robert McColley, William Gribbin, and D. R. Hickey read all or part of the manuscript at other stages and provided helpful comment.

The process of research could not have been completed without the kindness of the staffs at various manuscript repositories, particularly Duke University Library, the Southern Historical Collection at the University of North Carolina, the Alderman Library at the University of Virginia, and the Manuscript Division at the Library of Congress. Also of assistance were the staffs of the Massachusetts Historical Society, American Antiquarian Society, Yale University Library, Houghton Library at Harvard University, New-York Historical Society, Columbia University Library, New York Public Library, Historical Society of Pennsylvania, Virginia State Library, Virginia Historical Society, North Carolina Department of Archives and History, South Caroliniana Library at the University of South Carolina, Georgia Historical Society, University of Georgia Library, and Georgia Department of Archives and History. I was able to obtain much material on interlibrary loan through the efforts of librarians at Clarkson College, Fort Benjamin Harrison, and Southwest Texas State University. Financial assistance in purchasing research materials and paying typing expenses was generously provided by Clarkson College and Southwest Texas State University.

My wife Margaret helped substantially with the research, and each successive draft of the manuscript was improved by her critical reading. Without her the project would have taken much longer if, indeed, it would ever have been finished. Finally, I would like to thank my parents, who provided me the opportunity to inquire and learn both at home and at school, and to whom this volume is dedicated. Any errors of fact or interpretation in the work are of course entirely my own.

ONE Southern Federalists and the New Nation

Chapter 1 THE SOUTH IN 1800

THE South Atlantic states in 1800 were hardly a comfortable home for Federalism.[1] Their people were almost entirely rural and agricultural, and stubbornly independent small farmers comprised a large majority of the voting population. The most popular religious sects emphasized democratic principles, and the Great Revival was weakening the influence of more conservative churches. Southern voters, hostile to any hint of centralized or aristocratic national government, had opposed the adoption of the Constitution; and during the 1790s they grew increasingly dissatisfied with the Federalist party of Hamilton and Adams, of the financier and merchant, of the North and East.

Geographically the South exhibited three broad sections: Tidewater, Piedmont, and mountains. The coastal part of the Tidewater, with a much-indented shoreline and low swampy lands broken by many rivers and streams, had a climate unwholesome to humans but well suited to certain profitable crops. Beyond this fertile region lay the sparsely inhabited pine barrens, which, together with the fall line

1. To distinguish the federalism of 1788 (support for the Constitution) from Federalism after 1800 (the beliefs and policies of the Federalist party), the first letter of the word describing the latter will be capitalized herein.

that interrupted river navigation, formed a barrier to communication between the coast and backcountry. Westward lay the gently rolling Piedmont, whose fertile soil and healthy climate attracted a large white population. Farther west were the mountains, confined to a small corner of Georgia and South Carolina, widening in North Carolina, and spreading out to grasp in three long fingers all the western third of Virginia.[2]

Fully as diverse as the South's physical terrain was its human geography. Virginia alone contained nearly half the population of these four states, but she and the two Carolinas were growing very slowly, if at all. Only Georgia, still young and thinly peopled, was expanding rapidly. In every state slaves were heavily concentrated in the eastern towns and plantation counties; they were fewer in the Piedmont but were increasing yearly as planters sought better land.[3] Most whites were of English stock, especially in the Tidewater, with significant minorities of Scots, Scotch-Irish, Irish, and Germans in the west. Their national origins, dissenting religious convictions, and recent settlement on the frontier distinguished these groups from the coastal English majority. Ethnic feelings had weakened with time but even by 1800 still affected the political behavior of these minorities.

Religion had once been closely associated with nationality, but by 1800 the two had grown apart. By no means were all those of English background Episcopalians; in fact, few communicants remained in this once established church. Presbyterianism expanded to fill part of this gap but was itself beset, even among Scots and Scotch-Irish, by the Methodists and Baptists. These two sects, bubbling with enthusiasm and preaching on the common people's level, exploded into prominence after the Revolution. By the early 1800s they vied for numerical supremacy in the South, with the Presbyterians trailing distantly in size. There was often a difference in political outlook be-

2. Contemporary travel accounts are of great value in studying the physical and social aspects of southern life. Nearly all are listed in Thomas D. Clark (ed.), *Travels in the Old South: A Bibliography* (3 vols.; Norman, Okla., 1956–59), II, *The Expanding South, 1750–1825*. A good contemporary summary is D. B. Warden, *A Statistical, Political, and Historical Account of the United States of North America* (2 vols.; Edinburgh, Scotland, 1819), II.

3. Compare the distribution of slaves in 1800, 1810, and 1820 in Charles O. Paullin, *Atlas of the Historical Geography of the United States* (Washington, D.C., 1932), plate 67.

tween the democratic churches and the more conservative minority denominations, although religion never entered directly into partisan conflicts.[4]

In the material realm, agriculture thoroughly dominated the regional economy, since more than nine-tenths of the people lived in the countryside.[5] Wheat, corn, tobacco, rice, cotton, livestock, lumber, and naval stores were the chief products of soil and forest, their importance varying from state to state. Tobacco remained the great staple of the Virginia Piedmont and of northern North Carolina, while rice and Sea Island cotton flourished on the South Carolina and Georgia coasts. In the middle and upper country of the Carolinas and Georgia, wheat and other food crops were steadily retreating before the push of short-staple cotton. Growers of all these money crops looked to other states or abroad for cash markets, but many thousands of families barely raised enough to sustain themselves. Subsistence farmers populated every section of the South, living on poorer soil with less access to transportation than the staple growers, and sometimes behaving differently in politics.

Commerce, closely related to agriculture but far overshadowed by it, was important to the towns and the seaboard counties. Charleston was the premier southern port, drawing trade from both Carolinas and Georgia, though Norfolk handled the greater part of Virginia's commerce and much of North Carolina's. Other port towns included Alexandria in the District of Columbia; Petersburg and Richmond in Virginia; Wilmington, Newbern [New Bern], Edenton, and Halifax in North Carolina; and Savannah in Georgia. Inland, the need to market western crops supported such commercial centers as Augusta, Georgia; Columbia, South Carolina; Fayetteville, Salisbury, and Hillsborough [Hillsboro] in North Carolina; and Lexington, Staunton, and Martinsburg in Virginia. As might be expected, most commercial towns proved more receptive to Federalism than did the rural countryside. Even less important than trade, manufacturing above the household level never had much impact on the southern economy,

4. For a further treatment of ethnic and religious groups, see the relevant portions of Chap. 27, herein.

5. The southern economy in this period has been neglected. The chief work on agriculture is Lewis C. Gray, *History of Agriculture in the Southern United States to 1860* (2 vols.; Washington, D.C., 1933).

beyond the presence of local flour mills, whiskey stills, and the urban artisan class. A small number of townsmen followed professional careers, but even they were often tied to agriculture, and many became planters as soon as they were able.

Distinctions of social class paralleled those of occupation. At the top perched the rich planters with their vast acreage and many slaves. Just below them stood the lesser planters and the merchants, bankers, and professional men (who were often landowners as well). Next came artisans, tradesmen, and a large number of independent small farmers; although they constituted a majority of the electorate, this class usually accepted political leadership from the upper ranks.[6] Lowest were the landless whites, able to vote if they paid taxes; the free Negroes, deprived of political influence except in North Carolina; and the slaves. Class lines were still rather distinct in the early nineteenth century, but movement up or down the social scale was not uncommon. Frequent elections also forced the upper classes to maintain a necessary appearance of familiarity with the lower and gave the small farmer and tradesman a sense of importance in political society.

In this semistratified rural society where travel was difficult and communication slow, swaying public opinion was an arduous and drawn-out process. Newspapers had typical circulations of only a few hundred, and even though a single copy might pass through several hands or be posted in a public spot, only a fraction of the adult white male population could be directly reached. Nevertheless, newspapers became the chief weapons of political warfare. In the front rank of the southern Federalist press stood the *Charleston Courier, Norfolk Gazette and Publick Ledger*, Richmond *Virginia Gazette*, Raleigh *Minerva*, and *Augusta Herald*. They set the tone for their party, reprinting articles from the national Federalist press and carrying original editorials, which were in turn copied by the lesser party sheets throughout the South. During election campaigns, or when some event deeply stirred the people, newspapers alone were unequal to the task of shaping po-

6. Despite their numbers, small farmers were never an organized independent force in politics. However, a recent investigation of poll lists by Norman K. Risjord may indicate that the lesser landholders voted more independently than was previously thought: "How the 'Common Man' Voted in Jefferson's Virginia," in John B. Boles (ed.), *America: The Middle Period* (Charlottesville, Va., 1973), 36–64.

litical opinion. Printed circular letters by candidates and officeholders, mass meetings of citizens, militia musters, and even county and district grand juries—all served the cause of partisan controversy.

The most frantic efforts to sway opinion occurred during election time. Suffrage requirements were liberal enough so that candidates had to contend with a large electorate. Georgia and North Carolina allowed all taxpayers to vote, and since both states levied a poll tax, they had, in effect, universal white manhood suffrage. Virginia restricted the franchise to fifty-acre freeholders, whereas South Carolina allowed these and all three-shilling taxpayers to vote.[7] Qualified electors probably averaged 500 per county in Virginia, 1,200 in North Carolina, 500 in South Carolina, and 1,000 in Georgia. Congressional districts, of course, embraced a much larger number of voters.

Election campaigns might cover several months or only a few weeks, but they were often quite hectic. A candidate would announce himself with a few lines in the newspaper, a circular to the voters, or merely written or verbal notice to a few influential men.[8] Thereafter, he harangued militia musters, church meetings, tavern crowds, and any other gathering of voters, preferably in the vicinity of liquor. Even house-to-house canvassing, no easy matter in a land of scattered farms and poor roads, was sometimes necessary. Voting was by ballot except in Virginia, which required an oral vote in all but presidential elections. Sheriffs supervised the polling and officially certified the winners to the governor or legislature, but a permanent record of votes was seldom kept; consequently, election returns are scarce, existing primarily in unofficial fragmentary newspaper tabulations.[9]

7. The best single work on voting is Chilton Williamson, *American Suffrage: From Property to Democracy, 1760–1860* (Princeton, N.J., 1960), 29–35, 85–86, 104–14, 131–32, 151–57, 223–30.

8. At present one must go directly to the newspapers and manuscript collections for a full picture of election practices in the early republic, although the following are helpful: Noble E. Cunningham, *The Jeffersonian Republicans: The Formation of Party Organization, 1789–1801* (Chapel Hill, N.C., 1957) and *The Jeffersonian Republicans in Power: Party Operations, 1801–1809* (Chapel Hill, N.C., 1963); Charles S. Sydnor, *Gentlemen Freeholders: Political Practices in Washington's Virginia* (Chapel Hill, N.C., 1952); and Anthony Frederick Upton, "Political Structure of Virginia, 1790–1830" (M.A. thesis, Duke University, 1953), 30–44.

9. In Virginia, the governor appointed five commissioners in each county for presidential elections; in South Carolina, the legislature selected commissioners of election in each parish and district.

The incomplete evidence suggests that from 50 to 75 percent of those eligible usually cast ballots.

The political framework of each state was quite similar; constitutions written in the last quarter of the eighteenth century made the legislature clearly the ruling branch of government. Besides its lawmaking powers, the legislature chose the governor and other state officers (usually for one-year terms) and all judges above the county level. In addition, it elected the state's two senators and even instructed them to support or oppose specific measures in Congress. Local affairs also fell under legislative control, as did such individual matters as requests for divorce and for emancipation of slaves.[10] Despite this variety of activities, state expenses were small; in 1809 North Carolina's budget was only fourteen cents per capita and Virginia's only thirty-six cents. Salaries, legislative costs, and the administration of justice absorbed most of the money; hardly any went for education, welfare, or public improvements. To finance this modest establishment, the states taxed polls, land, town lots and improvements, peddlers, wholesale and retail merchants, slaves, and sometimes legal proceedings.

State problems such as taxation, representation, court reform, and banking often embroiled the legislatures in bitter controversy. However, these local issues had almost nothing to do with the partisan battle between Federalists and Republicans. After 1800, both parties in the South focused upon national and international problems and seldom showed any consistent position on a state issue. This had not always been the case. The party conflict begun in the 1790s was but the latest in a series of southern political divisions. Even during the Revolution the rebels were united only in desiring independence; on domestic matters they divided so often that opposing groups soon formed, whose altercations embittered the war and postwar years.

Many businessmen, large planters, and prosperous farmers joined in a conservative faction drawing strength from the seaboard, the towns, and the fertile valleys of navigable rivers. This group usually advocated government by the propertied classes (in other words, themselves), a sound metallic currency, flat-rate taxes on polls and

10. Fletcher M. Green, *Constitutional Development in the South Atlantic States, 1776–1860: A Study in the Evolution of Democracy* (Chapel Hill, N.C., 1930), Chaps. 2–3.

land, and a lenient attitude toward former Tories. Opposed to the conservatives was a "radical" or "democratic" element, led often by persons of wealth but supported by small farmers in the Piedmont and mountains and occasionally by urban artisans and mechanics. The radicals favored a larger voice for the backcountry, liberal issues of paper money, taxation according to wealth, and stern treatment of Loyalists.[11]

Besides these internal questions, the relation of each state to the Confederation government was a subject of controversy. As a rule, those whose vision was more national than local and who were willing to strengthen the authority of the Continental government were the same men who took the conservative side of disputes within the states. A sound and stable American society required, in their view, a powerful central government capable of dealing with foreign problems, strengthening the forces of order at home, and encouraging commerce. These conservative nationalists were quick to embrace the opportunity of creating a stronger government at the Philadelphia convention of 1787, and the South was well represented in that body.[12]

The new Constitution, however, was more nationalistic than many ordinary southerners wished, and there was widespread resistance to ratification. The old democratic faction raised strenuous objections to the document. Such "antifederalists" fought to protect state sovereignty and feared that the North might control a centralized government and trample upon southern interests. They demanded a specific

11. On southern state politics in this era, see Allan Nevins, *The American States During and After the Revolution, 1775–1789* (New York, 1924); Jackson Turner Main, *The Sovereign States, 1775–1783* (New York, 1973), especially Chaps. 5 and 11, and *Political Parties Before the Constitution* (Chapel Hill, N.C., 1973), Chaps. 9–13; and John Richard Alden, *The South in the Revolution, 1763–1789* (Baton Rouge, La., 1957), Vol. III, in Wendell Holmes Stephenson and E. Merton Coulter (eds.), *A History of the South*, Chaps. 17, 18, 20. The best state studies are George R. Lamplugh, "Politics on the Periphery: Factions and Parties in Georgia, 1776–1806" (Ph.D. dissertation, Emory University, 1973); Raymond G. Starr, "The Conservative Revolution: South Carolina Public Affairs, 1775–1790" (Ph.D. dissertation, University of Texas, 1964); Charles G. Singer, *South Carolina in the Confederation* (Philadelphia, Pa., 1941); Sheldon F. Koesy, "Continuity and Change in North Carolina, 1775–1789" (Ph.D. dissertation, Duke University, 1963); and Myra L. Rich, "The Experimental Years: Virginia, 1781–1789" (Ph.D. dissertation, Yale University, 1966).

12. H. James Henderson has recently explored the origins of this conservative southern attitude in *Party Politics in the Continental Congress* (New York, 1974).

Bill of Rights to protect individual liberties. The "federalists," favoring immediate ratification, consisted chiefly of the old conservative faction and many moderates.

The extent and seriousness of this debate varied from state to state. There was only minor opposition to the Constitution in Georgia, where frontier defense was the overriding need. South Carolina also fell in line, as the low-country planters and merchants, benefiting from malapportionment, pushed the Constitution through, probably against the wishes of a majority of the voting population. Virginians were almost equally divided, but after a lengthy convention debate against Patrick Henry's antifederalist bloc, the Constitution won approval by a narrow margin. In North Carolina the struggle was even longer and fiercer, producing at first a clear antifederalist victory. Only after the new Union had already begun to function did the state reconsider her judgment and grudgingly join her neighbors.[13]

Even after ratification the antifederalists remained a majority, or nearly so, in all the southern states but Georgia. They remained intensely suspicious of the new government. In fact, many federalists themselves were ready to repulse the first hints of overcentralization, favoritism to the North, or injury to agriculture.

Alexander Hamilton's plan for assuming state debts, funding both state and national debts at par, and creating a national bank seemed likely to produce all the evils which antifederalists had feared. Southerners drew back, alarmed. This violent anti-Hamiltonian reaction in the South created a new political alignment. Most of the local-minded democrats of Confederation years had become antifederalists in 1788, and nearly all of them now rose in anger against Hamilton. They were joined by many disillusioned former federalists, leaving the support-

13. On the ratification struggle, see particularly John Richard Alden, *The First South* (Baton Rouge, La., 1961), Chap. 4. See also Robert Allan Rutland, *The Ordeal of the Constitution: The Antifederalists and the Ratification Struggle of 1787–1788* (Norman, Okla., 1966), Chaps. 9, 10, 12; John P. Kaminski, "Controversy Amid Consensus: The Adoption of the Federal Constitution in Georgia," *Georgia Historical Quarterly*, LVIII (1974), 244–61; Robert E. Thomas, "The Virginia Convention of 1788: A Criticism of Beard's *An Economic Interpretation of the Constitution*," *Journal of Southern History*, XIX (1953), 63–72; Louise Irby Trenholme, *The Ratification of the Federal Constitution in North Carolina* (New York, 1932); and William C. Pool, "An Economic Interpretation of the Ratification of the Federal Constitution in North Carolina," *North Carolina Historical Review*, XXVII (1950), 119–41, 289–313, 437–61.

ers of Hamilton's program a small minority except in low-country South Carolina. Leaders in every state who had fought for the Constitution now turned against the administration, and congressional elections soon showed the broad extent of public dissatisfaction. Two-thirds of the southerners in the First Congress had originally been elected as friends of the Constitution. As the following table indicates, most quickly broke with the administration. This was only the beginning; in later Congresses the opposition steadily increased its margin over Hamilton's supporters.[14]

Table 1 **Voting Behavior of Southern Congressmen, 1790–1797**[15]

Congress (and Year)	*Pro-administration*	*Anti-administration*	*Wavering*
1st Cong. (1789–91)	4 (18%)	7 (32%)	11
2nd Cong. (1791–93)	4 (17%)	16 (70%)	3
3rd Cong. (1793–95)	4 (11%)	22 (61%)	10
4th Cong. (1795–97)	5 (13%)	30 (81%)	2

This emerging partisan division was hastened by events abroad, chiefly those growing out of the French Revolution. In its early years the Revolution received almost universal approval in the United States because the French seemed to be following America's example to a flattering degree. Gradually, enthusiasm for France began to sour as the Revolution turned militant, bloody, and aggressive. The French deposed and killed their king, destroyed their old ruling class, went to war with Britain, and invaded neighboring states to spread the gospel of revolution. All this alarmed conservative Americans. They were disgusted at the social upheaval and antireligious crusade within

14. Lisle A. Rose, *Prologue to Democracy: The Federalists in the South, 1789–1800* (Lexington, Ky., 1968), 10–15; Cunningham, *Jeffersonian Republicans, 1789–1801*, 22, 23, 50, 51; Delbert H. Gilpatrick, *Jeffersonian Democracy in North Carolina, 1789–1816* (New York, 1931), 39–50; John Harold Wolfe, *Jeffersonian Democracy in South Carolina* (Chapel Hill, N.C., 1940), 57–67; Richard R. Beeman, *The Old Dominion and the New Nation, 1788–1801* (Lexington, Ky., 1972), 67–85.

15. Sources for Table 1 are Joseph Charles, *The Origins of the American Party System: Three Essays* (Williamsburg, Va., 1956), 94, and Manning J. Dauer, *The Adams Federalists* (Baltimore, Md., 1953), 297.

France, angry at the war against Britain, and fearful that radical French ideas might infect the gullible "lower orders" in the United States.

Many southerners, though not a majority, experienced just such a reaction against revolutionary France. This occurred at all levels of the social and economic scale—among merchants, planters, and common farmers who set great store by stability, religion, and deference to "natural leadership." The split in southern opinion regarding France roughly paralleled that concerning Hamilton's program. Men who favored (or at least tolerated) Hamiltonian measures were likely to hope for a French defeat in Europe; those who opposed Hamilton felt that France was much less dangerous than Britain to American interests.[16]

Foreign affairs began to affect the shape of politics during the confrontation between French minister Edmond Genet and the Washington administration in 1793, when both pro- and anti-French groups first tried to marshal public opinion in their respective causes.[17] The long controversy over the Jay Treaty in 1795–1796 was even more important in stimulating the development of political parties. Resentment against Jay's Treaty was highest in the South. Jay had failed to gain any practical entry for American ships to the nearby West Indies trade or any compensation for southern slaves the British had carried off during the Revolution. Furthermore, the South's lively sense of national honor was offended by Jay's apparent abject surrender to every British demand. Opposition strategists, now beginning to call themselves Republicans, realized their opportunity and used the treaty issue to solidify their hold on southern opinion. Mass meetings hung Jay in effigy and condemned his work; legislatures censured the treaty; and the Republican press erupted with fiery articles.[18]

Friends of the administration, who had appropriated the name of

16. Richard Buel, Jr., *Securing the Revolution: Ideology in American Politics, 1789–1815* (Ithaca, N.Y., 1972), Chap. 2.

17. Harry Ammon, *The Genet Mission* (New York, 1973), especially Chaps. 4, 10.

18. Jerald A. Combs, *The Jay Treaty: Political Battleground of the Founding Fathers* (Berkeley and Los Angeles, 1970); Thomas J. Farnham, "The Virginia Amendments of 1795: An Episode in the Opposition to Jay's Treaty," *Virginia Magazine of History and Biography*, LXXV (1967), 75–88; Cunningham, *Jeffersonian Republicans, 1789–1801*, 77–84; and the state studies cited in note 14.

Federalist, were confused and divided. Some openly attacked Jay's Treaty, and in Congress three of the seven southern Federalists voted against appropriations for carrying it into effect. After a time Federalist leaders recovered themselves and fought back, using against Republicans the vast prestige of Washington and defending the treaty as the only alternative to war with Britain. Gradually, public opinion shifted and Federalists not only lived down the antitreaty agitation but actually made slight gains in the congressional elections of 1796 and 1797.

The treaty battle was crucial to southern politics, for it helped to mold what had been loose factions into formal political parties. Both Federalists and Republicans now worked consciously to seek effective ways of presenting issues before the people so as to cast odium on the other party and win approval for themselves. Inside Congress and in state legislatures, fewer men remained wavering between outright allegiance to one side or the other, and the opposing groups became clearly defined.[19]

Despite improved organization and encouraging results in the 1796–1797 elections, the southern Federalists remained a small minority in their section. John Adams won only two southern electoral votes for president in 1796 to Thomas Jefferson's forty-three. In congressional and legislative contests the party could dominate a few areas but did not threaten statewide Republican control anywhere except in South Carolina. The drift of former "federalists of 1788" (that is, proponents of the Constitution) into the Republican camp had eroded Federalist strength among the South's political leaders. Hamilton's nationalizing program, Jay's Treaty, and Federalist partiality to Britain in the European war had brought many supporters of the Constitution to distrust the actions of a Federalist government. Nearly all the antifederalist members of southern state ratifying conventions who were still active politically in the late 1790s had become Republicans, but only about half of the original federalist dele-

19. Rose, *Prologue to Democracy*, Chap. 3 and pp. 127–38; Charles, *Origins of Party System*, 91–140; Beeman, *Old Dominion*, 140–60; Buel, *Securing the Revolution*, Chap. 3. For a new look at the tightening of party allegiance, see Norman Risjord and Gordon DenBoer, "The Evolution of Political Parties in Virginia, 1782–1800," *Journal of American History*, LX (1974), 961–84.

gates were now affiliated with the Federalist party. The other half had, during the 1790s, permanently joined the opposition.[20] A similar defection occurred in the general electorate, for many counties that were pro-Constitution in 1788–1789 had become firmly Republican a decade later. By alienating these leaders and voters the Federalist party had reduced itself to dire circumstances by 1796.

Quite suddenly, however, this dismal picture was remarkably altered. By 1798 Federalists found themselves enjoying unaccustomed popularity. The French, regarding Jay's Treaty as an unneutral preference for Britain, increased their interference with American trade, refused to receive the South Carolina Federalist Charles Cotesworth Pinckney as minister, and in the famous XYZ Affair demanded bribes as the price of negotiations. The combination of commercial losses, insulted national honor, and fear of a French attack, upset southerners as much as other Americans. President Adams decided to prepare for war while hoping for peace, and resolutions of support poured in from the South.

In the face of such obvious popular approval of the president's stand against France, Republicans in Congress persisted in opposing Adams' defense measures. This attitude the voters soundly rebuked. The French crisis was almost the sole issue in the southern congressional campaigns of 1798–1799, and it hurt the Republicans deeply. In August and October, 1798, Federalists gained three additional seats in North Carolina and two more in South Carolina; in April, 1799, they captured two Republican districts in Virginia. In all, the South sent fifteen Federalists to the Sixth Congress, nearly doubling the party's preelection strength. Additionally, three "quasi-Federalists" were chosen from North Carolina and two from Georgia. Only seventeen districts were left in the hands of unswerving Republicans.[21]

Yet even as southern Federalists enjoyed these victories, their par-

20. Men who were later legislators, congressmen, or candidates for Congress; holders of or candidates for state office; party organizers or newspaper editors—all were considered as "politically active" in the late 1790s. An excellent new study is Norman K. Risjord, "Virginians and the Constitution: A Multivariant Analysis," *William and Mary Quarterly*, 3rd ser., XXXI (1974), 613–32.

21. Albert H. Bowman, *The Struggle for Neutrality: Franco-American Diplomacy During the Federalist Era* (Knoxville, Tenn., 1974), Chaps. 13–15; Alexander DeConde, *The Quasi-War: The Politics and Diplomacy of the Undeclared War with France, 1797–1801* (New York, 1966); John W. Kuehl, "The Quest for Identity in an Age of Insecurity:

ty's congressional behavior was insuring future defeat. Given the possibility of a serious maritime war with France, it was only prudent to expand the navy, fortify harbors, and finance these measures by borrowing and increasing taxes. But congressional Federalists went much further. They raised a large standing army, which seemed useless against France and gave rise to fears of domestic repression; they passed the Alien and Sedition Acts, designed to cripple domestic opposition; and they imposed a direct tax on all land, slaves, and buildings in the United States. There could scarcely be a more effective way to make Federalism unpopular than to couple an apparent attack on freedom of expression with the creation of an ominous standing army and direct taxation. Yet, so long as war seemed possible, the nation bore these impositions well. In fact, the southern Federalist election victories of 1798–1799 occurred months after passage of these stern bills. It was not until early 1800 that public feeling shifted from fear of France to resentment of Federalism at home, and for this change President Adams' peace policy was partly responsible.

The XYZ Affair and American Nationalism" (Ph.D. dissertation, University of Wisconsin, 1968), Chaps. 1–4, 7; Beeman, *Old Dominion*, 173–211; Gilpatrick, *Jeffersonian Democracy*, 82–102; Wolfe, *Jeffersonian Democracy*, 100–124.

Chapter 2 THE ELECTION OF 1800

BUOYED by public anger against France, Federalists hoped to hold power for some time after 1798. They enjoyed a three-to-two advantage in both houses of Congress and controlled most of the state governments, holding a firm grip upon New England and a slight majority in the middle states. Even in the South they were stronger than ever before. William R. Davie, a firm Federalist, was governor of North Carolina. Jacob Read and James Gunn represented South Carolina and Georgia in the Senate, and fully 40 percent of southern congressmen were Federalists. A large number of respectable and influential professional men, planters, and merchants provided able party leadership—men such as Congressmen John Marshall and Henry Lee in Virginia; North Carolina's Governor Davie and Congressman William Barry Grove; Senator Read, Congressman John Rutledge, Jr., and the brothers Thomas and Charles Cotesworth Pinckney in South Carolina; and, in Georgia, Senator Gunn and Thomas Gibbons, the mayor of Savannah. Many ordinary citizens from every background also had strong attachments to Federalism, and the elections of 1798–1799 had been very encouraging.

By 1800, however, the nation's war fever had cooled and a peaceful adjustment with France was possible. In this atmosphere the Federalist war program seemed expensive, oppressive, and now quite unnecessary. President Adams himself helped create this mood by sending a new team of envoys to Paris, evoking the wrath of the Hamiltonian "High Federalists" who wished to continue America's militant attitude toward France. Among southern Federalists there was no such criticism. Davie, himself one of the new ministers to France, never doubted the advisability of such an overture. Others expressed no opinion on the mission itself but agreed with Adams that Napoleon, who now controlled the French government, ought to be conciliated.[1] Even in Congress, where many northerners grumbled against the mission, a follower of Hamilton observed that the southern Federalists insisted that the whole proceeding was prudent and if it failed, would prove the "injustice and irreconcilable enmity of the French rulers."[2]

Although supporting the peace negotiations, some southern leaders were disturbed by other presidential actions. The dismissal of Hamiltonian cabinet members in May, 1800, never aroused in the South the bitter criticism voiced by some northern Federalists, but a few individuals did think this was unworthy treatment of meritorious men. Rumors that Adams intended to form an alliance with Jefferson also upset a number of southerners, most of them close friends of Charles Cotesworth Pinckney.[3] Overall, however, scarcely a handful of letters critical of Adams can be found. This may, of course, reflect only the high mortality of such correspondence and not widespread approval of the president, but he probably did stand higher with southern than with northern Federalists.

Whatever their opinion of Adams, nearly all Federalists recog-

1. Blackwell P. Robinson, *William R. Davie* (Chapel Hill, N.C., 1957), 323–29; Robert Goodloe Harper's letter to constituents in *Georgetown Gazette*, May 31, 1800; Arthur Campbell to Timothy Pickering, February 21, May 24, 1800, in Timothy Pickering Papers, Massachusetts Historical Society (hereinafter cited as MHS).

2. George Cabot to Rufus King, January 20, 1800, in Charles R. King (ed.), *The Life and Correspondence of Rufus King* (6 vols.; New York, 1894–1900), III, 813.

3. Henry William DeSaussure to Pickering, August 12, 1800, Charles Cotesworth Pinckney to Pickering, June 19, 1800, both in Timothy Pickering Papers; James Gunn to John Rutledge, Jr., May 12, 1800, in John Rutledge Papers, Southern Historical Collection, University of North Carolina (hereinafter cited as UNC); John Rutledge, Jr., to Alexander Hamilton, July 17, 1800, in Alexander Hamilton Papers, Library of Congress (hereinafter cited as LC); Rose, *Prologue to Democracy*, 240–42.

nized the need for a united effort to keep Jefferson from power. This was especially true after New York's election in April gave Republicans control of that pivotal state's legislature and electoral vote. To meet the danger, Federalist congressmen caucused in Philadelphia to make an official choice of candidates. Adams won renomination apparently without dissent, but there was some trouble selecting a running mate. Congressman John Rutledge, Jr., a Charleston lawyer and recent convert to Federalism, attended the caucus and summarized its results in a letter to Fisher Ames of Massachusetts. According to Rutledge, the Pennsylvania Federalists suggested Thomas Pinckney, the nominee for vice-president in 1796, but he declined. His brother, Charles Cotesworth Pinckney, then put forth John Marshall as most able to win support in heavily Republican Virginia; but this "was not liked by Genl. Marshall nor by the Federalists of the middle states," and finally Cotesworth Pinckney himself consented to run. The meeting ended with an agreement to support both men equally, although it was obvious that Adams was intended for president.[4]

The caucus appeal was universally approved in the South—grudgingly in South Carolina, cheerfully elsewhere. Several leading Charleston Federalists much preferred their neighbor Pinckney to Adams but felt unable to act openly. Pinckney himself was typical of this group; he harbored disloyal sentiments toward Adams but thought any desertion of the president should begin in New England, and if Adams kept his support there, then the South should stay with him also.[5] Outside this little band of South Carolinians, Adams was the clear choice of southern Federalists, especially of the local leaders most in touch with the common voter. In North Carolina, it was said that Adams was preferred to any man living, and the Federalist candidates there ran as Adams men only, not even mentioning Pinckney.

4. John Rutledge, Jr., to Fisher Ames, August 22, 1800, in John Rutledge, Jr., Papers, Houghton Library, Harvard University; William G. Morgan, "Presidential Nominations in the Federal Era, 1788–1826" (Ph.D. dissertation, University of Southern California, 1969), 41–44.

5. DeSaussure to Jedediah Morse, November 3, 1800, in Morse Family Papers, Yale University Library; Thomas Pinckney to John Rutledge, Jr., September 23, 1800, in Rutledge Papers, UNC; C. C. Pinckney to James McHenry, June 10 and July 19, 1800, in Bernard C. Steiner, *The Life and Correspondence of James McHenry: Secretary of War Under Washington and Adams* (Cleveland, Ohio, 1907), 459–61.

The election address of the Virginia central committee also emphasized the president alone. Even in South Carolina, despite the disaffection of some leaders, a local report claimed that "there is less of Pinckney than you would imagine. The Mass of sentiment seems to be divided between Adams and Jefferson."[6]

Nevertheless, the New England Adams men were concerned that southern Federalists might fall in with Alexander Hamilton's maneuvers to elevate Pinckney at the president's expense. The New Englanders threatened to retaliate by depriving Pinckney of votes in their section. Taking alarm at this, the very men who privately criticized Adams in South Carolina took pains to convince their northern colleagues that both nominees would receive an equal effort in the South. Several letters on this subject passed from Charleston and vicinity through John Rutledge, Jr. (then vacationing in Rhode Island), to the Federalist leaders of New England.[7] In the end, southerners did stand by the caucus agreement in the face of strong temptation, whereas one New England elector broke ranks and withheld his vote from Pinckney.

The most compelling reason for southern Federalists to accept Adams was their great fear that Jefferson's election would hurt the nation deeply. These men were not merely professional politicians seeking power as an end in itself; they truly believed a Republican victory would be an immeasurable national calamity. Federalist leaders told the public in newspapers, speeches, and pamphlets just what they told each other in their private letters. Their first concern was to defend John Adams and the unpopular war legislation of 1798. The president himself they held up as an honest, capable, well-intentioned man who desired peace and neutrality for America. Parrying Republican criticism of Adams' political principles, Federalist newspapers

6. Edward Carrington to Alexander Hamilton, August 30, 1800, in Alexander Hamilton Papers; advertisements for elector, in *North-Carolina Minerva*, March 18 and 25, July 1, 1800; *Virginia Herald*, June 3 and 6, 1800; Robert Goodloe Harper to Harrison Gray Otis, June 15, 1800, quoting "one of my correspondents," in Samuel Eliot Morison (ed.), *The Life and Letters of Harrison Gray Otis, Federalist, 1765–1848* (2 vols.; Boston, 1913), I, 192.

7. Thomas Pinckney to John Rutledge, Jr., September 23, 1800, John Rutledge, Jr., to Ames, October 15, 1800, Benjamin Stoddert to Rutledge, October 2, 1800, all in Rutledge Papers, UNC.

explained that he was no admirer of monarchical government and that he had served his country faithfully all his life.[8]

The huge standing army was passed off as merely a few soldiers necessary for defense against French insult and attack. Congressman Rutledge assured his constituents that there would be no danger of military tyranny; in fact, Congress suspended enlistments and voted to disband the ranks as soon as peace appeared likely.[9] Federalists likewise belittled the additional spending, taxation, and debt that the military preparations entailed. They said that despite the expense of fighting Indian wars, governing the western territories, putting down two insurrections, and arming against the French, the national debt had actually declined since 1790. The *Virginia Federalist* summarized their position thus: "Are we willing to estimate our sovereign rights as a nation at a *price*, and to put our purse in competition with our liberty?"[10]

The Sedition Act, too, was defended as hardly the oppressive measure Republicans made it out to be. The Federalists contended that it was not aimed in any way at true freedom of the press, and that it created no new crimes but merely punished by statute libels which were already illegal under the common law. No responsible critic would suffer, they held, because the law's only target was the blatant lie maliciously spread, and surely this was no infringement of liberty.[11]

Federalists did not merely brush away criticism of their controversial acts; they also extolled the positive side of the Adams years, especially the maintenance of peace and prosperity. Never within memory, they said, had economic conditions been so good. Led by George Washington and Adams, the nation had steadily advanced, and the two Federalist presidents should receive full credit. Furthermore, in a trying period John Adams had preserved America from both war and dishonor. Typical of the "peace and prosperity" issue

8. "A Federal Republican," in *South-Carolina State-Gazette*, July 2, 1800; "Agricola," in *Virginia Herald*, April 22, 1800.

9. "Bellisarius," in Alexandria *Columbia Mirror*, October 21, 1800; letter of John Rutledge, Jr., *ibid.*, June 21, 1800.

10. Henry Lee's letter to constituents, in *Georgetown Gazette*, July 12, 1800; *Virginia Federalist*, March 1, 1800.

11. "Freeholder," in *Virginia Herald*, March 21, 1800; *North-Carolina Minerva*, February 4, 1800; "Zenas," in *Augusta Herald*, quoted in *South-Carolina State-Gazette*, August 20, 1800.

was the declaration by Walter Alves, a planter of Orange County, North Carolina, in announcing his candidacy for presidential elector: "I cannot help attributing this Peace, Security, and Happiness which our country now enjoys (next to Divine Providence) to the wise, firm and patriotic measures which our government, under the administration of WASHINGTON and ADAMS, has adopted and pursued in these critical times."[12] Finally, the party cast over Adams the protective mantle of the Father of the Country, reminding voters that the president "had the approbation of our late much beloved, and deservedly much esteemed General Washington. This should weigh with us all."[13]

As for Thomas Jefferson, Federalists pictured him as the incompetent and irreligious candidate of a pro-French, anti-Constitutional party. They found him personally lacking the essential attributes of a good president; he had no firmness, courage, or honesty. His only reputation was as a visionary philosopher, and the practical task of managing a government was far above him.[14] Still worse, Jefferson was anti-Christian, and surely an unbeliever was not fit to preside over a Christian people.[15] His foreign policy was alive with danger. Federalists assured the voters that Jefferson "secretly and treacherously heads a faction, the object of which is to subject America to a foreign yoke"; he would league the United States with France, import dangerous ideas from that country, and plunge America into war on the side of the French.[16]

Above all considerations of personality or diplomacy, Federalists raised one most frequent and serious objection to Jefferson as president. They thought he was an enemy of the Constitution who wanted to dissolve the Union. Did he not, in his letter to Philip Mazzei, "tra-

12. "Juvenis," in *South-Carolina State-Gazette*, July 8, 1800; Walter Alves' announcement, in *North-Carolina Minerva*, March 18, 1800.

13. "Agricola," in *Virginia Herald*, April 22, 1800. "To the Freemen," in *Wilmington Gazette*, July 31, 1800; James Simons, *A Rallying Point, for All True Friends to Their Country* (Charleston, S.C., 1800), 5, 16.

14. *South-Carolina State-Gazette*, June 23, July 25, 1800; *Newbern Gazette*, August 15, 1800.

15. Letter to editor, in Alexandria *Columbian Mirror*, October 21, 1800; *North-Carolina Minerva*, October 14, 1800. On the impact of this issue, see Fred J. Hood, "Presbyterianism and the New American Nation, 1783–1826: A Case Study of Religion and National Life" (Ph.D. dissertation, Princeton University, 1968), 71–79, 84–88.

16. DeSaussure to John Rutledge, Jr., August 12, 14, 1800, in Rutledge Papers, UNC; *North-Carolina Minerva*, July 15, 1800.

duce and vilify" the Constitution, even while he was sworn to uphold it? Was his party not involved in two disgraceful insurrections against the government (the Whiskey and Fries rebellions)? Let all men who still held the Constitution sacred vote for Adams and Pinckney and cast aside Jefferson's impudent ambition.[17]

This Federalist publicity campaign was not tailored to the interest of any particular economic group. There was no special appeal to the merchant or the financier. The party required votes from both staple and subsistence farmers as well as from commercial men if Adams was to retain his office; Federalists therefore appealed to feelings that transcended economics. They sought to win the conservative-minded citizen in all walks of life—the man who, whatever his economic station, believed in orderly government, traditional religion, and a stable society; who venerated Washington; who distrusted political experiments; who abhorred the wild doctrines and bloody practices of revolutionary France; and who was satisfied with prosperous neutrality. Only by cutting across lines of social, occupational, and economic class could the Federalists hope for victory in the South.

The tone of Federalist propaganda was so bitter and fearful that one might have expected the party to campaign vigorously in every county and hamlet. Instead, the Adams–Pinckney organization was inferior to the Republicans almost everywhere in the South. This was partly due to the certainty of Republican victory in some areas—Georgia, for example. A more general cause of organizational weakness was simple apathy, despite the sharp partisan warfare in the press. It is a commonplace that disgruntled people are more readily stirred to action than those who quietly approve of things as they are; thus, Republican leaders found it easier to rouse opposition to the administration than Federalists did to rally those voters who saw more to praise than to condemn in the party's record.

Then, too, the Pinckney schism, though small, hurt the party's ef-

17. "Honestus," in *South-Carolina State-Gazette*, September 10, 1800; Robert Gamble to Alexander Hamilton, April 4, 1800, in Alexander Hamilton Papers; *Newbern Gazette*, August 15, 1800. See John R. Howe, Jr., "Republican Thought and the Political Violence of the 1790's," *American Quarterly*, XIX (1967), 147–65, and from a pro-Republican viewpoint, Charles O. Lerche, "Jefferson and the Election of 1800: A Case Study in the Political Smear," *William and Mary Quarterly*, 3rd ser., V (1948), 467–91.

forts to organize effectively. Another reason for the greater intensity of the Republicans' campaign is that while Federalists viewed Jefferson as a potential disaster for the country, Republicans believed that Federalist policies were already a present danger. Jefferson *might* uproot religion and tear down the Constitution; the Federalists actually *were* raising an army, multiplying taxes, and fining or imprisoning critics of the government.

Further hindering their campaign, the southern Federalist leaders did not adequately keep in touch with each other or with their northern colleagues. A few in South Carolina regularly exchanged advice and information with such men as Hamilton, Timothy Pickering, Harrison Gray Otis, and James McHenry; but nearly all these northerners were Hamiltonians, and most of their southern correspondents were Pinckney men who sympathized with Hamilton's scheme to defeat Adams. North Carolina and Virginia, whose Federalist leaders were more strongly attached to Adams, had very little contact with the northern party; and Georgia's handful of Federalists was entirely left out of intersectional consultations. Communication among the southern states was little better than between North and South. A few letters full of campaign strategy and election news passed between prominent southern Federalists, but newspapers were usually the only regular contact among the states. The southern party newspapers copied Federalist editorials, letters, and reports of meetings from each other and the northern press, keeping the most remote subscriber informed of party opinion and activity throughout the Union.

Within each southern state, the degree of Federalist organization varied with circumstances. Virginia had the only formal statewide party apparatus, the result of a new election law passed by the Republican legislature in January, 1800. In previous years presidential electors had been chosen from individual districts, and Adams might have won several even if he lost badly in the whole state. The General Ticket Law of 1800, an entirely partisan measure, was intended to secure an undivided vote for Jefferson by providing a statewide popular vote for all twenty-one electors. Any local Federalist majorities would be submerged in the general Republican tide.[18]

18. John B. Walton to Pickering, January 19, 1800, in Timothy Pickering Papers; Federalist electoral address in *Virginia Herald*, June 3, 1800.

One result of the law was to force each party to arrange a state list of electors. The easiest course was to have the party legislators, who were already in Richmond for the General Assembly session, meet privately to select the ticket. Although one Federalist protested this imitation of the Republicans' detestable caucus system, the party ignored such critics and followed the advice of "A Federalist" of Richmond, who urged an early caucus even though defeat was almost certain: "Shall the friends of the general government forever yield the palm of activity and zeal to their opponents? . . . If we continue supine . . . we should not only be conquered, but be conquered without the honor of resistance."[19] Accordingly, the Federalist assemblymen met, named twenty-one electoral candidates, and established a central committee that issued an election address over the signature of William Austin, a Richmond merchant. The state committee tried to follow the Republican example of setting up local campaign groups in each county, but with little apparent success. However, local Federalists made a disciplined effort in some of the April legislative contests and probably toiled diligently for Adams in the same counties that autumn.[20]

Angry and frustrated by the general ticket system, Virginia Federalists could at least make the law itself a campaign issue and possibly win some votes thereby. Even some Republican legislators disliked it, for the bill passed by only four votes in the house of delegates, where Federalists were outnumbered two to one. Indignant letters and editorials in Virginia's Federalist newspapers called the General Ticket Law a tyrannical and unexampled attack on the privileges of the people.[21] By ending any possibility of Adams electors from Virginia, the law discouraged an effective statewide Federalist organization. The prospect for November was so dismal that some party stalwarts refused to vote at all. Thomas Evans, the Eastern Shore congressman,

19. "Monitor" and "A Federalist," in *Virginia Herald*, February 21, March 18, 1800.

20. *Virginia Herald*, June 3, 1800; George Hancock to James Breckinridge, April 21, 1800, in Breckinridge Papers, Alderman Library, University of Virginia (hereinafter cited as UVa); Leven Powell to Burr Powell, March 5, 1800, in "The Leven Powell Correspondence," *John P. Branch Historical Papers of Randolph-Macon College* (hereinafter cited as *Branch Historical Papers*), III (1903), 237–38; R. B. Lee to Charles Simms, April 4, 1800, E. Brooke to Simms, April 10, 1800, both in Charles Simms Papers, LC.

21. "Agricola," in *Virginia Herald*, April 22, 1800; Alexandria *Columbian Mirror*, April 12, June 21, October 28, 1800.

hoped that "disgusting as is the mode of election . . . the people, seeing no alternative, will pretty generally turn out"; but many did not, especially in solidly Republican counties where they might be held up to ridicule. In Lunenberg County, for example, a crusty old Presbyterian minister and firm Federalist, expecting what would probably happen, "determined to avoid the Mortification, by staying at home with my Boys."[22]

This attitude was less prevalent in North Carolina, where the party's chances of success were much brighter. The state was divided into twelve districts, each entitled to choose one presidential elector, so that Federalists expected to carry several districts even if Jefferson should poll an overall majority. William Boylan, the youthful and very partisan editor of the Raleigh *North Carolina Minerva*, boasted that "the friends of government may count with certainty on NINE votes out of 12 in favour of Mr. Adams," and once he even claimed eleven. Others had less exalted hopes, estimating perhaps five districts for Adams and seven for Jefferson.[23]

Without a statewide contest, Federalists thought centralized direction for their campaign was unnecessary. Many letters passed between local leaders in various parts of North Carolina; but no one undertook the guidance of the general effort, and candidates either thrust themselves forward or were informally selected by the prominent Federalists of each area. This sometimes led to difficulties. In the Newbern district, for instance, two Federalists were in competition, and it took four months to induce one to withdraw so that a Republican would not win against a divided Federalist majority. Despite such problems, the Adams candidates and their supporters were generally energetic, waging a spirited campaign over most of the state.[24]

22. Thomas Evans to Leven Powell, October 30, 1800, in "Correspondence of Col. Leven Powell, M.C., Relating to the Election of 1800," *Branch Historical Papers*, I (1901), 56; John Cameron to Duncan Cameron, November 16, 1800, in Cameron Family Papers, UNC; William H. Cabell to Joseph C. Cabell, November 6, 1800, in Cabell Deposit, UVa.

23. *North-Carolina Minerva*, June 3, 1800; Charles W. Harris to Robert W. Harris, June 20, 1800, in H. M. Wagstaff (ed.), *The Harris Letters* (Chapel Hill, N.C., 1916), 74; Harper to Otis, August 28, 1800, in Morison (ed.), *Otis*, I, 193–94.

24. Thomas Blount to John Gray Blount, July 1, 1800, in Alice B. Keith and William H. Masterson (eds.), *The Papers of John Gray Blount* (3 vols. to date; Raleigh, N.C., 1952–65), III, 393–94; William Boylan to Duncan Cameron, October 31, 1800, in Cam-

Federalists drew comfort during the year from the much-publicized prosecution of vast land frauds which implicated James Glasgow, former North Carolina secretary of state, and the wealthy merchant brothers, William and John Gray Blount. All three were prominent Republicans, and the Federalist *Minerva* declared their trial "a severe blow to the Jefferson interest in this state. Those who have been unfortunate enough to receive their political creed from such politicians, will seek information from another source." Federalists planned also to benefit, or so the Republicans claimed, by postponing collection of the unpopular direct tax in North Carolina until after November.[25] Partly offsetting these advantages, the party had lost the services of its most popular leader, ex-Governor Davie, who was serving with the peace mission in France. Support was also lacking from some federal officeholders, a few of whom reportedly even worked for Jefferson.[26]

Although the Adams men looked for a few votes from North Carolina, they realized that South Carolina was the truly crucial southern state in 1800. Yet there was no central state party organization at all and, except in the Charleston area, local Federalists did not much exert themselves. Charleston was the great party stronghold and the residence of many eminent Federalists. Sending seventeen members to the state legislature (which chose presidential electors), the city was a fierce battleground, with both sides organizing slates of candidates and working vigorously to win votes. Federalists were more active than ever before or afterward, but even they conceded that the Republicans outdid them in energy.[27] Outside Charleston, some of the small coastal parishes were overwhelmingly Federalist, but these were insufficient to carry the legislature. The party had to win a number of seats in the vast middle and upper country, where Republicans

---

eron Family Papers; "A True Whig," in *Raleigh Register*, August 12, 1800; Archibald Henderson to Walter Alves, July 28, 1800, in Archibald Henderson Collection, UNC; the announcements of the two Newbern Federalists are in *Newbern Gazette*, May 23, 1800.

25. *Wilmington Gazette*, January 9, 1800; *North-Carolina Minerva*, June 24, 1800.

26. Letter from Newbern, in *North-Carolina Minerva*, December 16, 1800.

27. DeSaussure to Morse, June 27, 1800, in Morse Family Papers; DeSaussure to John Rutledge, Jr., August 14, 1800, in Rutledge Papers, UNC; *Charleston Courier*, November 8, 1804; letter of Wade Hampton, in Alexandria *Columbian Mirror*, December 2, 1800.

were usually dominant; yet there was little Federalist organization and no intensive canvass in this huge area. Disgusted with his party's halfhearted campaign, Congressman Benjamin Huger declared that in light of the Republicans' vigor, he would not be surprised to see Jefferson succeed.[28]

The party assumed that local pride would induce many legislators to support Charles Cotesworth Pinckney even if they rejected Adams. Most of the state's Federalists probably did work honestly for Adams, but they were sure that he was much less popular than Pinckney in South Carolina. They expected Hamilton's campaign against Adams to hurt the president even within the party and certainly among the voters. James Gunn, Federalist senator from Georgia, advised the South Carolinians to "make the *question* Genl. Pinckney against any other man, and say but little about Federal, or anti-Federal."[29] Most hoped for, and a few expected, a complete triumph in the state, but the presidential result depended upon the individual preferences of state legislators and was thus difficult to predict. A Charleston Federalist was confident that "the weight of talents & Character in this State is federal" but complained that "the demagogues never leave the people to a free unbiased choice." Thomas Pinckney, brother of the vice-presidential candidate, expected a sweep of Charleston's fifteen house seats but could obtain scant information about prospects elsewhere. While hoping to see a Federalist majority in the assembly, he confessed that the Republicans were equally sanguine.[30]

The choice of electors in Georgia was also by the legislature, which was almost entirely Republican. The two vigorous Federalist newspapers in Augusta and Savannah carried no report of any organized effort to send Federalists to the assembly, and no one thought the party had any chance at all there. As one local writer said, "That Mr. Jefferson will have all the votes of Georgia, admits of no doubt, con-

28. Benjamin Huger to Otis, July 7, 1800, in Harrison Gray Otis Papers, MHS; David Ramsay to King, January 28, 1800, in Robert L. Brunhouse (ed.), *David Ramsay, 1749–1815: Selections from His Writings* (Philadelphia, 1965), 150.

29. DeSaussure to Pickering, August 12, 1800, in Timothy Pickering Papers; Harper to Otis, August 28, 1800, in Morison (ed.), *Otis*, I, 193; James Gunn to John Rutledge, Jr., May 15, 1800, in Rutledge Papers, UNC.

30. DeSaussure to Pickering, August 12, 1800, in Timothy Pickering Papers; Thomas Pinckney to John Rutledge, Jr., September 23, 1800, in Rutledge Papers, UNC.

sidering the mode of our elections," though "if they were conducted otherwise, I have no doubt would give Mr. Adams at least an equal number with him."[31]

Aware of the South's importance in the national political balance, northern Federalists speculated often upon the southern elections. Most of them assigned Adams from one-half to two-thirds of North Carolina's twelve votes and saw at least an even chance to win South Carolina's eight. One exuberant journalist even thought Pinckney, if not Adams, could win the four Georgia electors, but events soon hinted that such predictions might be optimistic.[32] In April, just as the presidential canvass was beginning, Republicans increased their majority in Virginia's annual legislative election.[33] Although disappointing to Federalists, this did not necessarily indicate the presidential result, since legislative contests often turned upon local issues and personalities.

Shortly, there was a more definite forecast of doom for the Adams campaign. John Marshall's recent appointment as secretary of state had created a vacancy in the Richmond congressional district, and the contest to fill it was a clear test of party strength. Marshall had barely won in 1799 and Federalists knew they must retain the seat to have any chance of winning Virginia for the president. It was therefore a severe blow when Marshall reported a resounding Republican victory in his district and mourned that "there is a tide in the affairs of nations, of parties, & of individuals. I fear that of real Americanism is on the ebb." The Republican candidate won by nearly two to one, carrying every county and plunging Federalists into despair.[34]

The Carolinas provided in their August and September congres-

31. "A Georgian," in Savannah *Columbian Museum*, October 3, 1800; Gunn to John Rutledge, Jr., June 21, 1800, DeSaussure to John Rutledge, Jr., August 14, 1800, both in Rutledge Papers, UNC; DeSaussure to Morse, November 3, 1800, in Morse Family Papers.

32. Baltimore *Federal Gazette* and Boston *Centinel*, both quoted in *South-Carolina State-Gazette*, June 25, July 15, November 7, 1800; Ames to King, September 24, 26, 1800, in King (ed.), *King*, III, 306.

33. Joseph C. Cabell to John Breckinridge, May 20, 1800, in Breckinridge Family Papers, LC; James T. Callender to Thomas Jefferson, April 28, 1800, in Thomas Jefferson Papers, LC.

34. John Marshall to Otis, August 8, 1800, in Harrison Gray Otis Papers; *Virginia Argus*, August 8, 1800.

sional elections a more encouraging forecast of the presidential race. North Carolina Federalists worked vigorously in at least half a dozen districts and made the campaign a referendum on the Adams years. The total vote for Congress in North Carolina was about 36,000, of which Federalists polled some 43 percent, a very respectable share. Four of the party's candidates succeeded, the same number as in 1798, when Federalism was at its height of popularity in the French crisis.[35] If Adams could do equally well in the state he might yet have another term in office.

Little is known of the South Carolina congressional campaign, and complete returns exist for only three of six races. Two coastal districts saw a brisk contest between parties, and the Federalists won both by handsome margins; elsewhere, one Federalist and three Republicans succeeded against token opposition. Republicans won two-thirds or more of the nearly 12,000 votes cast and gained two new seats; but Federalists kept the three low country districts, which together would elect more than half the legislature. This left the party still with some hope of giving Adams the eight votes which would reelect him.[36]

South Carolina's importance became ever clearer as results from other states were known. Virginia had long been given up for lost, but the size of Jefferson's victory there was a bitter surprise. The county returns dribbled in for several weeks in November, with each successive report leaving Adams more hopelessly behind. In all, Jefferson's ticket polled over 21,000 votes; the Adams men polled about 6,000 (22 percent). The Federalists led in only eight counties, losing even Richmond and barely winning the commercial center of Norfolk. In many counties only a stubborn handful, "biting their lips with vexation" amid the Republican crowds, gave in ballots for Adams; and sometimes there were no votes at all for the president. Except for the two Eastern Shore counties, which went nine to one for Adams, the Feder-

35. The campaign may be followed from notices and election returns in the *Wilmington Gazette*, *North-Carolina Minerva*, and *Raleigh Register*, June–September, 1800.

36. DeSaussure to John Rutledge, Jr., October 22, 1800, in Miscellaneous Papers, New York Public Library (hereinafter cited as NYPL). The meager coverage of the congressional campaign may be found in the *South-Carolina State-Gazette*, Charleston *City Gazette*, and Charleston *Times*, August–October, 1800.

alist ticket did best in northwestern Virginia, with 47 percent of the vote. The president dropped to 36 percent in the Northern Neck, 33 percent in the valley, and only 20 percent in the Tidewater counties; and in the vast Piedmont, which cast nearly half the state's votes, Adams lost by a humiliating twelve-to-one margin.[37] The General Ticket Law probably did keep some Federalists at home, but even if electors had run by districts, Adams would have had no more than two of Virginia's twenty-one votes.

North Carolina, voting at the same time as Virginia, gave more pleasing results, though still below the Federalists' earlier predictions. They carried four electoral districts out of twelve and lacked only fourteen votes of winning another. In the statewide popular vote of some 24,000, the Adams men received about 10,500, or 44 percent. Federalists ran well in the western Piedmont and won handily in the southern Piedmont, the coastal counties around Newbern, and both the upper and lower Cape Fear Valley. All these areas except the lower Cape Fear had sizable Scottish and Scotch-Irish populations and all centered around commercial towns—Salisbury, Fayetteville, Newbern, and Wilmington. Only in the mountainous west and the plantation counties along the Virginia border was Jefferson far ahead.[38] In North Carolina and Virginia together, the president had won two electors more than in 1796. Georgia's legislature would choose four Jefferson men without opposition, but the Republican challenge might still be turned back if South Carolina remained true.

As Federalists gathered in Washington for the approaching session of Congress, they anxiously watched South Carolina. Outside that state Jefferson and Adams each had sixty-five votes; thus John Marshall warned Pinckney that "on your legislature I believe depends absolutely the election."[39] The October legislative elections had left the complexion of the South Carolina assembly still doubtful, and the evenly divided congressional voting further obscured the presidential

37. William H. Cabell to Joseph C. Cabell, November 6, 1800, in Cabell Deposit. Returns are in the Virginia State Library (hereinafter cited as VSL).

38. The North Carolina vote is estimated from incomplete returns in the state's newspapers and the *South-Carolina State-Gazette*, for November, 1800.

39. W. W. Burrows to Jonathan Williams, December 8, 1800, in W. W. Burrows Papers, UVa; John Marshall to C. C. Pinckney, November 22, 1800, photostat in Pinckney Family Papers, LC.

outcome.[40] Federalists were cheered by their victory in Charleston and felt confident that the seaboard parishes, containing few voters and dominated by great planters and merchants, would support the administration. Republicans, for their part, expected much from the up-country representatives. Both parties wooed the newly chosen legislators. Charles Pinckney, the vigorous Republican cousin of the Federalist brothers, lodged himself in Columbia to work for Jefferson. Meanwhile, the Federalists, anchored in Charleston, spread their arguments throughout the state and anxiously watched as the legislature met.[41]

A letter from Columbia in mid-November claimed sure victory because forty-eight of the first fifty-eight legislators to arrive were Federalists, and until the very eve of the election, South Carolina party leaders promised a full 8 votes for Adams and Pinckney. Then, suddenly, fully half the assembly attended a Republican caucus and the house chose a Republican speaker by nearly two to one. The Federalist cause collapsed. Meeting in joint session, the two houses gave eight Republican electors from 82 to 87 votes and the Federalists only 63 to 69. Nearly all the Charleston men voted for Adams, but the coastal rice and cotton plantation parishes were split. The president won a large majority in Beaufort and Charleston districts but lost the Georgetown area. In the entire up-country, only a handful of assemblymen supported the Federalist electors.[42] The national party was sorely "disappointed in the election at South Carolina, notwithstanding the indubitable assurances received from thence."[43] Adams was out, the Republicans in, and Federalists could only wait nervously for the new age to begin.

40. DeSaussure to John Rutledge, Jr., October 22, 1800, in Miscellaneous Papers; DeSaussure to Morse, November 3, 1800, in Morse Family Papers; *South-Carolina State-Gazette*, October 21, 1800.

41. Charles Pinckney to Jefferson, November 22, 1800, in Jefferson Papers; letter of Wade Hampton, in Alexandria *Columbian Mirror*, December 2, 1800.

42. *South-Carolina State-Gazette*, November 18, 1800; *Georgetown Gazette*, December 3, 1800; William Polk to John Steele, December 5, 1800, in H. M. Wagstaff (ed.), *The Papers of John Steele* (2 vols.; Raleigh, N.C., 1924), I, 193; Wolfe, *Jeffersonian Democracy*, 157–60; Cunningham, *Jeffersonian Republicans, 1789–1801*, 232–37.

43. Cabot to King, December 28, 1800, in King (ed.), *King*, III, 354.

Chapter 3 FACING THE NEW ORDER

FACING the gloomy prospect of a Republican era, southern Federalists searched frantically for ways to lessen the damage to a stable American society and to "rational liberty" as they conceived it. First they tried to block Jefferson by a desperate attempt to make Aaron Burr president, although local Federalist opinion doubted the wisdom of such a course. Failing in this, the southern party hoped at least to entrench Federalism within an expanded and strengthened judicial system and to restrain the violence of an increasingly partisan press by renewing the Sedition Act. Beyond this, they could only await the future with a growing despair.

After the unexpected defeat in South Carolina, Federalists resigned themselves to losing the presidency, but a quirk of the electoral system still gave them hope of blocking Jefferson. Under the Constitution each elector voted for two men equally. Whoever had the most votes (at least a majority) became president, and the runner-up vice-president. In 1800 the Republicans had intended Aaron Burr for vice-president, and at least one Republican elector should have omitted voting for him. Instead, Jefferson and Burr each had seventy-three votes, Adams sixty-five, and Pinckney sixty-four. This left the final choice of president to the House of Representatives, voting by states between the two leading candidates. Since the new Seventh Congress had not yet taken office—in fact, was still being elected in some states —the presidential deadlock would be decided by the old Federalist-dominated Congress.

Given this limited choice, most Federalists thought Burr would be less dangerous than Jefferson, though both candidates were highly offensive to them. Congressman Leven Powell, whose Virginia district adjoined Washington, considered for a time giving no vote at all and desperately sought advice from friends at home. He thought Burr lacked moral character but preferred his political principles to Jefferson's. When later reassured about Burr's character, Powell joined the other Virginia congressmen in supporting him. General Henry Lee, also in Congress, flatly refused a plea from Alexander Hamilton to support Jefferson. Lee explained that since the Republicans would abandon Burr, he would owe his office to Federalist votes and would have to support Federalist policies.[1]

John Rutledge, Jr., of South Carolina also ignored Hamilton's argument. He felt, as Lee did, that Burr's election would wreck the Republican party and force the new president to conciliate Federalists. He admitted that Burr might attempt an open assault on the Constitution; but this would be detected and easily foiled, whereas Jefferson's subtle subversion would be much more dangerous and more likely to succeed. The North Carolina delegation also fell in line. Expressing their position, Archibald Henderson of Salisbury saw Jefferson's election as a fatal blow to religion and order, and feared that America was fated to be another example of the fallibility of republican governments. He said that although Burr was not the Federalists' choice, he was at least a talented politician and was "at *heart* no *democrat*."[2]

Outside Congress, leading Federalists were sharply split. Two party newspapers, the *North Carolina Minerva* and the *South Carolina*

1. Leven Powell to Burr Powell, January 12, 19, 1801, in "Leven Powell Correspondence," I, 56–57, III, 244–45; Henry Lee to Alexander Hamilton, February 6, 1801, in Alexander Hamilton Papers.

2. John Rutledge, Jr., to Henry Dana Ward, January 3, 1801, in Rutledge Papers, UNC; John Rutledge, Jr., to Alexander Hamilton, January 10, 1801, in Hamilton (ed.), *Hamilton*, VI, 510; Archibald Henderson to Walter Alves, January 2, 1801, in Archibald Henderson, "A Federalist of the Old School," *North Carolina Booklet*, XVII (1917), 21; William Barry Grove to Alves, February 27, 1801, in Archibald Henderson Collection.

State-Gazette, preferred Burr, as did Charles Cotesworth Pinckney, the unsuccessful vice-presidential candidate. Other respected Federalists, such as John Steele of North Carolina (then comptroller of the currency), James Gunn of Georgia, and Secretary of State John Marshall, feared Burr more than Jefferson. And William R. Davie, among others, worried that a congressional deadlock might produce armed conflict in the country. He thought the Federalists should yield "at once to the public sentiment. . . . [Burr's election] will sink the Federalists in the opinion of the majority, and in its operation effect the entire destruction of the Federal party by [their] becoming responsible for an administration they can neither *control* nor *influence*, and consecrating beyond all doubt Mr. Jefferson in the eyes of the people."[3] Local opinion was also divided. According to Republicans, the Federalists in Virginia's northern Shenandoah Valley were strongly for Burr, but the "moderate and rational" Federalists around Williamsburg supported Jefferson. So did strongly Federalist Loudoun County, Virginia, and Davie claimed that in the Halifax section of North Carolina nearly all the "most enlightened friends of government" joined him in preferring Jefferson.[4]

Nevertheless, when the House began voting for president on February 10, 1801, the southern Federalist congressmen stood with Burr. On the first ballot three North Carolinians and three Virginians gave a token vote for Jefferson, one said, to show their acquiescence should he be elected. Thereafter, all but one southerner voted continually for Burr. United North and South, the Federalists gave Burr a majority of individual votes, but Jefferson led in states, eight to six, with two divided. After thirty-five such deadlocked ballots, Republicans began

3. *North-Carolina Minerva*, February 24, 1801; *South-Carolina State-Gazette*, January 20, 1801; C. C. Pinckney to Theodore Sedgwick, February 12, 1801, in Theodore Sedgwick Papers, MHS; John Steele to Ann Steele, January 3, 1801, and William R. Davie to Steele, February 2, 1801, in John Steele Papers, UNC; James Gunn to Alexander Hamilton, January 9, 1801, in Alexander Hamilton Papers; John Marshall to Alexander Hamilton, January 1, 1801, in Hamilton (ed.), *Hamilton*, VI, 502.

4. Statement of Thomas Brown, "Brown Lineage," I, 42, typed copy in Ambler-Brown Papers, Duke University; Henry Bedinger to George M. Bedinger, January 25, 1801, copy in Dandridge Papers, Duke University; Joseph C. Cabell to Nicholas Cabell, March 5, 1801, in Cabell Deposit; William R. Davie to Steele, February 2, 1801, in John Steele Papers. On Loudoun County see the letters to Leven Powell, February 5–20, 1801, in "Powell Correspondence," I, 57–73, and Henry Brooke to Powell, January 2, 1801, in Leven Powell Papers, LC.

hinting of violence if Jefferson were kept out. Faced with this prospect, a number of Federalist congressmen agreed with Archibald Henderson that a weak inefficient government under Jefferson was preferable to anarchy and confusion. Enough Federalists abstained or switched their votes on the thirty-sixth ballot to allow Jefferson's election.[5] Republicans were sure that the minority's vain attempt to elect Burr debased them in public opinion. But Leven Powell and his Federalist colleagues thought their opposition had won valuable promises of moderation from Jefferson's camp, if only the Republicans would live up to them.[6]

Besides the presidential struggle, there were lesser matters to occupy the lame-duck Federalist Congress in its last weeks of power. One was the Judiciary Act of 1801, which passed in January by a strict party vote. Establishing a layer of eighteen federal circuit courts between the existing district and supreme courts, the law relieved supreme court justices of riding circuit duty and also expanded federal judicial power at the expense of the states. The attack on state sovereignty and the cost of paying the additional officials aroused fierce Republican opposition, and Federalists were kept busy responding to these objections. The Judiciary Act was necessary, they said, to reduce the case load of federal judges to manageable size. It would also render justice more speedy and convenient, because the larger number of courts would save litigants and witnesses from long journeys. Surely the people would accept a small added expense to improve the administration of justice.[7]

Federalists argued further that the government could better enforce its laws, making it less dependent on the states and securing more firmly the allegiance of the people, by showing that it was strong enough to protect their lives and property in its own courts. "We are

5. Leven Powell to Burr Powell, February 16, 1801, in "Leven Powell Correspondence," III, 250; Henderson, "Federalist of the Old School," 22. The one southern Federalist to vote always for Jefferson was supposed by the newspapers to be Samuel Goode of Virginia.

6. Joseph Eggleston to Joseph Jones, February 17, 1801, in Joseph Jones Papers, Duke University; Leven Powell to Burr Powell, February 16, 1801, in "Leven Powell Correspondence," III, 250–52.

7. Archibald Henderson's circular letter, in *North-Carolina Minerva*, April 7, 1801; Robert Goodloe Harper's letter, in *Alexandria Advertiser*, March 18, 1801; John Marshall to William Patterson, February 2, 1801, in William Patterson Transcripts, NYPL.

too apt to view our Federal Government as a foreign one," remarked Henry Lee. "These prejudices . . . [are] unworthy of Americans." Privately, the southerners were as much concerned with the political as with the legal effect of the Judiciary Act, because the new offices were sure to be filled by good Federalists. Secure in their life tenure, the new judges could resist any Republican attempt to lay violent hands upon the Constitution. Davie stressed the importance of appointing "men of active and popular, as well as professional talents; on their exertions will depend in a great measure the course of Federalism in the Southern States."[8]

The Sedition Act of 1798 excited another hot debate. The law would expire shortly unless renewed, and Federalists were determined to extend it, despite Republican complaints of political repression. The southern congressmen insisted that no honest critic of government had ever been persecuted under the act. It was more lenient than the common law, they said, because it provided a jury trial and allowed truth as a defense against the charge of libel. Courts had declared the law constitutional; state legislatures had endorsed it. Even though the French danger had passed, the law was still necessary. As Archibald Henderson told his constituents, the press was the only vehicle of public information and if it should "teem with falsehoods and malicious abuse, they [the people] will be deceived" and thus prevented from forming just opinions.[9]

Only a few southerners broke ranks to oppose the law. John Marshall, though no longer in the House, had already declared his objections to the original Sedition Act in 1799. Benjamin Huger of South Carolina, a loyal party stalwart on other matters, thought the law was both inexpedient and unnecessary. It was a crisis measure and the crisis had passed. He did not think, as other Federalists professed to, that the people approved the Sedition Act. Certainly his own constituents did not. Huger agreed that unbridled expression of opinion

8. *Debates and Proceedings of the Congress of the United States* (Washington, D.C., 1834–56), 6th Cong., 2nd Sess., 901–903 (hereinafter cited as *Annals of Congress*); William R. Davie to Steele, February 21, 1801, in John Steele Papers; Kathryn Turner, "Federalist Policy and the Judiciary Act of 1801," *William and Mary Quarterly*, 3rd ser., XXII (1965), 3–32.

9. Henderson, "Federalist of the Old School," 26–28; remarks of John Rutledge, Jr., Henry Lee, and Robert Goodloe Harper in the House, *Annals of Congress*, 6th Cong., 2nd Sess., 929–40, 960–63.

was dangerous, but he felt this evil was outweighed by the advantages of completely free speech and press. Voting with him against extension were his neighbor, Abraham Nott of South Carolina, and two Virginians, Josiah Parker and Samuel Goode. However, the united support of the remaining Federalists, including eleven southerners, was sufficient to continue the Sedition Act in force.[10]

Consuming nearly as much time as these great matters of policy was the argument over a mausoleum to the memory of George Washington. Opposed by Republicans as a wasteful project that would honor Washington no more than a cheaper monument, the mausoleum found great favor with Federalist leaders. In their minds, it was a test of feeling toward the Father of the Country; the Republicans, in seeking to deny him this great memorial, showed their contempt for his life and policies. Robert Goodloe Harper declaimed in true Federalist style that "the greatest honor which this country ever has received . . . was derived from numbering with its sons the immortal WASHINGTON." Thirteen southern Federalists followed the lead of Huger and Harper and their votes provided the margin by which the great monument was approved.[11]

For all the length of these debates, their lasting importance was small. The Sedition Act soon lapsed, the Judiciary Law was repealed within two years, and Washington's monument was still decades from construction. Once out of office, the southern Federalists no longer urged the expansion of national power at state expense, as they had in the Judiciary Act debates; and they certainly found nothing repulsive about violent criticism of the government, as they had in the Sedition Act discussion. Yet this final exercise of power did exhibit certain traits which remained with the Federalists in defeat. The urgent desire that dependable party members hold federal office and that the courts act as a check on Republican excesses continued to concern Federalists in later years. Their distrust of newspapers and of uncontrolled public opinion was also to be a lasting theme in the party's political thought. And the veneration of Washington and the use of his

10. Albert J. Beveridge, *The Life of John Marshall* (4 vols.; Boston, 1916–19), II, 386–89, 451–52; Huger's speech in *Annals of Congress*, 6th Cong., 2nd Sess., 925–27.

11. *Annals of Congress*, 6th Cong., 2nd Sess., 801–803, 858–63, and vote recorded on 864–65.

name to sanctify their party was forever characteristic of Federalists, both northern and southern.

Turning reluctantly aside from their final months in authority, the southern Federalists anxiously awaited the new order of things. A Charleston attorney wondered whether the Virginians really intended important alterations of the Constitution. He asked those on the scene in Washington, "Are the . . . Establishments of the nation secure? . . . If they mean an entire alteration of our System . . . I fear a dissolution of the Union. . . . Straws will shew how the wind blows—that it may be a wholesome breeze, unaccompanied by storms & tempests, & lightning is my ardent prayer—for I would rather have my fears disappointed than realized."[12] Even men long in federal office were perplexed, but Jefferson's first official act temporarily dissipated this cloud of doubt and fear.

The new president, despite the bitterness of the preceding campaign, did not make his inaugural speech a tirade against the opposition. Rather, the moderate tone of his address and his assurance that "we are all republicans; we are all federalists," pleased many in the defeated party. Chief Justice John Marshall, who had sworn Jefferson into office, praised the speech as "well judged and conciliatory." William Boylan of the *North Carolina Minerva* boasted that the Federalists' approval of Jefferson's address showed their patriotism, and he expected their mildness to continue as long as the president maintained his tone of conciliation.[13]

Not all were willing to assume that Jefferson's conduct would be consistent with the creed laid down in his speech. One critic complained that the president's remarks had been so vague that they gave no real clue to his future policy. The South's only Federalist senator, lame duck James Gunn of Georgia, scornfully remarked that only the weak and disloyal Federalists—those ready and willing to desert to the enemy—were pleased with Jefferson's remarks. Others, who at first approved the address because they thought it forecast a policy of leaving the Federalist system untouched, soon realized their error.

12. H. W. DeSaussure to John Rutledge, Jr., January 12, 1801, in Rutledge Papers, UNC; Steele to wife, February 27, 1801, in John Steele Papers.

13. Marshall to C. C. Pinckney, March 4, 1801, in Beveridge, *Marshall*, III, 11; *North-Carolina Minerva*, March 31, 1801.

The first hints of Republican patronage policy shocked them into believing that, despite Jefferson's mild professions, the "fiery passions of party spirit and resentment" would lead him into dangerous behavior. William R. Davie thought the future was menacing and that things would "take their natural course and grow always worse and worse.[14]

14. *South-Carolina State-Gazette*, April 3, 1801; letter from Richmond, *ibid.*, May 4, 1801; Gunn to John Rutledge, Jr., March 16, 1801, and Thomas Evans to John Rutledge, Jr., December 8, 1801, in Rutledge Papers, UNC.

TWO Southern Federalists in National Politics: The Decline, 1801–1807

Chapter 4 DEFENDING FEDERALIST MEN AND MEASURES, 1801–1807

SENSIBLE Republicans doubted that the Federalists' initial satisfaction with the new president would long endure. Indeed, in their quiet tolerance of Jefferson in the spring of 1801, many Federalists assumed that he would not greatly alter existing policies nor unseat incumbent officeholders merely because they were of the wrong party. In the capital itself, Congressman William Barry Grove thought otherwise. In his view, there were "many hungry demagogues who have barked at the present [Adams] adminn. 'till they are hoarse, and they must be provided for." [1]

Events soon proved Grove to be far more correct than the optimistic Federalists. Much vexed by the nearly unanimous Federalism of the civil service and desiring to reward loyal Republican workers, Jefferson dispelled his initial appearance of moderate behavior by quickly ousting some incumbents from their posts. All whom Adams had appointed after he had clearly lost the election and all those guilty of misconduct were dismissed in short order. Still other Federalists in the judiciary, treasury, and military departments were to have their very offices abolished. Beyond this, Jefferson was unsure how

1. John Haywood to John Steele, December 16, 1800, in Wagstaff (ed.), *Papers of John Steele*, I, 198; William Barry Grove to William Gaston, December 12, 1800, in William Gaston Papers.

far to go. He wanted his party eventually to hold at least two-thirds of all government positions, but generally he was slow to dismiss Federalists merely for their politics.[2]

Still, the president made quite enough removals to scandalize the opposition, especially since vacancies went invariably to Republicans. By the summer of 1801, southern Federalists were already complaining of persecution, accusing Jefferson of dismissing many competent officials solely because of their politics. The partisan vengeance which Congressman Rutledge saw in these removals shocked, he said, even some Republicans "who are men of some sobriety and decency of Character (God knows there are but few such)." Although sympathetic toward those who were dismissed, Rutledge believed that Jefferson's rash actions would ultimately benefit the Federalists, for he was confident that public sentiment would rapidly turn against the president.[3]

Nothing irritated Federalists more than Jefferson's famous letter to a group of New Haven, Connecticut, merchants who had condemned his removal of the local customs collector. His reply included the first clear public statement of his intention to replace large numbers of Federalist officials with good Republicans. For Congressman Thomas Evans, who had always suspected Jefferson's initial mildness to be a fraud, the New Haven address only confirmed the president's duplicity. Henry William DeSaussure, a rising Charleston lawyer, agreed. "Never," the bitter Carolinian wrote, "was there such an open declaration of rotten principles—of a determination to be the head of a party & not of the Nation." He hoped that Federalists would republish the New Haven statement before every election, because it would disgust moderate men throughout the country.[4]

2. The best explanations of Jefferson's patronage policy are Dumas Malone, *Jefferson the President: First Term, 1801–1805* (Boston, 1970), Chap. 5, and Cunningham, *Jeffersonian Republicans in Power*, Chaps. 2–4. For the partisan nature of Adams' judicial appointments (including marshals and district attorneys), see Dwight F. Henderson, *Courts for a New Nation* (Washington, D.C., 1971). On the impact of Jefferson's policy, see Carl E. Prince, "The Passing of the Aristocracy: Jefferson's Removal of the Federalists, 1801–1805," *Journal of American History*, LVII (1970), 563–75.

3. Letter from Richmond, in *South-Carolina State-Gazette*, May 4, 1801; Bushrod Washington to Alexander Hamilton, November 21, 1801, in Hamilton (ed.), *Hamilton*, VI, 526; John Rutledge, Jr., to Theodore Sedgwick, May 10, 1801, in Theodore Sedgwick Papers.

4. Thomas Evans to John Rutledge, Jr., December 8, 1801, and H. W. DeSaussure

Party newspapers and their readers took up the same cry, even insisting that the removals were unconstitutional and that Jefferson should be impeached. Printing a protest by some Savannah merchants against the ouster of their Federalist customs collector, Abraham Hodge of the *North-Carolina Journal* consoled the unfortunate man, saying, "Dismissal is no disgrace. Should the present temper of the times continue, *holding* an office under the present administration will soon be considered a disgrace."[5]

Bitterness toward Jefferson's patronage policy continued for years, fed anew by each removal. As the southern Federalists saw it, there was an unceasing effort to rid every government department, even local post offices, of anyone who had the misfortune to be a member of their party.[6] Still worse was the dismissal of old revolutionary patriots like General Rufus Putnam, the surveyor-general, or William Heth, a Virginia customs collector. Such men had a double right to their offices—they were capable and had fought for their country.[7]

Federalists hoped that the army and navy at least would be free of partisanship. However, Jefferson found that nearly every officer in the armed forces was either a Federalist or entirely nonpolitical, since the previous administrations had consciously excluded Republicans from commissions. To right this imbalance, Jefferson dismissed some Federalists (though not necessarily because of their politics alone), and his new appointments were heavily Republican. This policy drew sharp protests from the Federalist press, whose editors hastened to defend "their" military men.[8]

In their hostility to Jefferson's patronage system, the southern Federalists spoke both as politicians and as men deeply concerned

---

to John Rutledge, Jr., August 25 and September 17, 1801, in Rutledge Papers, UNC; John Rutledge, Jr., to Harrison Gray Otis, September 15, 1801, in Harrison Gray Otis Papers.

5. "Americanus" and "A Virginian," in *South-Carolina State-Gazette*, August 1, October 12, 14, 27, and November 8, 1801; *North-Carolina Journal*, November 16, 1801.

6. *Charleston Courier*, April 23, 1804; Martinsburg *Berkeley & Jefferson Intelligencer*, January 20, 1804.

7. Raleigh *Minerva*, January 2, 1804. For an address of appreciation by Petersburg merchants to Heth, and his reply, see *Virginia Gazette*, August 25, 1802, and *South-Carolina State-Gazette*, August 31, 1802.

8. Cunningham, *Jeffersonian Republicans in Power*, 66–68; *Charleston Courier*, June 20, 1804; "An Eastern-Shore-Man," in *Norfolk Gazette and Publick Ledger* (hereinafter cited as *Norfolk Gazette*), November 8, 1804.

with the implications of his policy. As partisans, they of course objected to replacing any Federalist with a Republican. Yet they also felt a genuine fear that the new administration stressed political more than administrative capacity. Not merely Federalists, but able Federalists, were turned out of office; not merely Republicans, but inept Republicans, were put in. Jefferson seemed to regard government offices not as positions of public trust to be staffed by men of education, honesty, and community standing, but as mere rewards to party workers. Surely the man who distributed partisan literature, who roamed the taverns treating voters, who associated with the most dissolute persons to gain their suffrage, was not likely to have either the capacity or character to make a good civil servant. He would attend to partisan, not to public, business; and even if he wanted to do his job well, he would not know how. These beliefs, though seldom baldly stated, are implied in the Federalists' criticism. Before 1801, of course, the Federalists themselves had made party loyalty paramount in staffing government, but they honestly believed that their officeholders, in addition to being "safe" politically, were also highminded and able, whereas Jefferson's were not.[9]

Besides expecting a decline in the quality of public administration, Federalists also worried that the freedom of elections would be curtailed. Hordes of federal officers, owing their jobs to their support of the Republican party, would be a powerful force in maintaining that party in power. Any Federalist who might be allowed to keep his post would be afraid to campaign for his party and principles because a vengeful Republican executive might dismiss him. Thus Jefferson would have a host of servants paid by the public and adept at electioneering, who could keep the Republican party in office indefinitely.

This problem, however, would appear only gradually over the long term. Of more immediate concern, some Federalists were in danger of losing not only their positions but their reputations as well. Just before the first session of the Seventh Congress adjourned in the

9. Thomas Rhett Smith, *An Oration Delivered in Saint Michael's Church the Fifth of July, 1802* (Charleston, S.C., 1802), 16. As Sidney H. Aronson has shown, there was little difference in the background and social status of the high-level Adams and Jefferson appointees: *Status and Kinship in the Higher Civil Service: Standards of Selection in the Administrations of John Adams, Thomas Jefferson, and Andrew Jackson* (Cambridge, Mass., 1964).

spring of 1802, the Republican majority hastily approved and printed for wide distribution the report of a special House investigating committee. The report charged "that considerable sums of the public money have been greatly misapplied, and that much expense has been incurred without legal authority" by various former members of the Adams administration. Taken by surprise, the accused rushed into print with lengthy denials.[10] These stories all sought to discredit the committee, claiming that it had decided in advance to condemn the Federalist officials and that releasing the report on the eve of adjournment was simply a plot to make irresponsible charges without leaving time for a rebuttal. Federalists insisted that the accused men were blameless victims of Republican vengeance. William Barry Grove, who with the other Federalist congressmen had fought vainly against releasing the document, wrote of his contempt and indignation at the report of the "*Investigating* discriminating & Criminating Committee."[11]

Defending their officeholders against such threats was only part of the Federalists' task as an opposition party.They had also to defend party programs of the Adams years from vigorous Republican assaults. The most important battle involved the Judiciary Act of 1801, which the new Republican majority was determined to repeal. There was a certain need for the law, but Republicans were outraged that all the new judicial positions had been filled by Federalists. This seemed a blatant attempt to thwart the people's will by perpetuating Federalism in the courts after its rejection at the polls. Furthermore, the new judicial establishment was more expensive than the old, and Jefferson wanted to reduce the cost of government. As soon as the Seventh Congress convened in December, 1801, the Republicans undertook the repeal of the Judiciary Act.

Federalists both in and out of Congress vigorously resisted, with Archibald Henderson of North Carolina helping lead the defense in

10. *North-Carolina Journal*, May 17, 1802. Letters by Benjamin Stoddert, Oliver Wolcott, and Thomas Stanford appeared in numerous southern Federalist papers, for example, *Virginia Gazette*, September 22–October 22, 1802.

11. Grove to Steele, October 1, 1802, in John Steele Papers. The only three southern Federalists present in Congress at the end of the session had voted against releasing the report: *Annals of Congress*, 7th Cong., 1st Sess., 1285. For press comment, see *South-Carolina State-Gazette*, May 2, 1802, and "Decius," in *Virginia Gazette*, July 14–August 14, 1802.

the House of Representatives.[12] Repeal, he said, would overburden the remaining federal courts. There was already a huge backlog of cases in the judicial system, and reducing the number of courts would only compound the problem. Repeal would also force supreme court justices, even if aged and infirm, to traverse the country riding circuit court duty. This was unfair to the litigants, as well as to the judges, since a justice might decide a case on circuit and later sit in supreme court upon an appeal from his own ruling.[13]

Federalists also complained that the repealing bill was clearly unconstitutional. Judges were supposed to hold office during good behavior and were not removable at the mere pleasure of the president or Congress. This life tenure was directly spelled out in the Constitution. Republicans did not actually propose to remove the new judges, but they would achieve the same effect by abolishing the courts and thus set a dangerous precedent that would render the constitutional guarantee of life tenure valueless. As Chief Justice Marshall said, "the distinction of taking the Office from the Judge, and not the Judge from the Office" was "puerile and nonsensical."[14]

More important than the fate of individuals was the danger to the entire court system, which Federalists saw as the only protection against executive and legislative tyranny. They felt that future judges would shrink from opposing illegal acts of the president and Congress for fear of being swept from the bench. Even if a courageous judge should stand against the other branches, he would only find his office abolished and himself unemployed. Humbling the judiciary would be catastrophic, Archibald Henderson said. With the other Federalists, he believed that life and property would be safe only if judges held an independent tenure free of outside pressures. It would be criminal, he

12. Henderson, "Federalist of the Old School," 23; Ralph Wormeley to John Rutledge, Jr., February 25, 1802, in Rutledge Papers, UNC; William H. Hill to Duncan Cameron, January 28, 1802, in Cameron Family Papers.

13. Speeches of Archibald Henderson, John Stanly, Benjamin Huger, and John Rutledge, Jr., *Annals of Congress*, 7th Cong., 1st Sess., 523–30, 569–79, 665–93, 734–62; Abraham Nott to John Rutledge, Jr., February 20, 1802, in Rutledge Papers, UNC; John Marshall to William Patterson, April 6, 1802, in William Patterson Transcripts.

14. Marshall to [?], April 24, 1802, in Miscellaneous Papers; letter, in *Alexandria Advertiser*, February 10, 1802; "A Friend to an Independent Judiciary," in *South-Carolina State-Gazette*, July 16, 1802; Haywood to Steele, March 6, 1802, in Wagstaff (ed.), *Papers of John Steele*, I, 257.

said, for Republicans to destroy this safeguard merely to gratify their partisan designs.[15]

Joining the fight, Federalist newspapers bulged with reprints of congressional speeches and petitions from lawyers, all defending the Judiciary Act. Even a few southern Republicans, including Senator John Colhoun of South Carolina, broke with their party on the issue.[16] In spite of such defections and a united Federalist opposition, the Republican majority pushed the repealing bill triumphantly through Congress. Federalists despaired, moaning that the Constitution was no more.[17]

As discouraging as this defeat was, more was yet to come in the assault on judicial Federalism. Within two years after their successful repeal of the Judiciary Act, Republicans began a concerted effort to remove leading Federalist judges by impeaching District Judge John Pickering of Massachusetts, who was insane and often drunk. The ultimate Republican goal, if the Pickering case went well, was probably to clear the Supreme Court itself of its most prominent Federalists, especially Chief Justice John Marshall.[18] Impelled by political motives on both sides, senators conducted the Pickering trial in a partisan and irregular manner. Federalists defended him, ignoring his obvious unfitness for the bench. Republicans heard biased testimony from their own partisans, refused to allow Pickering counsel, and fi-

15. *Annals of Congress*, 7th Cong., 1st Sess., 687, 523–30, 569–79, 734–62, 855–62; Henderson to Samuel Johnston, January 24, 1802, in Hayes Collection, North Carolina Department of Archives and History (hereinafter cited as NCDAH); Walter Alves to Duncan Cameron, February 12, 1802, and Henderson to Duncan Cameron, January 7, 1802, in Cameron Family Papers.

16. *Augusta Herald*, May 12, 1802; *North-Carolina Journal*, March 1, 15, 1802. For examples of Republican opposition to repeal, see John Randolph to Joseph H. Nicholson, May 9, 1801, in John Randolph of Roanoke Papers, UVa, and John Shore to John Breckinridge, March 14, 1802, in Breckinridge Family Papers, LC; *South-Carolina State-Gazette*, April 10, 1802. On the tension between Republican moderates and radicals on the judiciary question, see Richard E. Ellis, *The Jeffersonian Crisis: Courts and Politics in the Young Republic* (New York, 1971), Chap. 3.

17. William R. Davie to Steele, March 13, 1802, in J. G. deRoulhac Hamilton (ed.), *William R. Davie: A Memoir, Followed by His Letters, with Notes by Kemp P. Battle* (Chapel Hill, N.C., 1907), 52–53; *South-Carolina State-Gazette*, March 18, 1802. The vigorous Republican effort to maintain party unity in the Judiciary Act repeal is shown in Alexander B. Lacy, Jr., "Jefferson and Congress: Congressional Methods and Politics, 1801–1809" (Ph.D. dissertation, University of Virginia, 1964), Chap. 2.

18. Lynn W. Turner, "The Impeachment of John Pickering," *American Historical Review*, LIV (1949), 485–507; Ellis, *Jeffersonian Crisis*, Chaps. 5–7; Malone, *Jefferson the President: First Term*, 468–70, 472–73.

nally voted to remove him, although he had committed no constitutional high crime or misdemeanor. Perhaps recognizing Pickering's unsuitability as a rallying point, the southern Federalists remained quiet during and after his trial. Only a handful of newspaper articles indicate that the party even cared whether one of its own was being cast from office.[19]

Far more worrisome was the Republican decision to strike next at Samuel Chase, an associate justice of the Supreme Court. No one claimed that Chase was a drunkard or had lost his wits; his offense was simply partisan behavior on the bench. On these grounds, Republican congressmen empowered a committee to investigate him with a view toward impeachment. Federalists, claiming that there were no charges worthy of investigation, strongly opposed the resolution. Thomas Lowndes, Charleston's Federalist congressman, protested that an investigation would intimidate the courts and make judges the tools of Congress.[20]

Such opposition had little effect. The House not only investigated Chase but formally impeached him by a strict party vote in March, 1804. Congress adjourned before senators could try the case, but Federalists expected the worst. They hardly thought the charges had any merit, but they feared Chase could not receive a fair trial before a partisan Senate loaded more than two to one against him. Because of the Chase trial, the repeal of the Judiciary Act, and Republican attacks on several state courts, Charleston's Federalists feared that paper sanctions could not protect the feeble judicial branch of government from legislative encroachment.[21]

Editors gave generously of their limited space to print Chase's lengthy memorial refuting the charges against himself. When the Senate trial began in 1805, Chase's reply was again spread liberally across their pages, often to the nearly complete exclusion of other

19. Turner, "Impeachment," 491–505; Martinsburg *Berkeley & Jefferson Intelligencer*, April 27, 1804; Raleigh *Minerva*, April 30, 1804.

20. Speeches of Thomas Lowndes and Thomas Griffin, in *Annals of Congress*, 8th Cong., 1st Sess., 825, 856–57.

21. DeSaussure to Timothy Pickering, February 26, 1804, in Timothy Pickering Papers; John Marshall to James Marshall, April 1, 1804, photostat in John Marshall Papers, LC; *Norfolk Gazette*, November 28, 1804; *Annals of Congress*, 8th Cong., 1st Sess., 1180–81.

news. The party press was sure no fair-minded person could doubt Chase's innocence after reading it. Some papers continued carrying portions of the judge's answer even after his acquittal, believing that its wide circulation was necessary to refute the "Republican slanders" against him.[22] To the Federalist mind, the trial was simply an attempt to gratify political malice and destroy the last judicial check upon Jeffersonian democracy. An anonymous writer protested that when impeachments "are made subservient to party views, they are a powerful engine of tyranny and oppression."[23]

After harboring such fears, Federalists were quite relieved by the Senate's unexpectedly decisive acquittal of Chase. Despite a Republican majority of 25 to 9, no more than eighteen senators voted for conviction on any one of the impeachment charges. Hearing the good news, a newspaper editor in predominantly Federalist Augusta County, Virginia, expressed pleasure "not from any political views, but from a belief that he has been justly acquitted—from a belief that he had been wrongfully charged—and from a belief that political rancour is upon the ebb."[24]

The judicial battle was not the only Republican attack on the men and institutions of the old Federalist system. Other policies of the Adams years also came under fire, particularly the internal taxes imposed during the 1790s. These were irksome to the public and costly to collect; therefore, in December, 1801, Congress willingly took up Jefferson's recommendation to repeal them. Expecting to run the government on the basis of strict economy, Republicans thought taxation could safely be reduced. And, as one admitted, cutting taxes would be the most popular thing the government could possibly do.[25]

22. Savannah *Columbian Museum*, April 25, 1804; Raleigh *Minerva*, April 23, 1804; *Charleston Courier*, January 24, February 23, 1805; Staunton *Candid Review*, January 18, 1805.

23. "Lucius," in Martinsburg *Berkeley & Jefferson Intelligencer*, December 28, 1804; Washington to E. S. Burd, January 7, 1804, in Howell J. Heaney (ed.), "The Letters of Bushrod Washington (1762–1829) in the Hampton L. Carson Collection of the Free Library of Philadelphia," *American Journal of Legal History*, II (1958), 165.

24. Staunton *Candid Review*, March 8, 1805; Richard B. Lillich, "The Chase Impeachment," *American Journal of Legal History*, IV (1960), 49–72.

25. Philip Norbone Nicholas to Wilson Cary Nicholas, December 14, 1801, in Wilson Cary Nicholas Papers, UVa.

Opposing abolition of the taxes, Federalists complained that the government would lose both revenue and a collection network built up at great effort. The taxes, once taken off, could not be levied again without enormous trouble and expense. Surely it was unwise to throw away a source of income that might later be sorely missed. Once the Republicans experienced the difficulties of running a government, they might be unable to make the economies they hoped for. "Would it not be more prudent," Congressman Huger asked, "first to make savings, and at the next session, if admissable, to take off these taxes?" Even excluding possible future needs, Federalists believed the internal revenue could be put to good use immediately. Why not apply these funds to reduce the national debt or to construct shore defenses and a large navy for protecting American coasts and commerce?[26]

Even if some taxes ought to be removed, Federalists wondered whether these were the proper ones. They boasted that their system of balanced internal and customs levies distributed the burden of taxation quite fairly. Perversely, the Republicans wanted to remove the internal tax on carriages (a luxury) and on spirits (a vice) but retain the import duties on brown sugar, molasses, and tea, which were necessities of the common people. Any equitable tax relief ought to start with these articles of general consumption. The complaint of discrimination against the lower classes became a major Federalist criticism of the repealing bill. A resident of northern Virginia wailed, "Things I need, are taxed now as high as they ever were. Things I do not need, but which are enjoyed exclusively by the rich, are now exempted from taxation."[27] In Congress, the southern Federalists voted consistently (but in vain) to continue taxes on luxury items and to repeal or reduce the levies on articles of everyday use. On final passage of the administration bill, the Federalists were split. Some opposed it to the end; but others, including southerners Benjamin Huger, John Stanly, and

26. Speeches of Huger and John Rutledge, Jr., *Annals of Congress*, 7th Cong., 1st Sess., 451–54, 1027; John Stanly, *Letter to His Constituents* (Washington, D.C., 1802), 14–16. For a critical look at the tax repeal question, see Alexander Balinky, *Albert Gallatin: Fiscal Theories and Policies* (New Brunswick, N.J., 1958), 138–51; and for a more favorable view, Raymond Walters, Jr., *Albert Gallatin: Jeffersonian Financier and Diplomat* (New York, 1957), 145–49.

27. "Vigilus," in Martinsburg *Berkeley & Jefferson Intelligencer*, March 25, 1803; *South-Carolina State-Gazette*, March 3, 1802; "Steady," in Savannah *Columbian Museum*, March 5, 1802.

Thomas Lowndes, preferred having some tax relief, even if the wrong type, to none at all.[28]

Next to the internal tax system and the judiciary, Federalists defended the American navy more jealously than any other institution of the Adams era. Always friendly to commerce, Federalists had begun in the 1790s creating a navy sufficient at least to protect American coasts and shipping. During the quasi war with France they made considerable progress toward building such a fleet. Since they believed Jefferson hostile to commerce and knew that he desired the utmost economy in government, Federalists were not surprised when he began to pare down the navy. Congressmen both North and South rose to its defense.

Huger of South Carolina conceded that he had "no objection to economical arrangements in the Army. . . . That establishment you can repair in a short time. But not so with respect to the Navy, for the establishment of which you must prepare for years beforehand." He warned that starving the navy would be false economy because American commerce would then lie unprotected from corsairs or foreign powers. Though unsuccessful in resisting this and other Republican steps to reduce naval expenses, Federalists continued to argue the desirability of a permanent, powerful fleet. They accused Jefferson of favoring agriculture and ignoring the merchant, saying that he burdened commerce with taxes and refused it protection.[29]

Federalists thought their case was proved beyond all argument when, for extended periods in 1803 and 1805, French privateers preyed upon vessels entering and leaving Charleston and Savannah harbors, while the navy was powerless to disperse them. Federalist papers throughout the South used these embarrassing and expensive invasions of American waters to prove the folly of Jefferson's antinavy policy.[30] As the country became increasingly involved in foreign difficulties and as commerce suffered more heavily, the Federalist demand for a strong navy was to grow yearly more strident.

28. *Annals of Congress*, 7th Cong., 1st Sess., 458, 461, 1019, 1020, 1022, 1042, 1055, 1056, 1073, contains the votes. John Stratton of Virginia and William H. Hill of North Carolina opposed repeal and three others did not vote at all.

29. *Annals of Congress*, 7th Cong., 1st Sess., 1198–1202; *Virginia Gazette*, June 23, 1802; *Charleston Courier*, November 9, 1803; *North-Carolina Journal*, February 6, 1804.

30. John Rutledge, Jr., to Robert Goodloe Harper, August 3, 1805, in Robert Good-

In defending Federalist men and measures against Republican attack, the southerners spoke not as champions of a narrow, elite economic interest. Except when urging a large navy, they tried to avoid appearing as the particular advocates of that commercial and financial class traditionally associated with their party. Instead, the southern Federalists in opposition sought broad support by representing themselves as the party of the people. Most of their arguments in behalf of the old Federalist system fell into two broad categories: defending the public interest and protecting the Constitution. As defenders of the public interest, Federalists argued that Jefferson's patronage policy would cripple public administration by replacing able, experienced officers with unqualified political appointees. The resulting waste, corruption, inefficiency, and inattention to business would harm every American who paid taxes or had any dealings with his government. Repealing the Judiciary Act would inconvenience everyone involved in any federal litigation and increase the cost of justice by requiring lawyers, litigants, and witnesses to travel much greater distances to the few remaining courts.

As a general argument, Federalists claimed that the nation could not be at peace with itself until Republicans ceased agitating the public mind and perpetuating "party spirit" by their vengeful campaign to overturn old policies. Federalists also aimed at several specific groups of voters. To win the support of veterans they recalled Jefferson's dismissal of many "old Revolutionary patriots" from office. In opposing repeal of the internal taxes on luxuries, the Federalists sought to cultivate lower- and middle-class voters. Finally, a strong navy was held up as a benefit to all farmers who grew staple crops for export, because it would secure them access to foreign markets.

As the defender of constitutional government, the party again attacked Jefferson's removal of Federalist officeholders. Persecuting men for their political views and making public office a reward for electioneering were dangerous extensions of executive and party influence. The entire civil service would soon be packed with men subservient to the president and his party. What then would become of

---

loe Harper Papers, LC; *Charleston Courier*, March 28, May 2, 1804; *Norfolk Gazette*, November 8, 1804.

balanced government and free elections? The Republican assault on the judiciary was seen as another threat to the Constitution. By removing independent-minded judges and cowing the rest, the system of checks and balances would be destroyed and Republicans would achieve absolute power in the United States. The people's rights would then be entirely at the mercy of Jefferson and his designing accomplices.

Chapter 5 ATTACKING THE JEFFERSONIAN PROGRAM, 1801–1807

IN THE years after 1800, southern Federalists were not merely rear-guard defenders of their party's traditional policies. They also opposed by word and vote almost every part of the Republican program. Of all the major Jeffersonian policies, only the most momentous—the Louisiana Purchase—won any significant minority support. The northern wing of the party was as firmly opposed to this as to every Republican idea, but southern Federalists were divided, and several party leaders who had never before said a word in favor of the administration spoke up to praise the Purchase.

Although American leaders knew by 1801 that Spain had ceded the vast territory to France, Louisiana did not become a public issue until the fall of 1802. At that time the Spanish intendant at New Orleans withdrew the right of free deposit for American goods, and the southern Federalists began to consider Louisiana a vital question. The intendant's act threatened the economy of the entire Ohio Valley, whose farmers had been sending their produce down the Mississippi and through New Orleans. Furthermore, the closing of the port was an ominous portent of what the more vigorous French might do when they officially took control of Louisiana.

A few Federalists were anxious for a peaceful settlement of the dispute, believing that the Spanish government had not authorized the intendant's hostile action. They cautioned against a rash move.[1] Others raised a different cry, calling for the use of force if necessary. North Carolina's Congressman William Barry Grove said flatly that if possession of Louisiana was essential to American honor and security, the territory should be seized at once.[2]

Such blustering declarations underscored the general Federalist belief that the Louisiana crisis involved much more than a rash action by a minor Spanish civil servant. The time was fast approaching when France would assume possession of all Louisiana, and if the weak Spanish had dared to shut off free entry to New Orleans, how much further might the proud and powerful French go? Federalists believed that French possession of Louisiana would be a "dagger now aimed at our vitals" and that Jefferson should use the indendant's closure of deposit as an excuse to occupy the territory with land and naval forces before France formally took control. If Napoleon once installed troops there, it might require a war to remove them. Indeed, one writer thought that Napoleon's chief aim in acquiring Louisiana was the subjection of the United States. Therefore, it was foolish to think he would sell the territory; Americans would have to take it by force.[3]

These men of warlike anti-French sentiments expected little from the president's decision to negotiate the purchase of New Orleans. The Savannah *Columbian Museum* jeered that this "chimerical scheme" was the ultimate example of the government's weakness. Federalists in Congress, too, doubted Jefferson's ability to resolve the question of Spanish insult and French menace by diplomacy alone. They pressed for full public information on the Spanish cession of Louisiana to

1. H. W. DeSaussure to John Rutledge, Jr., January 1803, in Rutledge Papers, UNC; *Virginia Gazette*, December 18, 1802. The amount of damage to the western economy by the closure of deposit is open to question: see C. Richard Arena, "Philadelphia-Mississippi Valley Trade and the Deposit Closure of 1802," *Pennsylvania History*, XXX (1963), 28–45; and Arthur P. Whitaker, *The Mississippi Question, 1795–1803* (New York, 1934), 189–201.

2. William Barry Grove to John Steele, February 25, 1803, in Wagstaff (ed.), *Papers of John Steele*, I, 367.

3. *Charleston Courier*, January 14, 1803; *Virginia Gazette*, February 2, March 19, 1803; Spruce Macay to Samuel Johnston, March 23, 1803, in Hayes Collection; Nathaniel Blount to Charles Pettigrew, May 9, 1803, in Charles Pettigrew Papers, NCDAH.

France, criticized the secrecy thrown about the crisis, and showed no enthusiasm for the attempt to buy New Orleans.[4]

All such fulminations were abruptly cut short by news that Napoleon had sold not only New Orleans but the entire Louisiana Territory to the American emissaries. Taken aback by the sudden success of the venture they had so loudly proclaimed a failure in advance, the southern Federalists lost their near unanimity on the Louisiana question. Some welcomed the Purchase because it removed America from an embarrassing difficulty and added valuable territory, while others who had been demanding Louisiana even at the price of war now condemned its acquisition by peaceful means.

Leading the chorus of praise were most Federalist editors in the South. One calculated that even if the new land were worth, on the average, only a dollar an acre, the United States had bought for $15 million a territory worth more than $600 million. Furthermore, possessing New Orleans would raise the value of all western lands by guaranteeing an outlet for their produce. Apart from economics, one editor said, "peace and good understanding, with a long prospect of enjoying each, appears to be of more consequence than a few millions of dollars." The *Charleston Courier* went so far as to frown upon "the honest, well-meant patriotic zeal of some of our brother federal editors" to the North who criticized the Purchase. "The objections against it," the paper said, "can be but few and unimportant, compared with the many circumstances of weighty advantage that will result from it." Most party leaders evidently agreed with William R. Davie and John Steele of North Carolina in approving the Purchase. Steele believed that future historians would rank it among the memorable events of the country.[5]

Samuel D. Purviance, the only North Carolina Federalist in the new Eighth Congress, took a middle ground. Explaining to the House his unusual support of Jefferson, he admitted that he had originally

4. Savannah *Columbian Museum*, April 8, 1803; speeches of Benjamin Huger, John Rutledge, Jr., and Thomas Lowndes in *Annals of Congress*, 7th Cong., 2nd Sess., 316, 326–27, 363–65.

5. Steele to Nathaniel Macon, September 12, 1803, William R. Davie to Steele, August 20, 1803, both in Wagstaff (ed.), *Papers of John Steele*, I, 406, 409–10; *Norfolk Gazette*, June 18, 1803; *Charleston Courier*, June 23, October 8, 1803; *Augusta Herald*, October 19, 1803.

favored outright seizure of Louisiana. Since the government had been too cowardly to take the territory, he preferred buying it to leaving it in French hands. Purviance stressed the dangers of Frenchmen on American borders and credited the renewed war in Europe, not any shrewdness by Jefferson's envoys, for inducing France to sell. Following his speech he voted for all appropriations necessary to carry out the treaty. This support was "purchased dear," another Federalist noted, for Purviance coupled his Louisiana remarks with "one of the severest philippics upon the present administration that were perhaps ever delivered."[6]

From this grudging acceptance of Louisiana it was but a step to the outright disapproval expressed by Federalist congressmen from Virginia and South Carolina. Thomas Griffin and Joseph Lewis, Jr., of Virginia both doubted the legality of the treaty because it granted special privileges to French and Spanish ships at New Orleans. Lewis and Griffin thought this violated the constitutional prohibition against giving one port preferential treatment over another. In fact, they claimed that the very attempt of the president and Senate to regulate commerce by treaty infringed the rights of the House as an equal branch of government. Therefore, along with fellow Virginians Thomas Lewis, Jr., and James Stephenson, they voted with the northern Federalists against carrying out the Purchase. John Rutledge, Jr., also had little use for the new territory. He agreed that New Orleans was an essential possession, but the rest of Louisiana would either remain a worthless wasteland or become a dangerous rival to the Atlantic states and perhaps even break up the Union.[7]

Even some newspapers that had earlier approved the Purchase now opened their columns to articles criticizing the entire Louisiana

6. *Annals of Congress*, 8th Cong., 1st Sess., 443–46. Samuel Purviance was joined in his support of the Purchase by Huger. Purviance's speech was widely reprinted in the southern party press. For comment on it, see Samuel Taggart to John Taylor, October 28, 1803, in George H. Haynes (ed.), "Letters of Samuel Taggart," *Proceedings of the American Antiquarian Society*, n.s., XXXIII (1923), 117–19.

7. See *Annals of Congress*, 8th Cong., 1st Sess., 440–43, for the congressional response. John Rutledge, Jr., to Harrison Gray Otis, October 1, 1803, in Morison (ed.), *Otis*, I, 279. In contrast to the division in southern opinion, the northern Federalists expressed almost solid opposition to the Louisiana Purchase: Jerry W. Knudson, "Newspaper Reaction to the Louisiana Purchase: 'This New, Immense, Unbounded World,'" *Missouri Historical Review*, LXIII (1969), 182–213.

business. Several editors condemned the Purchase outright as a waste of money. William Boylan of the Raleigh *Minerva* believed that removing the threat of a French military presence was reason enough for acquiring Louisiana, but he concluded that this benefit did not outweigh the huge financial cost.[8]

Whatever their feelings toward the Louisiana Purchase, most southern Federalists denied the Republicans any credit for it. Napoleon was not the man to be dissuaded from a long-planned venture in America merely by soft words and a little money. It was the war in Europe, Federalists said, which convinced him to sell Louisiana. Napoleon knew that the British, having command of the sea, could prevent his gaining any benefit from the territory and might even seize it themselves. Much better, then, to sell it to the United States for cash than risk losing all to Britain. The *Charleston Courier* concluded, "If war had not taken place between England and France, Messrs. LIVINGSTON and MONROE might have negociated to the end of their lives without success."[9]

Still, the administration was sure to claim political credit for the Purchase. Fighting just such a claim, Federalists in the South Carolina legislature voted against a resolution praising Jefferson's role in obtaining Louisiana. They formally protested in the house journal that the Constitution did not authorize a legislature to judge actions of the federal government and that the resolution tended to nourish political animosities. Federalists in Virginia's lower house were either more willing to give Jefferson a share of the credit or realized that resistance was useless, for a similar motion lauding the president passed unanimously in that body.[10]

Even more than the Purchase itself, the Republican arrangement for governing Louisiana displeased some Federalist editors. Instead of the elected legislature and appointed governor that had been granted the Northwest and Mississippi territories, Louisiana was to have a less democratic system. Nearly all power—executive, legislative, and

8. Raleigh *Minerva*, September 5, 1803; *North-Carolina Journal*, December 26, 1803, February 6, 1804; Savannah *Columbian Museum*, November 2, 1803.

9. *Virginia Gazette*, July 9, 13, 1803; *Charleston Courier*, July 4, August 13, 1803.

10. Thomas Lowndes to John Rutledge, Jr., July 13, 1803, in Rutledge Papers, UNC; *South Carolina House Journal*, 1803, pp. 42–45; *Virginia House Journal*, 1803, p. 107.

judicial—would be in the hands of officials appointed by the president. One newspaper, after digesting the provisions of the Louisiana Government Bill, concluded that "the Grand-Turk is not more absolute in Constantinople than Mr. Jefferson is" in the new territory. Others emphasized that the bill containing these "monarchical principles" had been "entirely the work of party," claiming incorrectly that it had been forced through Congress against strong Federalist opposition.[11] Whether such opinions extended much beyond the newspapers is uncertain. There are no extant letters from Federalists commenting upon the Louisiana government question; and on final passage of the bill in Congress, only one of the seven southern Federalist representatives was present; he voted *for*, not against, the measure.[12] Thus, newspaper opinion, even in an age of such partisan journalism, was not an infallible indication of an entire party's position.

Actually, Federalists regarded the Louisiana Government Bill as a very small affair compared to the battle over the proposed Twelfth Amendment to the Constitution, which would alter the method of casting electoral votes for president. Previously, electors had voted for two men without distinction of office; the candidate with most votes became president and the runner-up vice-president. Obviously a tie might occur, as in 1800, requiring the House of Representatives to choose between the two leaders. Or, as happened in 1796, the chief executive and the vice-president might be of different parties. To avoid such embarrassments, Republicans wanted to amend the Constitution so that electors would vote separately for president and vice-president. Federalists perceived this apparently innocuous proposal as a scheme to insure perpetual Republican control of the presidency; in Congress and later in the states, they opposed the amendment fiercely.[13]

Publicly, Federalists based their opposition on several grounds. They said the amendment would diminish the influence of small states

11. Raleigh *Minerva*, January 9, 23, September 17, 1804; *North-Carolina Journal*, December 26, 1803; Savannah *Columbian Museum*, January 21, 1804. On the Louisiana Government Bill, see James E. Scanlon, "A Sudden Conceit: Jefferson and the Louisiana Government Bill of 1804," *Louisiana History*, IX (1968), 139–62.

12. *Annals of Congress*, 8th Cong., 1st Sess., 1199.

13. Among the reprinted speeches were those of Benjamin Huger and Thomas Lowndes in the *Charleston Courier*, December 3–7, 1803, and the Savannah *Columbian Museum*, February 4, 1804.

in national politics by eliminating inconclusive or tied elections. So long as the House (voting by states, not by individuals) would often make the final choice of president, each small state would count as heavily as the largest. But if the electoral college gave a clear majority to one candidate for president, as it nearly always would under the proposed amendment, then a large state with twenty-four electoral votes would be as powerful as the six smallest states together. After all, said Benjamin Huger, the large states already controlled the House and had half the Senate. If they could elect the president as well, they would be far too powerful. This would destroy the balance between large and small states that was so vital a part of the original Constitution.[14] Furthermore, it was unwise to amend the Constitution overmuch. The document as completed in 1787 was "the deliberate result of the best talents and integrity of our country," Federalists said, and tampering with that masterpiece could only produce worse, not better, government.[15]

Although this defense of the small states and the unaltered Constitution was not merely for public consumption, the most serious Federalist objection to the amendment was, no doubt, a partisan one. They feared it would insure Jefferson's reelection and the subsequent victory of every future Republican candidate. Under the old system, each Republican elector was officially unable to specify which of his two votes was cast for the presidency or the vice-presidency. The few Federalist electors, assuming they had given up any attempt to elect one of their own, could at least choose which Republican would win by casting their votes for the least repulsive opponent. For example, in 1804 the Republicans ran Jefferson and George Clinton. Had the old electoral system still operated, Jefferson would have had 162 votes and Clinton a few less from Republican electors.[16] The Federalist electors could then have given their 14 votes to Clinton and to some third person, placing Clinton ahead of Jefferson in the total vote and

14. *Annals of Congress*, 8th Cong., 1st Sess., 518–35; DeSaussure to Timothy Pickering, February 26, 1804, in Timothy Pickering Papers; Savannah *Columbian Museum*, January 11, 1804.

15. Speeches of Huger, Thomas Lowndes, and Purviance in *Annals of Congress*, 8th Cong., 1st Sess., 519, 691–93, 708; *Virginia Gazette*, February 1, 1804.

16. I assume that one or two Republicans would have omitted Clinton's name to prevent a tie vote.

frustrating the Republicans' plans. Under the Twelfth Amendment this would be impossible. Republicans would vote for Jefferson as president and Clinton as vice-president, and any Federalist electoral votes for Clinton as president could not be combined with his Republican votes as vice-president to exclude Jefferson from the chair of state.

Federalist cries against the amendment were shrill indeed. "Mr. Jefferson to be President for LIFE!" screamed the Raleigh *Minerva*. Washington and Adams had been content to be elected in the old constitutional way; why must the Republicans now change the rules to benefit their leader?[17] Despite bitter opposition, the party was too weak to impede the amendment's passage or its ratification by southern legislatures. Federalists in Congress formed a solid front, but the amending resolution succeeded by 84 to 42, precisely the required two-thirds margin. There was a strong fight against the amendment in South Carolina, but the cause was hopeless; both houses finally ratified by more than two to one. Approval in the other three states was easily secured without even a roll call vote.[18]

Unsuccessful in opposing the Twelfth Amendment and divided on the Louisiana question, Federalists were reduced to minor sniping attacks on the Republican record. They concentrated on trying to destroy the popular image of Republican economy. Numerous claims of Jeffersonian extravagance appeared in Federalist newspapers, complaining of waste in the diplomatic service, the post office, the navy department, public works, and the handling of the national debt.[19]

Three particular incidents early in Jefferson's administration illustrate the Federalist argument that Republicans were profligate spenders. The first concerned repairs made at American expense to the French ship *Berceau*, captured in the naval war of 1798–1799. Under terms of the peace convention of 1800, each country was to return all such captured vessels. Federalists did not object to this, but to Jef-

17. Grove to William Gaston, March 12, 1804, in William Gaston Papers; Raleigh *Minerva*, January 9, November 5, 1804; *Virginia Gazette*, November 30, 1803.

18. *Annals of Congress*, 8th Cong., 1st Sess., 776; DeSaussure to Pickering, February 26, 1804, in Timothy Pickering Papers; *Charleston Courier*, May 19, 1804. *South Carolina House Journal*, 1804, May session, p. 25; *South Carolina Senate Journal*, 1804, May session, p. 195. The vote in South Carolina was 64–25 in the house and 22–9 in the senate.

19. For example, *Norfolk Gazette*, July 28, 1804; *North-Carolina Journal*, August 27, 1804; Savannah *Columbian Museum*, June 11, 1802.

ferson's decision to repair the *Berceau* before returning it. Was it not foolish, they asked, to spend $33,000 on a French ship, while selling entire American warships, fully equipped, for less than that amount? If the Republicans were disbanding the American navy because it was too expensive, how could they justify spending a single dollar on the *Berceau*? Congress had never authorized any such repairs, so Jefferson was shamelessly wasting public funds without any legal appropriation for that purpose. Pressing their point, the congressional Federalists urged an investigation. This demand caused the majority leaders much alarm and embarrassment. The Republican majority easily killed the motion, but the very act of suppressing an investigation might appear to the voters as proof that there was something worth hiding.[20]

Seeking further to mar the image of Jeffersonian economy, Federalists pointed to the increased executive salaries that Republicans voted themselves as soon as they gained power. During the Adams years Congress had passed, against strong Republican opposition, a law temporarily increasing the pay of several government officers. The law expired after 1800 but the Republicans, this time over Federalist protests, soon raised salaries to an even higher level. The minority in Congress accused Republicans of raiding the Treasury and of hypocrisy in proposing the very measure they previously had condemned.[21] Of course the Federalists were equally inconsistent. When in office, they had defended the salaries which now they condemned.

Another incident attracting particular attention was the sale of government-owned stock in the Bank of the United States. Secretary of the Treasury Albert Gallatin had arranged to sell a large amount of stock through Baring Brothers, a British financial house, and had used the proceeds to retire part of the national debt. Federalist critics of the transaction claimed that Gallatin had paid the Barings an excessive commission, had sold the stock below market price, and had given up an investment yielding 9 percent to pay off a 5 percent loan.

20. Archibald Henderson to John Rutledge, Jr., April 8, 1802, and Thomas Lowndes to John Rutledge, Jr., April 6, 1802, in Rutledge Papers, UNC; Savannah *Columbian Museum*, June 11, 1802; *Annals of Congress*, 7th Cong., 1st Sess., 1149–52.

21. *South-Carolina State-Gazette*, April 21, 1802; *Virginia Gazette*, April 14, 1802; *Annals of Congress*, 7th Cong., 1st Sess., 1085–93.

A Virginian demanded to know what had prompted Gallatin to such an unwise transaction. If the stock had been sold under pressure because the government badly needed money, "then all that is boasted about the overflowing treasury, must be a fable." On the other hand, "if the sale has been made from some capricious or worse motives, then let us hear no more concerning the *wise*, the *economical* and *virtuous administration*." As in the *Berceau* incident, congressional Federalists called loudly for an investigation, but again the Republican majority refused.[22]

Aside from these variations on the theme of financial mismanagement, Federalists tried to discredit Jefferson personally. They seized upon his friendship with Thomas Paine to portray the president as a church-hating atheist and an enemy of Washington. Paine, whose writings *Common Sense* and *The Crisis* had aided the struggle for American independence, later published vindications of agnosticism and the French Revolution and heaped abuse on Washington for not aiding the French. As a result, Paine's name became anathema to Federalists. Soon after taking office, Jefferson brought him to the United States in a public ship, touching off violent tirades from southern Federalists, who reviled Paine as a wretched Jacobin infidel. The *Charleston Courier* snidely remarked that "when the hoary headed incendiary, TOM PAINE, arrived in America, every man of sound judgment or sober reflection, who wished well to his country, felt the deepest regret. But the President of the United States, who differed from them, warmly greeted his return to this country." Other Federalists spoke with equal vigor against Jefferson and his "domesticated atheist."[23]

After his arrival Paine undertook to defend his views in a series of public letters and in a new edition of his agnostic work *The Age of Reason*. He drew a sharp reprimand from the southern Federalist press, which accused him of slandering Washington and "endeavoring to

22. "A Federalist," in *Virginia Gazette*, May 4–June 25, 1803; "Lucius J. Brutus," in Martinsburg *Berkeley & Jefferson Intelligencer*, August 26, 1803; *Charleston Courier*, March 22, 1803; *Annals of Congress*, 7th Cong., 1st Sess., 683–89. Balinky, *Albert Gallatin*, 99–101, criticizes the sale of the bank stock chiefly because of its political effect.

23. *Charleston Courier*, May 16, 1803, September 19, 1805; *Virginia Herald*, December 7, 1802; John Marshall to C. C. Pinckney, November 21, 1802, in Jack L. Cross (ed.), "John Marshall on the French Revolution and on American Politics," *William and Mary Quarterly*, 3rd ser., XII (1955), 646.

destroy that which alone solaces the unfortunate and proves an antidote to sins—the *Christian Religion.*"[24] Several readers took up their own pens to refute Paine, to decry his influence on the minds of gullible persons, and to brand Jefferson an infidel for aiding him.

Jefferson's connection with another Republican propagandist called forth still more denunciations. In the 1800 campaign James T. Callender, editor of the Richmond *Recorder*, had written a harsh attack on Washington, Adams, and the Federalists. To help finance Callender's partisan works, Jefferson had secretly made a small contribution. After the election Callender began to feel ignored and he broke with Jefferson, publishing evidence of the president's past financial aid. Federalists gleefully seized upon this revelation to brand Jefferson a liar, a coward, and a subsidizer of gross calumnies against the virtuous Washington. Augustine Davis led the attack in his *Virginia Gazette*, declaring that Jefferson's advocates would no longer be able to praise his political equity and patriotism.[25]

Even more than Jefferson's association with Paine and Callender, Federalists censured his persistent appointment of supposedly unqualified, dishonest, and disloyal men to office. Secretary of the Treasury Gallatin, a particular target of Federalist barbs, was frequently called a "Genevese renegade," an inciter of the Whiskey Rebellion, and reviler of Washington. Others such as Tench Coxe, supervisor of revenue in Pennsylvania, and William Stephens, district judge for Georgia, were denounced as having been Tories during the Revolution.[26] Editors of the leading Republican newspapers, many of whom Jefferson favored with patronage, were in Federalist eyes merely obnoxious foreigners, fugitives from justice in their own countries. Thieves were said to be numerous in the administration; among them was Edward Livingston, who was made district attorney for New York

24. Martinsburg *Berkeley & Jefferson Intelligencer*, October 14, 1803; "A Citizen of Virginia," in *Virginia Herald*, November 26, 1802; Savannah *Columbian Museum*, December 14, 1802. For the nationwide Federalist attack, see Jerry W. Knudson, "The Rage Around Tom Paine: Newspaper Reaction to His Homecoming in 1802," *New-York Historical Society Quarterly*, LIII (1969), 34–63.

25. *Virginia Gazette*, August 7–October 23, 1802, especially October 9; *Augusta Herald*, February 25, 1801.

26. *North-Carolina Journal*, March 29, 1802, July 4, 1803; *Virginia Gazette*, September 5, 1804; Thomas Gibbons to John Rutledge, Jr., April 15, 1802, in Rutledge Papers, UNC.

in return for his activity during the 1800 election. When Livingston confessed to being $100,000 short in his official accounts, one Federalist asked slyly whether Jefferson himself ought not to make good the default.[27]

In attacking Jefferson and his policies, as in defending the Adams administration, southern Federalists appealed to the widest possible electorate. They usually avoided any stand which might alienate rather than cultivate the voter. When the Louisiana Purchase aroused great public enthusiasm, for example, most Federalists did not openly criticize it. Instead, they tried to convince people that Jefferson deserved none of the credit for this fortunate acquisition. An even better point of attack, and one not fully exploited, was the president's plan of government for Louisiana. Here Federalists could touch the democratic strain in southern minds by protesting the nearly monarchical provisions of the Louisiana Government Bill. In fighting the Twelfth Amendment, Federalists accused their opponents of deforming the Constitution and crushing the influence of small states in order to reelect Jefferson indefinitely. The constant attempt to paint the administration as extravagant and corrupt and its officials as unworthy foreigners or unqualified hacks, was designed to attract voters of every occupation, section, and class. By harshly rebuking Jefferson for his aid to Paine and Callender, Federalists hoped for approval from all who valued the Christian religion and the memory of Washington.

In short, there was nothing exclusive or elitist in the propaganda barrage that the party aimed at the entrenched Republicans. Federalists put themselves forward, not as spokesmen of special commercial, urban, or upper-class interests, but as "watchdogs of the people," exposing what they said were attempts to steal the liberties or waste the money of ordinary citizens.

27. Martinsburg *Berkeley & Jefferson Intelligencer*, February 3, 1804; "Alfred," *ibid.*, February 10, 1804; *Charleston Courier*, July 23, 1805. Actually, the embezzlement was by a clerk, but Livingston took financial responsibility for it: William B. Hatcher, *Edward Livingston: Jeffersonian Republican and Jacksonian Democrat* (Baton Rouge, La., 1940), 93–99.

Chapter 6 SOUTHERN FEDERALISTS AND FOREIGN AFFAIRS, 1801–1807

FROM the outbreak of war between France and England in 1793 until Jefferson's election, foreign affairs dominated American politics. The war not only hurt neutral commerce but became a bitter political issue in its own right as Federalists championed Britain and branded the Republicans as partisans of France. During the quasi war of 1798–1799 the Federalists' anti-French stand helped them win substantial, if temporary, popularity in the South. If relations with France had continued tense after 1800, they might have used the same issue to offset the voter appeal of Jefferson's moderate domestic program.

Instead, the Franco-American convention of 1800 ended the crisis and soon thereafter the fierce European war itself abated, easing the precarious situation of neutrals such as the United States. For nearly half a dozen years into the new century, Americans worried little about foreign affairs, although Federalists never lost their own concern with this issue, as in this typical editorial: "We feel no desire to excite in our countrymen any animosity toward *France*, but we wish to warn them of the dangers to which they are exposed from the ambition of one [Napoleon] who appears to have no limits to his views."[1] The pub-

1. *Norfolk Gazette*, January 16, 1807.

lic, however, could not be convinced by mere words that France was any longer a threat. By concentrating their attention on the "French danger," Federalists were belaboring a subject in which voters were not interested, and this did nothing to improve the party's fading political appeal. French circumspection toward the United States contributed much to the rising popularity of Jefferson and his party until about 1807; after that year, the gradual return of problems with the French was partly responsible for the revival of southern Federalism.

The party did pay attention to some foreign matters not directly involving France, such as American troubles with Tripoli and Spain; but these never became major political issues. War with Tripoli began in a desultory fashion in 1801 when that Barbary state demanded an increase in the tribute that previous presidents had paid to protect America's Mediterranean commerce. Jefferson preferred to fight, in hopes of ending these embarrassing payments. Four years dragged by with little actual conflict. Besides an occasional mention in the newspapers, little attention was paid to the slow-moving war until 1804, when the warship *Philadelphia* ran aground and was captured by the enemy.[2] Federalist editors hastened to blame the president. To them the episode showed the absurdity of Jefferson's mania for economy in government. Because he had sold off or laid up the navy created by Washington and Adams, the *Philadelphia* had been lost. If only the United States had possessed sufficient sea power, Tripoli would long ago have been crushed. Instead, Jefferson had cost the nation a fine warship and probably a huge ransom to free the captured crew.[3]

Later the Federalists shifted position and began to criticize Jefferson for *not* ransoming the American prisoners. The president was reproached for doing nothing while the sailors rotted in enemy dungeons, and a Virginia newspaper publicized several "atrocity stories" of the captives' mistreatment. Even the war itself began to be a political issue, one editor complaining that it "has been so conducted, as, in a period of nearly four years, to afford no one solitary instance of advantage; no single circumstance to console the nation for the im-

2. *North-Carolina Journal*, September 6, 1802. On the Barbary situation, see Ray W. Irwin, *The Diplomatic Relations of the United States with the Barbary Powers, 1776–1816* (Chapel Hill, N.C., 1931), Chaps. 8–10.

3. *Charleston Courier*, March 26, 1804; Raleigh *Minerva*, April 16, 1804.

mense expense it has occasioned."[4] Here was a promising issue, but late in 1805, before the Federalist campaign could get well underway, the war ended. The American forces, far from doing nothing, had in fact assaulted Tripoli by land and sea with such vigor that her ruler agreed to make peace and return the captured sailors. This surprising victory left the Federalists only to grumble that it was long overdue.[5]

Relations with Spain offered even fewer chances to make political capital, for here Republicans were actively advancing American interests. Jefferson had convinced himself that Spanish West Florida (the coastal strip from the Mississippi River to the Perdido River) should have been included in the Louisiana Purchase. For several years he and Secretary of State Madison badgered Spain to give up West Florida. This belligerent stance brought the two countries near to a diplomatic rupture, if not to war, but Federalists made little protest. Instead, party editors became indignant about Spanish attacks on American commerce, and decried the administration's inability to extend naval protection to merchant shipping.[6] These stories were not numerous, however, and they soon merged into the larger stream of criticism generated by French depredations.

Only once did the Florida question enter party politics, and then indirectly. After failing to get West Florida by mere negotiations, Jefferson asked Congress in December, 1805, for a secret appropriation of $2 million to be used at his discretion to acquire the territory. The money was intended to bribe the French government into pressing Spain to give up West Florida. John Randolph of Virginia, who was once a Republican congressional leader but was now drifting toward opposition, denounced the secret proposal and Federalists immediately took up his cry.[7] Unable to block the appropriation in Congress, the party rushed into print to rouse public opinion. They criticized Republican pledges against secrecy in government as hypocritical promises made to win votes in 1800. Others condemned the measure

4. "An Old Ship Owner," in *Charleston Courier*, June 11, 1805; Martinsburg *Berkeley & Jefferson Intelligencer*, June 14, 1805.

5. *Norfolk Gazette*, September 4, 1805.

6. Savannah *Columbian Museum*, March 29, 1806; *Virginia Herald*, August 27, 1805.

7. Isaac J. Cox, *The West Florida Controversy, 1798–1813: A Study in American Diplomacy* (Baltimore, Md., 1918), Chap. 7; Clifford L. Egan, "The United States, France, and West Florida, 1803–1807," *Florida Historical Quarterly*, LXVII (1969), 227–52.

as a bribe to Napoleon under the new Republican principle of "Millions for tribute—Not a cent for defence." Even if the scheme worked, they said, West Florida was not worth the money; the whole territory was but a swampy wasteland.[8] Within a few months the controversy subsided, but Federalists brought up the charge of French tribute anew at each succeeding election.

These digressions involving Tripoli and Spain did not prevent the Federalists from centering their attention on France. They feared and despised Napoleon fully as much as they had the French revolutionary governments of the 1790s. From the constant raids by French privateers on American commerce, Federalists deduced that Napoleon had aggressive designs upon the United States. Furthermore, they believed that Jefferson was following a pro-French foreign policy and that many Republicans wanted to push America into a war against Great Britain, the one nation that could protect the world from Napoleon. The fear of France and of French influence increasingly occupied the party's attention, almost to the exclusion of domestic affairs, after Napoleon crowned himself emperor in 1804 and appeared to be master of Europe.

To southern Federalists it was evident that the French Revolution had destroyed a stable society and that the fruits of "Jacobin democracy" in France had been continual bloodshed, economic ruin, and the destruction of liberty itself, proving that an excess of liberty inevitably led to harsh despotism.[9] The Federalists regarded Napoleon's rule no more highly than revolutionary anarchy. The extremely antidemocratic *Charleston Courier* was sure that the French people longed to be rid of "such an exorbitant monstrous tyrant as BONAPARTE," and thought even the Bourbons were preferable. Others demanded to know why the Jeffersonians, who professed to love freedom, should befriend a man who destroyed it.[10] It would be bad enough, the party said, if Napoleon exercised his despotic powers only within his own

8. "An American," in Raleigh *Minerva*, May 19, 1806; Savannah *Columbian Museum*, May 14, 1806.

9. Nathaniel Blount to Charles Pettigrew, May 4, 1802, in Charles Pettigrew Papers; Frederick Rutledge to John Rutledge, Jr., July 24, 1804, in Rutledge Papers, UNC; Thomas Evans to John Cropper, December 15, 1800, in John Cropper Papers, Virginia Historical Society.

10. *Charleston Courier*, September 29, 1803, June 14, 1804; "Y. Z.," in *Virginia Gazette*, May 27, 1806.

nation. Instead, he brought neighboring countries under his sway as rapidly as he could; Switzerland, Holland, Italy, and other formerly happy lands now languished under French dictatorship.[11]

It was this appetite for external conquest that Federalists feared most in Napoleon, because they doubted that America could stand against him if he managed to subdue Europe. They depicted him as driven solely by ambition, willing to spend blood and treasure without stint to obtain world dominion. Could a man with such lust for power fail to covet the growing population and prosperity of the United States? If Napoleon did subject the Continent to his influence and force England to make peace, there would be nothing to prevent French armies from swarming over America.[12]

In fact, Napoleon was already inflicting serious injury on the United States by ravaging American neutral commerce. When war between England and France resumed in 1803, the editor of the *Virginia Gazette* hoped the United States might benefit by expanding her trade with the belligerents. But he warned the administration to stand ready to defend ships and sailors against harm, or Americans would suffer abuse from both France and England, and the nation's flourishing trade would be destroyed. It seemed to Federalists, as the European fighting wore on, that this melancholy prediction was being entirely fulfilled. Under headlines such as "French Piracy" and "French Insolence," newspapers increasingly reported American merchantmen burned, seized, or looted. Such stories were relatively few before 1808, but each one occasioned a new outburst of Federalist indignation against the French for committing the act and against the Republicans for not punishing it.[13]

Viewing France as the source of future invasion and present injury, Federalists were naturally drawn toward England as the first line of American defense. They believed that only the British navy kept Napoleon from American shores. John Rutledge, Jr., considered

11. *Charleston Courier*, March 4, 1803; *Norfolk Gazette*, August 22, 1806.

12. *North-Carolina Journal*, July 17, 1805. A series of "Thoughts and Reflections on the Present State of Affairs" dealing with French ambition ran in five Virginia and South Carolina papers, May–October, 1806.

13. *Virginia Gazette*, April 27, 1803; *Charleston Courier*, September 23, 1803. For the general background, see Clifford L. Egan, "Franco-American Relations, 1803–1814" (Ph.D. dissertation, University of Colorado, 1969), Chap. 5.

England "as but the advanced guard of our Country. . . . If they fall we do."[14] Of course Federalists could not ignore the fact that Britain, as well as France, threatened American neutral rights; and, until 1808, the party press carried nearly as many reports of British as of French injuries.[15] The shooting of an American sailor by the British warship *Leander* in April, 1806, particularly outraged Federalist editors. They quickly denounced the attack and hoped both parties would unite in demanding retribution against England.[16] On the heels of the *Leander* affair came reports of still more British indignities, and the long-continued practice of impressment drew special condemnation. The Federalists believed it to be a degrading practice and an affront to the rights of the United States.[17]

Even while publicizing such incidents, Federalists were careful to explain that the British were not really acting very badly. The *Charleston Courier*, the chief southern apologist for England, admitted that an occasional American ship ran afoul of British regulations but that, on the whole, the Royal Navy behaved correctly. Nothing would be gained by magnifying small injuries and stirring up resentment against Britain. Others agreed that English interference with American shipping was minute compared to the rapacity of the French.[18] At least in Britain reason still governed diplomacy, while Napoleon steered France on an irrational course with no guide but his own ambition. James Breckinridge, soon to become congressman from Virginia, explained to a Republican relative that the English government would not dare offend the United States seriously, for fear of losing the valuable American commerce.[19] In short, Federalists did not entirely ignore British injuries but did pass them off as trifling compared to the threat from Napoleon.

14. John Hamilton to Duncan Cameron, February 7, 1806, in Cameron Family Papers; John Rutledge, Jr., to Harrison Gray Otis, July 29, 1806, in Morison (ed.), *Otis*, I, 282.

15. For instance, *Charleston Courier*, January 27, 1806; *Norfolk Gazette*, February 14, 1806.

16. *Virginia Gazette*, May 7, 1806. Other editors were equally outraged.

17. Martinsburg *Berkeley & Jefferson Intelligencer*, May 23, 1806; *North-Carolina Journal*, October 21, 1805.

18. *Charleston Courier*, September 15, October 17, 1803; *Virginia Gazette*, June 19, 1805.

19. James Breckinridge to John Breckinridge, February 2, 1806, in Breckinridge Family Papers, LC.

They also complained that the Republican administration favored France in the conduct of American foreign policy. Long before 1800, Federalists had become convinced that their opponents were pro-French, and the events of Jefferson's first term only increased these fears.[20] First came the incident involving the repair of the *Berceau*.[21] Then, in the spring of 1802 Federalists heard stories that the administration secretly planned a large loan to France and that the French fleet was going to frighten Congress by entering the Chesapeake Bay. The rumor was soon exploded but it left its mark upon Federalist minds.[22] The next year Jefferson referred to Napoleon's government as "enlightened," prompting Federalists to ask why the president—a professed republican—was praising a despotic government. Surely this was a further sign that Jefferson was far from neutral.[23] More important than such minor incidents was the general attitude of Republicans, in which Federalists detected a strong pro-French bias. One editor accused Republicans of blowing out of proportion every British insult to American commerce, while ignoring the more numerous and more offensive French abuses. Federalists refused to ascribe this to mere chance. They saw a conscious, pervasive French influence in the opposite party stemming from acceptance of French bribes, fear of Napoleon's power, or infatuation with revolutionary ideas.[24]

Federalists also thought the government insisted upon more commercial rights than a neutral could reasonably expect. William Loughton Smith, a former congressman from Charleston, wrote the most lengthy and widely known Federalist criticism of this facet of Republican policy. Under the name Phocion, Smith published in the *Charleston Courier* a series of letters copied by other newspapers and later reprinted in pamphlet form. He warned that Britain was fighting for her life and Americans must not expect her to honor to the letter every neutral right. For military reasons England might have to interfere with certain types of commerce to and from French-occupied ports. If the United States objected, the issue surely could be discussed amica-

20. "An Enquirer," in *Virginia Gazette*, October 15, 1803.

21. See Chap. 5, herein.

22. *North-Carolina Minerva*, May 3, 1802; Thomas Lowndes to John Rutledge, Jr., April 13, 1802, in Rutledge Papers, UNC.

23. Savannah *Columbian Museum*, November 2, 1803.

24. "Falkland," in Raleigh *Minerva*, July 2, 1804; *Virginia Gazette*, August 27, 1806.

bly between the two nations. America should not threaten the British with reprisals; a pugnacious attitude would damage neutrality and poison relations on both sides.[25]

The party especially objected to Jefferson's rejection of the Monroe-Pinkney draft treaty with Great Britain. When the Jay treaty expired in 1805, Jefferson sent William Pinkney to join the regular American minister in London, James Monroe, with instructions to secure a new agreement. They were to negotiate an end to impressment, wider allowable trade with French ports, and restitution for ships previously captured by the Royal Navy. For reasons of domestic politics and wartime strategy, the British would yield little. Monroe and Pinkney, believing that an unsatisfactory treaty was better than none at all, then violated their instructions. They brought home a draft that gained none of Jefferson's conditions but might have led to unofficial adjustment of some points in dispute. The president found the draft treaty entirely unacceptable and would not even allow the Senate to consider it.[26]

Federalists, who were willing to go quite far in maintaining good relations with England, were shocked at Jefferson's actions. They warned that the United States should not try to take advantage of Britain, since she was the only barrier against Napoleon's power. As so often happened in Federalist thinking, the fear of France overrode all differences between the United States and Britain. Party newspapers took up the protest, insisting that the treaty would have helped American interests. The Raleigh *Minerva* expressed the common Federalist suspicion that French influence had caused Jefferson to reject it.[27]

Another irritant to Federalists was the passage in 1806 of a nonimportation act banning the entry of any British goods that could be produced in America or by other foreign sources. Although it was a weak measure, in effect sporadically for a few weeks in 1806 and 1807, the law met nothing but hostility from the minority. Nonimportation

25. "Phocion," in *Charleston Courier*, February 18–May 31, 1806.

26. Bradford Perkins, *Prologue to War: England and the United States, 1805–1812* (Berkeley and Los Angeles, 1961), Chap. 4; Patrick C. T. White, "Anglo-American Relations from 1803 to 1815" (Ph.D. dissertation, University of Minnesota, 1954), Chap. 3; Anthony Steel, "Impressment in the Monroe-Pinkney Negotiation, 1806–1807," *American Historical Review*, LVII (1952), 352–69.

27. Edward Carrington to Timothy Pickering, February 25, 1807, in Timothy Pickering Papers; Raleigh *Minerva*, April 15, 1807.

could scarcely affect Britain, they said, because of her vast worldwide markets; yet Americans would have to go without necessary imports or pay exorbitant prices for them. The law foolishly insulted Britain just when the United States needed to win concessions from her. The *Norfolk Gazette* asked what the British would think when they saw "that our President signed the nomination of the Commissioners for peace and friendship [Monroe and Pinkney] and the bill of exclusion with the same pen."[28]

Such partisan attacks abruptly ceased in June, 1807, when the *Chesapeake* affair suddenly brought war with Britain nearer than at any time since the Revolution. The English warship *Leopard*, lying off Norfolk harbor, hailed the American frigate *Chesapeake* and demanded the return of a few suspected British deserters among the crew. When the *Chesapeake* refused, the *Leopard* opened fire, forced the American ship to surrender, and forcibly removed the suspects. This open attack upon a ship of the United States Navy roused Americans everywhere to fury against the British.[29]

Federalists as well as Republicans joined the uproar. In Norfolk, the *Gazette*'s indignant editor urged his readers to discard party disputes in the face of such an insult to national honor and to place their faith in the government. The Richmond newspaper urged the most decisive measures, including invasion of any British territory within reach, if peace could not be maintained on honorable terms. And the *Charleston Courier*, though reaffirming its disgust with Jefferson, vowed to support him in the present crisis.[30]

Federalists throughout the South joined in public meetings denouncing Britain. At Richmond and elsewhere in Virginia, both parties advocated immediate war to avenge the insult. Scarcely less belligerent was the revenge demanded by Federalists at Charleston. The prominent citizens of Petersburg, Virginia, and Wilmington, North Carolina—Federalists among them—called the *Chesapeake* incident

28. *Norfolk Gazette*, April 28, 1806; *Charleston Courier*, November 5, 1806. On the background and details of nonimportation, see Herbert Heaton, "Non-Importation, 1806–1812," *Journal of Economic History*, I (1941), 178–98.

29. Edwin M. Gaines, "Outrageous Encounter: The Chesapeake-Leopard Affair of 1807" (Ph.D. dissertation, University of Virginia, 1960), 77–95 and Chap. 5.

30. *Norfolk Gazette*, June 24, July 1, 1807; *Virginia Gazette*, July 11, 15, 1807; *Charleston Courier*, August 24, 1807.

a virtual declaration of war by England and endorsed a ban on all trade with her until American honor was satisfied.[31] Other mass meetings across the South responded to the event in similar fashion, all castigating the British in language which, a few weeks before, Federalists would have sworn could come only from the mouths of Napoleon's "servile minions" in the Republican party. Each gathering pledged its unqualified approval in advance for whatever the government might do in the crisis, and no one raised a voice in dissent.[32]

In fact, Federalists rebuked Republican insinuations that they had not entered fully into the resentment against Britain. They protested that they loved their country and would not be backward in defending it. Could the party of George Washington, which had created and defended the American Constitution, do otherwise, they asked? Until well into the summer, Federalists gave almost blind support to the anti-British frenzy. John Rutledge, Jr., wrote privately of his preference for war over "a state of Peace in which a foreign Nation is to exercise the right of searching our National Ships"; and southern newspapers, regardless of party, bubbled with indignant letters and articles. The *Norfolk Gazette* even chided the northern Federalist press for not showing the proper spirit.[33]

This unaccustomed hostility toward Britain did not last long. When war did not immediately follow the *Chesapeake* attack, Federalist tempers quickly began to cool. The *Norfolk Gazette*, formerly so belligerent, took the lead in backing away from an anti-British atti-

31. *Virginia Argus*, July 1 and 18, 1807; *Charleston Courier*, July 4 and 9, 1807; Raleigh *Minerva*, July 16, 1807.

32. Federalists presided, acted as secretary, or served on the resolutions committees at mass meetings in at least the following places: Savannah and Augusta, in Georgia; Charleston and Columbia, in South Carolina; Fayetteville, Newbern, Orange County, and Wilmington, in North Carolina; and Richmond, Petersburg, Norfolk, Fredericksburg, Staunton, Clarksburg, New Kent County, and Westmoreland County, in Virginia. See Savannah *Columbian Museum*, July 7, 10, 14, 21, 1807; Savannah *Public Intelligencer*, July 21, 1807; Joseph Bryan to John Randolph, July 20, 1807, in Joseph Bryan Papers, UVa; Edward Hooker, "Diary of Edward Hooker," *American Historical Association Annual Report for 1896* (Washington, D.C., 1897), 905; *Raleigh Register*, August 6, 1807; Raleigh *Minerva*, July 16, August 6, 1807; *Virginia Argus*, July 4, 16, 18, 1807; *Virginia Gazette*, July 29, 1807; *Norfolk Gazette*, June 26, 1807; John G. Jackson to James Madison, August 2, 1807, in James Madison Papers, LC.

33. "A Georgian," in Savannah *Columbian Museum*, August 7, 1807; John Rutledge, Jr., to Otis, August 3, 1807, in Morison (ed.), *Otis*, I, 284; *Norfolk Gazette*, July 17 and 24, 1807.

tude before the end of July. Within a month or two the *Charleston Courier* and *Virginia Gazette* were also trying to damp the southern war spirit, warning against a hasty decision to fight.[34] Before the end of 1807 the southern party press had fully returned to its former policy of praising, or at least apologizing for, the British and criticizing France and the Republicans.

For some months war seemed a possibility. In July, Jefferson ordered all British ships from American waters and demanded satisfaction for the *Chesapeake* incident. Britain indicated a willingness to make amends but also published a stern decree emphatically claiming the right to search American vessels for deserters.[35] In this confused state of affairs, southerners hardly knew what to believe. As late as December the issue was still clouded. On Christmas Eve the *Charleston Courier* announced that the best informed men in Washington believed there would be war.[36]

Even as people speculated, Congress acted. The large Republican majority demanded retaliation for British misbehavior, yet few now wanted open war. Instead, the Embargo Act, forbidding any American ship to sail to a foreign port without special permission from the president, passed swiftly through the House and Senate; and Congress took various steps to improve the nation's fighting ability should war be unavoidable. John Culpepper of North Carolina and Joseph Lewis, Jr., of Virginia, the only southern Federalists in Congress, assumed a moderate position. With nearly everyone else of their party, they tried to soften the embargo bill on two occasions and then opposed it on final passage. At the same time, they did approve constructing more frigates and gunboats, and Lewis also voted to arm all the militia, although Culpepper was opposed.[37]

The embargo, which put a halt to all seaborne American commerce except the coasting trade, was bound to be a controversial policy. Fed-

34. "Hamilton," in *Norfolk Gazette*, August 24–September 25, 1807; "Cato," in *Charleston Courier*, August 29–September 4, 1807; *Virginia Gazette*, October 31, 1807.

35. Perkins, *Prologue to War*, 143–49; Dumas Malone, *Jefferson the President: Second Term, 1805–1809* (Boston, 1974), Chap. 25.

36. *Charleston Courier*, December 24, 1807; Archibald Henderson to John Steele, December 6, 1807, typed copy in Archibald Henderson Collection; James McDowell to Andrew Moore, December 29, 1807, in James McDowell Papers, UVa.

37. *Annals of Congress*, 10th Cong., 1st Sess., 853, 1049–50, 1171–72, 1218–22, 1227.

eralists hoped to rouse enough popular disgust to ride the embargo issue to victory in the elections of 1808, less than a year away. For half a dozen years, despite a vigorous attempt to portray themselves as the party of the people and to warn of the "French danger," Federalists had steadily lost support in the South. A succession of unrelieved defeats had drained the party of its will to resist the Republican tide, and the embargo election was their first real chance to redeem their decaying political fortunes.

Chapter 7 THE DECLINE OF SOUTHERN FEDERALISM, 1800–1807

"Two federalists meeting on the road, one of them exultingly exclaimed, 'Federalism begins to look up.' 'Very true,' replied the other; 'being now on its back, it can look no other way.'" Thus the Republican editor of the *Wilmington Gazette* aptly summarized the plight of Federalism throughout the South in the half decade following Jefferson's election. In 1800, Adams and Pinckney polled 22 percent of the popular vote in Jefferson's own Virginia and over 40 percent in North Carolina, and congressional elections in 1799–1800 sent thirteen southern Federalists to the House of Representatives. In the legislatures, Federalists held one-fourth of each house in Virginia, nearly half in South Carolina, and two-fifths of the lower house and nearly a third of the senate in North Carolina.

In the next six years Federalist strength everywhere fell sharply. Membership in the state assemblies dropped by half in Virginia and North Carolina and by nearly two-thirds in South Carolina.[1] The Federalist delegation to Congress also shrank. There were sometimes more contests between competing Republican candidates than be-

1. See Table 2, herein.

tween Federalists and Republicans, and by mid-decade a solitary Federalist sat in Congress from all the southern states.[2]

The erosion of congressional strength began with a stunning defeat in Virginia in April, 1801, just a month after Jefferson's conciliatory inaugural address had soothed many former opponents. Federalists suffered from public resentment of their recent attempt to elect Burr over Jefferson in the House of Representatives, and only one incumbent congressman could be persuaded to stand again. After a sharp campaign the party lost four of its five seats, with the single victor succeeding only by a technicality. State leaders were overwhelmed with disappointment, but most saw the poor result as a fluke and hoped to recoup in 1803.[3]

In that year a number of strong candidates appeared; six in Virginia, eight in North Carolina, and two in South Carolina came forth to search their districts for Federalist voters. Even Georgia's election the previous November had shown unusual activity. Matthew McAllister, a strong Washington-Adams supporter in the 1790s and probably still a Federalist, entered the statewide congressional race. The election received little publicity in either party's newspapers, but McAllister's past was well enough remembered to put him at the bottom of the poll. His 23 percent of the vote was a fine showing, however, in heavily Republican Georgia. Federalists in the more northerly states hoped to do even better in 1803.[4]

National issues dominated the election, as the party heaped abuse on Jefferson's administration and claimed that Republicans always had been, and still were, irreconcilable enemies of the Constitution. Repealing the Judiciary Act, abolishing internal taxes, removing Federalists from office, giving aid to Paine and Callender—these and other Republican actions were targets of attack. Federalists every-

2. Except in 1802–1803, three states held their congressional elections in even-numbered years: North Carolina (August), South Carolina (October), and Georgia (October). Virginia's election came in April of the following year. Because of reapportionment, North Carolina and South Carolina postponed their elections to the Eighth Congress from August and October, 1802, to April and February, 1803, respectively.

3. Fredericksburg *Courier*, May 1, 1801; John Marshall to C. C. Pinckney, November 21, 1802, in Cross (ed.), "John Marshall," 646.

4. *Georgia Republican*, November 10, 1802; *Louisville* (Georgia) *Gazette*, September 15, October 27, 1802; Obadiah Jones to Joseph Bryan, September 1, 1802, in Arnold-Screven Papers, UNC.

where expressed contempt for the "visionary, speculative government" that turned its back on George Washington's principles. The people's choice was clearly drawn. Those who fondly remembered the Washington and Adams years and detested Jefferson's new course were invited to protest by voting Federalist. All who perversely approved of Jeffersonian politics were given up as lost souls and there was no appeal whatever for their votes.[5]

While the battle of words raged in the press, many Federalists neglected the actual physical labor of courting voters. Congressman John Stratton complained that the great misfortune in Virginia was that the most influential Federalists were averse to public life and to campaigning. During the heated North Carolina campaign, one congressman saw the hard work of some Federalists undermined by others who thought it was "most politic to bend to the Storm, under the idea that the Vulgar & popular clamor of the day, will be the sooner exhausted and execrated, by giving it little opposition or alarm."[6]

Judging by the outcome in North Carolina's August election, a large number of former Federalists did prefer to bend to the storm. Only one of eight candidates succeeded, and that solely because two Republicans split a majority of the votes between them. In five districts the Federalists polled over 40 percent of the votes—a respectable share—but none exceeded 45 percent. Of the total statewide vote (including that cast for unopposed Republicans) the Federalists won 22 percent, only half as much as in 1800. Several prominent and able men had run—an incumbent congressman, a former governor, and a former speaker of the house of commons—but these had done no better than the five candidates of only local standing. It was not the quality of the nominee, but his party label, that defeated him. Jefferson was popular and his works were appreciated; the voters had rewarded his friends and rejected his detractors.[7]

5. "A Farmer," in *Alexandria Advertiser*, February 22, 1803; "Monitor," in Raleigh *Minerva*, July 18, 1803; addresses of Samuel D. Purviance and John Rutledge, Jr., in *Charleston Courier*, February 2, May 9, 1803.

6. John Stratton to [?], April 6, 1803, in Stratton Letter, UVa; H. W. DeSaussure to John Rutledge, Jr., February 14, 1803, William Barry Grove to John Rutledge, Jr., June 7, 1803, both in Rutledge Papers, UNC.

7. Returns are available in the newspapers for August and September, 1803.

South Carolina Federalists also lost ground in 1803, but here the caliber of the nominees did seem to influence the result. Two incumbents, Thomas Lowndes and Benjamin Huger, retained their Charleston and Georgetown districts by less than one hundred votes each against strong Republican opposition; and probably both seats would have fallen if anyone less prominent and popular had run. Elsewhere there were no Federalist nominees at all; even the seat held by John Rutledge, Jr., was surrendered without opposition as the party almost ceased to function in many areas.[8]

Against this poor showing in the Carolinas, Virginia voters appeared by contrast rather generous to Federalists in the April, 1803, elections. Three candidates won clear majorities, from 51 to 56 percent. Another, Thomas Lewis, Jr., appeared successful in his trans-Appalachian district, but his Republican opponent contested the result. After much debate, Congress ousted Lewis on a party-line vote and seated the Republican. Winning three districts certainly bettered the dismal performance of 1801, but still only ten of Virginia's nearly one hundred counties had given Federalist majorities and the party had not even contested three-fourths of the seats.[9]

The next round of elections, for president in 1804 and for Congress in 1804 and 1805, completed the dissolution of the Federalists as an effective opposition in the South. Ironically, the party had welcomed this contest, expecting that Charles Cotesworth Pinckney, the vice-presidential nominee in 1800, would again take a leading role in the campaign. In a semisecret caucus, northern Federalist leaders nominated Pinckney for president, and southerners were naturally pleased. The *Virginia Gazette* claimed that he was "universally acknowledged to be both a soldier and a statesman. Even the most daring among his

8. DeSaussure to John Rutledge, Jr., January, 1803, and February 14, 1803, in Rutledge Papers, UNC; *Charleston Courier*, February 9, 11, 19, March 1, 1803; Charleston *Carolina Gazette*, February 24, 1803.

9. *Virginia Gazette*, June 11, 1803; *Alexandria Advertiser*, May 2, 1803; James McDowell to Thomas Lewis, November 25, 1803, in James McDowell Papers; Lewis' protest at being unseated by Congress is in Martinsburg *Berkeley & Jefferson Intelligencer*, April 27, 1804. A full report on Lewis' contested election, which gives excellent information on electoral and voting practices in Virginia, is in Lexington *Virginia Telegraphe*, May 26, 1804. Partial election returns for several districts may be found in the newspapers for April and May, 1803.

opponents have neither impeached his integrity, his honor, or his talents."[10] Yet this editorial flourish marked the end, not the beginning, of the Federalist presidential campaign. Editors who never ceased to condemn Jefferson and all his works lifted not a finger to impede his return to office. A few Virginians stirred themselves to write indignant letters and editorials against the general ticket system of choosing electors, which prevented Pinckney from winning any of the state's two dozen votes. None of the protestors, however, undertook the nomination of a Federalist electoral slate. Election day saw a very low vote and, except for one or two counties, a completely unopposed Republican victory.[11]

In South Carolina and Georgia there was scarcely a grumble at Jefferson's reelection, much less any organized attempt to oppose it. The legislature in each state unanimously chose Republican electors, with the Federalist members either concurring or abstaining on the final vote. Only North Carolina saw the slightest concrete effort to deny Jefferson a few votes. Even here, no electoral candidate openly announced for Pinckney; but one in the Fayetteville district was a known Federalist, two others were firm Republicans, and a fourth had recently published his conversion to the Jeffersonian cause. Even with Republican votes divided three ways, the single Federalist managed only a small plurality and was later declared the loser on a technicality. This weak showing in what had been the most loyal Federalist district was a measure of the party's loss of vitality in North Carolina.[12]

The same lassitude crippled party prospects in the congressional elections. The two incumbent South Carolina Federalists, Benjamin Huger and Thomas Lowndes, did not care to face the voters again, and Huger's seat was among the seven that went to the Republicans

10. John Nicholas to John Rutledge, Jr., May 16, 1803, in Rutledge Papers, UNC; *Virginia Gazette*, February 15, 1804.

11. *Norfolk Gazette*, November 1, 16, 1804; *Petersburg Intelligencer*, November 9, 1804. Returns are in the Virginia State Library.

12. *Charleston Courier*, December 10, 1804; Peter Freneau to Thomas Jefferson, October 14, 1804, in Thomas Jefferson Papers, LC; Savannah *Southern Patriot*, November 21, 1804; Savannah *Columbian Museum*, March 17, August 29, 1804; *Raleigh Register*, October 15, November 12, 1804; Raleigh *Minerva*, October 8, November 19, 1804; *Wilmington Gazette*, November 27, 1804; George Anderson to Duncan Cameron, November 9, 1804, in Cameron Family Papers.

by default. In Lowndes' Charleston district, Federalists finally turned up a substitute candidate in Thomas Rhett Smith, a wealthy Charleston merchant; however, he was not popular enough to win. Smith lost Charleston, until then safe for Federalism, by a hundred votes, and in the whole district he polled only 38 percent of a very small turnout. Although one observer charged the defeat to Federalist apathy, surely deeper causes were at work.[13]

North Carolina Federalists contested only one of the dozen seats—their Fayetteville stronghold. Even in this oasis of Federalism one resident remarked upon the unusual quiet, as compared to the last election, when "newspapers and public places were crowded with addresses and candidates went abroad to solicit our votes." Although a popular Federalist faced two Republican challengers, the Raleigh *Minerva* surrendered in advance and refused to help save the party's last outpost. The result amply justified this melancholy attitude, as the Federalist ran behind both Republican candidates. In the northeastern Halifax district William R. Davie, not an active candidate, received a number of unsolicited ballots; but even he, a former governor and the best-known Federalist in the state, obtained only one-eighth of the votes in his home territory.[14]

Virginia, too, was disappointing. There were three seats to defend, yet the party scarcely stirred as the election approached. Joseph Lewis, Jr., won a second term in his Loudoun district near Washington, providing the only relief from an otherwise complete disaster. One incumbent was unseated because the strongly Federalist Eastern Shore turned out only two hundred votes, compared with eight hundred votes two years earlier; and another lost by only a hundred votes, a margin that surely could have been erased if fewer partisans had stayed home. The clearest evidence of the Federalists' sense of despair is that eighteen of the state's twenty-two seats had no candidate at all.[15]

13. *Charleston Courier*, June 7, August 23, 1804; "A Friend to the People," *ibid*., October 8, 1804; Frederick Rutledge to John Rutledge, Jr., August 28, 1804, in Rutledge Papers, UNC. Returns are in *Charleston Courier*, October 10–17, 1804.

14. *Raleigh Register*, July 23, 1804, quoting a letter from the Fayetteville district; Raleigh *Minerva*, August 6, 20, 1804; *North-Carolina Journal*, August 27, 1804; *Virginia Argus*, September 1, 1804.

15. *Virginia Gazette*, May 18, 1805; Martinsburg *Berkeley & Jefferson Intelligencer*, April 16, 1805; John G. Jackson to James Madison, April 19, 1805, in Madison Papers, LC.

The Virginia campaign of 1805 concluded a series of presidential, congressional, and legislative elections that recorded the near extinction—at least for a time—of Federalism in the South. Elections to the Tenth Congress in 1806 and 1807 affirmed this situation. Lewis of Virginia, the only incumbent Federalist below the Potomac, was joined by John Culpepper, as North Carolina's Fayetteville district again assumed its usual Federalism. Two candidates also ran in South Carolina, but both lost heavily. Aside from these four, not a single Federalist would even enter his name for the South's forty-six congressional districts.[16]

Table 2 **Results of Southern Congressional Elections, 1800–1807**

Election	*Federalist Candidate Won*	*Federalist Candidate Lost*	*No Federalist Candidate*
1800–01	8 (22%)	6 (16%)	23 (62%)
1802–03	7 (15%)	9 (20%)	30 (65%)
1804–05	1 (2%)	5 (11%)	40 (87%)
1806–07	2 (4%)	2 (4%)	42 (92%)

The collapse of southern Federalism after 1800 had several causes. To begin with, the party enjoyed an artificially high popularity between 1798 and 1800. The French crisis and Republican resistance to defense measures caused a temporary surge of public approval for the Federalist administration. From the Second Congress through the Fifth (1790–1797) Federalists had averaged only five southern congressional seats, but the sweeping tide of patriotic fervor gave them fifteen in 1798–1799. Thus the collapse after 1800 was, in part, a return to the party's normally weak position. Additional forces, however, must have been at work after 1800, because Federalist popular-

16. On the North Carolina campaign, see Raleigh *Minerva*, July 14, August 25, 1806; *Raleigh Register*, June 23, July 7, September 1, 1806; Robert Williams to John Haywood, June 7, 1806, in Ernest Haywood Papers, UNC; James Iredell, Jr., to Ebenezer Pettigrew, June 18, 1806, in Charles Pettigrew Papers, NCDAH. For Virginia, see *Alexandria Advertiser*, April 1, 3, 10, 1807; *Virginia Telegraphe*, February 21, May 9, 1807; *Virginia Argus*, April 14, 28, May 6, 9, 23, June 6, 1807; *Charleston Courier*, June 12, 1807; John McCampbell to James Breckinridge, February 21, 1807, in Breckinridge Papers, UVa.

ity did not cease declining at the level of the 1790s but dropped even lower.[17]

The party's own record in office was partly responsible. Many voters would for years carry resentful memories of the standing army, the direct tax, and the Sedition Act prosecutions of Adams' last years. At every election Republicans reminded southerners of the recent past. Consider the lament of one Federalist worker in North Carolina during the 1808 campaign: "You hear of nothing but tories, Monarchists, Warhawks, Oppressors, British partizans, taxmakers applied to the name of Federalists—Indeed the word Federalist alone without the aid of expletives represented to their affrighted imaginations every thing that is base and infamous."[18] This handicap was the more crippling because there was no way to correct it. Federalist behavior from 1798 to 1800 could only be forgotten with the slow passage of time, but by then the party itself might die.

Jefferson's astute conduct in office also helped reduce the number of Federalist voters. Many who had once feared Jefferson were reassured after 1800. The Constitution was not destroyed, religion was not uprooted, and the country was not overrun by ferocious Frenchmen. The Republicans turned out some Federalist officials and repealed some obnoxious measures, but the basic foundation established by Washington and Adams remained intact. When, in the face of this cautious behavior, Federalists continued to sound alarms, many southerners ceased to take either the party or its ominous warnings very seriously. Far from ruining the nation, Jefferson and the Republican Congress had slashed federal expenses, dismantled military power, reduced the debt, abolished internal taxes, and terminated the Alien and Sedition Acts—all much appreciated in the South. And, most importantly, the Louisiana Purchase won acclaim in a section that was jealous of the national government but eager to expand the national territory.

Economic prosperity also helped tie southerners more closely to the Republican party. Prices for farm products show that the livestock raiser; the cotton, rice, and tobacco planter; and the merchant,

17. For Federalist strength in the 1790s, see Chapter 1, herein, and Rose, *Prologue to Democracy*.

18. ? to Duncan Cameron, July 21, 1808, in Cameron Family Papers.

all enjoyed good times early in the new century. The average price for prime beef during 1804–1807 was nearly 8 percent higher than in January, 1801. Pork averaged almost 14 percent higher, rice 17 percent, and tobacco 18 percent. Thomas Lowndes of South Carolina confessed in 1805 that in spite of a Republican administration, the country had prospered beyond precedent. Whether the farmer, planter, and man of commerce consciously gave the administration credit for this prosperity is questionable, but rising prices at least meant that few southerners would be dissatisfied with Jefferson for economic reascns. The only major southern commodities to decline in price from 1801 to 1807 were wheat and its derivative, flour. Thus it is interesting that the area most stubborn in its Federalism during this period of eroding party fortunes was northwestern Virginia, a region heavily committed to wheat growing.[19]

These contributions to the Federalist collapse after 1800 were all things over which the party had no control, but the near-total lack of organization and the deadening apathy during election campaigns were impediments that need not have existed. A minority party, especially one having a traditionally weak voter appeal and facing a popular president, needs desperately to recruit able, energetic candidates and to turn out as many friendly voters as possible. Such "machines" were not unknown in this period. The Republican minority in several New England states was well organized even by the late 1790s, and so were Federalists after 1800 in many cities and counties from Maryland northward. But in the South, except for a very few localities, Federalists were content to fight their political battles as individuals or at best as isolated, informal groups. The great majority of congressional districts went year after year to the Republicans, without opposition. Eminent men who might have won election to the legislature or Congress refused to make the effort, and thousands of ordinary Federalists declined to vote even when important elections hung in the balance. Readers of party newspapers, men who had to be strong

19. Thomas Lowndes to John Rutledge, Jr., January 9, 1805, in Rutledge Papers, UNC. Commodity price levels are from Anne Bezanson *et al.*, *Wholesale Prices in Philadelphia, 1784–1861* (Philadelphia, 1936). For the similar impact of Jefferson's policies and economic prosperity on northern Federalists, see Robert A. East, "Economic Development and New England Federalism, 1803–1814," *New England Quarterly*, X (1937), 430–66.

partisans to tolerate such pro-Federalist sheets, consistently refused to pay their subscriptions, much less to support the papers with additional gifts. The southern Federalists were, by 1804 and 1806, an unorganized collection of bitter men convinced that America was going downhill; yet they were unwilling to spend their time and money trying to change that fatal course.[20]

Some of this unwillingness to organize actively can be laid to the fear of losing national and state patronage. Anyone who took an open part in Federalist electioneering knew he was reducing or eliminating his chance of receiving a patronage position. The diminished prospect for appointive office must have had a varying effect on individuals, depending on their social and political standing. To many in the upper ranks of society, an office was not a lucrative reward eagerly sought, but a tiresome duty involving sometimes a considerable financial loss. The difficulty that early presidents had in obtaining men for high office is well known.

Many prominent Federalists, however, were not at all dissuaded from party activity by the knowledge that they might be closing the door to preferment. A few even continued to hold office under Jefferson or were actually offered new positions. John Steele, for instance, served as comptroller of the Treasury until 1802, when he resigned voluntarily and against Jefferson's wishes. William Polk, a Federalist leader in Raleigh, continued through Jefferson's entire two terms as collector of revenue for the North Carolina district. Another ardent worker in the 1800 campaign, James Simons, was allowed to remain customs collector at Charleston, even though local Republicans argued that his removal would cripple Federalist strength in that city. William R. Davie of North Carolina and Joseph Habersham of Georgia, both eminent Federalists, were offered civilian appointments under Jefferson but declined; in Davie's case, his Federalist friends urged him not to accept the tendered office. Several party leaders received either army or militia commands, and even more were selected for judicial offices. Former congressman Thomas Evans of Virginia; former senator Samuel Johnston and prominent legislators William

20. The best account of Federalist organizations in the middle and northern states is David H. Fischer, *The Revolution of American Conservatism: The Federalist Party in the Age of Jeffersonian Democracy* (New York, 1965).

Watts Jones and Duncan Cameron of North Carolina; Abraham Nott, H. W. DeSaussure, and John F. Grimké, noted South Carolina Federalists; and John Macpherson Berrien of Georgia—all were chosen by Republican-controlled legislatures to serve in their states' judicial systems. For these men, Federalist affiliation or activity was no bar to obtaining state or national positions.[21]

At a lower level, however, lack of patronage may well have damaged the party. Many persons outside the social and political elite were active in politics and were important in their own counties. To this rank in society, an office paying even a small amount in salary or fees would be a great prize. Very few, if any, minor positions such as post-office and customhouse jobs and departmental clerkships were awarded to Federalists after 1800. For these local leaders, the obscure men who must staff any effective party organization, preferment and Federalism were incompatible. One writer in a North Carolina newspaper issued "A Friendly Invitation to Federalists," advising the county leaders of that party to give up their hopeless cause and become Republicans, "whereby you might stand better chances of being preferred into places of trust and profit."[22]

Besides the partial loss of patronage, general economic prosperity, Jefferson's popularity, and their own past record, Federalists suffered simply because the nation was at peace and unmolested. Throughout most of its history the Federalist party in the South was more deeply concerned with foreign policy, especially toward France, than with domestic matters. That nation had figured in nearly all the great events that helped to form the two parties—the Neutrality Proclamation, Genet's activities, the XYZ Affair, the quasi war, and, indirectly, the

21. John Steele to Nathaniel Macon, 1802, in Kemp P. Battle (ed.), *Letters of Nathaniel Macon, John Steele, and William Barry Grove* (Chapel Hill, N.C., 1902), 24; Jefferson to Steele, December 10, 1802, in Wagstaff (ed.), *Papers of John Steele*, I, 338; *Dictionary of American Biography*, XV, 43–44; James Simons to [?], June 2, 1801, in Rutledge Papers, UNC; Freneau to Jefferson, June 17, 1803, in Thomas Jefferson Papers; Robinson, *Davie*, 368–70; William R. Davie to Steele, August 3, 1801, in John Steele Papers; *Norfolk Gazette*, February 20, 1809; *North-Carolina Minerva*, December 16, 1800; Raleigh *Minerva*, December 22, 1808; William H. Hoyt (ed.), *The Papers of Archibald D. Murphey* (2 vols; Raleigh, N.C., 1914), I, 2*n*3; John B. O'Neall, *Biographical Sketches of the Bench and Bar of South Carolina* (2 vols; Charleston, S.C., 1859), II, 597; C. Jay Smith, Jr., "John McPherson Berrien," in Horace Montgomery (ed.), *Georgians in Profile: Historical Essays in Honor of Ellis Merton Coulter* (Athens, Ga., 1958), 169–70.

22. *Raleigh Register*, February 11, 1805.

Jay Treaty agitation. Hamiltonian economic programs of the 1790s and the Alien and Sedition Acts had driven from the Federalist party many who believed it hostile to southern agricultural interests, popular liberties, or the taxpayer's pocketbook. Who then remained loyal Federalists by 1800? Surely it must have been those who feared France and French ideas more than Hamiltonian government.

Soon after Jefferson attained office, this fear of France abated. The danger seemed to be over. Since the Federalist party by then subsisted largely on anti-French feeling, the truce in Europe removed the party's chief reason for existence. Domestic politics continued to blaze, but many formerly Federalist voters were not interested. The national government was remote and touched them little. It was not the issues of internal politics that gripped them, but the French threat to the American religious, political, and social order. France was quiet now and there seemed to be no need for an active, organized anti-French political movement. By 1805 John Steele wrote of his party "as *having been*, because it was in my opinion dissolved at the conclusion of the late general peace when the French revolution terminated."[23] The party had lapsed into a deep coma and would not revive until the fear of France once more gripped the public.

23. Steele to Nathaniel Macon, January 17, 1805, in Wagstaff (ed.), *Papers of John Steele*, I, 445.

THREE Southern Federalists in National Politics: The Revival, 1808–1816

Chapter 8 THE EMBARGO ELECTION, 1808

JEFFERSON'S controversial embargo and subsequent foreign troubles rescued Federalism from an early demise. In spite of the political heat it generated, the embargo was hardly an untried new weapon in American diplomacy. Colonial boycotts of British trade in the 1760s and 1770s had helped force the repeal of both the Stamp Act and the Townshend Acts. In the 1790s a Republican-sponsored embargo against Britain had spurred negotiations that produced the Jay Treaty. These precedents were quite familiar to Jeffersonians and encouraged them to think that economic pressure would again budge the stubborn British.[1] The embargo of 1807 differed, however, from earlier efforts; it prohibited trade with all countries, not only with Britain, and it had no time limit. Whatever its effect abroad, the embargo sorely hurt America's own economy. Although few southerners were directly engaged in foreign trade, many grew staple crops for export. Suddenly deprived of their markets, these men felt the pinch of economic distress and were unable to make their usual purchases or to repay loans. This in turn hurt creditors, tradesmen, and shopkeepers. Finally, legislative action to suspend the col-

1. William G. Moore, "Economic Coercion as a Policy of the United States, 1794–1805" (Ph.D. dissertation, University of Alabama, 1960), especially the conclusion.

lection of debts put many lawyers out of work and further crippled anyone who had sold goods on credit.[2]

From everywhere came tales of woe. A farmer of central North Carolina said "that he seen and heard of hard times, but, that these were the hardest, of hard times," and every large southern town heard complaints of business stagnating, merchants failing, and produce lying unsold. In Virginia, the cities of Norfolk, Richmond, and Petersburg, the nation's leading tobacco market, suffered from dull or completely paralyzed markets. Inland market towns and coastal ports in North Carolina fared no better.[3] In Charleston, the nation's fifth largest city and the funnel through which nearly all of South Carolina's exports passed, prices had collapsed by the end of January. In Georgia, too, business stagnated; one of her congressmen had "nearly 100 bales of cotton on hand commonly worth 10,000 dollars, now worth little more than nothing."[4]

Federalists hastened to flood the newspapers with criticisms of the economic damage wrought by the embargo. Neither England nor France could be brought to account by an embargo, they said; both countries would simply sell their wares and seek their supplies elsewhere. Long before the constriction of trade would make any impression in London and Paris, America would have strangled herself in her own noose.[5]

2. Louis M. Sears, *Jefferson and the Embargo* (Durham, N.C., 1927), Chap. 8.

3. Mary Cameron to Duncan Cameron, July 29, 1808, in Cameron Family Papers; Peter Bowdoin to Joseph Prentis, Jr., February 24, 1808, in Prentis Family Letterbooks, UVa; Moses Myers to Wilson Cary Nicholas, April 20, 1808, in Wilson Cary Nicholas Papers, LC; Halliday & Hinton to William Bond, January 7, 1808, in James Webb Papers, UNC.

4. David Anderson to John Steele, January 29, 1808, John Haywood to Steele, May 25, 1808, both in Wagstaff (ed.), *Papers of John Steele*, I, 538–39, 551; Robert Williams to Haywood, January 19, 1808, in Ernest Haywood Papers; Allen J. Davie to Thomas D. Bennehan, May 12, 1808, in Cameron Family Papers; Washington Norwood to William Lenoir, June 7, 1808, in Lenoir Family Papers, UNC; John Rutledge, Jr., to Harrison Gray Otis, January 19, 1808, in Harrison Gray Otis Papers; Shaler Hillyer circular to Lawrence Vansendren & Co., n.d., handwritten copy in Shaler Hillyer Letterbook, University of Georgia; Joseph Bryan to John Randolph, February 23, 1808, in Joseph Bryan Papers.

5. *Norfolk Gazette*, March 16, 1808; *Charleston Courier*, September 27, 1808. On the actual effect of the embargo, see Sears, *Jefferson and the Embargo*, Chap. 10; G. W. Daniels, "American Cotton Trade with Liverpool Under the Embargo and Non-Intercourse Acts," *American Historical Review*, XXI (1916), 276–87; W. Freeman Galpin, "The American Grain Trade Under the Embargo of 1808," *Journal of Economic and Business History*, II (1929), 71–100.

Hoping to exploit this widespread distress, Federalists focused their campaigns for the presidency and Congress almost entirely upon the embargo. To them it was a pro-French measure, the crowning absurdity of Jefferson's cowardly foreign policy. For weeks Federalists were complaining that the people were still ignorant of the causes that produced such a drastic measure with so little deliberation. One concluded that since America had no complaint serious enough to warrant an embargo, the law must have been designed to provoke a British declaration of war. Former congressman Henry Lee, long retired from active politics to his northern Virginia plantation, was so disturbed by this possibility that he wrote directly to Secretary of State Madison, warning him that Virginia wanted peace and would "pour forth her indignation against whomsoever she may believe to be the author of war."[6]

How had this dangerous crisis come about? The chief cause, in Federalist minds, was French influence upon the government. According to the *Carolina Weekly Messenger*, "Whether our ports are shut against Great Britain by a declaration of war, or by an embargo, it equally serves France and is precisely the thing which Bonaparte has been endeavoring to obtain."[7]

Although it was easy to stir public anger against the embargo, electing a president on that issue was far more difficult work, made no easier by the party's weak southern organization and by confusion and delay in choosing a national ticket. The Republicans had settled on James Madison and George Clinton for president and vice-president as early as January, 1808, but Federalists waited until late August to hold a nominating caucus in New York. Even then there was but one representative from the entire South—John Rutledge, Jr., of South Carolina, who happened to be traveling nearby at the time. Two maverick Republicans, James Monroe and Clinton,[8] were already in the field against Madison; but after spirited debate the caucus declined

6. *Norfolk Gazette*, January 8, 1808; Henry Lee to James Madison, January 18, 1808, in Madison Papers, LC; "A North Carolina Soldier of '76," in Raleigh *Minerva*, February 25, 1808.

7. Raleigh *Minerva*, January 8, 14, 28, 1808; Charleston *Carolina Weekly Messenger*, January 12, 1808.

8. At the same time that he was Madison's running mate on the regular Republican ticket, Clinton was supported for president by antiadministration Republicans in New York and elsewhere.

to support either of them and instead renominated the 1804 Federalist candidates, Charles Cotesworth Pinckney for president and Rufus King of New York for vice-president.[9]

Once made, the caucus decision was slow to reach the southern Federalists. Pinckney himself asked Rutledge on September 8, "Could you not inform us who met? . . . From what States? How long were you together? Were any propositions made immediately from the C[linton] party? &c. &c." On the same day a letter from Rutledge arrived giving details of the caucus and Pinckney quickly replied, accepting the presidential nomination but admitting, "I still continue of opinion that our exertions will not be ultimately successful. I however think they ought to be vigorously made, in order to show that federalism is not extinct, and that there is in the Union a formidable party of the old Washingtonian school, alert to detect & expose any weak or visionary plans which may endanger the prosperity or safety of our Country." Even at this late date, southern party leaders decided —it is not clear why—to keep the nominations from the public for a few weeks longer.[10] Partly because of this secrecy, Federalist campaign efforts were hopelessly divided.

In Virginia, where the General Ticket Law required a statewide electoral vote, the wisdom of a strictly Federalist slate was doubtful. Pinckney and King might carry some counties but could hardly be expected to win the state. Most Federalist leaders therefore concluded that the only chance to deny Madison Virginia was to throw their own party's small strength to the antiadministration Republican, James Monroe. A former senator, governor, and minister to France and England, Monroe had broken with Jefferson and Madison chiefly because he felt they had ignored and slighted him. He avoided a public announcement but allowed his Virginia friends to press a vigorous campaign for him.[11] In January, 1808, when the regular Republican

9. Fischer, *Revolution of American Conservatism*, 84–87; Samuel Eliot Morison, "The First National Nominating Convention," *American Historical Review*, XVII (1912), 744–65; C. C. Pinckney to John Rutledge, Jr., September 8, 1808, in Rutledge Papers, UNC.

10. C. C. Pinckney to John Rutledge, Jr., September 8, 1808 (two letters of this date), Rutledge Papers, UNC.

11. Harry Ammon, "James Monroe and the Election of 1808 in Virginia," *William and Mary Quarterly*, 3rd ser., XX (1963), 33–56.

legislative caucus endorsed Madison for president, one-third of the General Assembly met separately to choose a Monroe electoral ticket and state and county campaign committees. Several Federalists attended this rump meeting.[12]

As the election approached, the Monroe revolt gained more adherents, including all but one of the state's Federalist newspapers. The *Virginia Gazette*, for instance, argued that "we can render no service *in this state* by voting for such [Federalist] Ticket" as Pinckney and King. Monroe "differs in political opinion from us; but he is an honest man . . . we have no fears of his marking out the Federalists as a political sect, upon whom he will have vengeance!!!" A local meeting in Richmond, given weight by the presence of several prominent leaders, also joined Monroe, explaining that a separate Pinckney ticket would merely divide the anti-Madison vote.[13]

Some Federalists could not bring themselves to such action, for no matter how much Monroe opposed the government, he was still a Republican. They were unwilling to abandon their traditional principles, especially with no significant proof that Monroe would adopt a course substantially different from Jefferson's. Five weeks before the election, a freeholders meeting in Staunton gave an organized voice to such opinions and set up a corresponding committee for Pinckney and King. In early November—far too late to gain wide publicity—the committee published a formal slate of Pinckney electors, denying any intention to dictate to Federalists elsewhere but showing determination to put a "pure" party ticket in the field.[14]

Still other Virginia Federalists preferred even Madison himself, though John Marshall's claim that most of them did so is surely a great exaggeration. Francis Corbin, a Federalist merchant, assured

12. Edward Carrington to Timothy Pickering, January 30, 1808, in Timothy Pickering Papers; Frederick Hamilton to David Campbell, January 25, 1808, in David Campbell Papers, Duke University; *Virginia Argus*, January 22, 26, 1808; Richmond *Enquirer*, February 2, 1808.

13. *Virginia Gazette*, October 18, 1808; *Virginia Argus*, October 18, 1808; John Marshall to C. C. Pinckney, October 19, 1808, in Cross (ed.), "John Marshall," 648–49; Robert Beverly to John Rutledge, Jr., July 3, 1808, in Rutledge Papers, UNC.

14. Robert Anderson's letter in *Virginia Gazette*, November 8, 1808; Winchester *Gazette*, quoted in *Charleston Courier*, July 18, 1808; Staunton *Political Censor*, quoted in *Alexandria Advertiser*, September 28, 1808.

the secretary of state that despite the Richmond and Staunton meetings, many of his party would support his ticket

> under a firm persuasion that you are still attached to the Fedl. Const[itution] & that you will not suffer it to be impaired, . . . That you will consult the Interests of the U.S. exclusively without favor or partiality for any foreign Country. . . . That you will promote the Interests of Commerce. . . . That you will be the President of the U.S. and not the President of a Party. That you will rule by principle and not by Faction. That you will respect the Rights of the Minority, not merely in Word but in deed. . . . Believing all these things We pray for the success of your Election.

In another part of the state a Republican congratulated Madison on getting Federalist votes that even Jefferson had lost. Still, this should not be exaggerated; county election returns confirm the consensus of contemporaries that the great majority of Virginia Federalists enlisted with Monroe.[15]

The three-way division among candidates meant that Federalists had even less formal organization than in 1800. Those who supported Madison acted entirely as individuals, and the Staunton mass meeting for Pinckney occurred much too late in the year to stimulate local organizations in other counties, as the very low vote for Pinckney suggests. The Richmond leaders who endorsed Monroe never intended to become an official central committee directing party efforts in the whole state, nor is there any evidence of organized Federalist groups aiding Monroe in their counties. Probably local Federalists worked through the structure already established by the Monroe Republicans, who as early as February had a central committee in Richmond and county campaign groups throughout the state. Some Madison Republicans complained of these mergers, as in Halifax County, where at election time "three lawyers—five parsons—one doctor—the whole tribe of federalists—monarchists—and British adherents—(a curious coalition)—appeared on the field of action early in the day" flushing out votes for Monroe.[16]

15. Francis Corbin to James Madison, October 29, 1808, William Pope to James Madison, October 31, 1808, both in Madison Papers, LC; *Virginia Argus*, October 14, 1808; William H. Cabell to Joseph C. Cabell, October 19, 1808, in Cabell Deposit.

16. Letter from Halifax County in *Virginia Argus*, November 25, 1808.

North Carolina Federalists also floundered in search of a candidate. They liked the New York caucus nomination of Pinckney and King, but it came too late to untangle their confusion, partly because the state leaders gave that news only to confidential friends and did not publicize it until shortly before the election.[17] Since no one could be sure whether Pinckney or one of the maverick Republicans would prove strongest against Madison, the anti-Madison electoral candidates scattered their preferences widely. Some supported both Monroe and Clinton, hoping to attract the maximum of disgruntled Republican voters. At least one stuck to the straight party ticket of Pinckney and King; another promised to vote for either Pinckney or Monroe, whoever seemed most likely to defeat Madison. Other Federalists said simply that they would vote for men favoring free commerce. Even after the November balloting, the confusion continued. William Gaston, one of the successful Federalist electors, wrote to friends in Washington and South Carolina, asking them to recommend the most expedient course of action for Federalist electors in other states.[18]

The confusion might have been eased greatly by a statewide party organization, but there was none. The choice of presidential electors by districts removed the chief incentive for a guiding state committee, and even within the districts there was no formal party framework. Occasional informal meetings were held, as in the Raleigh district, where Federalist leaders were able to agree on a single nominee pledged to vote against Madison, or in the neighboring Hillsborough district, where the leadership resolved a dispute between two candidates by inducing one to withdraw;[19] but usually there was not even this small degree of concerted effort.

South Carolina, as Pinckney's home state, was spared most of the uncertainty that plagued the party elsewhere. The Charleston Feder-

17. Archibald Henderson to John Rutledge, Jr., September 9, 1808, in Rutledge Papers, UNC; William Barry Grove to Walter Alves, September 19, 1808, in Walter Alves Papers, UNC.

18. See the announcements of various candidates in Raleigh *Minerva*, July 21, September 8, October 6, 13, 1808, and *Raleigh Register*, February 25, 1808; William Gaston to John Rutledge, Jr., November 8, 1808, in Rutledge Papers, UNC. The winning Federalist electors did finally vote for Pinckney and King.

19. William Polk to Walter Alves, October 6, 15, 1808, Grove to Alves, September 19, 1808, Alves to Lemuel Benton, October 27, 1808—all in Walter Alves Papers.

alists had been shocked that some New England leaders were considering supporting Clinton during the summer and were relieved when their neighbor finally secured the presidential nomination at New York. One writer emphasized that Pinckney had been born among them and was known to them all; another urged quick action to organize the low country.[20] A few letters for Clinton appeared in the *Charleston Courier*, but these probably came from dissatisfied Republicans, not Federalists.[21]

Since the legislature cast South Carolina's presidential vote, the October elections for the house and senate would be decisive. In Charleston and surrounding coastal parishes the campaign was vigorous. Within the city, Federalists put together a full legislative ticket and waged an unusually active campaign, even sending pamphlets into the surrounding low-country parishes.[22] In the rest of South Carolina it was a different story; Republicans had the middle and upper country to themselves, disturbed by only an occasional Federalist candidate.

Despite their lack of organization, southern Federalists hoped to make a good showing in every state by their sustained attack on Republican foreign policy. The embargo they saw as a mere symptom of the general Republican partiality for France.[23] And shortsighted Republican "economy" had left the nation defenseless, so that instead of protecting commerce, ships and sailors were hidden at home.[24]

The ghost of Washington, so long useful to Federalists, was again conjured up to curse the Republican party. A resident of the general's old Virginia district asked whether voters would "travel the old plain level road, marked by the immortal Washington" or "encounter the

20. John Rutledge, Jr., to Otis, September 18, 1808, in Harrison Gray Otis Papers; letter to the "Federal Republican Committee, Charleston, South Carolina," September, 1808, in Morison (ed.), *Otis*, I, 314–15; "A Voter" and "Gustavus Vasa," in *Charleston Courier*, August 11, 19, 1808.

21. "Thousands" and "A Clintonian," in *Charleston Courier*, August 13, 16, 23, September 6, 15, 26, 1808.

22. Charles Pinckney to Thomas Jefferson, October 23, 1808, in Thomas Jefferson Papers; Charles Pinckney to Madison, October 12, 1808, in Madison Papers, LC; C. C. Pinckney to John Rutledge, Jr., September 8, 28, 1808, in Rutledge Papers, UNC.

23. *Wilmington Gazette*, November 22, 1808; *Virginia Gazette*, September 12, 1808.

24. Steele to Wade Hampton, August 28, 1808, in Wagstaff (ed.), *Papers of John Steele*, II, 559.

dark zigzag path" of Jefferson and Madison.[25] Federalists also claimed that eight years of Republican misrule had deprived the United States of respect abroad and prosperity at home and had left her scorned and insulted, impoverished and bankrupt. Madison would continue this downward course; only a change of men and parties could bring a change of fortune. The *Wilmington Gazette* summed up the "Probable Consequences of the Next Election":

> MADISON—Embargo, no sales for produce, internal taxes, empty Treasury, loans, a subservient judiciary . . . a probable separation of the states . . . collisions with all nations, general ruin & disgrace, war.
> PINCKNEY—No Embargo, an honest and perfect neutrality, commercial treaties, extensive commerce, no internal taxes, an overflowing treasury, no French or British tribute, a dignified, independent, honorable reparation from England . . . no impressment of American seamen; an upright, learned & independent judiciary, respect from all nations, peace with all the world.[26]

Northern Federalists hoped that the pressure of the embargo would be enough to pry loose four or five electoral votes in North Carolina and to win South Carolina's ten as well.[27] The southerners themselves were more pessimistic. South Carolina, they knew, was out of reach; local victories might reduce the Republican legislative majority there but surely could not erase it. Virginia, too, was hopeless, although a few wild optimists thought Monroe, at least, might deprive Madison of her votes. Only in North Carolina did close observers really expect to win any electors, and even there one candidate worried that apathy born of despair would cost Federalists the election.[28]

The final results amply bore out the melancholy predictions. Madison carried Virginia by four to one over Monroe in a very low turnout,

25. "Firelock," in *Virginia Herald*, September 16, 1808.

26. *Wilmington Gazette*, November 3, 1808.

27. Baltimore *Federal Gazette, Connecticut Herald*, and Washington *Federalist*, all quoted in *Virginia Gazette*, June 7, July 1, September 30, 1808.

28. H. W. DeSaussure to Ezekiel Pickens, September 12, 1808, in H. W. DeSaussure Papers, University of South Carolina (hereinafter cited as USC); C. C. Pinckney to John Rutledge, Jr., September 28, 1808, Gaston to John Rutledge, Jr., November 8, 1808, both in Rutledge Papers, UNC; John Marshall to C. C. Pinckney, September 21, 1808, in Cross (ed.), "John Marshall," 646–47; *Norfolk Gazette*, October 12, 1808; Raleigh *Minerva*, October 13, 1808.

with Pinckney gaining less than 1,000 votes in a total of 19,000. North Carolina went Republican by a larger margin than Federalists expected, but they did at least win three electors. The state's popular vote was about 10,000 for Pinckney, 1,500 for Monroe, and 21,000 (or 65 percent) for the Madison electors. South Carolina was even worse; the October legislative elections returned scarcely twenty-five Federalists out of one hundred sixty-one members in the house and senate combined. Reduced to such standing, the party avoided the useless gesture of presenting a Pinckney ticket, and the Assembly chose ten Madison electors without opposition. Madison also had an easy race in Georgia, which had no Federalist organization and very few, if any, Federalists in its legislature. John Macpherson Berrien, a young party activist in Savannah, claimed that many assemblymen might support Pinckney if they received persuasive letters from prominent northern Federalists; and there was also some Monroe sentiment among anti-administration Republicans. In the end, neither group made any visible challenge and Madison won Georgia's six votes.[29]

During the presidential contest, Federalists also made an unaccustomed effort in southern congressional elections. There was even a Federalist candidate in Georgia, where the party had shrunk almost to the vanishing point and the label *Federalist* was never used in public except as an accusation. The congressional candidate in 1802 had not done well, and neither did John M. Dooly in 1808; but at least he gave Federalists a chance to cast a vote of protest. Six men put themselves forward for Georgia's four House seats, and Dooly was the only one whose Republicanism was not certified in the newspapers. His entry was announced "with pleasure" by the Federalist *Augusta Herald*, which merely listed the five other names without comment. The

29. Virginia official returns are in Virginia State Library; see also Randolph to Joseph H. Nicholson, November 14, 1808, in Randolph Papers, UVa. North Carolina popular vote is estimated from incomplete returns in the newspapers for November, 1808. For South Carolina, see Thomas Lehre to Jefferson, November 1, December 6, 1808, in Thomas Jefferson Papers; letter from South Carolina in *Virginia Argus*, December 16, 1808; Samuel House to Elizabeth Trist, November 17, 1808, in Nicholas P. Trist Papers, UNC; DeSaussure to Josiah Quincy, December 7, 1808, in Edmund Quincy, *Life of Josiah Quincy of Massachusetts* (Boston: Ticknor & Fields, 1867), 189. On the Georgia election, John M. Berrien to John Rutledge, Jr., October 3, 1808, in Rutledge Papers, UNC; Bryan to Randolph, July 26, September 5, 1808, typed copies in John Randolph Papers, UNC; Charleston *City Gazette*, November 19, 1808.

few active Federalists left in Georgia did little in the campaign, and Dooly finished last with 4,800 votes in a total of about 16,000. However, this was a remarkably high percentage for a Federalist, and obviously many people voted for him with no idea of his party membership. He ran very well, for instance, in the area surrounding his up-country home, which was otherwise heavily Republican.[30]

In contrast to Georgia, the South Carolina election was quieter than in previous years; only one Federalist dared to challenge the solidly Republican delegation. Former congressman Thomas Lowndes fought to regain his old Charleston district, but after a brief campaign as an antiembargo man he failed by more than two to one.[31] Farther north there was more activity. North Carolina and Virginia had each returned only one Federalist to the previous Congress, but now the embargo seemed to bring many other seats within grasp. The Federalists of Rockbridge County, Virginia, echoed the tone of their party's whole campaign, declaring the embargo utterly mad, "repugnant to the habits of the people, and inconsistent with the spirit of the constitution."[32]

Actually, the embargo issue was largely irrelevant in North Carolina. In the four most hotly contested races, every candidate, Republican as well as Federalist, opposed the law. The Fayetteville district had no Republican nominee, but the sitting Federalist faced a strong challenger from within his party. In three other districts incumbent Republicans had voted against the embargo in Congress, although Federalists tried to chain them all tightly to the unpopular measure, and with some success. Two of the three were unseated, as Federalists polled about 12,000 votes across the state to perhaps 38,000 for the administration men. It was impossible not to gloat over the great improvement from two years ago. The Raleigh *Minerva* found the election results very pleasing, considering that North Carolina had es-

30. *Augusta Chronicle*, September 17, 1808; *Augusta Herald*, August 11, 1808; Savannah *Columbian Museum*, August 12, 1808; Savannah *Republican*, August 11, November 15, 1808; and letters from Bryan to Randolph, January 31, February 23, and September 5, 1808, in Bryan Papers.

31. C. C. Pinckney to John Rutledge, Jr., August 24, September 8, 1808, in Rutledge Papers, UNC; *Charleston Courier*, August 23, September 7, 1808. Thomas Lowndes polled only 30 percent of the vote compared to 44 percent for William Loughton Smith, the party's candidate in 1806.

32. Staunton *Political Censor*, February 22, 1809.

caped the worst effects of the embargo and that many Republicans were unopposed. From his Salisbury plantation John Steele commented: "a little more Embargo—a little more mystery concerning our affairs with France . . . will cure the people everywhere of their delusions."[33]

Although Virginia's election was not until April, 1809, Federalist candidates had begun to come forth as early as the preceding summer; one district even held county mass meetings and formed corresponding committees to choose a nominee. There were reports of a statewide campaign plan centralized in Richmond, but there is no firm evidence for this. Probably the Federalists of each congressional district worked independently, occasionally exchanging information across the state but having no formal channels of cooperation.[34] In all, nine Federalists ran for Congress and four succeeded, gratifying the party faithful. In addition, three antiadministration Republicans entered the field and all won. Since thirteen districts had no Federalist candidate, the popular vote in 1809 is hardly an exact expression of the party's true strength throughout Virginia. As nearly as can be estimated, about 7,000 votes (22 percent) were cast for Federalists, 3,400 (11 percent) for the opposition Republicans, and 22,000 (67 percent) for the administration Republicans. Here, as in North Carolina, the Federalist share was considerably better than in the previous few years.[35]

Was this series of presidential and congressional elections truly a referendum on the embargo? If so, the verdict is hazy. Federalists gained several House seats in Virginia and North Carolina, but Republicans still held thirty-nine of the forty-six southern congressional districts. Furthermore, the embargo was a direct party issue only in

33. Steele to Hampton, August 28, 1808, in Wagstaff (ed.), *Papers of John Steele*, II, 558–59; Raleigh *Minerva*, August 25, 1808; James C. Johnston to James Iredell, Jr., n.d., in Charles E. Johnson Papers, NCDAH. Returns are estimated from incomplete figures in the newspapers.

34. *Norfolk Gazette*, July 11, 1808; *Alexandria Advertiser*, July 21, 1808; Martinsburg *Berkeley & Jefferson Intelligencer*, September 23, October 14, December 2, 1808; Allen Taylor to James Breckinridge, January 1, 1808, in Breckinridge Papers, UVa.

35. *Norfolk Gazette*, May 3, 8 (letter from Staunton), 1809; *Alexandria Gazette*, April 18, 1809; Robert Gamble to James McDowell, May 1, 1809, in James McDowell Papers. For the partial returns, see the newspapers for April and May, 1809, and John G. Jackson to Madison, May 1, 1809, and William McKinley to Madison, May 1, 1809, both in Madison Papers, LC.

those few districts where a Federalist opposed a pro-Embargo Republican. The presidential race offered a clearer choice—Madison versus Pinckney or Monroe—and in this contest the Federalists actually did worse than in 1800. Then, Adams had polled 23 percent of the vote in Virginia; Pinckney and Monroe combined had but 21 percent in 1808. Adams reached 44 percent in North Carolina; Pinckney and Monroe, only 35 percent. Of South Carolina's legislators, nearly half had supported Adams, but in 1808 less than one-seventh were Federalists. The fourteen Federalist congressmen from the South in 1800 had dwindled to only seven, even after the sharp gains of 1808 and 1809.

There are several reasons why the embargo was not more painful politically for the Republicans. Economically, it was not nearly so harmful as in the North. Merchants, staple planters and farmers, and their satellite professional men were the chief victims. Subsistence farmers and those who sold to local markets may have known the embargo's effects more by hearsay than from harsh personal experience. These people, easily a majority of the population in most of the South, lived on the very fringes of the money economy. Seldom seeing much cash even in good times, they had little to lose from falling prices. Even in the towns, everyone who did not grow his own crops would benefit by the depressed cost of food and fiber. Within the commercial class, some eased their lot by smuggling.[36] Those who partly or entirely escaped the embargo's hardships were under no great personal economic compulsion to cast a protest vote. So the South, being more rural, more agricultural, and less dependent upon commerce than the North, reacted less violently against the Republicans in 1808.

Besides, there seemed to be no real alternative to the embargo; at least the Federalists did not suggest any. Taking up arms in active defense of neutral rights or suffering quietly while those rights were violated seemed to be the only other courses open to Americans. Neither war nor submission was acceptable to a people fiercely jealous of their national honor but deeply reluctant to maintain a military force. The embargo might possibly make Britain and France respect neutral rights at less sacrifice than an open war. Throughout the 1808 cam-

36. On smuggling, see Sears, *Jefferson and the Embargo*, 241.

paign Republicans emphasized this argument in defense of their policy, asking that people "nobly, patiently, suffer a temporary evil, to procure a lasting good."[37] One indication that southerners heeded the plea to accept the embargo as a necessary burden is the striking absence—except in a few heavily Federalist counties—of mass protests. In 1793 and 1798, and again in 1807 and 1812, when the South was deeply incensed against France or England, many localities passed resolutions of indignation. Even in 1808, outside the South, there were numerous city and county antiembargo meetings, but from Virginia to Georgia there was silence. Both common voters and local opinion leaders seemed to approve (or at least to tolerate) the measure.[38]

Even those who did wish to protest the embargo might be apprehensive of voting for a Federalist president or congressman. Memories of the oppressive Adams years were too fresh in the minds of many to allow them to support Federalists, whatever the economic aggravation of the embargo. Perhaps most decisive in preventing heavier Federalist gains was simply the firm attachment of most southerners to the Republican party. Party loyalty is an extremely durable bond, broken only once or twice in a voter's life, if ever. Those unattached to either party might well vote Federalist if affected adversely by the embargo, but those who consciously considered themselves firm Republicans were much less likely to do so. For some, this was a traditional allegiance going back to the struggle against the Constitution; nearly all the antifederalist leaders of 1788 later became Republicans and often took their followers with them. Others, firm federalists in 1788, went into opposition over Hamilton's financial program and remained thereafter in the Republican ranks. The Jay Treaty dispute and the French crisis, with its repressive legislation, helped solidify the attachment of these converts to Republicanism. Finally, the first Jefferson administration brought many formerly hostile or wavering voters into the fold and filled the Republican party to overflowing.

37. "Pacificus," in *Raleigh Register*, February 4, 1808; Richmond *Enquirer*, June 21, 1808.

38. In fact, when the citizens of Wilmington and vicinity in North Carolina heard of men circulating antiembargo sentiments, a public meeting was held to pass resolu-McPherson (ed.), "Unpublished Letters from North Carolinians to Jefferson," *North Carolina Historical Review*, XII (1935), 361–62.

By 1808 these southerners had become accustomed to voting Republican and to receiving their political information from Republican sources. They had absorbed at least some of the arguments of their party about the need for effective but peaceful resistance to Britain and France. The temporary discomfort of the embargo could not shake the voting habits of these loyal Republicans, and this doomed the Federalists' hopes for a major revival of strength similar to the one in the North. Archibald Henderson, the retired congressman, recognized that the party's gains in 1808 were not permanent; "it was the Embargo," he said, "and not Democracy, that lost popularity." And he resigned the Federalists to a dismal future, in the belief that the people would have to become far better informed or else continue to be duped by "those who profess themselves the devoted admirers of equal liberty."[39]

39. Henderson to John Rutledge, Jr., January 17, 1808, in Rutledge Papers, UNC.

Chapter 9 FEDERALISTS AND DOMESTIC AFFAIRS, 1807–1812

FOREIGN policy increasingly absorbed public attention after 1807, but domestic matters were not forgotten. The most spectacular issues involved three Republican personalities: Aaron Burr, the former vice-president; James Wilkinson, commanding general of the army; and John Randolph, the maverick congressman. Perhaps the most interesting episode was the changing Federalist attitude toward America's foremost political chameleon, Aaron Burr.

Before 1801, while Burr was a Republican political leader, Federalists condemned him equally with Jefferson as a scheming Jacobin, dangerous to the country. In the 1801 election deadlock between the two Republicans, congressional Federalists became friendly toward Burr, preferring him to Jefferson. After Burr became vice-president the southerners practically forgot him until 1804, when he killed Alexander Hamilton in a duel and incurred the fury of all Federalists, who then considered him little better than a murderer. This loathing continued unabated for some years.[1]

1. *Norfolk Gazette*, March 13, 1805.

In the autumn of 1806, reports began arriving from the West that Burr was involved in a scheme of disunion and rebellion. In January, 1807, the rumor became accepted fact and the press of both parties bulged with details of a plot to amputate the Southwest from the Union. Federalists hastened to make the affair a party issue, denouncing both Burr's conspiracy and Jefferson's casual attitude toward it. They accused Napoleon of financing the plot and criticized the president for having disbanded most of the standing army and leaving the citizens' protection in the hands of an unreliable militia who were more likely to join the conspiracy than oppose it. One Georgian proclaimed that after Burr had received unanimous Republican support in the 1800 election, no attempt "to pass him off for a federal character, or as having ever been a federal favorite" should be allowed.[2]

Yet when the administration did move against Burr, the Federalists abruptly reversed themselves and began to attack his accusers. After waiting for months while news of Burr's suspicious behavior flowed in, Jefferson at last decided that treason was afoot. Once convinced, he had Burr arrested and brought to Richmond for trial before Chief Justice Marshall, the most prominent of all southern Federalists. It soon became obvious that the judge and the president had very different ideas about the trial. Jefferson, sure of Burr's guilt and determined to see him punished, was supported by most Republican leaders. Marshall saw this as simple political persecution, and in presiding over the trial he gave Burr at least a fair hearing, if not favoritism.

Marshall's view was a common one among southern Federalists. Those who earlier had been convinced of Burr's treason and who had criticized Jefferson for not acting firmly, were now equally sure that the Republicans were shamefully hounding a man who was perhaps entirely innocent. Some denounced the Republican press for declaring Burr guilty before his trial commenced. The Richmond Federalists were the most outspoken, and the city's party newspaper insisted

2. Raleigh *Minerva*, November 24, 1806, January 12, 19, February 9, 1807; Robert Mackay to his wife, January 10, 1807, in Walter C. Hartridge (ed.), *Letters of Robert Mackay to His Wife* (Athens, Ga., 1949), 56–57; *Augusta Herald*, quoted in *Charleston Courier*, April 22, 1807.

throughout the trial that Burr was a victim of political harassment. Local Federalists wrote long articles upholding Burr's innocence and denouncing the Republicans for wishing him hung. Others went beyond mere correspondence; John Wickham, Richmond's leading Federalist lawyer, was one of Burr's defense counsel; and Edward Carrington, a party stalwart and local officeholder, openly patronized the defendant. All this led one Republican to exclaim in disgust, "Burr killed Hamilton, and the Federalists denounced him! He traduces the administration, and forms a plot to dissever the union, and now, forsooth, they are offering their lives, their *fortunes*, to protect the traitor!"[3]

Soon Republicans were accusing Chief Justice Marshall himself of partiality to Burr, and the jury was said to be so packed with antiadministration men that it would never return a fair verdict. When the chief justice attended a dinner at which Burr also was present, the outcry from Republicans was quick and shrill; here surely was proof of Marshall's bias. Federalists in Richmond excused the judge, saying that he had no idea Burr would be at the dinner and could hardly leap from the table and walk out once he discovered Burr's presence. There is little evidence to suggest what southern Federalists in general thought of this incident, but a few in rural Virginia did object to Marshall's conduct and to the Richmonders' defense of it.[4]

Burr's final acquittal, not only of treason but even of a misdemeanor, brought more Republican blasts against Marshall. Jefferson himself joined in, declaring Burr quite guilty and casting doubt upon Marshall's honesty. Again the Federalists hastened to protect their most eminent officeholder and accused the Republicans of trying to "overwhelm [Marshall] with their noisome venom" merely because he would not persecute Burr as the president wished. One, who claimed that Republicans needed no evidence against Burr and were a law unto themselves, feared impeachment for Marshall. Most efforts in defense of Marshall emanated from Virginia, his own state; but the

3. Demands for a fair trial are in *Norfolk Gazette*, April 29, June 5, 17, 1807; Raleigh *Minerva*, May 21, 1807; and *Virginia Gazette*, May 6, 1807. See also "Investigator" and "Philo-Investigator," in *Virginia Gazette*, June 24–October 10, 1807.

4. *Virginia Gazette*, April 29, 1807; William H. Cabell to James C. Cabell, April 12, 1807, in Cabell Deposit.

Federalists farther south were no less convinced of Marshall's rectitude and of the grossness of Republican attacks upon him.[5]

Shortly after Burr's trial he and Marshall were replaced as subjects of controversy by one of Burr's accusers, Brigadier General James Wilkinson, whom Federalists had come to despise nearly as much as they did Jefferson himself. Wilkinson, the commanding general of the army, had participated in the western conspiracy but then deserted Burr and was one of the chief witnesses against him. Evidence during the trial revealed Wilkinson's ties to Burr and further indicated that he had been in the pay of Spain for years. Witnesses said they had long ago informed the government of this but Jefferson had done nothing. Federalists quickly demanded an investigation, hoping to embarrass the administration. The Raleigh *Minerva* led off, piously asking whether Americans should not feel astonished and indignant at the government for keeping Wilkinson in charge of the army. Federalists in Virginia's lower house supported a resolution against the general, with substantial help from Republican members.[6]

As soon as Congress met in October, 1807, the maverick Republican John Randolph asked for a special committee to weigh the charges against Wilkinson. In this demand Randolph won the consistent backing of Joseph Lewis, Jr., one of the two southern Federalists then in Congress, but the motion was unsuccessful. Instead, the president summoned a special military court to try Wilkinson on the accusations of wrongdoing. Since all the members of the court-martial were subordinate in rank to the general, it was doubtful from the beginning that they would vote to convict him. When the court finally acquitted Wilkinson in the summer of 1808, most Federalists were unaccountably silent, although one editor was disgusted by the verdict. "Without attempting to attach censure to the court martial before which this Hero has been tried," he sarcastically wrote, "we will only observe, that two of the court, Burbeck & Williams, are relations and

5. *Virginia Gazette*, September 30, 1807; Raleigh *Minerva*, September 24, 1807; *Norfolk Gazette*, November 25, 1807; Beveridge, *Marshall*, III, Chaps. 7–9; Robert K. Faulkner, "John Marshall and the Burr Trial," *Journal of American History*, LIII (1966), 247–58. For the Jeffersonian view of Burr's trial, see Malone, *Jefferson the President: Second Term*, Chaps. 17–19, especially pp. 335–42.

6. Raleigh *Minerva*, January 14, 21, 28, 1808; *Virginia House Journal*, 1807, p. 150.

completely subject to the will of Wilkinson—and Cushing, we are also credibly informed, is a cringing, crouching, fawning sycophant, a mere creature in shape only of an human."[7]

Federalists continued to criticize Wilkinson and also flayed Jefferson for allowing the suspect to remain in command of the entire army and to receive $55,000 more than his official salary. Two newspapers ran a long series of scathing articles that as much as branded Wilkinson a traitor. Nor were this rascal's schemes even yet ended; the *Norfolk Gazette* claimed that he was planning an expedition against Florida or Mexico and that the government had full knowledge of it. Yet Jefferson and Madison still kept him in office.[8]

Finally, in 1809, Congress appeared ready to notice the serious charges against Wilkinson. In the first regular session of the Eleventh Congress, the North Carolina Federalist Joseph Pearson took up Randolph's cause of two years past and pressed for a special investigating committee. There was certainly ample reason for one, Pearson said, and "the only wonder is, why this subject had been permitted to remain uninvestigated so long." Supported by nearly all Federalists and many Republicans, the Pearson resolution eventually passed, only to have Congress adjourn without actually implementing it.[9]

When the House reconvened in December, 1810, Pearson renewed his efforts. He reminded members of the evidence supporting Wilkinson's connection with the Spanish agents. Surely it was desirable to learn the truth about these suspicions. Joined by more than a score of Republicans, the Federalist bloc again voted for an investigation that some thought would implicate Jefferson himself. If Burr was a traitor, as the Republicans had claimed in 1807, then Wilkinson was one also. And, if Wilkinson was a turncoat, what could his patron, Jefferson, be called?[10] But despite congressional resolutions and Federalist

7. The other Federalist, John Culpepper of North Carolina, sided with Wilkinson once but was absent on the four other votes: *Annals of Congress*, 10th Cong., 1st Sess., 1268, 1322–23, 1357, 1458, 1487; Staunton *Political Censor*, July 20, 1808.

8. Winchester *Gazette*, February 25, 1809; *Norfolk Gazette*, March 3, September 18, 1809; "The Commander in Chief" series, in the *Virginia Gazette*, September 15–October 10, 1809 and the Raleigh *Minerva*, September 14–October 19, 1809.

9. *Charleston Courier*, November 4, 1809; *Annals of Congress*, 11th Cong., 2nd Sess., 1606, 1746–54, 2035.

10. *Annals of Congress*, 11th Cong., 3rd Sess., 434–50. For speech by Pearson and editorial comment, see Raleigh *Minerva*, January 10, 1811.

accusations, Wilkinson remained untouched by investigation, for the prospect of war with Great Britain soon pushed this and all other secondary matters aside.

Although the Burr and Wilkinson affairs were easy to dramatize, some Federalists thought more could be gained by attacking the financial side of Republican government. Nothing would sway the voters more surely than to convince them that Jefferson, Madison, and other important Republicans were profligate spenders of the people's money. To hear Federalists tell it, huge sums were wasted yearly through the stupidity, carelessness, and even thievery of the party in power. Jefferson spent more than Washington on presidential household items; a Republican editor drew $1,350 yearly as an army colonel, though he was fit only for journalism, if that; and the War Department wasted $100,000 by abolishing the efficient quartermaster's office and relying instead on incompetent military agents to procure supplies. The supposedly economical and antimilitary Republicans spent even more on the army and navy than the Federalists had. An individual sailor cost twice as much to maintain under Jefferson as under Adams, a fact that prompted hints of fraud and mismanagement. The *Charleston Courier* ran an entire series of articles entitled "Science of Draining Money from the Treasury," detailing similar instances of extravagance.[11]

Federalists thought the most flagrant example of waste was Jefferson's plan of replacing American warships with tiny gunboats. Always proponents of a strong navy, southern Federalists scoffed at the gunboats as being expensive, unseaworthy, and unable to perform even their limited purpose of defending American harbors. In 1807, Congress asked the president for information on the efficacy of gunboats before it would authorize sixty more of them. The *Norfolk Gazette* wondered why the House had not investigated that question before it built the first sixty-nine. When Madison gave signs of abandoning the gunboats, the same editor praised his willingness to end a wasteful and useless project. The little craft had cost almost $1 million and now that the government was in a more rational mood "they are no

11. Raleigh *Minerva*, May 24, June 14, July 19, 1810; Leesburg *Washingtonian*, July 24, 1810; *Charleston Courier*, May–July, 1810; "Junius," in Savannah *Columbian Museum*, September 6, 1810.

longer the rage—they are the sport of everybody—& will be sold or rather *given away*."[12]

Another extravagance, said Federalist critics, was the $2 million appropriated secretly in 1806 to bribe France into helping the United States obtain Florida. During the 1808 campaign, Federalists reminded voters that the money had been voted two years before. Had it been given to Napoleon or not? The *Wilmington Gazette* accused Republicans of malfeasance in the transaction, saying that they had either committed a disgusting act of international bribery or had shamefully deceived the American people by spending the money for some other purpose.[13]

Taking all government expenses together, Federalists calculated that Washington and Adams, despite the burden of putting down two insurrections, fighting an Indian war, fending off France, and creating a navy, spent only $26 million in twelve years; but the "economical" Jefferson ran through $28 million in eight years, and Madison was spending at an even faster rate. Burdened with this extravagance, the government was sinking into fiscal quicksand. While Madison was proclaiming national prosperity, the *Minerva* jeered that Albert Gallatin had confessed to a $1 million budget deficit. S. L. Campbell, a Virginia Federalist, hoped the party would do its utmost to publicize the deplorable condition of national finances by drawing up a comparative statement of government revenues and expenses under Washington, Adams, Jefferson, and Madison. Campbell thought many Republican policies were reprehensible, but he shrewdly observed that "none strike so forcibly on the mind of the multitude as money matters."[14]

The most important money matter, however, concerned the Bank of the United States, whose charter would expire in March, 1811, unless renewed. The whole body of Federalists favored recharter, as did some Republicans who had come to realize the bank's usefulness. Both Congress and the press discussed the issue for nearly two years, preparing for the final struggle in early 1811. To the Raleigh *Minerva*,

12. *Norfolk Gazette*, May 3, 31, 1809; Raleigh *Minerva*, May 4, 1809; Joseph Pearson to John Steele, June 8, 1809, in Wagstaff (ed.), *Papers of John Steele*, II, 596.

13. *Wilmington Gazette*, October 18, 1808.

14. Raleigh *Minerva*, January 5, July 6, 1809, April 26, 1810; S. L. Campbell to James Breckinridge, February 15, 1810, in Breckinridge Papers, UVa.

the most outspoken of the bank's southern supporters, denying a new charter would be at once unwise and disgraceful; besides, the bank, if allowed to continue, was expected to establish a branch in North Carolina. Both the *Minerva* and the *Carolina Federal Republican* at Newbern argued for the bank, but other party newspapers virtually ignored the issue, although several editors personally favored recharter.[15]

In Congress, John Stanly of North Carolina was the only southern Federalist to speak. The young Newbern lawyer implored his colleagues to spare the bank, brushing aside the argument that Congress had no constitutional power to charter it. He reasoned that the bank was a necessary and proper means to aid Congress in carrying out its express powers to collect taxes, borrow money, and pay debts. Stanly had no fear that the availability of bank credit would tempt the government to amass a huge debt, because congressional approval was required for all federal loans.

Those opposing recharter claimed that foreigners could control the bank and, through it, the entire American economy. It was true, Stanly said, that foreign interests had bought heavily of the bank's stock, but where was the danger? Only American stockholders could vote for directors. Besides, "if it be a sin to have sold stock to foreigners, lay the blame at the right door"; it was the Republicans who had sold to English merchants the government's entire holdings of bank stock. Next, Stanly fought the contention that the state banks could provide the investment capital America needed. All parts of the growing economy, he said, required an expanding credit which only a large national bank could furnish. How could any sensible person oppose a bank approved by Hamilton, Washington, and now even by Gallatin? This was no time for dangerous financial experiments that might harm national prosperity.[16]

According to Congressman Archibald McBryde, the large commercial towns already trembled with fear at the bank's impending death. Refusing a new charter would eliminate $20 million of commercial capital and bankrupt thousands. Despite such warnings, Republicans carried by sixty-five votes to sixty-four a motion to post-

15. Raleigh *Minerva*, January 17, 1811; Newbern *Carolina Federal Republican*, February 25, 1811.

16. *Annals of Congress*, 11th Cong., 3rd Sess., 797–809.

pone indefinitely (and thus kill) the bank bill. All the seven southern Federalists opposed postponement, but in vain.[17] Their only satisfaction came in being vindicated during the war, when the nation endured chaos partly because there was no national bank.

Although frustrated at the outcome of the bank struggle, Federalists were more satisfied than in the past with Republican patronage policy. The ousting of Federalist officers had abated after Jefferson's first term, and complaints on this score had grown weaker. Still, occasional dismissals did occur, calling forth the usual protest; the *Charleston Courier*, for example, objected to the removal of two customs collectors in 1809, declaring that their only crime was Federalism. A disappointed office seeker might also still protest, as one North Carolinian did, that his being a Federalist prevented his success.[18]

In reality, the party was not entirely excluded from office except at the very highest civilian level. Lower federal posts such as clerkships were still sometimes within reach. One Republican newspaper claimed that Federalists had more than their share of lesser posts in Washington, and this after nearly a decade of "Republican persecution." In military appointments, even the highest ranks were open. Robert B. Taylor of Virginia, Duncan Cameron of North Carolina, and Jacob Read of South Carolina were all appointed or retained as generals in the state militia by Republican legislatures or governors. In Washington a prominent South Carolina Federalist was asked by the administration whether any of his comrades would be able and willing to accept a military command. In preparation for the approaching war, the army was expanded early in 1812, and the only two new southern generals were both Federalists—Thomas Pinckney of South Carolina and William Polk of North Carolina.[19]

17. Archibald McBryde to Archibald D. Murphey, January 20, 1811, in Hoyt (ed.), *Papers of Archibald D. Murphey*, I, 46–47; *Annals of Congress*, 11th Cong., 3rd Sess., 826. On the bank question, see Anthony F. Turhollow, "The Struggle for the Recharter of the First Bank of the United States: A Study in Early American Politics" (Ph.D. dissertation, University of California at Berkeley, 1955), especially Chaps. 5–6.

18. *Charleston Courier*, March 14, 1809; A. D. Moore to John Haywood, February 22, 1810, in Ernest Haywood Papers.

19. *Raleigh Register*, September 13, 1810; Robert B. Taylor to Governor of Virginia, December 23, 1812, in H. W. Flournoy (ed.), *Calendar of Virginia State Papers* (11 vols.; Richmond, Va., 1875–93), X, 176; Wagstaff (ed.), *Papers of John Steele*, II, 701*n*.4; Charleston *Carolina Weekly Messenger*, December 20, 1808; Timothy Pickering to Rufus King, January 11, 1808, in King (ed.), *King*, V, 53; *Norfolk Gazette*, April 1, 1812; William Polk to Duncan Cameron, April 19, 1812, in Cameron Family Papers.

Not content with these token posts and unable to prevail in any aspect of domestic politics, Federalists drew their only real comfort from observing the internal bickering that plagued Republicans. These feuds were nothing new; they had begun to flare by the end of Jefferson's first term. During President Madison's first year the estranged wings of the party had for a time drawn more closely together under the pressure of increased Federalist strength, but in 1810 the old conflicts began to sputter again. When a newspaper war broke out among several of the most prominent Republican editors, the Raleigh *Minerva* treated its readers to the spectacle of the enemy at each other's throats. Next, John Randolph wrote, under the pseudonym Philo-Laos, a series of long attacks on Madison. These essays restated every criticism the Federalists themselves had made of the president and found a ready welcome in party newspapers, along with other antiadministration letters by lesser men.[20]

There was even a battle within Madison's own cabinet that finally led the president to dismiss the chief malcontent, Secretary of State Robert Smith, in the spring of 1811. Smith was not a man to be fired quietly. He dashed off a pamphlet defending himself and accusing Madison of pampering "court favorites," toadying to the French, and violating the Constitution. Southern Federalists had previously condemned Smith's conduct as secretary, but now the same newspapers gladly printed his pamphlet, saying that it proved the president's unsuitability for office. Madison's friends replied that Smith was an untrustworthy incompetent, and the delighted Federalists hoped that the new civil war would reduce the public stature of both combatants. If Smith's charges were true, Madison stood convicted by one of his own official family of duplicity, secrecy, corruption, and partiality to France. On the other hand, if the president's defenders were correct, Smith had bungled his job for two years, and this also reflected poorly upon the president. If Smith was substandard, why was he ever appointed?[21]

20. Raleigh *Minerva*, June 14, 1810, April 26, 1811; "Philo-Laos," in *Charleston Courier*, February 6 and 13, 1810, and Raleigh *Minerva*, January 25, 1810.

21. "Brutus," in Savannah *Columbian Museum*, August 5, 1811; *Martinsburg Gazette*, August 2, 1811. At least four papers reprinted Smith's attack on Madison in June and July, 1811. John S. Pancake, "'The Invisibles': A Chapter in the Opposition to President Madison," *Journal of Southern History*, XXI (1955), 27–33, covers the Smith episode in general.

With Republicans so busily engaged in exposing and denouncing each other's faults and misdeeds, who could doubt that their years in power had been disastrous for the country? The feuds only confirmed the Federalists' low opinion of Jefferson and Madison—an opinion aptly summarized by the *Augusta Herald* in 1810. Recalling the successful Republican campaign of 1800, the editor asked: "Have any of the *promises*, or the expectations of those who were deluded by them, been realized? Where is the planter, the merchant, or the mechanick, who has been benefitted by the national change of rulers? Has not our country indeed been advancing backwards ever since that unfortunate period?"[22]

22. *Augusta Herald*, quoted in *Charleston Courier*, February 3, 1810.

Chapter 10 FEDERALISTS AND THE DRIFT TOWARD WAR, 1809–1812

AFTER the election of 1808, the attention of southern Federalists focused on the increasingly tense discussion between the United States, Britain, and France about the rights of neutral commerce in the European war. When President Madison tried by negotiation and coercion to induce greater British respect for American ships and seamen, the Federalists snorted in disgust. France was the real enemy, they said. Napoleon's mania for world dominion and a powerful clique of French partisans in the Republican party were the twin devils dragging America toward an inferno of war, revolution, and dictatorship.

The partisan division over foreign policy was evident in the bitter debate on Jefferson's embargo, still the most prominent issue early in 1809. Federalist newspapers always found room to report northern mass meetings and congressional speeches flaying the embargo, and the southern Federalists in Congress did their feeble best to help repeal or at least weaken it.[1] Editors enlarged upon the law's economic

1. Newbern *Carolina Federal Republican*, February 23, 1809; *Norfolk Gazette*, January 6, 1809. For the congressional debate, see *Annals of Congress*, 10th Cong., 2nd Sess., 500, 513, 987–99, 1022–25, 1332, 1502, 1534–35.

damage to the South, sympathizing with farmers who had sold their goods for little more than the cost of bringing them to market. Also, Federalists were fearful of the extensive police powers Jefferson used to enforce the embargo, pointing to numerous violations of civil liberties.[2]

Republicans, too, finally concluded that their experiment was not working and, after much confused debate on alternative policies, Congress replaced the embargo in March, 1809, with the Nonintercourse Act. Under the new law Americans could trade with any foreign port not British or French, and if either belligerent repealed its decrees against neutral commerce, trade with that nation would be reopened. Southern Federalists were not enthusiastic about nonintercourse; the *Charleston Courier* and the *Norfolk Gazette* both dismissed it as scarcely better than the old embargo. The *Gazette* explained that the exclusion of French imports meant nothing, since the British navy kept French goods off the seas anyway; but Britain would suffer heavily from the loss of her large American markets. Thus the law would directly help Napoleon. Furthermore, government revenue would drop sharply because of the reduction of imports. The rest of the law, prohibiting exports to the belligerents, was useless, since American goods could be reshipped through a neutral port.[3] The two southern Federalist congressmen were also dubious; they tried at every opportunity to impede the progress of the bill. On final passage they divided, John Culpepper of North Carolina voting "aye" because the last section of the bill provided for its own repeal and that of all embargo laws, after the end of the next congressional session.[4]

Soon after nonintercourse became law, the new British minister at Washington, David M. Erskine, declared his country's willingness

2. Raleigh *Minerva*, January 19, February 16, 1809. *Charleston Courier*, February 6, 1809. A large Virginia mass meeting was reported in the Charlestown *Farmer's Repository*, March 3, 1809, and David Stuart to Timothy Pickering, January 24, 1809, Pickering to Abraham Shepherd, February 28, 1809, both in Timothy Pickering Papers.

3. *Norfolk Gazette*, February 15, 1809; *Charleston Courier*, March 9, 1809; Edward Carrington to Pickering, February 23, 1809, in Timothy Pickering Papers; Shaler Hillyer to John Lawrence, April 5, 1809, copy in Shaler Hillyer Letterbook; Malone, *Jefferson the President: Second Term*, 641–49.

4. *Annals of Congress*, 10th Cong., 2nd Sess., 1517–18, 1525–34, 1541; Joseph Pearson to John Steele, June 8, 1809, in Wagstaff (ed.), *Papers of John Steele*, II, 595.

to revoke the Orders in Council aimed at American trade.[5] Responding according to the promise in the Nonintercourse Act, President Madison proclaimed commerce with Britain open again as of June 10, 1809. Federalists welcomed the renewal of trade, and news of it caused celebrations across the South. Before the proclamation, four ships a week were clearing Edenton, North Carolina; now the rate jumped to eleven per week. At Charleston, the *Courier* boasted that thirty-three vessels had sailed for foreign and sixty-three for American ports by the end of May. Along with the increase in shipping came a satisfying rise in prices at the various market towns.[6]

Federalists hailed the president's action because it represented an abandonment of Jefferson's "anti-British" and "Frenchifying" policies. Some who had been suspicious of the new president were now willing to be converted. The *Virginia Gazette*, for instance, disclaimed any hostility toward Madison, saying "We mean to give him *time* and a *fair trial*.—if he administers the government according to the constitution; if he acts fairly and impartially towards *foreign nations*; far from being opposed to him, he will find us in company with his warmest friends, admiring and approving—if he will pursue the path that *Washington* marked out, he cannot go wrong." Federalist newspapers praised Madison's inaugural address and his first message to Congress for being conciliatory toward Britain. If these statements were any guide, the president seemed to the minority to be honestly neutral in foreign affairs, friendly to a stronger navy, and anxious to reduce partisan warfare. If he would live up to these professions, his former opponents were willing to pledge him unstinting support.[7]

5. The Orders in Council of January 7 and November 11, 1807, declared a blockade of French Europe and forbade neutral ships to trade from one French port to another or even to enter ports that excluded British ships.

6. Savannah *Columbian Museum*, June 22, 1809; *Virginia Gazette*, June 13, 1809; *Charleston Courier*, May 29, 1809; *Edenton Gazette*, various issues of 1809, lists ship clearances; John Dunlop (from Petersburg) to Duncan Cameron, May 6, 1809, and John A. Cameron (from Fayetteville) to Duncan Cameron, May 8, 1809, in Cameron Family Papers; Joseph Turner (from Tarborough) to John Haywood, June 11, 1809, in Ernest Haywood Papers.

7. *Virginia Gazette*, May 19, 1809; Raleigh *Star*, June 22, July 20, 1809; *Charleston Courier*, May 22, 30, 1809; H. W. DeSaussure to Ezekiel Pickens, July 3, 1809, in DeSaussure Papers, USC; Thomas Lesesne to Robert Brown, January 23, 1809, in Robert Brown Papers, USC.

The premature enthusiasm for Madison proved no more lasting than the illusory accommodation with England that inspired it. Even as southerners celebrated, the British government disavowed Erskine's agreement and reaffirmed the Orders in Council. In answer to this rebuff, Madison again prohibited trade with Britain on August 9, as required by the Nonintercourse Act. At first, Federalists shared the general outrage against Britain. On the strength of Madison's original reopening of the British trade, countless southern ships had cleared port. The owners of these ships and cargoes, who were often Federalists, had sent their property to sea believing that the Orders in Council no longer restricted American trade. Now Erskine's promises meant nothing, and a fortune in American property was sailing unaware into the British blockade. To some the whole affair seemed a trick to entice American vessels to sea and then scoop them up wholesale.[8] Federalist newspapers in three major exporting towns—Richmond, Norfolk, and Charleston—reacted indignantly to the British disavowal. They accused Erskine and his government of deceiving the United States and predicted that all Americans, regardless of party, would rally to support national honor.[9]

The displays of anger faded very soon to cautious waiting and then even to apology for Britain. The *Norfolk Gazette*, which had expressed outrage on July 28, was appealing within a week for Americans to suspend judgment on Britain until all the facts were known. By August 14 the editor concluded that there was, after all, no cause for anger, since Erskine had merely misconceived the situation. Other Federalists took a similarly tolerant view, and by the middle of August the party had returned once again to advocating forebearance and even friendship toward England. In Charleston, the foremost southern port and probably the hardest hit by the British action, many Federalists attended a mass meeting in a vain attempt to defeat a resolution expressing indignation at Britain and confidence in Madison.[10]

If the British government was blameless, then either Erskine or

8. Perkins, *Prologue to War*, 209–19.

9. *Virginia Gazette*, July 25, 1809; *Charleston Courier*, July 27, 28, 1809.

10. *Norfolk Gazette*, July 28, August 2, 7, 14, 1809; "A Farmer" in *Virginia Herald*, September 6, 1809. On the Charleston meeting, see Charles Pinckney to Thomas Jefferson, received September 30, 1809, in Thomas Jefferson Papers; and *Charleston Courier*, September 6, 1809.

the American negotiators were at fault. Perhaps Erskine exceeded his instructions out of zeal for better relations with America; if so, resentment should be directed toward the man himself, not toward the government at London. More typical was the party's disposition to blame Republicans for the incident. Either through bumbling or deliberate calculation the administration must have taken advantage of Erskine and worked him into an agreement that violated his instructions. The Federalists' ultimate regret about the affair was that it gave "the French faction" another chance to excite hostility against England.[11]

Because of the Erskine trouble and the resulting nonintercourse with Britain, Federalists turned permanently sour on Madison and thereafter classed him with the other leading Republicans as anti-British and partial to France.[12] The so-called Jackson incident later in the year confirmed their low opinion of the president. Francis James Jackson, a new English envoy, came to Washington to renew discussions over the Orders in Council, but in November the administration accused him of insufferable conduct and refused to deal with him further. Jackson left Washington and the American minister in London also went home, practically severing diplomatic relations between the two countries at a time of great tension.

As in the earlier *Chesapeake* and Erskine disputes, some southern Federalists temporarily supported their government, though more feebly than before. Soon the party swung around, as usual, to defend England, denying that Jackson had insulted anyone and finding clear evidence of a pro-French taint in the administration.[13] The controversy became more heated when Congress met in November, 1809. William B. Giles, a Virginia Republican, introduced resolutions approving the government's conduct, and the seven southern Federalists in the House quickly took issue with him. Jacob Swoope of Virginia went so far as to argue that the whole incident was caused by Republican officials "whose intrigues were covered by a veil too trans-

11. Raleigh *Minerva*, August 3, 1809; *Virginia Gazette*, October 27, 1809; *Charleston Courier*, February 22, 24, 1809. However, some Federalists were still angry at Britain: David Ramsay to James Madison, September 5, 1809, in Brunhouse (ed.), *David Ramsay*, 164.

12. This was, of course, merely a return to the pre-1809 view of Madison.

13. White, "Anglo-American Relations," 158ff; *Virginia Patriot*, March 23, 1810; "Pelopidas," in *Charleston Courier*, January 18, 1810.

parent to deceive, and whose rooted animosity to England was as notorious, as their devotion to France was wicked." The real motive of the Giles resolutions, according to the Federalists, was to provoke England into declaring war. Party newspapers helped spread these sentiments by reprinting speeches and circular letters for subscribers everywhere to read. Far too weak to block the resolutions, Federalist members at least showed that a vocal minority in the South opposed antagonizing England.[14]

When Congress turned to the more general problem of continued violations of American neutral trade, the solid Federalist bloc broke apart. Few in either party liked the current policy of nonintercourse with British and French territories, which barred American exports from their best markets. As an alternative, proadministration Republicans produced the so-called Macon's Bill Number One, allowing American ships to trade anywhere in the world, while excluding British and French vessels from American ports. This had the advantage of throwing open immediately the markets of both belligerents, provided American ships could elude the cruisers of the other nation. Against the bill stood the extreme Republicans who wanted a sterner attitude toward England, and the northern Federalists who demanded absolutely free trade.[15]

Southern Federalists were torn by conflicting desires. They did want American commerce free to trade where it dared, but the exclusion of British and French ships from America might provoke retaliation. Joseph Pearson, representing a western North Carolina district, said that he would vote for the bill only because it would liberate American trade from the chains of nonintercourse. Archibald McBryde also believed it was better to settle for an unsatisfactory bill than risk getting something worse. In the end, the three North Carolinians—Pearson, McBryde, and John Stanly—along with Jacob Swoope of Virginia, were among the handful of Federalists supporting the first

14. Swoope circular letter in *Alexandria Gazette*, May 5, 1810; Breckinridge circular letter in *Charleston Courier*, June 2, 1810; Pearson to Hutchins G. Burton, December 21 or 25, 1809, in Hutchins G. Burton Papers, UNC; John Stanly's speech in *Annals of Congress*, 11th Cong., 2nd Sess., 1121–43; Joseph Lewis, Jr., to James McHenry, December 26, 1809, in Charles Hamilton Autographs, UVa.

15. Perkins, *Prologue to War*, 239–42.

Macon's Bill on final passage. The three other Virginians—Joseph Lewis, Jr., James Stephenson, and James Breckinridge—voted with the northern Federalists against it. The party press was uncommonly quiet; only two newspapers expressed themselves, and both were favorable to the bill.[16]

In the Senate the bill was roughly handled; a coalition of Federalists and antiadministration Republicans virtually destroyed it. In its place arose another plan known as Macon's Bill Number Two, although Nathaniel Macon himself disowned it. The second bill, like the first, allowed Americans to trade wherever they could, but it also threw American ports open to all foreign ships. Most significantly for the future, the bill promised that if either Britain or France rescinded her commercial decrees, the other must do the same or face a renewal of nonintercourse. In this revised form, Macon's Bill met nearly unanimous Federalist opposition. Southern members were silently hostile, content to let their northern colleagues denounce the bill; but on the final roll call, all seven Virginia and North Carolina Federalists voted "nay." Perhaps the editor of the *Augusta Herald* best expressed Federalist feelings; he was not concerned so much with the bill itself as with giving the country a chance to recover from the economic damage wrought by the previous two years of embargo and nonintercourse.[17]

In their constant opposition to Republican foreign policy, congressional Federalists usually tried to thwart military preparations for a possible war. The southerners voted unanimously against arming the state militia, against having it serve with the regular army, and against allowing it to be sent outside the United States (for instance, to invade Canada). They also tried to reduce the standing army, despite the tense state of foreign affairs. In their eagerness to eliminate any possibility of a British war, the southern congressmen even reversed their usual preference for a strong navy. The three North

16. Pearson to Steele, January 26, 1810, in Wagstaff (ed.), *Papers of John Steele*, II, 620–21; Archibald McBryde to Archibald D. Murphey, January 27, 1810, in Hoyt (ed.), *Papers of Archibald D. Murphey*, I, 35–36; *Annals of Congress*, 11th Cong., 2nd Sess., 1329–30, 1354; *Norfolk Gazette*, January 12, 1810; *Virginia Patriot*, May 1, 1810.

17. *Annals of Congress*, 11th Cong., 2nd Sess., 1931; *Augusta Herald*, quoted in *Virginia Patriot*, June 15, 1810.

Carolinians voted ten times against, and never in favor of, naval preparations; the Virginians, whose state had more at stake upon the seas, cast five votes for, but seven against, the navy.[18]

The Federalists' negative attitude was more than opposition for its own sake. During the spring of 1809, many of them had been genuinely optimistic about the future course of Madison's administration. Then the bellicose Republican reaction to the Erskine and Jackson incidents, the anti-British tone of Giles' resolutions, and the willingness of some Republicans to contemplate war with England—all rekindled the old Federalist fears. They deeply believed that the prosperity and safety of the United States depended entirely on friendly relations with England. Southern staple growers had especially close ties to Britain. Hundreds of ships yearly carried southern tobacco, cotton, rice, wheat, and flour to British markets, and each disturbance in Anglo-American diplomacy caused staple prices to drop in southern market towns.[19]

More important than economics was the Federalist belief that only British sea power kept Napoleon from lunging at the unprotected throat of America, because above all else, Federalists feared aggressive French imperialism. War with Great Britain would be disastrous whatever its outcome. If England won, Americans might again become subjects of the king; at least, they would suffer heavy losses. If America defeated England, the Royal Navy would no longer bar Napoleon's way, and he would quickly overrun the United States.[20]

True, the British might occasionally impress American seamen or seize cargoes, but such injuries could well be borne. France was far more predatory; insurance premiums were twice as high on voyages to British ports as to French or Spanish ports, reflecting the danger of French interference. Records of the Marine Insurance Company at Norfolk showed that French ships (and Spanish ships under French orders) had captured nearly $250,000 worth of property insured by that company. The British, by comparison, had seized only $50,000

18. *Annals of Congress*, 11th Cong., 2nd Sess., 1529, 1570–77, 1604–05, 1884–85, 1977, 1996, 2013.

19. *Virginia Gazette*, November 17, 1809; *Wilmington Gazette*, May 23, 1809.

20. "A Virginian," in Martinsburg *Berkeley & Jefferson Intelligencer*, February 26, March 4, 1808; *Charleston Courier*, May 5, 1810; John A. Cameron to Duncan Cameron, November, 1809, in Cameron Family Papers.

worth and, to offset this, had recaptured nearly the same amount from the French and restored it to American owners. No wonder that Federalists had difficulty understanding why public opinion was so much more hostile to England than to France.[21]

Party opinion of France had become fixed in the 1790s and had not mellowed since. The memory of revolutionary upheaval and the guillotine cast a long shadow upon the Federalist mind. In 1808 the editor of the Staunton paper exclaimed "It is Sixteen Years this night, since the principles of murder and massacre were established in France—and from that period to the present, Good God! what bloodshed—what butchering and inhuman massacres, have marked the tracks of the French nation!!" Napoleon had brought France only slavery, poverty, and death—a fate no better than the previous years of revolution and anarchy.

The ambitious Bonaparte was bent upon extending his tyranny beyond his own country as rapidly as his military might permitted. When he had finished with the Old World, Federalists did not doubt that his appetite would encompass the United States as well. Even now he waged undeclared war, as his privateers ravaged American commerce on the seas and his officials seized ships and cargoes in French ports. In his *Virginia Patriot*, Augustine Davis sought to rouse the country against the "universal plunder of everything American" in the harbors of France and her satellites. "Act like men," he urged, and speak to Napoleon "from the mouths of your cannon."[22]

The effect of this anti-French campaign was blunted, however, by the sudden news that Napoleon had revoked his Berlin and Milan decrees (so far as they affected the United States), effective November 1, 1810.[23] Taken by surprise, Federalists could only mutter that it was all

21. *Norfolk Gazette*, July 8, 1808; *Alexandria Advertiser*, July 13, 1808.

22. Staunton *Political Censor*, August 10, 1808; *Virginia Patriot*, quoted in *Charleston Courier*, September 24, 1810. The fear of France was a constant theme in these years; see, for example, "A Virginia Farmer," in *Virginia Herald*, June 10, 1808; Raleigh *Minerva*, November 16, 1809; and "Hamilton," in *Charleston Courier*, April 16, 1808. Accounts of French attacks on American commerce may be found in Leesburg *Washingtonian*, May 7, 1811; Newbern *Carolina Federal Republican*, August 18, 1810; Savannah *Columbian Museum*, December 4, 1809.

23. The Berlin and Milan decrees (November 21, 1806, and December 17, 1807), declared a blockade of Britain and said that all ships submitting to the British Orders in Council could be legally seized by France.

a trick. The French foreign secretary, the duke of Cadore, had written a letter promising repeal if the British would revoke their Orders in Council and ease their blockade of Europe, and if the United States would force England to respect her neutral rights. To the Federalists, these requirements were absurd; Britain would not agree to them and therefore the supposed French repeal would never be effective. Cadore's promise was only a ruse to lure American ships to sea where they could be captured, or to strain the relations between the United States and Great Britain even further. Federalist editors warned Americans not to be taken in by the deception, not to overlook the conditional nature of the promised repeal.[24]

President Madison brushed off such warnings, assumed that Napoleon was sincere, and officially proclaimed that he considered the decrees repealed on the first of November. Under the terms of Macon's Bill, this meant that England had to revoke her Orders in Council within three months or face a total suspension of Anglo-American trade. Federalists regarded the proclamation as highly inequitable. They believed that Macon's Bill should apply only to an actual, and not merely a promised, repeal of the decrees. Besides, even if there would be no more French pillaging, none of the millions of dollars' worth of property confiscated in the past had been restored. The president's action was a national disgrace. He had proved himself to be an obedient pupil of Jefferson and slavishly partial to France. Well into 1811 the party continued to dispute the Cadore letter, monthly displaying new evidence that the decrees were yet in force. Under sarcastic headlines came numerous reports of American ships seized and their cargoes confiscated, and always there were editorials condemning French treachery and Republican gullibility.[25]

Meanwhile, the British government was not so trusting as the president and refused to accept the Cadore letter as an actual repeal of the Berlin and Milan decrees. Therefore, the Orders in Council remained fully in effect, and at the end of ninety days Madison duly invoked nonintercourse toward Britain. Hastening to support him, congres-

24. *Charleston Courier*, October 8, 10, 27, 1810; *Norfolk Gazette*, October 29, 1810.

25. Pearson to Steele, December 23, 1810, in Wagstaff (ed.), *Papers of John Steele*, II, 645; "Plato," in Savannah *Columbian Museum*, December 10, 1810; *Martinsburg Gazette*, April 12, 1811.

sional Republicans introduced a bill approving the ban on British trade, which excited a warm debate early in 1811. Federalists asked again for proof that Napoleon had really nullified the decrees. They complained that American merchants and staple producers would suffer greatly from nonintercourse with Britain while gaining no real entry to French markets. There was the additional danger that Madison's action would lead Britain to declare war or at least to retaliate against American property in English ports. Congressman Joseph Pearson believed nonintercourse was another evidence of devotion to France and harmful to both private commerce and government revenue. To Archibald McBryde, whose district adjoined Pearson's, it was evident that Great Britain could not purchase American goods if the United States did not buy hers in return; the result would be a collapse of American produce prices and ruin to farmers. The other southern Federalists agreed with Pearson and McBryde, all voting on several occasions to weaken or postpone nonintercourse. In all, they cast fifty votes against, and none in favor of, various parts of the bill, although only Jacob Swoope of Virginia was present to oppose it on final passage.[26]

By the end of the congressional session the southern Federalists were in a frustrating and uncomfortable position. The relaxation of Franco-American relations, which began with the Cadore letter, had deflated their chief political issue; yet they were convinced that the easing of tension was an illusion created by Napoleon for his own purposes. Even worse, Republicans had demanded real concessions from Britain to match the paper promises by France. When the British government declined, it was easy for Republicans to rouse public support for nonintercourse. What irked the Federalists most was their inability to convince voters of this interpretation of events. Most people accepted the Republican view that France had ceased violating American neutral trade and Britain had not, and therefore Americans should act mildly toward France and harshly toward Britain.

The mid-term elections of 1810–1811 took place amidst this rising

26. *Charleston Courier*, January 15, 1811; *Raleigh Minerva*, March 28 and April 5, 1811, has Pearson's speech in the House; Pearson to Steele, January 18, February 5, 1811, in Wagstaff (ed.), *Papers of John Steele*, II, 645, 650, 655; McBryde to Murphey, January 20, 1811, in Hoyt (ed.), *Papers of Archibald D. Murphey*, I, 47; *Annals of Congress*, 11th Cong., 3rd Sess., 894–96, 979, 1028–29, 1035–36, 1062–63, 1087–90, 1094–95.

anti-British feeling, and Federalists glumly expected the state of foreign relations to depress their chances in the South. There was a distinct decline in the party's willingness to compete at the polls. South Carolina, for the first time, had not a single Federalist candidate; even Charleston, whose numerous Federalists had always supported one of their own for Congress, gave up the battle this year.[27]

In Georgia, normally their weakest state, Federalists showed more vigor. John Elliott, a low-country lawyer, was one of six candidates for Georgia's four congressional seats at large. There was little or no organized effort on Elliott's behalf, but some individual Federalists took up his cause. One of them deplored the party prejudice against Elliott, claiming that a candidate should be judged on his ability, not on his party label. Another writer, "Aristides," begged Georgians to close their ears against "the poison of democracy." Whatever his actual merits, Elliott's party affiliation doomed him. The most popular Republican drew nearly 18,000 votes; the least popular, over 6,500; and Elliott, less than 2,500. Since each person could vote for four men, the total of 73,000 votes may have been cast by as few as 20,000 individual voters, of whom about 12 percent marked one of their four ballots for Elliott. This was scarcely half the share given to John M. Dooly two years earlier, and it marked the end of active Federalism in Georgia.[28]

North Carolina showed more activity, but the fight was mainly restricted to defending the three Federalist seats. The Fayetteville district was so one-sided that no Republican ventured to run, and two Federalists could safely wage a sharp intraparty fight. In two rather quiet contests, incumbent Joseph Pearson of Salisbury easily turned back the challenge of a Republican preacher, but on the coast the Republican congressman and future vice-president, William R. King, defeated his Federalist opponent even more handily.[29]

By all accounts the most heated race was in the marginal Newbern district. Here a Federalist incumbent retired, leaving a young

27. *Charleston Courier*, October 15–23, 1810, and Charleston *City Gazette*, October 11–23, 1810, have the election returns.

28. Savannah *Columbian Museum*, October 22, 1810; "Decius," *ibid.*, September 27, 1810; *Georgia Express*, October 6, 1810; *Charleston Courier*, October 19, 1810.

29. See Gilpatrick, *Jeffersonian Democracy*, 241–44, and the various candidates' announcements in the press.

lawyer, William Gaston, the task of holding the seat against a former Republican congressman. Gaston, after hanging back for some time, addressed a circular letter to the voters criticizing in good Federalist fashion the president, France, Republican policy, the deceased embargo, and Jefferson's entire administration. The Republican, William Blackledge, replied with his own address, and a war of pamphlets ensued. In all, Gaston issued at least three circulars and Blackledge at least two, while the rival Newbern papers, the *Carolina Federal Republican* and the *Herald*, debated with each other the merits of the candidates. Despite his vigorous canvass, Gaston failed by a margin of five to four. Federalists therefore lost one of their three districts although their share of the state's congressional vote—25 percent—was about the same as in 1808. It was not a very encouraging election. Less was attempted and less achieved than two years before.[30]

The same was true of the Virginia Federalists, who defended their four existing seats in April, 1811, but made almost no attempt to add to them. Of the sixteen districts east of the Blue Ridge, only two had Federalist candidates: the Loudoun-Fairfax district, where incumbent Joseph Lewis, Jr., won easily without organized opposition, and the Eastern Shore district, which remained narrowly Republican. In the west, Federalists kept two seats by respectable majorities and captured another when Republican John G. Jackson retired. Jackson complained to his father-in-law, President Madison, that the new Republican candidate was responsible for losing this Ohio River district; he "never was here before & his coming ruined our hopes, as his manners &c are unpopular, & here the People vote for men more than principles." However, Republicans won back the Staunton district, leaving Federalists with the same number of seats as before. Overall, the party took only 18 percent of the total vote against 22 percent in 1809.[31]

Altogether, these elections to the Twelfth Congress indicated a

30. *Raleigh Register*, June 21, July 26, 1810; Newbern *Carolina Federal Republican*, June 30, July 28, August 4, 11, 18, September 1, 1810; Raleigh *Minerva*, July 5, 1810; Gilpatrick, *Jeffersonian Democracy*, 177. Returns are estimated from incomplete figures in the newspapers for August–September, 1810.

31. *Virginia Argus*, October 16, 1810; Charlestown *Farmer's Repository*, October 5, December 14, 1810; *Alexandria Gazette*, April 11, 17, 1811; John G. Jackson to Madison, April 19, 1811, in Madison Papers, LC. Election returns are in the newspapers for April–May, 1811.

slight decline in Federalist vigor and popularity, an impression confirmed by state legislative results. Considering the state of foreign affairs, this was to be expected. Increasing coolness toward England and warmer relations with France could not but hurt the Federalists. Their traditional anti-French argument seemed discredited.

Also working against them was the return of economic prosperity. With the repeal of the embargo, American trade flowed again, though subject to some restrictions. Prices for wheat, tobacco, cotton, rice, corn, beef, pork, and flour rose by an average of 50 percent between January, 1809, and January, 1811. Federalist candidates no longer had an ally in economic hardship, and southern farmers no longer saw in their empty pockets a reason to vote against the Republican administration.

As the year wore on, all political calculations became wrapped up in the drift toward war. In August, 1811, Madison summoned Congress to an early session, stirring Federalist fears that a conflict with Great Britain was unavoidable. Yet there was no immediate rush to war, and as late as October, John Rutledge, Jr., traveling through Richmond, was pleasantly surprised at the moderation of many Republicans there and in Congress. The president, however, sent a belligerent message to Congress in November, and soon all could see the tide running against peace. Gradually, reluctantly, most Republicans became convinced that there was no honorable alternative to war. Federalists could do little but anxiously rebuke the rising war spirit, chiding "those, who unwisely think, that in *every* discussion between ours and a foreign government, that ours is always right." By early January, some Federalists were convinced that the nation stood upon the verge of a bloody war.[32]

Except for a score or so of cautious members, the Republicans in Congress soon voted a number of bills anticipating war. Even some Federalists wavered in their usually steadfast attitude against military preparations. Together the six southern Federalists cast fourteen votes for, and only eight against, various attempts to strengthen the

32. Raleigh *Minerva*, August 2, 1811, January 10, 1812; John Rutledge, Jr., to Harrison Gray Otis, October 22, 1811, in Harrison Gray Otis Papers; Newbern *Carolina Federal Republican*, January 11, 1812.

army and the militia, and they were nearly unanimous in voting to reinforce the navy. This was partly a sheer political tactic to make the war measures as expensive as possible in hopes of defeating them later, but some Federalists may have been sincere, especially in their support of a strong navy. Party newspapers were divided, some reprinting articles and speeches against the army bills but urging heavy additions to the fleet. The Federalist editor in Norfolk wrote in some disgust that if the United States had begun building up its army and navy five years before, there would have been no trouble from Britain or France. The editor omitted mentioning that five years ago Federalists would have been the last to propose such expensive military preparations.[33]

For a time during February the war fever seemed to abate, as Albert Gallatin's gloomy report on the necessity for heavy war taxes cooled the Republicans' ardor. They well knew the unpopularity of laying financial burdens on the people, for they had won office themselves in 1800 by declaiming against just such obnoxious taxes. The lull, though, was only momentary; the War Hawks soon regained the initiative and persuaded Congress to accept the necessary taxes. Greatly increased customs and tonnage duties, new salt, sugar, and liquor taxes, and still other levies were put upon the books—all to go into effect at the outbreak of war. Each had almost unanimous Federalist opposition in the House, including the six southerners, none of whom voted for a single one of the tax resolutions.[34]

In March the Republicans proposed a temporary embargo to pull American vessels off the seas and out of danger until war was official, leading the Raleigh *Minerva* to predict that a declaration of war was imminent. Others were not so sure; the Newbern Federalists John Stanly and William Gaston both believed the war talk would subside in Washington after a good deal of blustering. This, however, was a minority view; those on the scene were much more pessimistic. On

33. *Norfolk Gazette*, December 11, 1811, January 31, 1812; *Charleston Courier*, January 20, 1812; *Annals of Congress*, 12th Cong., 1st Sess., 566–67, 691, 800–801, 938–39, 999–1005, 1084–85.

34. *Charleston Courier*, January 22, 1812; "The Crisis," in Savannah *American Patriot*, April 21, 24, 1812; Pearson to Steele, March 2, 1812, in Wagstaff (ed.), *Papers of John Steele*, II, 668–70; *Annals of Congress*, 12th Cong., 1st Sess., 1108–53.

his way to Washington, Archibald McBryde had thought peace would prevail, but after a few days in the capital, he wrote home that there would soon be a war.[35]

In a last vain attempt to prevent what they feared was inevitable, the Federalists repeated every possible argument against war. New reports of French attacks on American property appeared in issue after issue of the party newspapers from Virginia to Georgia. To Chief Justice John Marshall, the president's claim that Napoleon had revoked his decrees was "one of the most astonishing instances of national credulity . . . that is to be found in political history." If the French depredations went unprotested, then why snarl at England for her lesser insults?[36] Federalists could not ignore British impressment of American seamen, but they said it occurred on far too small a scale to warrant armed conflict. According to the secretary of state's own figures, only 6,257 native Americans had been impressed in ten years, and of those only 400 to 600 were still held to British service.[37]

Moreover, it would be economic suicide to fight England, the best customer of the United States. American commerce with France was only $4 million yearly, compared to almost $39 million worth of trade with Britain and her allies.[38] The financial cost of war would be ruinous. Even if an army should manage to conquer Canada, that empty territory would be useless and would certainly not repay the expense of lives and dollars. To fight England when it was not really necessary and to load future generations with debt and taxes appeared to the Federalists of Hampshire County, Virginia, to be "the extreme of folly, little short of madness."[39]

35. Raleigh *Minerva*, April 10, 1812; Pearson to Steele, April 6, 1812, in John Steele Papers; James Stephenson to Abraham Morgan, May 17, 1812, in Joseph D. Hamilton Papers, UNC; William Polk to Duncan Cameron, April 10, May 6, June 1, 11, 1812, in Cameron Family Papers.

36. John Marshall to John Randolph, June 18, 1812, in Simes Collection, Harvard University; Pearson to Steele, May 27, 1812, in John Steele Papers. Nearly every Federalist newspaper took this stand; see for example, *Virginia Herald*, March 28, 1812. On French harassment of American trade after the "repeal," see Egan, "Franco-American Relations," Chap. 8.

37. *Norfolk Gazette*, November 11, 1811; Joseph Lewis, Jr., quoted *ibid.*, June 17, 1812; Newbern *Carolina Federal Republican*, April 25, 1812.

38. Raleigh *Minerva*, February 14, 1812; "A Loudoun Farmer," in *Alexandria Gazette*, January 22, 1812.

39. *Martinsburg Gazette*, October 25, 1811; address of Hampshire County Federalists, *ibid.*, March 27, 1812; Newbern *Carolina Federal Republican*, January 11, 1812.

To Federalists it was evident that the nation was opposed to war. As proof of this claim, they pointed to the dismal reception of Gallatin's $11 million war loan in May, 1812. Nearly everywhere subscriptions were far below what the government had hoped for; only $4 million was placed—barely one-third of the required sum. The *American Patriot*, a new Federalist newspaper in Savannah, crowed over the loan's failure, saying that it reflected a public repudiation of the administration and that men of principle should never support an unjust cause. To further the impression of widespread resistance to war, party newspapers gave full play to accounts of peace meetings in northern towns and counties.[40]

Finally, the Federalists warned of French tyranny as the fruit of war. Only a British victory over Napoleon could save the United States from the French grasp; it would be absurd to fight England, America's one protector, and to aid a despot whose reward might be the yoke of slavery. The case against war was summarized by Congressman Joseph Lewis, Jr., in an open letter to his constituents. If Britain invaded the United States, Lewis said, then of course Americans should spring to arms without thought of the cost. But an aggressive war, merely to gratify pride or ambition, was another matter. Even if there were just cause to fight England, no rational man could believe that the prospective benefits would justify the tremendous expense.[41]

All such words of protest the War Hawks brushed aside, and the House formally declared war on June 4, with the Federalists and a handful of Republicans dissenting. The Senate concurred on June 18. Among southern Federalists there were two views of the coming struggle. In the ranks of the pessimists were men such as Joseph Pearson, who wrote on the day after the declaration of war that "the *die* is cast —Democratic folly & blindness is consummated. . . . France is our loving friend & will no doubt soon be our ally—In what these dreadful measures will end—God only knows—If the people do not interpose their constitutional power—I fear all is lost." The former governor of North Carolina, William R. Davie, had another opinion. Although he

40. *Norfolk Gazette*, June 12, 1812; Savannah *American Patriot*, quoted in *Charleston Courier*, May 13, 1812; Pearson to Steele, March 2, 1812, in Wagstaff (ed.), *Papers of John Steele*, II, 669.

41. Raleigh *Minerva*, June 5, 1812; Lewis' address in *Norfolk Gazette*, June 17, 1812; address of Richmond Federalists in *Charleston Courier*, June 24, 1812.

disliked the war as much as Pearson did, he saw in it the potential salvation of the country: "Upon the whole, perhaps it will be better, two or three rattling fights, 30 or 40 thousand men killed, and a debt of as many millions will bring us all to our senses—You will remember some years ago giving me your serious opinion that we must touch the extreme point of public wretchedness before the people could be set right."[42] If the people could be "set right" by the miseries of war, Davie and the rest of his party would soon know it, for the presidential campaign of 1812 was already under way. If the Federalists could not regain power in these the worst of times (as they believed), their future as a political party would be bleak indeed.

42. Pearson to Steele, June 19, 1812, in John Steele Papers; William R. Davie to Steele, February 10, 1812, in Hamilton (ed.), *William R. Davie*, 70. On the war vote, see Ronald L. Hatzenbuehler, "Party Unity and the Vote for War in the House of Representatives, 1812," *William and Mary Quarterly*, 3rd ser., XXIX (1972), 367–90.

Chapter 11 THE ELECTION OF 1812

THE war would clearly be the determining issue in the election of 1812, and Federalists realized early that their best course was to rally all disgruntled citizens to the banner of peace and say little of party affiliation. John Marshall, among others, advocated this action soon after war was declared. Even with a fusion of parties, however, would the friends of peace be numerous enough to put an end to the current administration and its war? The leading antiwar Republican, John Randolph, reluctantly thought not. Voters might dislike the war but they would still help fight it, he believed; and they would brand its opponents as disloyal. A Federalist in central Virginia agreed that there was little party spirit there, and most people were willing to support the administration.[1]

Others were more optimistic about the war as a political issue. James Stephenson, Federalist congressman from western Virginia, found no war spirit among the people; and William R. Davie, the former governor of North Carolina, was absolutely sure the Republicans

1. John Marshall to Robert Smith, July 27, 1812, in Dreer Collection, Historical Society of Pennsylvania; John Randolph to Josiah Quincy, August 2 and 16, 1812, in Quincy (ed.), *Quincy*, 269–70; Elijah Fletcher to his father, July 4, 1812, in Martha von Briesen (ed.), *The Letters of Elijah Fletcher* (Charlottesville, Va., 1965), 57.

were doomed. They must pay for the war with enormous taxes or risk military defeat for want of money; either course would ruin them at the polls.[2] Basing their entire election campaign upon the war issue and talking of practically nothing else, the Federalists were shortly to discover whether Davie was a shrewd analyst of popular feeling or wildly out of touch with political realities.

This was the first wartime presidential campaign in the nation's history. In 1800, it is true, French and American ships had been skirmishing for two years, but neither side had attempted to invade the territory of the other. There was no formal state of war, and peace was being negotiated during the election campaign. In 1812 there was war in earnest. American ships were harrying enemy commerce, scooping in prizes by the score. In return, the British navy mounted an increasingly effective blockade against the United States. On the northern frontier, one American army had already unsuccessfully invaded Canada, producing nothing but casualties. Another had surrendered at Detroit almost without a shot, leaving the entire Northwest open to British incursions. The country was pitifully unready to fight, even months after war had been declared.

Although American efforts were largely wasted and ineffectual during the first half year of combat, the country still had to endure the sacrifices of war. Purely as a statistic, the number of men killed, wounded, captured, or dead of disease by the fall of 1812 was not large. Yet each casualty was a personal tragedy not soon forgotten by family, friends, and neighbors. Those voters who were spared personal loss still felt the war's financial burden; taxes were heavy and were likely to be increased. Many southerners who grew wheat, tobacco, cotton, or rice for export were losing their overseas markets. It was hard to accept this heavy toll in good spirits and to discount it as the price of victory, for victory was nowhere in sight. To compound the frustration, all these hardships were quite possibly needless because the British Orders in Council had already been repealed before the outbreak of war. If ever the American people were to become disgusted with Republican rule and restore the Federalists to power, surely 1812 was that time.

2. James Stephenson to Abraham Morgan, May 17, 1812, in Joseph D. Hamilton Papers; William R. Davie to John Steele, October 15, 1812, in John Steele Papers.

Still, the war held dangers as well as political opportunity for the opposition party. Given the tendency of citizens to rally to their government in a crisis, some would support the president's reelection merely because the country was at war. Also, the usual advantages of an incumbent were magnified by the larger number of offices in the gift of the administration. Commissions in the army, contracts for military supplies, new positions in the civilian bureaucracy—all had to be filled. Recipients of the new patronage could be expected to aid the party that had secured them an office and a salary.

More important was the question of how far a minority party could safely go in opposing a wartime government. For years Federalists had accused Republican administrations of hostility to England and had opposed a war with that nation as unnecessary, expensive, and dangerous. How would the voters now react? Would America embrace the Federalists as the only hope of ending a senseless and mismanaged war, or scorn them as slackers, cowards, and friends of England? The nearest precedent for 1812 was the quasi war of 1798–1799. At that time the party which opposed war measures and seemed partial to the enemy was convincingly defeated, but by 1800 that same party returned to win both the presidency and Congress. The Federalists were now in the position the Republicans had been in then. Would the party be spurned as the Republicans were in 1798, or would an angry public bring the opposition to power as it had in 1800?

One way in which the political complexion of 1812 resembled that of 1800, and which gave the Federalists hope for victory, was the severe split within the governing party. As President Adams had been opposed by Hamilton's clique in 1800, so Madison was now rejected by the "peace Republicans" who followed DeWitt Clinton. They considered the dominant southern wing of their party pro-French, anticommercial, and too ready to jump into war. Twenty-two Republicans in Congress, chiefly Clintonians, had joined the Federalists to vote against declaring war. Since there was no chance of preventing Madison's renomination by the Republican congressional caucus in May, the Clinton men had stayed away in protest, and only 82 of the 138 Republican senators and representatives were present. Pressing toward an open rebellion against Madison, Republican members of the New York legislature officially nominated Clinton and published a letter "To the People of the United States" urging his cause. This address, reprinted by the southern Federalist press, indicated that Clinton would stand as a peace candidate and that, in all but party label, his foreign policy would resemble that benevolent neutrality toward England which Federalists had long advocated.[3] The Republican split increased the likelihood of defeating Madison but reduced the possibility of electing a Federalist, since disgruntled Republicans could now vote for Clinton against Madison and still remain within their party. Federalists had to decide whether their primary goal was a victory of principle (to alter Madison's policies by ousting him from the presidency) or of party (to nominate a true Federalist even if this insured Madison's reelection and continued the war).[4]

To settle this question, Federalist committees in New York and Philadelphia asked party leaders in various states to gather at New York City in September or at least to send written advice on the political situation in their states. From North Carolina, Congressmen Joseph Pearson and Archibald McBryde, former Congressmen John Stanly and Archibald Henderson, and William Gaston, soon to be in Congress, all were invited. They were asked also to send any other talented and influential Federalists of various opinions and from different parts of the state. In South Carolina the Federalist nominee of 1804 and 1808, Charles Cotesworth Pinckney, received notice of the meeting and informed his associates in the Charleston area and in Columbia, the state capital. There was also contact with the Virginia party, and letters of reply reached the caucus from Supreme Court Justice Bushrod Washington and from John Hopkins, a prominent Federalist merchant in Richmond.[5]

Despite the effort to secure southern delegates, there was little response. The shortness of notification and the hazards of travel prevented Federalists in either of the Carolinas from attending, although

3. Newbern *Carolina Federal Republican*, May 30, 1812. The address of the New York Clinton committee appeared in the *Virginia Patriot*, September 1, 1812, and several other papers.

4. For one opinion, see a letter in the Staunton *Republican Farmer*, October 11, 1811.

5. Jacob Radcliffe *et al.* to William Gaston, August 25, 1812, and James Milnor *et al.* to Gaston and John Stanly, August 13, 1812, in William Gaston Papers; C. C. Pinckney to Milnor, August 24, 1812, in Pinckney Family Papers; King (ed.), *King*, V, 280–81, has information on the opinions of Washington and Hopkins.

four South Carolinians who happened to be near New York did show up. As Pinckney said, "No gentleman will like at this period to venture by sea to New York, lest he should be captured; or to take a land journey of 800 miles and as many to return at this inclement season of the year for a session of two or three days."[6] Virginia, though much less distant, was busy organizing its own state convention and presumably could not spare its key men for the two weeks necessary to make the round trip and participate in the New York caucus.

Even so, southern opinions were not ignored. Besides the four men present from South Carolina (one of whom was John Rutledge, Jr., the former congressman), there were advisory letters from Pinckney, Pearson, Hopkins, and Washington. There was an attempt, originating in Maryland and the District of Columbia, to stir up sentiment for John Marshall among the southern Federalists. Two Virginians, Hopkins and Joseph Davies, fell in with this group, believing that any respectable Federalist would do as well as Clinton in their state. Most North Carolina Federalists were also said to be attracted more strongly to John Marshall than to anyone else.[7]

Unfortunately for the Marshall enthusiasts, Pinckney took a different view. He begged the caucus not to run any southern Federalist for president because the South was so thoroughly Republican that he would not get a single electoral vote there. Northern Federalists such as Rufus King or John Jay, who could attract wide support in their own section, would be much better choices. If even they would have little chance of election, then Pinckney proposed ignoring party labels and endorsing Clinton. It would be prudent, he wrote, to support any Republican who would promise "speedy and honourable peace, and unshackled Commerce, & who would avoid all french influence & alliance, would keep up such a navy & army . . . as would ensure us respect from foreign nations." In short, the party should vote for a Republican who "in essential points would act most feder-

6. C. C. Pinckney to Milnor, August 24, 1812, in Pinckney Family Papers.

7. Elias B. Caldwell to Gaston, August 22, September 7, 1812, Stanley to Gaston, August 28, 1812, Gaston to David B. Ogden *et al.*, September 11, 1812—all in William Gaston Papers; Benjamin Stoddert to James McHenry, July 15, 1812, in Steiner, *McHenry*, 581–82; letter to John Hopkins, mentioned by Rufus King in King (ed.), *King*, V, 280–81. A letter from Gaston and Stanly arrived too late to be read to the gathering; Ogden to Gaston, September 21, 1812, in William Gaston Papers.

ally." Eventually the delegates adopted his view, reluctantly concluding that no Federalist had a chance at the presidency. The meeting dissolved in a general but informal agreement to work for DeWitt Clinton's election.[8]

The decision pleased many Federalist leaders in the South. The *Charleston Courier* had already begun printing a series of pro-Clinton letters and, without flatly stating his preference for Clinton over a true Federalist, the editor asked all who favored peace and commerce to forget party distinctions and to unite against Madison. Clinton also won the loyalty of Federalists in North Carolina because he could attract those Republicans dissatisfied with the policies of the present administration and ready for a change.[9]

There was strong opposition to Clinton only in Virginia, where Federalists were preparing to hold their own nominating convention. Because Virginia chose electors on a statewide ticket, each party had to draw up a list of twenty-five men and decide who they would support for president. This task required some form of communication among state party leaders, and Republicans had always used a legislative caucus at Richmond. Federalists could not employ the caucus system after 1800 because they had only a few dozen seats in the assembly, leaving three-quarters of the state's counties unrepresented. In 1804 there was no Federalist electoral ticket at all and in 1808 most Federalists supported Monroe's dissident Republican slate, so that in neither case was there any statewide party consultation. The election of 1812 resembled none of the previous three. Unlike 1804, Federalists were strongly opposed to the incumbent president and were determined to fight his reelection; and unlike 1808, they had no home-state Republican as a natural magnet for their support.

To answer its need the party produced the most nearly modern political convention ever seen in the South before the days of Jackson. The idea for a convention began in the Federalist stronghold of

8. C. C. Pinckney to Milnor *et al.*, August 24, 1812, in Pinckney Family Papers; Ogden to Gaston, September 21, 1812, in William Gaston Papers; Morison (ed.), *Otis*, I, 308–309*n*38; Robert Goodloe Harper to Col. Lynn, September 25, 1812, in Steiner, *McHenry*, 583–86; King (ed.), *King*, V, 266, 280–81; John S. Murdock, "The First National Nominating Convention," *American Historical Review*, I (1896), 681–82; Harper's letter in Raleigh *Minerva*, November 27, 1812.

9. *Charleston Courier*, July 24, 29, August 5, 1812; Raleigh *Minerva*, September 11, 1812; letter, in *Alexandria Gazette*, September 16, 1812.

Loudoun County, possibly in the mind of Charles Fenton Mercer, a young lawyer and state legislator. At an August 22 county mass meeting, the Loudoun Federalists proposed a state party convention at Staunton on September 21. They chose two delegates of their own and published an address asking Federalists everywhere to cooperate. Mercer himself wrote "to the amount of one whole newspaper & two quires of paper—rode 170 miles & made two speeches—all in the course of 16 days" to promote the venture.[10] The first response was encouraging. Federalists in several other counties held public meetings and chose delegates to Staunton. Some also established county committees to correspond with Federalists elsewhere and to canvass locally for the party's nominee. From Staunton itself the Federalist newspaper, the *Republican Farmer*, hailed each meeting and urged other counties not to dally at a time when vigorous activity was necessary.[11]

A disappointing thirty-two delegates from eighteen of the state's ninety-nine counties and cities finally assembled at Staunton. The preconvention activity had indeed been feverish, but it had been confined to a small area. Not all the Federalist counties had participated; proximity to Staunton or to Loudoun County was more decisive than party strength in determining whether a county sent representatives. Augusta County, of which Staunton was the seat, and five of the six counties bordering it chose delegates; so did Loudoun and all five counties touching it. Together these accounted for nearly two-thirds of the members; the others came chiefly from the northern Shenandoah Valley and the neighboring eastern slope of the Alleghenies, areas with fairly easy access to Staunton. Only one county west of the Alleghenies and only one in the entire Tidewater and southern Piedmont were represented. Neither the two largest towns, Richmond and Norfolk, nor the two most heavily Federalist counties, Accomac and Northampton on the Eastern Shore, sent anyone to the convention.

Once assembled, the Federalists had difficulty choosing a candidate except to agree that it would not be Clinton. Even delegates who

10. Staunton *Republican Farmer*, August 27, 1812. Proceedings and resolutions of the Loudoun convention are in *Alexandria Gazette*, September 5, 8, 9, 1812. Randolph to James M. Garnett, September 15, 1812, copy in John Randolph Papers, LC.

11. Staunton *Republican Farmer*, September 10, 17, October 8, 1812.

had previously found no objection to him deserted after seeing the address of the New York Clinton committee, which praised Jefferson, urged a vigorous war against Britain, and demanded territorial gains for the United States. "It promises nothing," one delegate said, "but the gratification of New York as a reward for our exertions to elect Mr. Clinton." A large number of those present, including the venerable Henry Lee and the vigorous Charles Fenton Mercer, opposed endorsing any particular candidate. They wanted to leave the electoral nominees a free choice and to appeal for the votes of all antiwar men, regardless of party. An unpledged Federalist ticket might attract all voters who were disgusted with the administration for any reason, and not merely those who preferred King, Marshall, Clinton, or any other single individual to Madison.[12]

By the extremely close margin of 16 to 15, this idea failed, and the convention resolved to recommend specific candidates. Baldly ignoring the New York caucus, delegates passed over Clinton and endorsed two strict Federalists, Rufus King of New York and William R. Davie of South Carolina (formerly governor of North Carolina). A central committee of five in Augusta County was detailed to notify the electoral nominees and to solicit their efforts for the entire ticket. The committee was also to write to the antiwar men in each county, asking them to form local committees for distributing campaign material. To the voters at large the convention addressed a lengthy condemnation of Madison and his party. Virginians were asked to consider the folly of the current war. Madison had chosen the wrong nation for an enemy, because France had surely far outdone England in injuring commerce and treating Americans with contempt. He had been too eager to fight, for the British Orders in Council were repealed even before Congress declared war. Even worse, Madison had kept America utterly unprepared for war. Only a change of presidents could save the nation; the address went on to say: "As friends of Commerce, we ask your co-operation in removing from office an administration which has nearly accomplished its total annihilation. As Friends of Peace, we invite your solemn protest against the authors of an impolitic and unnecessary War. As friends of Union, we invoke you to arrest the

12. Letter from an anonymous delegate, in *Virginia Patriot*, October 6, 1812; Staunton *Republican Farmer*, October 1, 1812.

progress of a system tending to its speedy and awful dissolution."[13]

With this, the convention adjourned and campaigning began in earnest, though only a few counties followed the central committee's recommendation to form local canvassing groups. Besides poor organization, Federalists had difficulty with their electoral slate. Its members had been chosen without being consulted, and at least one of them publicly announced that he would not vote for the ticket upon which he was listed. Even with such embarrassments, this was the most vigorous presidential campaign since 1800. The war was the chief issue, but Federalists also made a point of attacking the state law that required general ticket elections for president, calling it a Republican scheme to suppress the voice of the minority.[14]

The effect of the General Ticket Law was evident on election day. In the face of a bitter campaign, many freeholders were still apathetic, and less than 21,000 voted out of some 50,000 eligible. One Republican opponent of the war, John Taylor of Caroline, blamed the low turnout on the voters' equal dissatisfaction with Madison and with the only alternative, a Federalist president; but the tendency to stay at home was evident also in strongly Federalist counties. Probably the belief that statewide victory was hopeless kept many Federalists from making the arduous ride to their courthouses, while Republicans abstained because they were equally certain of victory. The Federalist candidates won the Eastern Shore nearly unanimously as usual and managed also to carry northwestern Virginia beyond the valley. Everywhere else, Madison won easily, his margins reaching 90 percent and more in the Piedmont and Tidewater counties. It was quite a satisfying victory for the president. The total vote was about 20,700, of which the electors pledged to King and Davie drew just 5,600 (27 percent). The Federalist share was only slightly above that given President Adams twelve years before, when he bore the burden of a standing army, war taxes, and the Sedition Act. Still, five districts voted

13. Letter from an anonymous delegate, in *Virginia Patriot*, October 6, 1812; Staunton *Republican Farmer*, October 1, 1812; address of the Staunton convention to the freeholders of Virginia, in the *Martinsburg Gazette*, October 9, 1812, and several other papers.

14. "A Citizen of Charlotte," in *Virginia Patriot*, October 16, 1812; Fletcher to his father, October 2, 1812, in von Briesen (ed.), *Elijah Fletcher*, 63; Maria Hamilton Campbell to David Campbell, October 25, 1812, in David Campbell Papers; "Senex," in *Virginia Herald*, October 24, 1812.

Federalist, where only two had done so in 1800; and but for the General Ticket Law Madison would have lost those five electors.[15]

In North Carolina the result was similar—a clean sweep for Madison—but it was achieved by a different method. In December, 1811, the General Assembly had adopted a Republican plan to vest the choice of electors in the legislature. In previous years they had been chosen popularly by districts, and the Federalists were strong enough locally to win four of twelve in 1800 and three of fourteen in 1808. Doing away with district elections would insure an entirely Republican vote, since there was almost no chance of the Federalists' ever controlling the legislature. When the electoral bill was debated in December, Federalist members were joined in stubborn opposition by a few Republicans who disliked taking away the people's direct vote, but the measure passed easily. All now depended upon the election of legislators in August, 1812. There was only slight prospect of a Federalist victory. The party normally held less than one-third of the legislature, and it would require a gain of more than ten senate and thirty house seats to oust the Republicans from control. An upheaval of this magnitude was virtually impossible. Instead, the Federalists aimed merely to repeal the electoral law and return to the district system. If the antielectoral forces could win a majority in August and induce the governor to call a special session, the districts might be restored in time for a popular presidential election in November. In that case Clinton would certainly win several votes.[16]

Federalists employed every device to inflame public opinion, beginning with bitter editorials in the Raleigh *Minerva* and the *Carolina Federal Republican*. As the *Minerva* explained it, the evil purpose of the law was to dilute the voting power of the more populous counties and to prevent the expression of a minority opinion in the state. Another writer called the law tyrannical and corrupt, saying that it

15. John Taylor to James Monroe, November 8, 1812, Thomas Jefferson to Monroe, November 3, 1812, both in James Monroe Papers, LC; Staunton *Republican Farmer*, November 5, December 3, 1812. Official returns are in the Rare Book Room, Virginia State Library.

16. John A. Cameron to Duncan Cameron, December 24, 1811, in Cameron Family Papers; Stanly to Gaston, August 28, 1812, Gaston and Stanly to [James Milnor], September, 1812, both in William Gaston Papers; Hoyt (ed.), *Papers of Archibald D. Murphey*, I, 63–64*n*.2; Raleigh *Minerva*, January 3, 1812; *North Carolina House Journal*, 1811, pp. 51–52; *North Carolina Senate Journal*, 1811, pp. 36, 42, 45, 52, 54.

would lay the assembly open to bribery by partisans of the various presidential candidates. In an open letter to the people, a Rutherford County Federalist proposed a threefold scheme of action: citizens should vote only for legislative candidates pledged to repeal, county grand juries should present the law as a grievance, and the people should petition for a special legislative session to draw new electoral districts.[17]

It was not very difficult to arouse indignation against the electoral law. Even many Republicans opposed it, and several had signed an official protest against it in the 1811 legislative journals. At least sixteen county grand juries across the state protested the law; only two approved it. Cumberland County called the law unconstitutional; the jurors of Orange County found its principles threatening to republican institutions; and many other juries expressed themselves in similar language. The Republican *Raleigh Register* passed off these grand jury presentments as the work of two or three influential Federalists in each county, but some of the protests came from counties which were solidly Republican and very unlikely to be "misled" by Federalist intrigues.[18] With two such controversial and interrelated issues as the presidential election and the electoral law depending upon the makeup of the next assembly, the summer legislative campaign was the most vigorous since 1800.[19]

Sifting through the county returns in August, Federalists were elated. In Orange County, John A. Cameron hailed his brother Duncan's victory "over the wild ravings of democracy," and the *Wilmington Gazette* reported a Federalist sweep of Craven County, which had been Republican until then. A distraught Republican feared that resentment against the electoral law had split his party so badly that Clinton would carry off the honors in the presidential voting. Surveying the entire state, William Boylan claimed that three-fourths of the members opposed the electoral law and that ninety (only eight short of a majority) were against Madison and the war. He predicted that

17. Newbern *Carolina Federal Republican*, July 4, 1812; letter of William Porter, *ibid.*, April 18, 1812; "A Friend of the People," *ibid.*, June 27, 1812; Raleigh *Minerva*, April 3, 1812.

18. Hoyt (ed.), *Papers of Archibald D. Murphey*, I, 63–64*n*.2; Raleigh *Minerva*, March 20, June 12, 1812; *Raleigh Register*, April 17, 1812.

19. *Raleigh Register*, August 7, 1812.

the president would not get a single electoral vote in the state. On September 5 Boylan sat down to list by county the probable strength of the "peace party" in the legislature. He counted ninety-nine votes, a bare majority, if there were a real chance of defeating Madison in the national election. If not, he expected only seventy-six to eighty firm Clinton votes.[20]

More sober heads, mulling the returns, realized that some legislators who opposed the electoral law would not necessarily support Clinton for president. Peter Browne, a Halifax Federalist, admitted that, despite his party's legislative gains, there was still a clear Republican majority, at least on the question of Madison's reelection. The politically neutral Raleigh *Star* came to approximately the same conclusion, estimating a Republican majority of about twenty seats and predicting a Madison victory in North Carolina. Republican papers generally agreed.[21] Actually, the Federalists had gained only about ten seats in the house and two in the senate, hardly denting the normal Republican majorities. A bloc of ten counties on the central Atlantic coast around Newbern, and another group of eleven in the northern Piedmont, produced the only striking Federalist victories; from these two regions the party elected thirty-three senators and representatives as against only eighteen in 1811. The counties of the south central Fayetteville congressional district were loyal as always, sending twenty Federalists and only four Republicans to Raleigh. But in the remaining half of the state the Federalist party actually lost five assembly seats in 1812, keeping only nine against eighty-five for the Republicans. This failure to enlarge the Federalist appeal beyond a few areas of the state doomed the Clinton campaign in North Carolina. Although some of the Republicans would support repeal of the electoral law, few if any would desert Madison in the presidential vote.

After the August elections, events moved steadily against the Fed-

20. John A. Cameron to Duncan Cameron, August 18, 1812, in Cameron Family Papers; *Wilmington Gazette*, August 25, 1812; letter in Newbern *Carolina Federal Republican*, September 26, 1812; Raleigh *Minerva*, September 4, 1812; William Boylan to Steele, September 5, 1812, in Wagstaff (ed.), *Papers of John Steele*, II, 686–87.

21. Peter Browne to James Iredell, Jr., September 28, 1812, in James Iredell, Jr., Papers, Duke University; Raleigh *Star*, November 6, 1812; *Raleigh Register*, September 11, 1812; *Edenton Gazette*, September 29, 1812.

eralists. Legislators from several counties petitioned for a special session to reinstate electoral districts, but the governor and Council of State declined to act. When the legislature finally did meet in its customary year-end session, a coalition of Federalists and antielectoral Republicans tried and failed to repeal the law, losing at one point by only a single vote. The assembly then proceeded to choose electors, and a prestigious slate of Clinton men suffered an unexpectedly crushing defeat. After much canvassing and wheedling, the Republicans held a caucus to whip their forces into line, and the Madison ticket triumphed by the huge margin of 130 to 60. No Republicans deserted their candidate, and even a few Federalist members forgot Clinton and voted instead for the very president their party leaders had been denouncing for years as a bumbler and a tool of France.[22]

Compared to the sharp contest in North Carolina and the introduction of a state nominating convention in Virginia, the election in South Carolina was mild, producing little effort and no innovations. The state legislature, as usual, would pick the electors, so that the presidential issue would really be decided in the October assembly elections. Inasmuch as the Federalists had steadily lost ground since 1800 and now held only about 10 percent of the legislative seats, no one expected anything but a substantial Madison victory in 1812. Even holding their existing handful of seats might be beyond the Federalists' capacity.

Two recent constitutional changes had altered the political balance in South Carolina more heavily than ever against their party. Both houses of the legislature had been reapportioned in 1808, giving the up-country districts a larger voice and the coastal parishes a comparatively smaller one. Since Federalists rarely won elections outside the Tidewater, nearly all the new up-country members would be Re-

22. Events in the legislature must be pieced together from a variety of sources: Raleigh *Minerva*, August 7, October 2, December 4, 1812; Newbern *Carolina Federal Republican*, October 10, December 12, 26, 1812; Raleigh *Star*, October 2, 1812; *Raleigh Register*, November 27, 1812; William Hawkins to Duncan Cameron, September 19, 1812, in Cameron Family Papers; *North Carolina House Journal*, 1812, pp. 3, 9; *North Carolina Senate Journal*, 1812, p. 4. There were about 127 Republican members and 130 votes for Madison and about 66 Federalists but only 60 votes for Clinton. Advance reports said that some Federalists were going to support Madison in preference to another Republican (Clinton): Raleigh *Star*, November 6, 1812; Boylan to Steele, September 5, 1812, in Wagstaff (ed.), *Papers of John Steele*, II, 688.

publican. The second change threatened the Federalists' existence even where they were still strong, in Charleston and vicinity. The right to vote, previously restricted to three-shilling taxpayers, was extended in 1810 to all adult white males. The infusion of thousands of additional voters, all of them on the lower economic level, could only hurt the Federalist party, which—in South Carolina, at least—drew its greatest support from planters, merchants, and professional men.[23]

In 1812 the party made an unusually energetic campaign in Charleston but was dormant everywhere else. A citywide Federalist caucus nominated a full ticket for the one senate seat and sixteen house seats at stake. In the weeks before election day the candidates and their supporters showered upon the voters of Charleston countless campaign leaflets in support of Clinton and those pledged to his cause. Much of this material arrived by mail from the North, but the local party received considerable aid from anti-Madison Republican defectors. The Republican *City Gazette* admitted that "quids and apostate republicans" added probably two hundred voters to the Clinton legislative ticket.[24] While the votes were being tallied, the *Charleston Courier* looked back with pride upon the vigor of the campaign; even if the Federalists lost they had proved "that the large and highly respectable body of citizens who are opposed to the present ruinous measures . . . were not disposed to sit down quietly, and submit to being *branded tories and traitors*." This may have been true of Charleston itself and a few neighboring parishes, but elsewhere on the coast and throughout the up-country, Federalists did as little as ever.[25]

Even in Charleston most of the voters were determined to retain James Madison as President. The lowest of sixteen candidates on the Republican legislative ticket received 858 votes; the highest Federalist, 823. The average vote for each ticket was a more accurate measure of basic party strength, and on this the Federalists lost by a wider margin—1,089 to 770. Outside the city, a few Federalists were successful in the coastal parishes, but in most districts their situation was

23. See Chap. 16, herein, for the effect of reapportionment and suffrage extension on South Carolina politics.

24. John Geddes to James Madison, September 26, 1812, in Madison Papers, LC; Thomas Lehre to Jefferson, August 1, September 21, 1812, in Thomas Jefferson Papers; *Charleston Courier*, July 24, 1812; Charleston *City Gazette*, October 15, 1812.

25. *Charleston Courier*, October 14, 1812; Charleston *City Gazette*, October 16, 1812.

hopeless. Before the election there had been only about 10 Federalists out of 124 in the house and less than half a dozen out of 45 in the senate. The new assembly was, if anything, even more Republican. After such a crushing defeat, there was not much to be gained from presenting a slate of Clinton electors, and in December the legislature chose 11 firm Madisonians without opposition.[26]

The Georgia Federalists were even weaker than their friends in South Carolina and made no attempt at all to place a large bloc in the legislature, which chose the electors. However, this did not stop some from hoping that Madison could be denied at least one vote. John Rutledge, Jr., after talking with many Georgia Federalists, wrote about one Republican candidate for elector who was so esteemed that no pledge of his presidential vote would be required and who, if chosen by the legislature, might vote for Clinton. If there was such an effort, it did not succeed; a few weeks later the Georgia legislature selected a complete slate of eight loyal Madison men.[27]

The net result of the 1812 presidential campaign in the South was, from a Federalist view, very mixed. The search for electoral votes had failed in every state. Even worse, the Federalist candidates (except Rufus King in Virginia) fell short of John Adams' showing in 1800 and could not even equal the performance of 1808. This outcome would surely have convinced an impartial observer that the Federalist party had no chance of riding the war issue to victory in the South, as it did in New England and some other states.

At the same time, the election did show the continued existence of a respectable minority of voters in Virginia and North Carolina and of a stubborn if much smaller number in South Carolina, who were determined to oppose Madison and the war against England. Whether this minority could survive the patriotic pressure for unity during wartime and the incessant Republican attempts to brand opposition as disloyalty, was another question entirely.

26. Charleston *City Gazette*, September 22, 1812; *Charleston Courier*, December 7, 1812. Election returns, very incomplete, are in the papers for October, 1812. South Carolina was perhaps the only state in the Union in which Republicans gained ground because of the war. Margaret K. Latimer has undertaken an explanation of the state's unique attitude in "South Carolina—A Protagonist of the War of 1812," *American Historical Review*, LXI (1956), 914–29.

27. John Rutledge, Jr., to Harrison Gray Otis, November 10, 1812, in Harrison Gray Otis Papers.

Chapter 12 THE SEMILOYAL OPPOSITION, 1812–1815

THE Federalists' stubborn opposition to the approach of war left them in an awkward spot once the fighting actually began. They had spoken and written so ardently and voted so consistently against war that their loyalty was now suspect. In the South as well as in New England, Federalism was to some people synonymous with Toryism. Henry Bedinger, a western Virginia Republican, wrote that he would "watch, and denounce all such as may be dangerous, & such as take part with the enemy"—a category in which he included most Federalist leaders.[1]

Federalists were quite aware of the suspicion they had brought upon themselves, and they labored to escape it. Although disgusted with the war and with the administration that declared it, they announced their support for a vigorous military campaign. As early as August, 1811, party newspapers had promised that if war came, the Federalists would be among the firmest supporters of their country.[2]

1. Henry Bedinger to George M. Bedinger, July 6, 1812, copy in Dandridge Papers. For the overall view, see Myron F. Wehtje, "Opposition in Virginia to the War of 1812," *Virginia Magazine of History and Biography*, LXXVIII (1970), 65–86; and Sarah M. Lemmon, "Dissent in North Carolina During the War of 1812," *North Carolina Historical Review*, XLIX (1972), 108–18.

2. *Norfolk Gazette*, August 9, 1811; Raleigh *Minerva*, September 6, 1811.

In the summer of 1812 these sentiments were repeated in the press and at public gatherings. In Virginia, the Federalists of Rockbridge and Frederick counties denounced the onset of war but resolved to risk everything in defending the country "from every peril and from every enemy, foreign and domestic." Party newspapers cheered the volunteers who passed through their towns on the way to the front. The *Raleigh Minerva* even publicly chided the New England Federalists, noting with disapproval a vehement antiwar article in a Boston paper. All these were certainly unexceptionable sentiments, remarkable only because Federalists thought it necessary to express what should have been taken for granted—that they would support their government against the enemy. This says a good deal about the public image of the Federalist party in 1812.[3]

The Federalists themselves diluted the effect of their patriotic declarations by continuing to criticize the war's origins, expense, and aims. They saw nothing inconsistent in reviling the government for declaring an evil war, while aiding the same government to fight that war. Many voters, however, did not see such a broad distinction between criticism and disloyalty. By constantly refighting the partisan battles of 1811 and early 1812, and by reminding everyone of their party's opposition to the onset of war, the Federalists reduced the credibility of their wartime protestations of loyalty. Still they persevered, for they were convinced that the war would soon become unpopular and voters would turn in disgust from the guilty Republicans and reward the friends of peace.

There was also a real concern among Federalists that the Republicans were playing, perhaps unconsciously, Napoleon's game. "What do you think of this war measure?" one North Carolinian asked another in a private letter. "Don't you think we are adding another link to Bonys Chain?" A correspondent of the *Charleston Courier* could scarcely believe that while all Europe battled for its freedom against

3. Staunton *Republican Farmer*, November 19, 1812; Raleigh *Minerva*, July 10, 1812. Several Federalist mass meetings were held from July through October, 1812. For an example of concrete Federalist help in the war effort, see John Cropper to James Barbour, March 28 and 29, 1813, in S. Bailey Turlington (ed.), "Letters from Old Trunks," *Virginia Magazine of History and Biography*, XLV (1937), 42–45; and "Richmond During the War of 1812: The Vigilance Committee," *Virginia Magazine of History and Biography*, VII (1900), 225–41.

Napoleon, "we alone, who boast so much of the rights of man, should fight on the side of the Tyrant against those liberties." The party felt its case immeasurably strengthened when Americans learned in midsummer, 1812, that Britain had repealed her Orders in Council. Did this not put the United States in a most awkward position? The *Norfolk Gazette* affected amazement that "the Berlin and Milan decrees are not revoked, yet we are at peace with France! The British Orders in Council are rescinded, yet we are at war with Great Britain!" The only way to right this incredible blunder was to elect a Federalist government capable of making a swift and just peace.[4]

Since the war was needless, the heavy burdens it imposed on the nation were entirely indefensible. Besides the heavy war taxes and the huge debt for future generations, Federalists worried about the danger to constitutional liberties.[5] Those who denied the necessity of fighting England risked being branded traitors and were sometimes even in physical danger. The most extreme example of this, and the one that Federalists denounced in their sharpest language, was the "Baltimore massacre." For years, Republicans had considered the Baltimore *Federal Republican* one of the most obnoxious newspapers in the country, and the coming of war only sharpened its opposition to the government. Baltimore was an extremely Republican town and in the summer of 1812 a mob of Republican sympathizers, stung by the newspaper's antiwar propaganda, attacked its offices and put it out of publication for some time. Later, a second mob savagely beat a number of Federalists, killing several and crippling others for life. Among the victims was the old revolutionary general, Henry Lee of Virginia. The city and state officials, all Republican, had done little or nothing to halt the mobs.

Federalists everywhere were enraged and frightened. They rushed to denounce the violence as a savage crime and accused local officials of consenting to political murder. Federalists feared the massacre was only the beginning of a "DOMESTIC WAR of terror and proscription" in which all antiadministration opinion would be ruthlessly

4. Thomas Trotter to Ebenezer Pettigrew, July 18, 1812, in Charles Pettigrew Papers; *Charleston Courier*, July 5, 1813; *Norfolk Gazette*, quoted in Staunton *Republican Farmer*, November 19, 1812.

5. Savannah *Columbian Museum*, October 17, 1814. Timothy Pickering wrote a series of letters on the burdens of war, which several papers printed in April, 1813.

eradicated. Either the opposition would be threatened into silence or it would actually be crushed and a dictatorship established. The letter of an obscure North Carolinian, bubbling with indignation, nicely expresses this combination of anger and fear: "I am so Horrably Vexed at the D——d Vile Licensious Democratic Mob's Conduct in Baltimore that I solemnly declare there has not been 10 minutes together since I first Heard of it that it has been out of my mind, unless I was asleep—Gratious Heaven—to what a situation is our distracted Country Rappidly arriving? . . . it would almost seem dangerous to raise a Voice against Democracy yet I am resolved to decry it to my last breath."[6]

A scattering of similar, though less serious, actions seemed to foretell a wholesale repression of dissent. In Richmond the editor of the *Virginia Patriot*, Augustine Davis, said he had received anonymous threats of a Baltimore-style attack if he did not change his politics. Farther south, a Federalist editor in Savannah, who had just started his new paper with a broad criticism of the president and the war, was badly beaten by a Republican mob. He closed his newspaper permanently two days afterward. A Virginia gentleman who had spoken against the war was threatened by a "military mob" in Nottoway County, and at Williamsburg a captain interrupted an election to warn that "if no other method could be found to reclaim the federalists, that cutting their throats must follow." Complaints of this sort continued throughout the war whenever the Federalists could find examples to put before the public—outrages by soldiers against civilians, an officer discharged from the army for voting Federalist, a newspaper editor threatened again, letters being opened by Republican officials.[7]

One should not exaggerate; some of these are only Federalist claims, not proven incidents of repression, and they never became widespread

6. "A Civilian," in *Charleston Courier*, September 2, 1812; Loudoun County resolutions in *Alexandria Gazette*, August 27, 1812; Francis Taylor to William Johnson, August 17, 1812, in William Johnson Papers, UNC.

7. "C.B.," in Staunton *Republican Farmer*, November 5, 1812; *Virginia Patriot*, May 4, 7, August 6, October 29, November 5, 1813; John E. Talmadge, "Georgia's Federalist Press and the War of 1812," *Journal of Southern History*, XIX (1953), 493–98; Raleigh *Minerva*, April 16, 23, 1813; *Martinsburg Gazette*, September 22, 1814; *Charleston Courier*, March 25, 1815; William R. Davie to John Steele, November 29, 1814, in John Steele Papers.

enough to curb the antiwar minority. Federalists continued, therefore, to criticize the war as unnecessary and costly, and insisted that nothing worthwhile could be gained by it. The three possible fruits of American victory, as Federalists summarized them, were repeal of the Orders in Council, an end to impressment, and the conquest of Canada. The first of these was already won. The second was so trifling that it was not worth a skirmish, let alone a war, to obtain.

The introduction of a seamen's bill in Congress (to prevent foreigners from serving on American ships) led to an extended congressional and newspaper debate in 1813, during which Federalists repeated their old arguments on the legality and extent of impressment. They still believed that Britain had a perfect right in international law to reclaim her own subjects from American ships and that nearly every person impressed was in fact British. The number of American citizens seized by mistake or design was almost nil. In short, the Federalists accepted, as in past years, the British view that citizenship was indelible. They rejected the Republican claim that a British-born subject who became a naturalized American thereby lost his previous citizenship (and his obligation to serve the crown) and was entitled to the same protection as a native-born American. Republicans complained of more than 6,200 Americans impressed since 1796, but Federalists insisted that very few of those were native-born, and of that smaller figure all but about 100 had been released upon proving their citizenship. There was no point in fighting a long and bloody war to protect such a small number of native Americans—about 6 or 7 a year—from impressment. The larger goal, protection of naturalized as well as native citizens, could not be justified morally or legally, according to the Federalists and the British.[8]

The supposed third war aim, the conquest of Canada, was absurd, the minority said. Canada was little more than a stretch of vacant land, and there was already land aplenty south of the border. Besides, Federalists were sure that no invasion of Canada could succeed. The embarrassingly fruitless military campaigns on the northern frontier

8. Newbern *Carolina Federal Republican*, February 27, 1813; "A Virginian," in *Alexandria Gazette*, March, 1813; Joseph Pearson's speech in Congress, reprinted in *Wilmington Gazette*, February 12, 1813.

convinced them that their pessimism was justified. As early as February, 1813, the *Virginia Patriot* complained that it would take at least five years to overrun Canada at a cost of almost $500 million and countless American dead and wounded. A standing army of ruinous proportions would be required to hold down the conquered territory, leaving the United States larger but much weaker.[9]

Since criticism of the war's origins and aims generated public suspicion of the Federalists' loyalty, some Federalists tried to gain advantage by charging the Republicans with incompetence in waging war. Had not the Jeffersonians always opposed a strong navy, the most essential weapon in a war against Britain? Had they not shamefully neglected to fortify ports and harbors? Surely the catastrophic defeats on the Canadian front proved the Republicans' inability to fight effectively.[10] The Federalists' particular tactic was to play up the contrast between defeat in land operations, often led by Republican generals, and the successful exploits of the navy. This enabled them to display their patriotism by showing that the naval heroes were Federalists. The *Wilmington Gazette* celebrated Oliver Hazard Perry's victory on Lake Erie by acclaiming him as "the American Nelson" and reminding voters that naval officers were almost all Federalists and that only "Federal Valor on the Ocean and on the Lakes" saved the administration and the nation from complete disgrace.[11]

Federalists also emphasized that after years of "cursing and wrecking" the navy, Republicans were now being forced in the midst of war to adopt the old Federalist position in favor of more ships. If Federalists had been in power since 1800, America would have been better served by the creation of a strong fleet.[12] The neglect of southern coastal defense was another point of attack. When the British threatened the Chesapeake Bay and later blockaded it, Virginians complained loudly of being left alone against the enemy. And in Charles-

9. *Virginia Patriot*, February 9, 1813, February 16, 1814; "A Friend to Peace," in *Charleston Courier*, June 18, 1813.

10. *Virginia Patriot*, September 4, 1812; *Augusta Herald*, September 8, 1814; William R. Davie to William Gaston, February 14, 1815, in William Gaston Papers.

11. *Virginia Patriot*, March 23, 1813; *Wilmington Gazette*, quoted *ibid.*, October 12, 1813.

12. *Martinsburg Gazette*, January 15, 1813; Newbern *Carolina Federal Republican*, March 13, 1813.

ton the local Federalists circulated the charge that Madison cared nothing for the exposed and defenseless Carolina coast.[13]

Pointing out the military shortcomings of the administration allowed Federalists to blunt somewhat the charge of treasonable behavior. If the Republicans who mismanaged the war were loyal, then surely the minority which pointed out such fumblings was no less patriotic.[14] In fact, the Federalists genuinely resented as much as any other American the invasion of their land and the killing of their fellow citizens. Despite Republican claims of disloyalty, there is no evidence of it among southern Federalists. Instead, there was a spirit of firm resolution against the enemy, even though some fretted about having to fight and perhaps die because they were fellow citizens with the Republican majority. Francis Corbin of Virginia, long retired from active politics but still a strong partisan, hoped for unity against the enemy, saying, "'If we don't kill them, they will kill us'—this motto should now be inscribed on every Musket." A former congressman summarized the southern Federalist viewpoint; he was totally convinced that the war was unwise and unjust, but he could not see British troops on American soil "without feeling that indignant spirit against the invaders, that I am sure is felt by every American."[15]

Nevertheless, the party's effort to prove its loyalty was not fully effective, and many voters continued to look on the Federalists as a suspect group of latter-day Tories. Three things in particular contributed to this feeling: party opposition to the vital war loans of 1813 and 1814, the calling of the Hartford Convention, and the undisguised Federalist happiness at the fall of Napoleon, Britain's enemy in Europe.

Even during the 1812 presidential campaign, when charges of hobbling the war effort were more than usually damaging, southern Fed-

13. *Charleston Courier*, July 26, 1814; Newbern *Carolina Federal Republican*, February 13, 1813; "An Old Soldier," in *Virginia Patriot*, May 4, 1814; Thomas Lehre to James Madison, March 26, 1813, in Madison Papers, LC. The inability of the administration to defend the South, especially Virginia and North Carolina, is well covered in Edward J. Wagner II, "State-Federal Relations During the War of 1812" (Ph.D. dissertation, Ohio State University, 1963), 115–18, 121–22, 146–57.

14. *Virginia Patriot*, April 9, 1814; *Augusta Herald*, October 27, 1814; William Polk to William Hawkins, November 17, 1814, typed copy in George W. Polk Papers, UNC.

15. Joseph Caldwell to Walter Alves, April 22, 1813, copy in Norwood Papers, UNC; Francis Corbin to Wilson Cary Nicholas, February 13, 1815, in Edgehill-Randolph Papers, UVa; William Barry Grove to Gaston, July 8, 1813, in William Gaston Papers.

eralists had turned their backs on the first war loan and rejoiced when subscriptions fell far below the amount sought. Their attitude was no different in 1813 and 1814 when Madison's administration, staggering under the cost of the expanded armed forces, came forward with two additional loan requests. In Congress the North Carolinians Joseph Pearson and William Gaston did their best to discredit the new bond issues. Raising these huge sums would give the national government too much financial power, they warned. There was no limit on the rate of interest and no provision for repaying the principal. Such a large infusion of paper currency would depreciate rapidly in value, as the 1812 loan had already done, and would defraud the trusting citizens who bought the bonds at face value.[16]

Newspapers gave wide circulation to the congressional arguments and added their own objections as well. The *Virginia Patriot* explained that Federalists could not approve an immense loan to be wasted in a hopeless attempt to conquer Canada, although they would gladly endorse a loan for purely defensive purposes. Another Virginian hoped that if the loan failed, Republicans would have to make peace because they would have no money to fight any longer. Indeed, the 1813 bond issue did fall very far short of supplying the funds desired, partly because the wealthy Federalist areas withheld their support. This attitude did not make the party very popular among those who endorsed the war.[17]

Even so, opposing war loans was not nearly so serious as plotting to destroy the Union, a sin that many Republicans were convinced was in the hearts of New England Federalists. Disaffection in that section was so obvious and of so dangerous an aspect that even the southern Federalists became alarmed.[18] The unrest continued and finally led to a regional convention of New England delegates at Hartford in the winter of 1814–1815. The stated purpose of the convention was to protect the economic and political interests of a section that

16. Gaston's and Pearson's speeches in Congress, reprinted in *Virginia Patriot*, April 13–May 18, 1814. William R. Barlow, "Congress During the War of 1812" (Ph.D. dissertation, Ohio State University, 1961), Chaps. 4–6, deals with Federalist opposition to war measures in Congress.

17. *Virginia Patriot*, April 2, 1814; *Martinsburg Gazette*, February 12, 1813; Isaac A. Coles to David Campbell, March 18, 1813, in David Campbell Papers. Various congressional speeches are reprinted in *Virginia Patriot*, March–June, 1814, and in other papers.

18. *Virginia Patriot*, August 4, 1812.

contained a smaller and smaller minority of America's population. The actual purpose, some opponents said, was to foment secession.

A few southerners such as the old aristocrat Carter Beverly of Virginia, welcomed the convention idea, hoping that a firm protest might compel the Republicans to alter their policies. The *Charleston Courier*, alone among the Federalist newspapers, praised the convention as a temperate meeting of sufferers seeking relief from misgovernment. The majority of Federalists, though, shared the fears of other men that the convention might not stop at moderation and that extremists might attempt disunion and ruin the country even if they failed in their goal.[19]

More than one southern Federalist worried that Congress would never meet again, that the Union would not last two years more, and that Madison would finish his career "amidst the ruins of his country." William R. Davie reported such fears to be common among the minority in South Carolina. If the New Englanders actually did lay hands upon the Union, what then? An obscure Georgia Federalist spoke for many of his southern comrades. Writing to a Bostonian, he recalled his firm party loyalty of many years past and promised to support all efforts for Federalist victory by every means available under the Constitution. But if the New England men stepped one foot "beyond that Sacred Boundary," they would deserve only contempt and rejection from all good men forever.[20]

Such protestations, especially when private, could not entirely erase the widespread suspicion that Federalists were only semiloyal in this war against their great idol, Britain. The party's attitude toward European affairs after 1812 contributed heavily to this feeling. The fact that British troops, ships, and money were primarily committed to the struggle against Napoleon was of considerable importance in convincing the Republicans to declare war. France, there-

19. Carter Beverly to Thomas M. Bayly, October 31, 1814, in Timothy Pickering Papers; *Charleston Courier*, January 2, 1815; H. W. DeSaussure to Benjamin Silliman, July 5, 1814, in H. W. DeSaussure Papers, Duke University. The *Martinsburg Gazette* printed the convention's proceedings at length, January 19, 1815.

20. William R. Davie to Steele, November 29, 1814, in John Steele Papers; William R. Davie to Gaston, November 17, 1814, copy in Davie Papers, UNC; Shaler Hillyer to Oliver Whyte, August 8, 1813, copy in Shaler Hillyer Letterbook; Richard Drummond Bayly to Cropper, November 10, 1814, in John Cropper Papers.

fore, was an accidental and unofficial ally of the United States, and the greater the success of French arms in Europe, the less effort Britain could devote to America. Thus, when Federalists cheered England on in the European war and rejoiced at the defeat of France, they seemed to be encouraging the enemy.

Federalists had, of course, long been afraid of Napoleon; they vilified him even more than Jefferson or Madison and were immensely gratified after 1812 to see his career rapidly declining. The retreat from Moscow, coming just at the beginning of the Anglo-American war, had given the party hope that he might soon be quelled for good. After the allied victory at Leipzig a year later, Federalists finally allowed themselves to believe that Napoleon's downfall was near. Early in January, 1814, word of the battle reached America, cheering Federalists throughout the country. Newspapers hastened to give their readers every detail of the battle and the allied pursuit, while leading men wrote each other the news, hardly able to believe their good fortune.[21]

Later reports of Napoleon's retreat into France and the allied occupation of Paris redoubled the Federalists' joy, and when the French emperor finally surrendered, their relief was unbounded. Europe was free of French control and this alone was cause for gratification. Much more to the point, America itself was free of the threat of French conquest and of the malignant French influence that Federalists had always seen at work in Washington. William Gaston heard the "momentous intelligence from Europe with gratitude and awe," and William Barry Grove could not refrain from congratulating his friends on the downfall of "that Tyrant & wretch Napoleon." Many Federalists dispatched letters to their newspapers extolling the new era in Europe and heaping contempt on the fallen emperor. Editors, too, sighed their relief that the welfare of the world and the interest of humanity had been saved by the provident defeat of Napoleon. Federalists thought it shocking, but all too natural, that Republicans were unhappy at Bonaparte's fate. One editor professed amazement that so many Re-

21. John Rutledge, Jr., to Harrison Gray Otis, March 1, 1814, in Harrison Gray Otis Papers; Grove to Duncan Cameron, January 12, 1814, in Cameron Family Papers; *Augusta Herald*, January 20, 1814.

publicans could "groan and grieve, at the downfall of the arch cut throat of modern times."[22]

Federalists rejoiced not only because they believed Napoleon's defeat freed Europe of tyranny and removed the French threat to America, but also because it might bring peace with England. It was no longer possible for the government to sustain its morale in a fruitless war by hoping that a French victory in Europe would force England to make a generous peace with the United States. On the contrary, British forces were now freed from continental battlefields to reinforce the assault against America. This bleak prospect might cause even the most warlike Republican to think of drawing the conflict to a close. Also, Federalists assumed that Bonaparte's fall would destroy any possible French hold upon the American government. With her upstart emperor crushed and the Bourbon monarchy restored, France could neither threaten Americans nor offer them "Jacobin ideas" to worship. Since the administration was now free to consider only American interests, it must soon see the absurdity of the present war. Most importantly, the end of the European struggle removed all the major causes of the war against Britain. Impressment of American seamen, depredations upon commerce, and interference with normal trade patterns were all products of England's war for survival against Napoleon. Therefore, an end to the American war must inevitably follow the end of the European war.[23]

In view of the Federalists' wartime performance—condemning the war itself as wrong and ruinous, refusing to support vital loans, attacking the country's quasi ally Napoleon—it is remarkable that they did not suffer crushing losses at the polls, especially in the prowar southern states. Yet in the wartime elections from 1812 through 1815 Federalists did comparatively well. They did not make striking gains in the South (as they did elsewhere) but neither were they decimated. In the presidential election of 1812, Federalists had maintained

22. Gaston to John F. Burgwin, May 20, 1814, in William Gaston Papers; Grove to Duncan Cameron, June 1, 1814, in Cameron Family Papers; *Martinsburg Gazette*, March 31, 1814. A good nationwide survey, including the South, is Guillaume de Bertier de Sauvigny, "The American Press and the Fall of Napoleon in 1814," *Proceedings of the American Philosophical Society*, XCVIII (1954), 337–76.

23. *Augusta Herald*, June 23, 1814; "The Certain Prospect of a Speedy Peace with Great Britain," in *Virginia Patriot*, January 20, 1814.

—and in Virginia even increased—their prewar strength. Although they could not hope for a statewide victory anywhere, they remained popular in their traditional strongholds.

The congressional contests of late 1812 and early 1813 reinforced this impression. In Georgia there was no sign of life, but Federalists elsewhere made these elections a referendum on the war and enjoyed their best showing since 1800. There were three congressional candidates in South Carolina, of whom the most energetic was John Rutledge, Jr., in Charleston. He was nominated by a citywide Federalist caucus that appointed a central committee to draw up and distribute a circular throughout Charleston and neighboring parishes. The *Charleston Courier* ran articles defending Rutledge's attachment to republican government, challenging his opponents to "put your finger on the act which Col. RUTLEDGE has done, in his life, that is opposed in any manner to your Republican Constitution, to its Laws, or its Institutions. You cannot!" Despite these efforts, Rutledge lost by nearly two to one, and Federalist candidates in the other coastal districts, Beaufort and Georgetown, did even worse. Still, this was the best result and the most energetic campaign since 1803, ending nearly a decade of uninterrupted decline for South Carolina Federalism.[24]

There was also a surge of activity in North Carolina, where congressional elections had been moved from August of even-numbered years to April of odd-numbered ones. Hoping to capitalize on military defeats and higher taxes, the party campaigned almost entirely on the war issue, repeating all the usual arguments and pointing to new American disasters as evidence of Republican incompetence. The *Carolina Federal Republican* summed up the consequences of war, saying that it had "lost us territory, lost us armies . . . stopped the course of justice, deprived honest industry of its reward, destroyed our commerce;" the "corrupt or the insane" were its only advocates.

24. Circular addressed to William Sinclair, St. Stephen's Parish, signed by the Federalist committee of correspondence in Charleston, dated September 24, 1812, in Rutledge Papers, USC. See the following in *Charleston Courier*: September 15, October 4, 1812, "Hundreds of Voters," October 2, 1812, and "An American," October 15, 1812. Returns are in the papers for October, 1812. "An American" laid the defeat in Charleston to "the exertions which were made by French emissaries to bring to the polls every subject of Napoleon, to aid in the subjugation of our country's happiness," but even subtracting the three hundred "French votes" that he claimed were cast, the Republican candidate outran Rutledge by a good margin.

Waiting lazily until only a month before the election, Federalist leaders finally began to coordinate plans for contesting as many districts as possible. They were able to find six active candidates, the largest number in a decade, although seven Republicans still escaped opposition.[25]

Both sitting Federalists, Joseph Pearson of Salisbury and John Culpepper of the Fayetteville district, easily won another term. Culpepper's only serious challenge was from another Federalist; his Republican opponent took only 10 percent of the district's vote. In a sharp contest on the Atlantic coast, William Gaston, who had lost by five hundred votes in 1810, now unseated the Republican incumbent by almost a three-to-one margin. In the western Piedmont another Federalist missed election by only twenty-six votes, and a fifth district north of Newbern might have gone Federalist except that Republican Congressman William Kennedy was himself an antiwar man. For years Kennedy had contested the seat against an administration Republican, and Federalists had become so used to voting for him that some continued to do so even against a candidate of their own party. Over the whole state, Federalists won about 30 percent of the popular vote and would have done even better if they had nominated candidates in the remaining seven districts. In those few counties which the party contested in both 1810 and 1813, the Federalist vote jumped from 54 to 67 percent of the total.[26]

Virginia gave further cheer to the party by returning the largest Federalist congressional delegation since 1799. Spurred by the hope of widespread antiwar sentiment, at least ten Federalists ran for Congress, covering every district where victory was even conceivable. As always, the real two-party battle was west of the Blue Ridge, where five of seven seats had Federalist candidates; but this year even eastern Virginia had at least five, and possibly seven, party contests, more

25. Newbern *Carolina Federal Republican*, March 20, 1813; William Gaston to voters of Newbern district, in North Carolina Broadsides (1813), UNC; Polk to Steele, March 27, 1813, in Wagstaff (ed.), *Papers of John Steele*, II, 706; Polk to Gaston, March 23, 1813, in William Gaston Papers; Archibald D. Murphey to Duncan Cameron, March 29, 1813, William Boylan to Duncan Cameron, April 25 and May 13, 1813, in Cameron Family Papers; Bartlett Yancey to Thomas Ruffin, March, 1813, in J. G. deRoulhac Hamilton (ed.), *The Papers of Thomas Ruffin* (4 vols.; Raleigh, N.C., 1918–20), I, 132–34.

26. Boylan to Duncan Cameron, April 25 and May 13, 1813, in Cameron Family Papers. Returns are in the newspapers for May, 1813.

than ever before. The Federalists ran as "Friends of Peace, Commerce, and No Foreign Alliances." In December and January some counties began planning their campaign, but most candidates waited until March, just a month before the voting, to announce themselves. Deviating from the usual custom of self-nomination, leaders in at least two districts formed party committees to search for acceptable Federalist candidates.[27]

The voting showed that Federalists did make progress, though not as much as they had hoped. Two incumbents were returned with comfortable margins: Joseph Lewis, Jr., for the Loudoun seat (by 57 percent) and James Breckinridge in the upper valley (by 54 percent). In another valley district there was no Republican opponent at all. The party lost the Ohio River seat when President Madison's son-in-law John G. Jackson reversed his defeat of two years before, but this was balanced by a gain in extreme eastern Virginia, in the district that spanned Chesapeake Bay and included the heavily Federalist Eastern Shore counties. For eight years a Republican had won this seat, sometimes narrowly, sometimes easily; but in 1813 he fell to a young Federalist lawyer who had not even been a candidate until a few days before the polling. A Federalist also won a newly created western district, making a total of five congressmen, which was a gain of one over 1811 and the largest delegation in history except for 1799. West of the Blue Ridge, Federalists had polled nearly 40 percent of the entire popular vote (even without contesting two districts), and an antiwar Republican won an additional 12 percent. Less than half the voters of western Virginia were willing to support candidates who approved of the war.[28]

Altogether, eighteen southern Federalists ran for Congress in these first wartime elections, and eight actually won. Both figures were the highest since the turn of the century. The first nine months of war with

27. Two easterners may have been either Federalists or antiwar Republicans. Letter "To the people comprising the Congressional District of Henrico," in *Virginia Patriot*, March 23 and 26, 1813; William Rice, *ibid.*, February 19, 1813; letter to the voters of Culpepper district, in *Virginia Herald*, December 2, 1812; Allen Taylor to James Breckinridge, January 20, 1813, in Breckinridge Papers, UVa; public letters to central committees in Rockingham and Berkeley districts announcing Federalist nominees, in Staunton *Republican Farmer*, March 18, 1813, and *Virginia Patriot*, March 30, 1813.

28. Samuel Taggart to John Taylor, February 11, 1813, in Haynes (ed.), "Letters of Taggart," 427; John Teackle to Timothy Pickering, December 27, 1812, in Timothy Pickering Papers; letter from Northampton County, in *Virginia Patriot*, April 2, 1813. Returns are in the newspapers for April–May, 1813.

England, instead of hurting the party that had long taken England's side, actually brought forth a greater campaign effort and a greater share of votes for Federalists than in the prewar elections. Much the same thing occurred in state legislative contests. There was a mild revival of Federalist membership in the Virginia house of delegates between 1811 and 1815, and a gain in North Carolina to the highest level since 1800. Only in South Carolina was there no recovery; that state was so much a "protagonist of the War of 1812" that Federalists actually lost most of their already small representation in the assembly. However, the state's only large city, Charleston, saw a distinct Federalist quickening in both local and legislative races. The office of intendant (mayor) of the city, which had been in Republican hands for some years before the war, fell to a Federalist in 1813, 1814, and 1815, after sharp partisan campaigns in each case; and the Federalist slate of assembly candidates, though never successful, polled a sizably increased vote in the 1812 and 1814 contests.[29]

Elections to the Fourteenth Congress, held during the last months of war and the first of peace, ratified this trend in voter preference. When South Carolina chose her new congressmen in October, 1814, the war had dragged on for nearly thirty months with little to show. The British had thoroughly blockaded the Atlantic coast, burned Washington, and hurled back every American attempt to invade Canada. At the same time, Federalists had persisted in their halfhearted support of the war effort, and some in the North were issuing extreme statements about the fragility of the Union. Both sides were thus handicapped in appealing for votes—the Republicans by their administration's ineptness and the Federalists by their northern friends' extremism. The war and its subsidiary issues clearly dominated the campaign. Benjamin Huger, announcing his candidacy as a Federalist for the coastal Georgetown district, declared that the objects of the war were obviously unattainable, and he asked voters to use the election as a chance to express themselves in favor of peace.[30] Huger had

29. The campaigns for intendant and for legislators are reported in the Charleston papers for September–October each year; see especially *Charleston Courier*, September 22, 1812, September 20, 21, 24, 1813, and September 9, 20, 1814; Charleston *Times*, September 17, 1816; and in Charleston *Southern Patriot*, "A Voter," September 19, 1814, and "An Adopted Citizen," April 11, 1815.

30. Benjamin Huger's address, in *Charleston Courier*, September 20, 1814.

often been sent to the legislature by the Republican voters of his parish. He was an excellent candidate in this district because his personal attraction could overcome the handicap of his party label. Charleston also offered strong possibilities for Federalist success. Like Georgetown, it had once been a Federalist stronghold and it still had the most active, and perhaps the only, party organization in the state.

The Federalists as usual began both contests very late. Huger announced on September 20 and Thomas Rhett Smith, the Charleston nominee, was not publicly proclaimed until September 28, only two weeks before the election. This hardly left time for an adequate canvass, and the *Charleston Courier*, despairing of success, did not give its customary wide publicity to either candidate. In Charleston itself these shortcomings, added to the popularity of the incumbent Republican, were decisive. After a quiet campaign Smith polled only 37 percent of the votes—no improvement at all over 1812, but better than in any prewar year since 1803. However, Benjamin Huger did win the Georgetown seat, owing his majority of barely 100 votes to personal popularity rather than party. He carried one county, for example, by 359 to 15, even while it was choosing an all-Republican delegation to the assembly. Since no South Carolina Federalist had been in Congress for more than a decade, his victory was an event of some national interest; but this was so obviously an individual success that it reveals nothing about voters' attitudes toward the war.[31] Only the Charleston result allows any comparison with immediate past years, and in this most mercantile and most Federalist of areas there was no change in party strength at all.

Georgians also voted in the fall of 1814, but there was not a single Federalist in the field of nine candidates. The vigorous voice of local Federalism, the *Augusta Herald*, contented itself with a mild editorial asking voters to defeat every sitting member. Even though their replacements would all be Republicans, they would not be bound by past actions and might be more willing to end the war quickly. In Savannah a greatly exasperated Federalist signing himself "Veritates" condemned the incumbents for their "imbecility and paucity of un-

31. Thomas Rhett Smith's announcement, in *Charleston Courier*, September 28, 1814. Returns are in the newspapers for October 12–24, 1814. Taggart to John Taylor, November 2, 1814, in Haynes (ed.), "Letters of Taggart," 432.

derstanding . . . cohesive degeneracy of favouritism, and the madning delusions of party." Since no Federalists were running, "Veritates" could only recommend electing different Republicans, and even this wish was not granted. Four of the five incumbents who ran were reelected, and although two new men were chosen, two others ran at the foot of the list.[32]

Strictly speaking, this was the last of the wartime elections, since peace intervened before North Carolina and Virginia voted in April, 1815. The long negotiations at Ghent had at last produced an agreement. Peace—the party's incessant demand for nearly three years—was restored, and Federalists were unrestrained in welcoming it. Their newspapers printed the story in great detail and with appropriate applause. Even so bitterly partisan a sheet as the *Charleston Courier* suspended its attacks on the administration and devoted much of its space in February and March to hailing the return of peace. The editor of the *Augusta Herald* also spread the glad news upon his pages but could not help wishing that Americans had learned from experience and that Republicans would abandon any thought of future embargoes or other commercial restrictions. Thoroughly convinced of the government's incapacity for waging war, Federalists congratulated their country on the timely end of a struggle whose continuation would have meant disaster. Charles Fenton Mercer, the most active Federalist in northern Virginia, assured a Republican friend that the peace treaty was the happiest event since the adoption of the Constitution because it saved the country from "bankruptcy, disunion, and civil war, combined with foreign invasion; in fine, from national dishonor and ruin."[33]

Virginia's congressional campaign had already begun before news of the treaty reached America, and the voting in April came less than two months after peace was known. The recent war was still the foremost issue in the public mind. Federalists contested a record number

32. "A Voter," in *Georgia Argus*, June 1, 1814; "A Georgian," in Savannah *Republican*, September 22, 1814; *Augusta Herald*, August 18, 23, September 1, 1814; "Veritates," in Savannah *Columbian Museum*, October 3, 1814. Election results are in *Georgia Journal*, October 19, 1814.

33. *Augusta Herald*, February 23, March 2, 1815; John A. Cameron to Duncan Cameron, February 12, 1815, and John Dunlop to Duncan Cameron, February 23, 1815, both in Cameron Family Papers; Charles Fenton Mercer to W. C. Nicholas, April 14, 1815, in Nicholas Papers, LC.

of seats in the most determined challenge since 1799, and opposition Republicans of the John Randolph stripe ran in five other districts. This was the most serious challenge that Virginia's ruling faction had yet faced, although the last weeks of the campaign passed in something of a political vacuum. In some districts both parties fell back upon the wartime issues for lack of anything better. The chief argument made in favor of Joseph Lewis, Jr., the Federalist incumbent in the Loudoun-Fairfax district, was that he had opposed conscription and the invasion of Canada. The main Republican charge against Lewis was the same, that he had not supported the war effort. Probably elsewhere in the state the same thing occurred. The great question that Virginia's voters could now answer was whether peace would destroy Federalist hopes or whether the failure to obtain any of the proclaimed goals of the war would damage the administration.[34]

Other things, too, would influence the result. The Federalists suffered, for instance, from lack of a proper organization. In the most essential point—the selection of candidates—the party blundered, and four districts each had a pair of Federalists in the field. In one, the lower valley, there was no Republican running and the entrance of a second candidate posed no danger. In fact, Magnus Tate, who took pains to explain in his address to the people why he had run "without the sanction of a committee," actually defeated the regularly nominated Federalist. On the Eastern Shore a former Congressman, Thomas Griffin, and a former unsuccessful candidate, John Eyre, both entered the race; but here the Federalists were rather well organized and were used to consulting from county to county. Eventually the leadership persuaded Griffin to withdraw, allowing Eyre to concentrate the entire Federalist vote. But in the remaining districts nothing was done to correct the presence of two Federalist candidates, and the party's vote was badly split, insuring Republican victory. In yet another district the Federalist nominee suddenly withdrew late in the campaign and no replacement could be found before election day.[35]

34. Lewis' address, in *Alexandria Gazette*, March 11, 1815; "A Fairfax Farmer," *ibid.*, March 21, 1815.

35. For the Virginia campaign, see the newspapers for April, 1815, and also the *Virginia Patriot*, November 10, 1813; *Martinsburg Gazette*, January 19, 1815; Robert Saunders to Joseph Prentis, Jr., March 5, 1815, in Prentis Transcripts, UVa; Maria Hamilton Campbell to Jefferson Campbell, January 20, 1815, in David Campbell Papers.

Even with such handicaps, Federalists made their best showing ever in terms of actual votes received. Of a total poll approaching 33,000 (including votes cast for unopposed Republicans) the Federalist candidates took 6,500, or nearly 20 percent, and won three seats. Opposition Republicans polled about 3,700 more votes (11 percent), leaving the administration candidates about 22,500 (or 69 percent). The Federalist total was greater than the vote for presidential candidates in 1800 and 1812 and also exceeded the party's total congressional vote at any past election. This record was more apparent than real, because the Republican vote rose also. In percentage terms the Federalist share fell below both the 1800 and 1812 presidential figures and the 1809 and 1813 congressional contests. The best analysis is to compare the Federalist vote in those few districts and counties that had two-party battles in both 1813 and 1815. On this basis, the party increased its share of the ballots by just over 1 percent. Measured by the number of seats actually won, the result is just the opposite. There had been five Federalist congressmen in 1813 and now there were three.[36]

North Carolina's election, coming four months after Virginia's, was less dominated by the recently ended war and the rejoicing over peace. Little attention was given to the campaign, though it was notable in showing the vigor of Federalism in this Republican state. Eight of the congressional districts had Federalist contestants, the most since 1800, and for one other seat the party supported an opposition Republican. The quality of Federalist nominees was unusually high, including three popular congressmen and three prominent state legislators; and in the Newbern and Fayetteville districts the incumbents were so strongly entrenched that no Republican cared to oppose them.[37] In the voting itself Federalists made a mixed but respectable showing. Although their only two victories were in the unopposed districts, four of the losing candidates received more than 45 percent in their races. In the northeastern Halifax district, where so prominent a man as William R. Davie had lost heavily in 1803, a Federalist legislator came within 170 votes of unseating a veteran Repub-

36. For election returns see the Virginia papers for April–May, 1815, and Robert Porterfield to Harry Heth, May 30, 1815, in Harry Heth Papers, UVa.

37. Raleigh *Star*, August 18, 1815.

lican congressman. Three other districts were lost by less than 350 votes each. Even in areas where no Federalist candidate had dared to run since before 1800, the party did well. It polled 40 percent in the Rockingham district along the Virginia border and about 35 percent against the formidable Nathaniel Macon, never before challenged by a Federalist.

The probable vote in the entire state, including unopposed races, was just over 18,000 (or 35 percent) for the Federalist candidates; about 2,100 (4 percent) for Richard Stanford, the opposition Republican; and just under 32,000 (61 percent) for the administration candidates—the lowest Republican percentages since 1800. If one compares only those counties having two-party races in both 1813 and 1815, the Federalist share of popular votes dropped slightly, from 46.5 percent to 44 percent.[38] In all, this series of elections certainly did not indicate any wave of public disgust toward Federalists because of their wartime activity. If the party was to disappear in the South after 1815, it would do so by choice and not from necessity.

38. Partial election returns are in the newspapers for August–September, 1815, and a sheriff's certificate dated August 17, 1815, in William Gaston Papers.

Chapter 13 WHAT BECAME OF THE SOUTHERN FEDERALISTS?

SURVIVING and even prospering during the war, Federalists nevertheless welcomed the news of peace, even though it eliminated their chief political issue. North Carolina's William Gaston recognized that "the political effect operated by the Peace . . . is more or less favorable to the administration," but there was no immediate exodus of voters from the Federalist ranks.[1] In fact, the first postwar elections showed the party to be nearly as strong in the South as it had ever been since 1800.

If American armies had stormed victoriously through Canada, if the navy had cleared the oceans of British ships, if the negotiators had wrung large concessions from England at Ghent, then the return of peace might have destroyed the Federalist party. Instead, as the Federalist press took pains to make clear, the peace treaty won not a single point that Republicans had claimed as causes of the war. Britain did not back down on impressment or "paper" blockades or any other issue. The blood, the taxes, the ruin of commerce, the deprivation of civil liberties—all had been useless. The war had accom-

1. William Gaston to Morris S. Miller, April 28, 1816, in Gratz Papers, Historical Society of Pennsylvania.

plished nothing. That was the Federalist view, best expressed in the anecdote about an Irishman who was listening to a Republican read the peace treaty. He listened to the reader until the conclusion, and then asked, "*Pray sir, did you read the whole of it*? . . . Is there nothing in it about 'Free Trade and Sailors' Rights?' No said the gentleman, not a word.—*Then what the devil have we been fighting for*? asked Pat. Why for peace said the gentleman. *For pace* reiterated the Irishman! By——, we had pace before the war was commenced."[2]

The continuing popular support of Federalism was clearly shown in the early postwar legislative and congressional elections of 1816 and 1817. Georgia was the exception, as usual; the state had for years been so hopeless that there was not a ripple of Federalist effort. South Carolina was also disappointing. Carolinians had sent one Federalist, Benjamin Huger, to the Fourteenth Congress but had retired him in October, 1816, though the difference in popular vote was not dramatic. However, a Federalist was reelected intendant (mayor) of Charleston by a substantial margin; and the Federalist candidate for Congress in that coastal district, William Crafts, polled 43 percent of the ballots, a marked improvement over previous elections. He was able to capitalize on a split between Republican factions and might have won except that he entered the race only two weeks before the voting.[3] Apart from these three contests, there was little party activity in South Carolina, and the legislature contained no more than the usual handful of Federalists in each house.

North Carolina, which had chosen two Federalists to the Fourteenth Congress in 1815, gave the party a surprising victory in a special election the next year. Richard Stanford, an antiadministration "peace Republican," had for years represented the Hillsborough district in the central Piedmont, fending off both Federalist and proadministration challengers. When he died in 1816 the seat was thrown open to a straight battle between Samuel Dickens, a Federalist legis-

2. "Decius," in *Virginia Patriot*, April 5–26, 1815; Joseph Pearson to constituents, in Raleigh *Star*, March 31, 1815; *Augusta Herald*, March 30, 1815.

3. *Charleston Courier*, September 16, October 5, 17, 21, 1816; Charleston *City Gazette*, October 19, 1816; Charleston *Times*, September 28, 1816; Charleston *Southern Patriot*, October 16, 1816. The *Courier* declined even to take part in the 1816 campaign (October 5 editorial). The *Courier* and the *City Gazette*, October, 1814 and 1816, have congressional returns, and the *Courier*, September of each year, has city results.

lator, and John Craig, a loyal Republican. In an extremely heavy poll Dickens won by two hundred votes, the first time his party had ever captured the district.[4] His victory raised Federalist strength to the same peak reached in 1808 and 1813, but Dickens lost in the regular 1817 elections the following year, again reducing the party to two seats. A veteran Federalist legislator, Jesse Slocumb, won the Newbern seat being vacated by William Gaston; and in the loyal Fayetteville district the incumbent John Culpepper (who had boasted of voting to raise his own salary) lost to fellow party member Alexander McMillan. Elsewhere in the state there probably were no Federalist candidates.[5] The elections therefore indicated a small reduction in party popularity, but nothing to signify a drastic loss of public support. Elections to fill the state house and senate in the fall of 1816 had shown the same pattern; between 35 and 40 percent of each house was Federalist—percentages well above the prewar average.

In Virginia there was also no anti-Federalist reaction in the wake of peace. The party made a strenuous effort in at least half a dozen congressional districts for the April, 1817, elections. The result was quite a turnover of members but no net change in the party balance. Joseph Lewis, Jr., was succeeded in his district near Washington by Charles Fenton Mercer, a capable Federalist who had been influential in the state house of delegates; but Mercer secured only a small majority, probably reflecting the substitution of his less familiar name for that of Lewis. The Berkeley district in the northern valley also remained in friendly hands, as Edward Colston won a hard-fought battle to replace the incumbent Magnus Tate. James Breckinridge's retirement allowed a Republican to win the Botetourt district straddling the middle valley; but this loss was redeemed in extreme northwestern Virginia, where a Federalist was chosen without opposition to replace James Madison's son-in-law. In the East, determined Federalist campaigns in the Northern Neck and Eastern Shore districts fell short because the legislature had possessed foresight enough to drown the few strongly Federalist counties in a surrounding sea of Republican

4. *Raleigh Register*, August 16, 1816; *Charleston Courier*, August 20, 1816; Raleigh *Minerva*, May 24, 1816.

5. *Raleigh Register*, August 8, 15, 22, 29, 1817.

votes.[6] In state legislative elections Federalists held their existing strength of about 20 percent in each house.

As these results show, the Federalist party in the South was not crushed by popular revulsion against the Hartford Convention or antiwar activities generally. The party did gradually disappear, but only by the voluntary decision of its leaders that there was no longer any point in wearing the label *Federalist*. Just when this occurred is uncertain; it was a slow process and probably an unconscious one, decided on an individual basis. Candidates in Georgia had not used the name of Federalist in public since 1800; elsewhere the shift came within a few years after the war. The first positive evidence that southern Federalists were in the process of dissolving their party came in the presidential contest of 1816.

Most northern states that year saw a spirited campaign on behalf of Rufus King, the Federalist presidential candidate, even though he had no chance whatever of national victory against James Monroe. But in the South nothing stirred. Men who had eagerly joined the hopeless fight for anti-Madison electors in 1808 and for Clinton in 1812, now refused to bother. They would not even rally behind a southern Republican, William H. Crawford, who had shown great sectional strength in the Republican caucus earlier in the year. Not that the Federalists were eager for Monroe; many were hostile, and even those who could tolerate the candidate were disgusted with the caucus system of nomination. The press spoke out against this method of nominating presidents, and some North Carolina grand juries even issued official protests.[7]

The Richmond *Virginia Patriot* pleaded for at least a show of oppo-

6. Winchester *Gazette*, April 26, 1817; Leesburg *Genius of Liberty*, March 18, April 14, 22, 29, May 20, 1817; in *Virginia Patriot*, Andrew Stevenson to freeholders of Henrico District, October 2, 1816, and Henry Lee, Jr., to electors of Stafford District, October 31, 1816; *Lynchburg Press*, December 26, 1816; James H. Roy to John Cropper, April 29, 1817, in John Cropper Papers; David J. Russo, "The Southern Republicans and American Political Nationalism, 1815–1825" (Ph.D dissertation, Yale University, 1966), 146–52.

7. "Phocion," in *Virginia Patriot*, September 7, 1816; *Augusta Herald*, March 28, April 25, 1816. Jury presentments are in Morgantown *Monongalia Spectator*, June 8, 1816, and Raleigh *Star*, April 5, May 17, 1816. On the caucus, see William G. Morgan, "The Congressional Nominating Caucus of 1816: The Struggle Against the Virginia Dynasty," *Virginia Magazine of History and Biography*, LXX (1972), 461–75.

sition; Federalists could attract disgruntled Republicans and defeat Monroe. "Forever, we say forever, be scouted the idea of dissolving the federal party." Still, the party *was* dissolving. Just after the congressional caucus, when Crawford's friends were smarting from his narrow defeat by Monroe, some Federalists hoped to fan the discontent into open rebellion. Their newspapers gave wide circulation to the *Exposition*, in which the anti-Monroe Republican congressmen set out their reasons for opposing his nomination. If the Crawford men would carry their dispute into the election, they might receive the aid of Federalist voters, as the Clinton faction had in 1812. For a time this seemed possible; in March there were efforts to unite the anti-Monroe voters of all parties in North Carolina behind one electoral ticket. Yet nothing came of the grand scheme, and even the Federalist newspapers soon fell silent on the subject of the election. In November there was no opposition to Monroe and very few persons voted: in Virginia only 7,000 and in North Carolina about 10,000—far below the normal vote in each. A Republican editor took this as "a pleasing evidence of that harmony which has so happily subsisted between the two parties for some time past."[8]

And why should there not be harmony? There were no longer any major issues separating the national parties. Struggles over domestic policy, except for the bank dispute of 1810–1811, had virtually ceased after Jefferson's first term. The European peace in 1815 ended the only foreign policy dispute of any substance, as Britain and France ceased to violate American commerce, and the specter of Napoleonic conquest no longer frightened the Federalists. On the state level, strong two-party competition—based sometimes on substantial issues—continued in several northern states, but the South was different. Here, the national parties had seldom extended their disagreements to state issues. There was no consistent Federalist or Republican position on such matters as taxation, banking, internal improvements, constitutional revision, slavery, court reform, or any other major local problem. The southern Federalists looked to national politics only,

8. *Virginia Patriot*, May 25, 1816; Charles Pinckney to Thomas Jefferson, August 27 [?], 1816, in Coolidge Collection, MHS; *Charleston Courier*, May 29, 1816; William R. Davie to Gaston, April 7, 1816, in William Gaston Papers; Raleigh *Star*, March 6, 1816; Norfolk *American Beacon*, February 23, November 5, 1815. North Carolina results are in Raleigh *Star*, November 29, 1816; Virginia returns are in Rare Book Room, VSL.

and when national issues ceased to matter, there was no longer any need for a Federalist party. Federalist politicians saw, too, that casting aside old labels and attaching themselves to one or another Republican faction offered a much greater chance for advancement than keeping alive a perpetual minority party based upon dead issues. Left with no great policies to champion and no Jefferson or Napoleon to fight, and being no longer the most useful vehicle for the political ambitions of its leaders, the Federalist party could quietly disappear in the southern states.

Speeding the voluntary dissolution of organized Federalism was a sharp reduction in the strength of the party press. Perhaps one reason for the long-continued (although mostly fruitless) activity of Federalists in the North was the lasting vigor of many party newspapers after 1815. In the South, by contrast, most of the active newspapers changed hands or gave up publishing entirely. When the war began, there were nine leading Federalist organs in the South. In 1816, two of these papers, the *Norfolk Gazette* and the *Wilmington Gazette*, went out of business. The *Carolina Federal Republican* at Newbern followed in 1818. Of the other six, three lost their vigorous partisan editors; Abraham H. Boylan left the Raleigh *Minerva* in 1813, and Philip Wohlhopter and William J. Hobby retired from the Savannah *Columbian Museum* and the *Augusta Herald* in 1817. Only the *Charleston Courier*, the *Virginia Patriot* at Richmond, and the *Martinsburg Gazette* continued until after 1820 under their former operators.[9] New editors were free to avoid the old party battles. They were not bound by years of constant partisan editorializing and were not used to playing the key role in activating the minority party. They had little to gain by adhering to the Federalist cause; this would limit their subscription lists to a smaller and smaller circle. It made good journalistic sense to change a paper's politics when editors changed, or to be neutral if not actively Republican when starting a new paper.

Whether Republicans would allow old party lines to dissolve was quite another question. There was no compelling reason for them to

9. Clarence S. Brigham, *History and Bibliography of American Newspapers, 1690–1820* (2 vols.; Worcester, Mass., 1947), has the editorial histories of the various papers. On the continued vigor of northern Federalist journalism, see Shaw Livermore, *The Twilight of Federalism: The Disintegration of the Federalist Party, 1815–1830* (Princeton, N.J., 1962), especially Chaps. 3 and 4.

do so. Federalist leaders, so long excluded from government and cut off from nearly all patronage, could not easily win wholesale acceptance from the Republicans. Why should a group of politicians already in power voluntarily welcome men who for years had tried to oust them from office? Nationally, there was very little relaxation of barriers. When President Monroe professed the hope that party distinctions would fade, he meant not to create an amalgamated party but to see the Federalists die out entirely, leaving his Republicans as the only organized political group. This did occur in the South, but Federalists elsewhere kept their name and what remained of their organization, contesting and sometimes winning local and state elections into the 1820s. If they themselves kept alive the traditional party warfare, they obviously could expect no offices from Republicans. This was Monroe's conclusion, and in adhering to it for eight years he denied national office to all Federalists—even to southerners, who had ceased firing well before 1820.[10]

Within the South the acceptance of Federalists into the "era of good feeling" was spotty. Traditional party strongholds in Virginia and North Carolina continued to send former Federalists to Congress. Charles Fenton Mercer held his northern Virginia district well into the 1830s; and John Culpepper and Archibald McNeill alternately represented North Carolina's Fayetteville district from 1819 through 1827. Each state also sent one or two other Federalists to Washington during all of these years. In 1817, North Carolina and Virginia together had chosen six Federalists to the Fifteenth Congress; from the Sixteenth through the Nineteenth (elected 1819–1825), they sent four each time, and South Carolina also elected a one-time Federalist to the Nineteenth Congress. The average Federalist delegation from 1816–1817 through 1824–1825 was, therefore, just over 4.5 congressmen compared to the average of 5.5 for the years 1800–1815.[11]

10. Livermore, *Twilight of Federalism*, Chaps. 3 and 4; Harry Ammon, *James Monroe: The Quest for National Identity* (New York, 1971), Chap. 20.

11. *Biographical Directory of the American Congress* (Washington, D.C., 1961), 85–93 and biographies; Emily B. Reynolds and Joan R. Faunt (eds.), *Biographical Directory of the Senate of the State of South Carolina, 1775–1964* (Columbia, S.C., 1964), 37–38; Leesburg *True American*, April–May, 1817 and 1819; Philip F. Wild, "South Carolina Politics: 1816–1833" (Ph.D. dissertation, University of Pennsylvania, 1949); Daniel M. McFarland, "Rip Van Winkle: Political Evolution in North Carolina, 1815–1835" (Ph.D. dissertation, University of Pennsylvania, 1954).

Above the congressional level it had been nearly impossible for a Federalist to win office, and after 1815 it was still difficult at times. Virginia, especially, continued her long-standing policy of excluding Federalist leaders from office, even into the 1840s. No senator, governor, other state officer, or speaker of the house or senate ever came from the ranks of former Federalists. However, the minority was well represented on one occasion of importance. The Virginia constitutional convention of 1829–1830, the culmination of two decades of agitation, contained among its 106 delegates 48 who had been politically active before 1816. Of these, 15 were old Federalists and 33 were former Republicans, a ratio of almost one-third Federalist. This was a higher percentage than the party had ever been able to elect to the legislature during the years after 1800.[12]

The other southern states were more generous in their postwar treatment of Federalists. A former leader of that party, John Elliott of Georgia, sat in the national Senate from 1819 to 1825, and several other Georgia Federalists, one of whom later became governor, were elected judges of the state superior court. The most successful was John Macpherson Berrien, whose Federalist politics had never been a secret. He served as judge of the circuit court until 1821, senator from 1825 to 1829, United States attorney general in 1829–1831, and senator again from 1841 to 1852. He was also briefly a justice of the Georgia Supreme Court in 1845. South Carolina was equally willing to allow some Federalists a share in public life. None was ever governor, but former congressman Abraham Nott served as judge of the circuit court until 1830, Daniel Elliott Huger was a judge of the state superior court in the 1820s and United States senator in 1843–1845, and Benjamin Huger presided over the state senate from 1819 to 1822. Other formerly active Federalists served in various judicial and local positions.

It was in North Carolina that the old party lines were most nearly forgotten. Men who had been firm Federalists before 1816 held almost every office within the gift of the state, including governor, sen-

12. Robert P. Sutton, "The Virginia Constitutional Convention of 1829–1830: A Profile Analysis of Late-Jeffersonian Virginia" (Ph.D. dissertation, University of Virginia, 1967). Party identification of delegates was based on their public or legislative record, 1800–1816.

ator, and many lesser posts. For almost a decade Federalists presided over the state house of commons: James Iredell from 1816 to 1818, Alfred Moore in 1823 and 1824, John Stanly in 1825 and 1826, and Iredell again in 1827. After his terms as speaker, Iredell was elected governor of the state, judge of the superior court, and finally United States senator. Several others, including former congressman William Gaston, Willie P. Mangum, and George E. Badger were also made judges, and the last two went on to serve in the national Senate as well. Federal appointments went to Badger (secretary of the navy), James I. McKay (United States attorney), and John A. Cameron (territorial judge).[13]

As Federalists were abandoning their party label after 1815, they tried to smooth the way by proclaiming loudly that traditional party lines no longer existed. What they meant, of course, was that they *hoped* party lines would not exist. There were still occasional hints of the old partisanship, as when Charles Fenton Mercer told Congress that he had opposed Monroe's election, or when Edward Colston said more bluntly that he felt no respect at all for the president. But many antiadministration Republicans could have made the same confession. The issue of previous party affiliation seldom crept into election campaigns, and the complaint of John A. Cameron, running for the North Carolina assembly in 1820, was unusual: "You are told that I am a *Federalist*! and this with some of those who are opposed to me, is the head and front of my offending." The more prevalent comments were those of conciliation. Mercer, Huger, Gaston, and others disavowed any fixed opposition to the administration; parties, they said, no longer existed. The *Monongalia Spectator* of Morgantown, Virginia, spoke the desire of all Federalists in asking, "Is the mere triumph of a name at an election an object of sufficient magnitude to set one half of our fellow citizens in battle array against the other half? . . . *These parties must, under some other name, be amalgamated*."[14]

13. For the later careers of old Federalists, I have relied heavily on various biographical information such as *Biographical Directory of the American Congress* and the *Dictionary of American Biography*; also, Wayland F. Dunaway, "Charles Fenton Mercer" (M.A. thesis, University of Chicago, 1917), particularly 15–53; Thomas P. Govan, "John M. Berrien and the Administration of Andrew Jackson," *Journal of Southern History*, V (1939), 449–63.

14. *Annals of Congress*, 14th Cong., 1st Sess., 446–47, 699–718, 1053; 14th Cong., 2nd Sess., 499; 15th Cong., 1st Sess., 1262, 1285; 15th Cong., 2nd Sess., 484; John A.

One might expect that the assimilation Federalists hoped for would be hastened by the Republicans' own turn to nationalism after the war. Henry Clay, John C. Calhoun, and other leading southern Republicans brought forward a postwar program of vigorous and expensive government, causing some Federalists to welcome them as men who were renouncing the errors of their predecessors. Federalist editors crowed that "hardly anyone now disputes the superiority of the Washington system of politics." As one said, "A navy *was* a ruinous appendage of monarchy—a navy *is* a desirable thing . . . a standing army *was* the devil all over—a standing army *is* a necessary thing—Taxes *were* a proof of a bad administration—Taxes *are* evidence of the patriotism of the people—a public debt *was* a curse—a public debt *is* a public blessing."[15]

Nevertheless, it would be misleading to judge the Federalist attitude by such comments. If the nationalism advanced by Clay, Calhoun, and company after 1815 was "neo-Federalism," then the southern Federalists became "neo-Republicans," for they opposed nearly every point of this program. The Fourteenth and Fifteenth Congresses (1815–1819) faced a variety of issues involving the question of nationalism. Men who followed Clay and Calhoun's vision of a strong, vigorous, growing nation approved such things as internal improvements at federal expense, a new Bank of the United States, a protective tariff, the direct tax, a large peacetime army, rapid admission of new states into the Union, and Andrew Jackson's invasion of Spanish Florida. Hamilton himself would have endorsed nearly all these measures except the speedy admission of new states. The southern Federalists did not. The only feature of postwar nationalism that they found at all attractive was the internal improvement program. They cast a majority of their votes against the bank, against the tariff, against the direct tax, against a large army, against early admission of Mississippi, and against Jackson's military operation. Of the thirteen southern Federalists who served in these two postwar Congresses, only one, Ben-

---

Cameron to the voters of Fayetteville, in Raleigh *Minerva*, July 7, 1820; Morgantown *Monongalia Spectator*, July 13, 1816.

15. *Annals of Congress*, 14th Cong., 1st Sess., 456; *Augusta Herald*, November 30, 1815, April 18, 1816; *Virginia Patriot*, April 17, 1816.

jamin Huger, nearly always sided with the nationalists. Three others—Gaston, Colston, and Mercer—wavered back and forth depending on the issue, and the other nine voted almost every time against nationalism and in favor of a small, inexpensive, restricted central government. They were voting like a Jefferson of the 1790s, even as many Republicans were new-modeling themselves after Hamilton.

At the core of the Clay-Calhoun program were three primary goals: a system of federal internal improvements, a new national bank, and a protective tariff. In approving the first of these, the southern Federalists acted as much from local economic interests as from general sympathy with the nationalists. In the Fourteenth and Fifteenth Congresses, there were six Virginia Federalists, all from the northwestern part of the state, which most needed better roads and navigation. They consistently voted for federal internal improvements, and Mercer, who was one of them, even thought Calhoun's Bonus Bill did not go far enough. On this particular question only, these men took a broad view of the Constitution and spent some time refuting strict-constructionist arguments against congressional financing. Huger also upheld the nationalist view on this topic as on most others, but the six North Carolinians were divided. Three of them, perhaps recognizing their state's desperate need for internal improvements of all kinds, joined the Virginians in urging congressional action. The other three voted with that group of southern Republicans who, from motives of strict construction or simple parsimony, disapproved a federal scheme for better transportation.[16]

Once they left the subject of internal improvements, the southern Federalists became almost entirely negative. The new bank was the most clearly Hamiltonian nationalist proposal, and their opposition to it might seem extraordinary. But the bank was the one measure not entirely free of traditional party considerations, because one-fifth of its directors were to be chosen by the president of the United States. Thus the nation's premier financial institution would be influenced,

16. *Annals of Congress*, 14th Cong., 2nd Sess., 922, 934, 1062; 15th Cong., 1st Sess., 1278–82, 1284–1318, 1340–50, 1384–86, 1388–89, 1398, 1400, 1657, 1664, 1679; 15th Cong., 2nd Sess., 514, 530; Russo, "Southern Republicans," 129–44. Calhoun's Bonus Bill would have converted the "bonus" that the Bank of the United States paid the government for its charter into a fund for internal improvements.

and possibly controlled, by Republican politicians. The unanimous Federalist support for the original Bank of the United States had derived not only from its financial usefulness but also from the knowledge that its operations were directed by Federalists.

Opposition to the new bank came not from a sudden shift of opinion on its financial or constitutional propriety but from the political fear that it would become a powerful Republican machine. William Gaston, among others, asked the House to drop the idea of government directors who would inevitably be appointed, not for business ability, but for their political service, past or to come. The other southerners agreed, and all voted with Gaston in a vain attempt to strike out the five presidential directors. This failing, they turned against the bank itself, which they now regarded as a political more than a financial institution. The roll call on final passage of the bank bill therefore showed an unusual result. In favor were the "new nationalist" Republicans. Opposed on constitutional grounds, from dislike of all banks, or from personal interest in state bank stock, were the southern "old Republicans," joined by the half-dozen representatives of the supposedly Hamiltonian Federalist party.[17]

Even after its creation, the second bank had few friends among the southern Federalists, and sometimes their opposition was framed in economic rather than in political terms. When the bank asked Congress for power to expand its operations early in 1818, none of the six southerners who had opposed its formation two years earlier remained in the House; but the six new Federalists were equally hostile to the institution. They joined other antibank congressmen in rejecting the proposed expansion. Charles Fenton Mercer feared that the bank might become too powerful and even drive state banks out of existence.[18]

The next year, after the Panic of 1819 was underway—its origin traced by some to the bank's sudden contraction of credit—there was serious talk of repealing the charter entirely. Most Federalists were

17. *Annals of Congress*, 14th Cong., 1st Sess., 1147–48, 1210–11, 1219; Gaston to Miller, March 12, 1816, in Gratz Papers; Raymond Walters, Jr., "The Origins of the Second Bank of the United States," *Journal of Political Economy*, LIII (1945), 115–31; Samuel Hopkins to John Cropper, November 6, 1814, in John Cropper Papers; Russo, "Southern Republicans," 101–10.

18. *Annals of Congress*, 15th Cong., 1st Sess., 1752–55, 1762.

not willing to go so far; they voted with the great majority of congressmen to allow the bank's continuation. But one southerner, James Pindall of Virginia, broke with his colleagues and used remarkably un-Hamiltonian language in attacking the bank. He objected in principle to corporate charters that granted privileges to a favored few, and he hoped that the House would not allow the establishment of a moneyed aristocracy. Answering those who said Congress had no right to repeal a charter once granted, Pindall warned that "this bank, if not subject to the legislative authority of congress, is incapable of subjection by any power on earth"; and he proposed sternly that "if this great corporation has thus become too powerful for the Government, and acknowledges itself subject to no law, and yet retains all its capacity to sin, I would aim a blow at its existence." Forget the year of the speech and the politics of the speaker, and it might have been Andrew Jackson giving the bank its death blow in 1832.[19]

In addition to creating the new bank and improving transportation, postwar nationalists hoped to protect American industries from foreign competition by imposing heavy duties on certain imported goods. Such a tariff would furnish protection and also provide revenue for the expensive transportation projects and the large military force that the nationalists wanted. Did the Federalists welcome this conversion of onetime Jeffersonian agrarians to the gospel of Hamilton? They did not. Although many southern Republicans spoke and voted in favor of protection, not one of the thirteen southern Federalists in the two postwar Congresses would endorse the idea. Samuel Dickens of North Carolina was not present to vote on this question, and the two Virginians, Colston and Pindall, divided their votes (though both were inclined against protection). All the remaining ten, including the otherwise nationalistic Huger, were solidly opposed. Huger even spoke several times on the floor against high tariffs that would tax farmers and consumers for the benefit of merchants and give a monopoly to a few large manufacturers. The rest held the same view, voting heavily against high duties on woolens, cottons, iron, and sugar, and against the entire tariff bill on its final passage. In the Fifteenth

19. *Annals of Congress*, 15th Cong., 2nd Sess., 1268–71, 1411–12.

Congress there were a few individual votes for high duties on iron, but again all the Federalists opposed the final tariff bill itself.[20]

Aside from these three great programs, several other issues tested the strength of national- versus state-minded sentiment. Southern Federalists were far more often found among the ardent antinationalists than were the bulk of southern Republicans. In early 1816, for instance, the first important matter that the Fourteenth Congress had to decide was whether to continue the wartime direct tax on property. It was an unpopular levy but a lucrative one, and the nationalists wanted to keep the flow of revenue undiminished for a time. As William Gaston, a reluctant supporter of the tax, explained, the heavy national debt made a "vigorous system of finance" necessary. In the late 1790s Federalists had defended such a tax as a powerful force for creating national feeling and a way to lessen the government's dependence on customs duties. Gaston and Huger joined the nationalist Republicans in wishing to keep the direct tax, but the other four southern Federalists fought to repeal it entirely.[21]

One of the reasons advocates of strong government needed high taxes was their insistence upon keeping peacetime military strength at a respectable level. This was hard to accomplish, given the traditional American hostility toward a standing army (encouraged greatly by the Republicans themselves at an earlier day). In the spring of 1815, just as the war officially ended, there was a strong effort to cut military expenses by reducing the peacetime army from 10,000 to 6,000 men and by halving the appropriation for artillery horses. Every southern Federalist who voted favored both reductions. A year later, four voted also to slash the army's ordnance appropriation, with only Gaston of North Carolina against. In the Fifteenth Congress the new delegation of six Federalists was scarcely more favorable to the military than their predecessors. Altogether in the three Congresses from

20. *Annals of Congress*, 14th Cong., 1st Sess., 676, 1258, 1274, 1312–13, 1315, 1326–27, 1336–37, 1347–49, 1352, 1438; 15th Cong., 1st Sess., 1736, 1741–43; Norris W. Preyer, "Southern Support of the Tariff of 1816: A Reappraisal," *Journal of Southern History*, XXV (1959), 306–22.

21. *Annals of Congress*, 14th Cong., 1st Sess., 871–73, 875, 967, 979, 1135; Norman K. Risjord, *The Old Republicans: Southern Conservatism in the Age of Jefferson* (New York, 1965), 191–92.

Table 3* **Votes of Southern Federalists on Nationalist Measures in Congress, 1815–1818**[23]

	Internal Imprvmts	*Bank*	*Tariff*	*Direct Tax*	*Large Army*	*Invade Florida*	*Admit Miss.*
Breckinridge (VA)	NATL	anti	anti	anti	anti	—	anti
Colston (VA)	NATL	anti	anti	—	NATL	anti	—
Culpepper (NC)	NATL	anti	anti	anti	anti	—	—
Dickens (NC)	anti	—	—	—	—	—	anti
Gaston (NC)	NATL	anti	anti	NATL	NATL	—	anti
Huger (SC)	NATL	NATL	anti	NATL	—	—	NATL
Lewis (VA)	NATL	anti	anti	anti	anti	—	anti
McMillan (NC)	—	—	—	—	—	—	—
Mercer (VA)	NATL	anti	anti	—	NATL	anti	—
Owen (NC)	anti	anti	anti	—	—	NATL	—
Pindall (VA)	NATL	anti	anti	—	—	anti	—
Slocumb (NC)	NATL	anti	anti	—	anti	anti	—
Stewart (NC)	anti	anti	anti	—	anti	anti	—
Tate (VA)	NATL	—	anti	anti	anti	—	—
Nationalists	10	1	0	2	3	1	1
Antinationalists	3	10	12	4	6	5	4

*Each congressman is categorized on each issue according to the way he cast a preponderance of his votes. See Note 24 for the list of roll calls involved.

1815 through 1818, ten Federalist members cast a majority of their votes against a large army while only four favored it. Here, surely, was one of the first requirements of a nationalist, whether of the Hamiltonian or the Clay-Calhoun variety—that he be willing to support a well-equipped army for defense. In opposing such plans, southern Federalist congressmen stood with the small-government, states' rights men and against the advocates of postwar nationalism.[22]

Perhaps the most spectacular expression of American national feeling after the war was Andrew Jackson's raid into Spanish Florida

22. *Annals of Congress*, 13th Cong., 3rd Sess., 1251–52, 1256; 14th Cong., 1st Sess., 975, 977–78; 15th Cong., 2nd Sess., 457–60, 484, 535, 1165.

23. The following roll call votes were used in the construction of the table (all citations are to the *Annals of Congress*): internal improvements—14th Cong., 2nd Sess., 922, 934, 1062; 15th Cong., 1st Sess., 1384–86; 1388–89; Bank of United States—14th Cong., 1st Sess., 1211, 1219; 15th Cong., 1st Sess., 1762; 15th Cong., 2nd Sess., 1411–12; tariff—14th Cong., 1st Sess., 1312–13, 1315, 1326, 1336–37, 1347–49, 1352; 15th Cong., 1st Sess., 1741, 1743; direct tax—14th Cong., 1st Sess., 875, 967, 969; large army—13th Cong., 3rd Sess., 1251–52, 1256; 14th Cong., 1st Sess., 975, 977–78; 15th Cong., 2nd Sess., 1165; Florida invasion—15th Cong., 2nd Sess., 1135–36, 1138; admission of Mississippi—14th Cong., 1st Sess., 1301; 14th Cong., 2nd Sess., 1026–27.

in 1818. He was in search of hostile Indians, and he captured several Spanish posts. Political opponents of Jackson, joined by those who feared serious trouble with Spain, put themselves on record denouncing the invasion. They brought forward two resolutions censuring Jackson and condemning his capture of Pensacola, but both were buried by the votes of expansionists, who saw Jackson's incursion as a broad hint to Spain that she had best surrender Florida. Among the minority who disapproved of Jackson's raid were five of the six Federalists in the Fifteenth Congress. James Owen of North Carolina supported the general, but Virginia's Colston and Mercer accused Jackson of military usurpation and of waging an unconstitutional, undeclared war against the Indians and Spanish.[24]

The picture, then, of southern Federalist congressmen in the era of postwar nationalism is of men who resisted the new spirit of the age and shrank from an active and expensive central government. They joined the "Old Republicans" in an almost Jeffersonian distrust of power, while most of Jefferson's own party, North and South, rushed to strengthen the federal role in American life. Why should this be so? There is no truly satisfying explanation for the sudden burst of antinational feeling in a party that, as late as 1811, defended the First Bank of the United States in strongly Hamiltonian terms.

Two approaches to understanding the postwar Federalist attitude suggest themselves. To begin with, "power makes policy." When in office, Federalists might well have supported vigorous measures that they would have decried in a government controlled by their opponents. Certainly the Republicans displayed this characteristic in reverse. As the "outs" before 1800, they bitterly attacked many of the same measures they supported as the "ins" later. It was only natural, then, for Federalists to favor a bank controlled by members of their party in 1810–1811 and to oppose a similar institution in 1815–1816 because it was Republican-controlled. On several occasions after 1800, one could see the southern Federalists taking the "popular" or "country" side of issues, claiming to defend individual liberties and pocketbooks against oppressive or expensive Republican measures. This attitude stemmed partly from sheer politics but also from a genuine

24. *Annals of Congress*, 15th Cong., 2nd Sess., 446–47, 797–820, 824–31, 1135–36, 1138.

fear that Republicans were mere place-hunters devoid of principle, who actually might harm the public for party benefit. Even some Republicans shared this concern, as the growing uneasiness of the "Old Republicans" indicates. In opposing nationalist programs after 1815, therefore, Federalists were in part simply showing that they still feared the exercise of expanded governmental power by "demagogic" Republican politicians.

The second explanation for postwar antinationalism is that the Federalist congressmen were simply "voting their districts." Most of the congressmen from Virginia and North Carolina, Republicans as well as Federalists, were suspicious of nationalism in these years. The great surge of national feeling came from elsewhere—South Carolina, Georgia, and the Southwest. On the three great postwar issues—bank, tariff, and internal improvements—the southern members voted thus: Federalists (all from Virginia and North Carolina except one), 6 for and 11 against; Republicans from those two states, 32 for and 41 against; Republicans from South Carolina, Georgia, Kentucky, Tennessee, and Louisiana, 48 for and 27 against.[25] Foreign policy had always been the one great unifying bond for Federalists everywhere; on domestic issues the party was often divided after 1800. Even within the southern states one could seldom find Federalists standing together on a local problem. Each legislator represented his county or his conscience; there was almost no effort to think or act together as Federalists on a state issue. After the war, each congressman did what he thought best for his district. When so many Virginia and North Carolina Republicans were driven to oppose the plans of their party's most active leaders in 1815 and 1816, it is hardly surprising that Federalists from the same two states, under no constraint of party loyalty to Clay or Calhoun, might also oppose.

Neither of these explanations is completely convincing, and one cannot even know whether the antinationalist congressmen truly reflected the opinions of ordinary southern Federalist voters. A quick but misleading test would be to ask whether the congressmen were reelected. In fact, none of the seven Federalists serving in the Four-

25. *Annals of Congress*, 14th Cong., 1st Sess., 1219, 1352; 14th Cong., 2nd Sess., 934.

teenth Congress returned to the Fifteenth; four retired, two lost to Republicans, and one was unseated by another Federalist. At the next elections in 1818–1819 three of the new representatives were returned, one was defeated by a fellow Federalist, and two retired. In spite of appearances, this rapid turnover probably was not a repudiation of the sitting members in either Congress, since the new Federalists elected in 1816–1817 and 1818–1819 were at least as much opposed to nationalism as their predecessors.

From their voting records in Congress and their often expressed hope of political acceptance in the years of "good feeling," one might expect the Federalist leaders to move wholesale into the Crawford campaign during the presidential election of 1824. Until the mid-1820s few Federalist politicians, despite their claims that party distinctions were now meaningless, had been able to advance into the Republican ranks. By about 1822 or 1823 this rigid attitude against Federalist converts was decaying. The eagerness of half a dozen prominent Republicans for the presidency and the obvious impending breakdown of the caucus as an acceptable means of deciding the succession, made each candidate's supporters willing to accept allies wherever they could be found. In this highly competitive situation the former "exclusive Republicans" decided that Federalist votes were as good, and Federalist leaders as able, as any others. As the end of Monroe's term approached, southern politicians began sorting themselves into more or less cohesive groups behind William H. Crawford, John Quincy Adams, Andrew Jackson, and Henry Clay.

As the leading exponent of limited federal government at a time when most other candidates were thoroughgoing nationalists, Crawford should have been especially attractive to the antinationalist southern Federalists. Yet there was no general movement of ex-Federalists into his camp; if anything, most appeared aloof or even hostile to Crawford. Virginia's state legislative caucus, for example, nominated Crawford by an overwhelming vote of 112 to 6 each for Adams, Clay, and Jackson, and 4 for Nathaniel Macon of North Carolina. However, attendance was low; nearly a third of the members stayed away from the caucus. The twenty-five most heavily Federalist counties (out of one hundred in the state) cast only twenty-six caucus votes for Crawford, while thirty-six legislators were absent or supported other candidates. The remainder of the state, containing very few old Federalists, was heavily for Crawford by a margin of 86 to 15, with thirty-five absentees. When supporters of each candidate drew up their statewide electoral tickets, the same pattern emerged. Three Federalist names appeared on the Clay ticket, two on Adams' list, one on Jackson's, but none on the list of twenty-four Crawford electors.[26]

In the other southern states information is scantier, but clearly the Federalists were dividing their loyalties and Crawford fared poorly. Two of North Carolina's most prominent ex-congressmen, William Gaston and John Stanly, enlisted in the Adams campaign, and Jackson's statewide effort was led by another Federalist, William Polk of Raleigh. The only Crawford organizer who had Federalist ties was young Willie P. Mangum, who had come of age too late to have been an active partisan. South Carolina Federalists were rather quiet, but Charleston's editor-politician, William Crafts, was a vigorous Adams supporter in a heavily Jacksonian state. Even in Georgia, John Macpherson Berrien and Senator John Elliott were for Crawford, but the only other Federalist active in presidential politics, John M. Dooly, was a Jackson man.[27]

The popular vote in Virginia and North Carolina bore out the impression of Federalism divided but generally hostile to Crawford. Virginia gave the Georgian a handsome victory with 8,500 votes (56 percent) to 3,500 for Adams, 3,000 for Jackson, and a few hundred for Clay. The twenty-five most heavily Federalist counties were only 35 percent for Crawford while the fifty most heavily Republican counties gave him 67 percent of their votes. Adams ran up 30 percent of the to-

26. Horace L. Bachelder, "The Presidential Election of 1824 in Virginia" (M.A. thesis, Duke University, 1942), especially 30–32, 37, 57, 67, 71, 80–81; Francis T. Brooke to Henry Clay, July 12, 1824, in James F. Hopkins (ed.), *The Papers of Henry Clay* (5 vols. to date; Lexington, Ky., 1959–), III, 793.

27. Albert R. Newsome, *The Presidential Election of 1824 in North Carolina* (Chapel Hill, N.C., 1939); McFarland, "Rip Van Winkle," 160–82; Joseph H. Schauinger, *William Gaston, Carolinian* (Milwaukee, Wis., 1949), 112, 114; William Polk Papers, NCDAH, contain many letters of Polk's pro-Jackson activity; Wild, "South Carolina Politics," 222–25; Josiah S. Johnston to Henry Clay, August 24, 1824, in Hopkins (ed.), *Papers of Henry Clay*, III, 818; Jack N. Averitt, "The Democratic Party in Georgia, 1824–1837" (Ph.D. dissertation, University of North Carolina, 1957), 175, 180–81.

tal in the Federalist areas but only 15 percent in the most strongly Republican counties, and Jackson received 26 percent in the Federalist counties but only 17 percent in the Republican. Overall, only thirty of Virginia's counties were carried by someone other than Crawford; sixteen of these were in the top twenty-five Federalist counties and only seven were in the bottom fifty. The situation in North Carolina was more complicated, since the anti-Crawford forces combined in a coalition People's ticket whose electors carried the state by 20,000 to 15,000 and finally voted for Jackson. The sixteen most strongly Federalist counties went 67 percent for the People's ticket, and the thirty most strongly Republican counties were almost evenly divided. It is impossible to distinguish accurately between the Jackson and Adams supporters in the People's campaign, but contemporary opinion and a few unofficial polls agreed that in the old Federalist areas most of the People's ticket voters were Adams men.[28]

After 1824 John Quincy Adams continued to hold the loyalty of a sizable number of ordinary Federalists, but the leadership gravitated toward Jackson. There were six former Federalists serving in the Nineteenth Congress (elected 1824–1825), of whom one may be called a wavering Adams supporter. Another was a moderate Jacksonian and the remaining four were all strong Jackson men. In the next Congress there were three steadfast Jacksonians, one moderate, and again only one halfhearted Adams man. By the next presidential election, in 1828, Jackson displayed a remarkable ability to obtain public support from old Federalist partisans. He carried both Georgia and South Carolina with hardly a dissenting voice. Joining his crusade were the few remaining Federalist leaders—John M. Dooly, Augustin S. Clayton, John Macpherson Berrien, and William Schley in Georgia; William Drayton and Daniel Elliott Huger in South Carolina; William Polk, John Stanly, James Iredell, Jr., and James I. McKay in North Carolina. Only in Virginia did the leading Federalists remain distant from Jackson.

The popular vote in 1828 was somewhat different from the leadership alignment. Georgia was almost unanimous for Jackson, and he carried North Carolina by better than three to one and Virginia by

28. The popular vote returns are in Bachelder, "Election of 1824," 80–81, and Newsome, *Presidential Election of 1824*, 156–63.

nearly two to one. The legislative vote for electors in South Carolina was also overwhelmingly for Jackson. Examining the popular returns in the two northernmost states, however, it is clear that Adams was supported proportionally far better in Federalist areas than in Republican. He carried almost half the traditionally Federalist counties in both Virginia and North Carolina but won almost none of the traditionally Republican counties.[29]

Beyond 1828 the impact of Federalism in the South faded rapidly. Not only did fewer and fewer people survive who still remembered the partisan conflicts of an earlier age, but also the remaining Federalist leaders and voters diffused their support between both the new parties, Whig and Democratic. The initial favorable reaction that Jackson made on some ex-Federalists soured within a few years; like Adams, he ended his term with less support from this group than when he began. In Georgia, John Macpherson Berrien, a member of Jackson's own cabinet, split with the president to help form the opposition party; in North Carolina, Willie P. Mangum did the same. By the mid-1830s Federalist influence was spread rather evenly between the two new parties. If one examines the leadership, there were nearly two dozen former Federalists who held high position in the 1830s and 1840s. Exactly half became Whigs and half Democrats. On the local level the same division occurred. The following table shows the relationship between Federalist voting strength in 1800–1816 and Whig voting in 1836–1848, by county. In North Carolina the old Federalist and old Republican counties were not very different from each other politically in the 1840s; in Georgia the old Federalist areas were actually less Whig-oriented than the Republican areas. Only Virginia showed a clear but marginal correlation between Federalist and Whig voting. In sum, there was no great connection between Federalism

29. George R. Nielsen, "The Indispensable Institution: The Congressional Party During the Era of Good Feelings" (Ph.D. dissertation, University of Iowa, 1968), 186–90 and 248–52, discusses the factional affiliation of members in the Adams years; Averitt, "Democratic Party in Georgia," 205–206, 212, 239, 456–57; Wild, "South Carolina Politics," 372–73; William S. Hoffman, *Andrew Jackson and North Carolina Politics* (Chapel Hill, N.C., 1958), Chap. 3; Paul Murray, *The Whig Party in Georgia, 1825–1853* (Chapel Hill, N.C., 1948), especially Chaps. 1–3; Charles S. Sydnor, *The Development of Southern Sectionalism, 1819–1848* (Baton Rouge, 1948), 192–94, 342–43; McFarland, "Rip Van Winkle," 228–42.

before 1816 and Whiggery after 1836. Even the mild relationship evident in Virginia may be related more to sectional than partisan causes. In general, southern Federalist voters (or their descendants) were absorbed with equal facility by both the new major parties.[30]

Table 4 **Relation of Federalist Strength, 1800–1816 and Whig Strength, 1836–1848**[31]

	Virginia			*North Carolina*			*Georgia*		
Counties Ranked by Fed. Vote	*Median Whig %*	*Number of Counties Whig*	*Dem*	*Median Whig %*	*Number of Counties Whig*	*Dem*	*Median Whig %*	*Number of Counties Whig*	*Dem*
Top fourth	56%	16	8	65%	12	4	52%	6	3
Next fourth	49%	10	14	45%	5	11	61%	5	3
Bottom half	45%	16	33	57%	19	11	61%	15	2

30. The debate over the relationship between the Whig and Democratic parties and the old Federalist and Republican parties is still unresolved. Studies such as Donald B. Cole, *Jacksonian Democracy in New Hampshire, 1800–1851* (Cambridge, Mass., 1970), Chap. 6; and Mark H. Haller, "The Rise of the Jackson Party in Maryland, 1820–1829," *Journal of Southern History*, XXVIII (1962), 307–26, find the Jacksonians strongest in the old Republican counties and the National Republicans and Whigs carrying the old Federalist areas. Others, such as Richard P. McCormick, "Party Formation in New Jersey in the Jackson Era," *Proceedings of the New Jersey Historical Society*, LXXXIII (1965), 161–73, and Max R. Williams, "The Foundations of the Whig Party in North Carolina," *North Carolina Historical Review*, XLVII (1970), 115–29, find the old Federalist leaders becoming Jacksonians, though they draw no conclusions about the mass of voters.

31. Popular vote for the 1836–48 elections is from W. Dean Burnham, *Presidential Ballots, 1836–1892* (Baltimore, Md., 1955).

FOUR The Southern Federalists in State Politics

Chapter 14 THE VIRGINIA FEDERALISTS

IN A sense, there was no single southern Federalist party; there were four individual state parties, each existing in a different political climate. The Virginia Federalists claimed among their number two of the nation's most prominent figures, George Washington and John Marshall. Unfortunately for the Federalists, Virginia was also home to the Republican national leaders—Jefferson, Madison, Monroe, Giles, and Randolph. Furthermore, Washington was dead by 1800 and Marshall was politically muted as chief justice, while these Republicans were still active men of influence in state politics.

In numbers alone the Federalists were not particularly starved for talent; but the list of leading Republican names was well balanced by section, occupation, and previous political alignment, whereas the Federalist leaders were not representative even of the political elite, much less of the general electorate. The typical Virginia Federalist who put his name forward for Congress or presidential elector, became a veteran in the assembly, or organized his county for the party, was a town-dwelling lawyer or commercial man. He lived in the western half of the state or in the large eastern towns, and if he was politically active in the 1780s he had supported the movement for a stronger

Constitution. The large majority of Virginia voters who were farmers, who lived in rural areas east of the Blue Ridge, or who had opposed the Constitution, could seldom identify with men in the higher circles of Federalism. In the entire eastern half of the state, prominent Federalists were concentrated in four localities only: Richmond, Norfolk, the Eastern Shore, and the vicinity of Alexandria. Outside these centers, almost none of the chief men in eastern politics could be found on the Federalist side. This dearth of local talent in the Tidewater and Piedmont, damaging enough in itself, was made a crippling handicap by Virginia's political system.

To begin with, elections for the legislature and Congress were by voice vote at the county courthouse. With the candidates or their representatives present and the sheriff presiding, each voter declared his choice aloud, and it was then entered next to his name on a tally sheet. Every individual had to face the consequences if his vote displeased his neighbors. Where the political elite was divided between parties, the common man could be sure of having some influential men on his side whichever way he voted; but if all the prominent citizens were Republicans, any ordinary farmer wishing to vote a Federalist ticket could be made to feel quite uncomfortable. Since the political leaders also dominated the county's social and economic life, even a man of some standing might quail from declaring Federalist opinions if he found his "betters" to be unanimously Republican.[1]

Fear of censure was not the only thing inclining lonely Federalists to keep quiet in the Republican countryside. There was also the county court to think of. Governing nearly every aspect of local affairs and acting as a combined executive, legislative, and judicial body, the court was a self-perpetuating closed corporation. Its members included most of the prominent men in a county (providing their politics were correct), and vacancies were filled nominally by the governor but actually on recommendation of the court itself. If a sizable fraction of the larger planters, merchants, and professional men was Federalist, the party could perhaps count on some representation in the court. However, if all the justices were vigorous Republicans, the

1. On the deferential nature of Virginia politics in the early Republic, see Sydnor, *Gentlemen Freeholders*, and Beeman, *Old Dominion*.

handful of Federalists in a rural county might fear reprisals if they openly supported such a despised party.[2]

Of course any hint of pressure from the county court would be unnecessary if there were no Federalist candidates to vote for. This was very often the case in the Piedmont and Tidewater, illustrating another handicap associated with the lack of county-level leadership. The inconvenience of officeholding and the expense of campaigning made it necessary for legislative and congressional candidates to be men of at least moderate substance. If there were none such in a county or congressional district who were willing to stand forth as Federalists, then the party could never run a candidate in that area. The seriousness of this problem may be seen by tabulating the number of Federalist congressional nominees by region from 1803 through 1815. West of the Blue Ridge, Federalists ran in twenty-eight of forty-four possible contests, and sometimes there were even two men vying for a single seat. In the five eastern districts where at least a significant minority of the political elite was Federalist, the party ran sixteen candidates in thirty-five elections. In the remainder of the Tidewater and Piedmont—about half of the entire state—only four Federalists ever offered for Congress in the seventy-seven separate district elections.[3]

Even if more Federalists had run in the eastern congressional districts, they would have found it difficult to canvass effectively in those counties that had no local party leadership. It was, of course, possible for a would-be congressman to mail out or nail up broadsides announcing his intentions. He could even make a personal tour of the weaker counties, speaking at various occasions or going from farm to farm. But the most important part of electioneering in early nineteenth-century Virginia was to gain the support of a few leading men in each county. Enlisting a number of the local elite was a tremendous advantage in any election; and having the support of no prominent man in an entire county was usually fatal. Even if a Feder-

2. On county courts and their dominant role in local politics, see Tadahisa Kuroda, "The County Court System of Virginia from the Revolution to the Civil War" (Ph.D. dissertation, Columbia University, 1969), Chap. 3.

3. Names and affiliations of candidates may be found in the various Virginia newspapers in February–May of odd-numbered years.

alist launched an active campaign for Congress and won the endorsement of party leaders in his own area, he might lose the election if no one would sponsor him in the heavily Republican counties of the district.[4]

In addition to the handicaps imposed on Federalists by the nature of Virginia's political system, Republicans added some of their own devising. The general ticket for president was probably the worst of these.[5] Although Federalists won a majority of votes in several electoral districts in 1800 and 1812, and the anti-Madison ticket backed by Federalists carried some districts in 1808, the General Ticket Law submerged these local majorities and produced a unanimously Republican statewide electoral vote. Since the Federalists had no chance whatever to carry the whole state, they became understandably apathetic in presidential campaigns. On the Eastern Shore nearly 700 voters might turn out for congressional or legislative contests, usually dividing nine to one or more for the Federalist nominees. In the presidential election of 1800 only 476 voted, and only 505 showed up in 1812. There was little point in making a long trip to the courthouse when everyone knew that the Eastern Shore vote would inevitably be swamped by the Republicans elsewhere.[6]

The General Ticket Law also required every voter to cast a written ballot containing the names of all presidential electors he favored. It was not enough merely to know that John Adams or Rufus King was the Federalist candidate for president; one must know all the names on the electoral ticket. Of course lists of electors could be prepared ahead of time by party workers and passed out on election day, so persons who had no idea of the identity of the Federalist electors could still vote for them. This, however, required some person in each county to write to one of the party newspapers or to a political friend for a copy of the electoral ticket, and then to produce a sufficient number of ballots for his county. If no one was willing to do this, then no votes

4. See the source in Note 1 and also Anthony F. Upton, "The Road to Power in Virginia in the Early Nineteenth Century," *Virginia Magazine of History and Biography*, LXII (1954), 259–80, and "Political Structure."

5. The background and passage of the General Ticket Law may be found in Rose, *Prologue to Democracy*, 227–28, 261–64, and Beeman, *Old Dominion*, 215–16.

6. Federalist defeatism may have been balanced by Republican overconfidence, since there is not much difference between Federalist and Republican counties in the falloff of votes from congressional to presidential years.

could be cast for the Federalist presidential candidate in that county. The lateness with which the party nominated its electors compounded the problem of preparing and distributing ballots, and in 1800 there was not a single Federalist vote for president in six of the state's counties. In 1808, eleven counties cast no votes for either of the anti-Madison electoral tickets, and in 1812 nineteen counties reported no votes for Rufus King.[7]

So effective was the general ticket in stifling Federalist efforts in presidential elections that some feared the Republicans would impose a statewide ballot for Congress also.[8] Congressmen in several states were chosen at large, usually to the detriment of the minority party, but none had more than half a dozen seats. For Virginia to elect her nearly two dozen congressmen in a statewide ballot would have been politically impossible. Too many local Republican interests would have been offended by being deprived of an individual member in touch with the particular desires of a single district.

Although Republicans could not use the general ticket to eliminate Federalists from Congress, they did the next best thing by gerrymandering individual districts. In the 1801 redistricting, western Virginia (with a high proportion of Federalists) was given only six congressional seats, although its white population entitled it to eight. Even in the overrepresented east, Federalist areas received short shrift. The two Eastern Shore counties, which were heavily Federalist and would have dominated any normal-sized congressional district, were grouped with enough new Republican counties to reduce greatly the chance of sending a Federalist to Congress. The addition of Republican voters pushed the district's federal population to 42,000, compared with the state average of 33,000. The Federalists complained, but to no avail. The same sort of gerrymandering occurred following the 1810 census. After a heated debate in the lower house, one disgusted Federalist delegate protested that nearly "every alteration made in the Districts West of the Blue Ridge . . . is believed to have been the result of calculation, and designed to be subserviant to the views of the dominant party," and that rearrangements in the eastern

7. Official returns are in the Rare Book Room, VSL.

8. H. Brooke to Leven Powell, December 22, 1800, in Leven Powell Papers, LC; John Marshall to C. C. Pinckney, November 21, 1802, photostat in Pinckney Family Papers.

districts, "although supported and inforced by every claim of justice and equality, were refused from the same motives."[9]

A similar malapportionment, though not deliberately partisan in origin, reduced Federalist strength in the legislature. Virginia's constitution assigned each county two members of the house of delegates, regardless of population. Small eastern counties, which after 1800 happened to be strongly Republican, had an equal representation with larger western, Federalist-leaning counties. Even with an equal apportionment of members by white population, Federalists would never have approached a majority in the house, but they would have enjoyed greater influence than under the existing system. In 1800, Federalists had only 27 percent of the house members, but they represented counties with 33 percent of Virginia's white population. A dozen years later, Federalist members made up only 17 percent of the house, but their counties had 23 percent of the total white population. The situation in the senate was even worse; the west had only four out of twenty-four members, but it should have had nine on the basis of white population. Several of the "lost" western senators would have been Federalists in any normal election year.[10]

Within the legislature itself, Federalists faced an additional problem. Centralization of government in the assembly was common to all the southern states, but only in Virginia was this a serious political handicap to the minority. Partisanship in legislative operations was stronger here than in the more southerly states, perhaps because Federalists were more organized in Virginia and were therefore deemed more menacing. There was, at any rate, a very evident legislative prejudice against Federalists. A resident of Greenbrier County complained in 1800 that "the treatment we have recd. from the Assembly for several years past is unparalleled in any government in the world towards their own citizens." He was sure the county was being punished for its Federalist voting record. A few years later another westerner grum-

9. John Stratton to constituents, April 2, 1800, in John Cropper Papers; Samuel Blackburn to citizens of Bath County, in Staunton *Republican Farmer*, March 4, 1813. The federal population was the whole number of free persons plus three-fifths of slaves —the constitutional formula for distributing congressmen.

10. Federalists are credited with representing half the white population if they elected one of the two delegates from a county, and the whole population if they elected both delegates.

bled against a legislative attempt to humiliate Federalist stockholders in the Bank of the Potowmac by changing the banking laws. Another form of discrimination was shown in 1803 when the house of delegates expelled a Federalist member because he held a federal contract for mail delivery, which supposedly made him ineligible to serve in the legislature. At the same session the state senate declined to expel a Republican senator who also held a mail contract. In 1808 and 1810 the house majority refused to allow a number of Federalist motions even to be entered on the pages of the journal, and one Republican even moved to throw them on the floor. Such efforts to hinder minority participation in legislative operations prompted the *Virginia Patriot* to lecture the Republican assemblymen in a long editorial. "It is the usual custom in the House of Delegates of Virginia," the editor scolded, "to stop any member who attempts to utter disagreeable truths, *by making STRANGE NOISES*!"[11]

Another expression of the deep partisanship in state politics was the extremely one-sided distribution of patronage. Many important officers were chosen by the legislature: the speakers of both houses; the governor, his council, and the other members of the executive branch; the two United States senators; judges; and even militia generals. In filling these positions of trust and profit, the majority party excluded Federalists much more stringently in Virginia than in other southern states. The policy of proscription was applied as soon as Republicans seized undisputed control of both houses in the election of 1800. So evident was their determination to allow no Federalist to be elected, that the minority did not think it worthwhile even to put up nominees for most positions.[12]

Since no active Federalist ever became a candidate for governor or senator, the party was reduced to cheering feebly for the least ob-

11. John Stuart to James Breckinridge, May 8, 1800, and John McCampbell to James Breckinridge, February 3, 1810, in Breckinridge Papers, UVa; Thomas Jones' letter in *Virginia Gazette*, May 11, 1805; Martinsburg *Berkeley & Jefferson Intelligencer*, May 20, 1803; letter from a legislator in *Alexandria Advertiser*, February 10, 1808; *Virginia Patriot*, February 9, 1810. The power of the Republican "Richmond junto" in the state is well discussed in Joseph H. Harrison, Jr., "Oligarchs and Democrats: The Richmond Junto," *Virginia Magazine of History and Biography*, LXXVIII (1970), 184–98.

12. James Breckinridge to John Breckinridge, December 6, 1800, in Breckinridge Family Papers, LC; John Wayles Eppes to Thomas Jefferson, December 23, 1802, in Edgehill-Randolph Papers.

noxious Republican whenever there was a battle within the majority ranks. Next in stature was the Council of State, which acted as a cross between a cabinet and a third house of the legislature. It was of little consequence except in its power to veto executive appointments. However, one of the prime goals of the energetic Republican majority after 1800 was to sweep the council clean of Federalists, who then held four of the eight seats. This was not difficult, since by law the councilors had to be removed periodically; thus, by the session of 1802 the last Federalists were ousted. One Republican delegate reported with pride, "We have purged the Council of all aristocracy." Since it had so obviously been marked off limits, no Federalist ever again sought a place on the council.[13]

It was only natural for these openly political offices to be closed to Federalists; it would have been unusual indeed for a predominantly Republican legislature to elevate a member of the opposition to the governorship or send him to the Senate. The meek acceptance of such proscription, however, was unique to Virginia Federalism. In the two Carolinas and even in Georgia there was at least an occasional partisan challenge for these high offices. Equally unusual was the extension of a "no-Federalist" policy to elections for relatively nonpolitical offices such as the speakers of the house and senate, judge, and militia general. No Federalist ever presided over either house of the legislature; indeed, none bothered to try. Speakers were often elected unanimously, and when there were any contests, all the candidates were Republicans.[14]

13. For the gubernatorial elections, see Richmond *Examiner*, December 8, 1802; *Virginia Argus*, December 13, 1808; *Norfolk Gazette*, January 21, December 9, 1811; *Petersburg Daily Courier*, November 11, 1814; Andrew Russell to David Campbell, December 6, 1808, and John Campbell to David Campbell, December 7, 1810, in David Campbell Papers. On the senate contests, see *Virginia Argus*, January 4, 1811; *Martinsburg Gazette*, November 24, 1811; and Allen Taylor to James Breckinridge, January 3, 1811, in Breckinridge Papers, UVa. The purge of the Council of State is covered in Harry Ammon, "The Republican Party in Virginia, 1789 to 1824" (Ph.D. dissertation, University of Virginia, 1948), 268; "No Pot-Boiler," in *Virginia Federalist*, April 19, 1800; Garland Anderson to David Watson, December 14, 1802, in Watson Papers, UVa; William H. Cabell to J. Cabell, December 14, 1802, in Cabell Deposit; and Richmond *Examiner*, June 8, 1803. The extreme partisan Republicans also attempted to oust the state's auditor in 1804 because of his politics: Charles D. Lowery, "James Barbour: A Politician and Planter of Ante-Bellum Virginia" (Ph.D. dissertation, University of Virginia, 1966), 93–94.

14. The election of speaker is listed in the first day's proceedings in the annual journal of each house. Unless so stated, the election was not unanimous. For informa-

Since Federalists drew a disproportionate number of their leaders from the legal profession, several of them were undoubtedly well qualified for the bench. Yet in Virginia alone of the southern states, this avenue of professional advancement was closed. When choosing judges for the appeals, chancery, and district courts, legislators carefully excluded Federalists. One who already happened to be on the bench in 1800, and who even Republicans admitted was "one of the best men in the world, and one of our ablest Judges," was passed over for a place on the appeals court in 1811 because of his politics. A prominent western legislator was denied a judgeship in the same year for making "one or two rank federal speeches" during that session. Most of the time Federalist lawyers avoided such embarrassment by leaving the field entirely to Republican contestants.[15]

Even generals in the state militia were subject to political approval. It was not enough for a man to be a respected officer and have the endorsement of legislators from his vicinity; he also had to be a sound Republican, or at least not an open Federalist. The single exception to this rule after 1800 was the selection of Robert Barraud Taylor, a prominent Norfolk Federalist, as brigadier general; but in his instance there were simply no Republican candidates for the job. On each of the half-dozen occasions when members of both parties were nominated for generalships, the Republicans always won. Sometimes the Federalist assemblymen even declined to vote for their political comrade, so hopeless were his prospects.[16]

Although shut out of office themselves, the Virginia Federalists

---

tion on names of candidates and votes cast, see Richmond *Examiner*, December 7, 1803; *Virginia Herald*, December 7, 1804; Staunton *Eagle*, December 18, 1807; *Alexandria Advertiser*, February 15, 1809; *Alexandria Gazette*, December 8, 1809; *Virginia Patriot*, December 4, 1812; and John Campbell to Elizabeth Campbell, December 4, 1810, in David Campbell Papers.

15. William H. Cabell to Charles Yancey, January 20, 1811, in Cabell Deposit; Allen Taylor to James Breckinridge, February 12, 1811, in Breckinridge Papers, UVa; and John Campbell to David Campbell, February 1, 1811, in David Campbell Papers. See reports of judgeship elections in *Virginia Argus*, December 7, 1805; *Petersburg Intelligencer*, December 6, 1806; *Virginia Gazette*, December 16, 1808; and *Alexandria Gazette*, February 15, 1809.

16. For the names of candidates and their vote totals, see Richmond *Examiner*, December 22, 1802; *Alexandria Advertiser*, December 22, 1806, December 17, 1807; *Virginia Herald*, December 12, 1806, January 28, 1809; Allen Taylor to James Breckinridge, January 23, 1811, in Breckinridge Papers, UVa; and John Campbell to David Campbell, January 21 and December 9, 1815, in David Campbell Papers.

did sometimes manage to influence elections by attaching themselves to one of two competing Republicans. In 1805, for example, Federalists became alarmed at what they claimed to be extreme partisanship in the legislature, and one warned that unless there was a timely "*union of honest men*," the "rage for democracy" would plunge Virginia into anarchy. Therefore, at the beginning of the December, 1805, session, the Federalist bloc aided the successful election of a "moderate" governor and judge, who had run against the candidates of the "high-toned" or "Dantonian wild-eyed" Republicans. The Republican leadership scoffed that Federalists were manufacturing an ideological schism where none existed, but Federalist newspapers insisted that the extreme Republicans had received a severe check.[17] Half a decade later the same thing occurred. James Monroe was a candidate for governor and was supposedly less thorough in his support of national Republican policies than his opponent. Two Federalist leaders in the house of delegates, Allen Taylor from the Shenandoah Valley and Charles Fenton Mercer of Loudoun County, asked their party's delegates to unite behind Monroe. Although not all agreed to this scheme, most apparently did. Again, in 1814, Federalists were reported to be marshaling support for the incumbent Republican state treasurer, but he won by such a huge majority that his Federalist backing was purely incidental.[18]

On occasional matters of national policy, Federalists sometimes worked with a Republican faction. In 1807 they tried to strike out any praise of Jefferson from a resolution approving James Monroe's conduct as minister to England, so that they might align themselves with the antiadministration group which later supported Monroe for president. In the same session, Federalists claimed to have support from the Randolph faction in the House for a resolution attacking General James Wilkinson's continuing as commanding general of the army.[19]

17. Thomas Jones, quoted in *Virginia Gazette*, May 11, 1805; *Alexandria Advertiser*, December 17, 1805; *Norfolk Gazette*, December 11, 16, 30, 1805; *Virginia Argus*, October 25, 1808.

18. Allen Taylor to James Breckinridge, January 8, 1811, in Breckinridge Papers, UVa; John Campbell to David Campbell, January 20, 1811, November 24 and December 10, 1814, in David Campbell Papers; William Wirt to Dabney Carr, December 10, 1814, in William Wirt Papers, VSL.

19. Frederick Hamilton to David Campbell, December 22, 1807, in David Campbell Papers; letter from a legislator, in *Alexandria Advertiser*, February 1, 1808.

Handicapped so much by Virginia's political system, the Federalists' only chance for even modest success was to assume popular stands on important state issues. This was difficult because there was no strictly Virginian problem that could readily be made a partisan issue. The most prominent and lengthy disputes in state politics involved legislative apportionment, constitutional revision, and judicial reform—all of which were primarily sectional concerns. On these issues both parties divided into eastern and western wings. On either side, a strong public stand as a party would have angered, embarrassed, and perhaps defeated the Federalist legislators from the other section. Since Federalist strength lay primarily in the west, the party might have increased its hold on western voters by taking an official position in favor of better representation, a new constitution, and court reform. But this would have required some formal statewide Federalist organization to issue policy statements, and no such structure existed. Also, the eastern element in the party contained the major newspapers and many of the most prominent leaders, and it would doubtless have fought bitterly against an open endorsement of western interests. Finally, Federalists could gain from supporting western demands only if the Republicans took an antiwestern position. In fact, western Republican legislators were no less committed than western Federalists to their section's desires. The question of new counties illustrates this.

In the house of delegates every county, whatever its population, had two members. The ever-growing western half of the state felt entitled to a larger share of the legislature as time passed, and the only way to accomplish this was to create more western counties. Since politicians east of the Blue Ridge did not like reducing their dominance of the legislature, delegates from the Piedmont and Tidewater generally stood against dividing any western county. From 1800 through 1816 there were twenty-one roll call votes in the house on creating new counties; the division of Harrison County appeared six times, Kanawha County five times, Amherst County four times, Monroe County twice, and three other counties once each.

On all twenty-one votes, Federalists were more favorable to dividing a county than Republicans were. Twenty times a majority of Federalists voted for division, while Republicans favored new counties on only eight roll calls. Altogether, 74 percent of Federalists and 47 percent of Republicans voted in favor of additional counties. This seems to indicate a strong partisan split on the issue, but such an impression is deceptive. There were simply far more Republicans than Federalists from east of the Blue Ridge, and the party affiliations mask what was in fact a sectional alignment. Within each half of the state, Federalist and Republican delegates took generally the same attitude, westerners of both parties favoring division and easterners opposing.[20]

A more drastic solution to western underrepresentation in the legislature was to revise the state constitution itself, giving each side of the Blue Ridge a share of house and senate seats more in keeping with relative populations. Periodically the question of calling a constitutional convention came before the house of delegates, sometimes even introduced by eastern members. In 1801, 1806, and 1816, resolutions for a convention passed the house by margins of as much as three to one, but each year the senate objected. Sectional representation in the upper house was even more lopsided than in the lower, with the west having only about one-fourth of the seats. Easterners who wished to preserve their ironclad control of at least one house were always hostile to a convention, especially since threats had been made of actually abolishing the senate altogether.[21]

Although the convention issue frequently arose in the assembly, it did not much concern the general voting public. There were no sustained newspaper campaigns either for or against revision, nor was there ever a flurry of pamphlets, mass meetings, or other activity aimed at bringing popular pressure upon the legislators. Until 1816 there was little evidence that western voters were nearly as anxious about representation or constitutional revision as their delegates in the assembly were. Possibly the Federalists missed a chance to create

20. *Virginia House Journal*, 1801, pp. 33, 38; 1803, p. 55; 1804, pp. 19, 45, 89; 1805, pp. 29, 67; 1806, pp. 26, 27; 1807, pp. 28, 34, 63; 1809, p. 41; 1810, p. 42; 1811, p. 103; 1813, pp. 131, 140; 1815, p. 119.

21. William H. Cabell to Joseph C. Cabell, December 16, 1802, in Cabell Deposit; George P. Stephenson to Peter Carr, January 1, 1807, in Carr-Cary Papers, UVa; John Campbell to David Campbell, December 12, 1810, January 20, 1811, in David Campbell Papers; Martinsburg *Berkeley & Jefferson Intelligencer*, January 16, 1807. On the general question of representation and suffrage, see J. R. Pole, "Representation and Authority in Virginia from the Revolution to Reform," *Journal of Southern History*, XXIV (1958), 16–50.

a popular issue in the west, but it would have been both difficult and risky for a bisectional party to take a firm stand on a very sectional issue.

In fact, party alignments on the convention question were not at all clear. In the thirteen separate votes on calling a convention, both parties divided almost evenly, with 48 percent of Federalists and 51 percent of Republicans voting in favor.[22] A comparison between party support for a convention and for the less drastic creation of new counties shows Federalists much less willing to change the constitution than to divide a county (48 percent for revision versus 74 percent for division). Republicans, however, viewed both issues about equally (51 percent versus 47 percent). The vast difference in the Federalists' outlook toward these two ways of increasing western representation is difficult to explain. It may stem partly from the Federalist reverence toward constitutions generally. To solve the problem of western underrepresentation gradually by dividing large counties might be perfectly acceptable; but to subject the state constitution to outright amendment, opening up the possibility of other drastic changes in the fundamental framework of government, was too bold a step. This is purely a conjecture, because no Federalist explained, or even noticed, the party's relative reluctance to support a convention.

Another point that eludes explanation is the drastic oscillation in Federalist attitudes toward a convention during this decade and a half. On the four roll calls taken between 1801 and 1803, Federalists voted 58 percent for revising the constitution; on the six votes between 1805 and 1811 they were only 30 percent in favor; but in the three roll calls of 1815–1816 they voted 70 percent for revision. There was no such variation in Republican voting (57, 47, and 51 percent for revision in the three time periods). These wide swings in Federalist opinion do not seem connected with events in state politics or with variations in the level of Federalist party strength.

The third major issue in Virginia was judicial reform. Virginia's courts, like those of most states, were being found increasingly unsuited to the needs of the early nineteenth century. The growth of

22. The votes are in *Virginia House Journal*, 1801, pp. 52, 54; 1802, p. 65; 1803, p. 71; 1805, p. 82; 1806, p. 68; 1807, p. 99; 1808, p. 83; 1810, p. 85; 1811, p. 95; 1815, p. 167; 1816, pp. 170, 184.

population and litigation had revealed faults in jurisdiction, overly large court districts, and other insufficiencies; and court reform was discussed at nearly every assembly session. Several bills reached the point of extended debate and even passage, but there was always something left to be improved upon in the future.[23] The first half-dozen years after 1800 saw various uncoordinated attempts at reform frustrated or postponed. Bills to alter the chancery court system, to extend the jurisdiction of local justices of the peace, and to speed up trials were debated and usually defeated. In these early years the Federalist minority generally supported reform. On five house votes in the sessions of 1800, 1801, and 1802, 57 percent of Federalists voted for the proposed alterations in the judicial system, but only 46 percent of Republican delegates did so.[24]

A package of reform laws won approval in the 1806–1807 session, but there is no record of the yeas and nays. The next year, still another plan was introduced to abolish the existing district courts, to set up a superior court in each county, to add a layer of circuit courts above them, and to combine common law and equity jurisdiction in a single system. For nearly a month there was spirited debate, and strong opposition finally forced the continued separation of law and equity courts. The main point, to create a superior court above the county court in each county, did carry, with Federalists falling away from the reform campaign. They voted only 12–7 in favor of superior courts, while Republicans were 108–47 in favor. Even after losing the fight against superior courts, some opponents continued to question whether the change was in fact a reform at all. A Shenandoah Valley man, noticing that the law created 158 new offices to be filled by lawyers, cried "GRACIOUS HEAVEN! How long will our fellow citizens suffer themselves to be the dupes and slaves of this class of men?" Opponents also claimed that the addition of so many new courts would impose a heavy burden on taxpayers and that the new circuit court judges would be spending a week or less in each county, hardly enough time

23. Watson to Joseph C. Cabell, December 14, 1801, in Cabell Deposit; James Breckinridge to John Breckinridge, January 3, 1802, in Breckinridge Family Papers, LC. On the court reform issue, see Albert O. Porter, *County Government in Virginia: A Legislative History, 1607–1904* (New York, 1947), 159–61.

24. *Virginia House Journal*, 1800, pp. 47, 59; 1801, p. 57; 1802, p. 52.

to weigh properly the merits of the many cases they would hear.[25]

Within a few years, such objections began proving true in practice. Circuit court terms were too brief, the convenience of a superior court in every county clogged the judicial system with a mass of new litigation, cases were argued by inexperienced lawyers before a single judge in superior court, and too many cases were being appealed to higher courts.[26] Meanwhile, the arrangement of the chancery courts (which dealt in equity rather than common law) was coming under attack. One petition expressed a general western sentiment against the inconveniences, delays, and enormous expense caused by the existing system. The single chancery district west of the Blue Ridge covered scores of miles in each direction and contained one-third of Virginia's population. The difficulty of travel compounded the problem of obtaining justice in this mountainous region. Responding to demands for change, western legislators lobbied in a body for a better distribution of chancery courts in 1810, and in this and the two succeeding years there were roll call votes on amending the system. The great majority of Federalist delegates twice supported reform and once opposed it; Republicans were narrowly against reform in 1810, strongly in favor the next year, and strongly against in 1812. With such widely varying positions from year to year, party affiliation obviously had no consistent relationship to this issue.[27]

One final stage in the movement for judicial reform was the attempt during the War of 1812 to provide regular paid prosecutors in the superior courts, which were the first step of appeal above the justice of the peace. An official prosecutor could see to the more efficient disposition of cases and could better prepare the state's side of each case. The desire of most delegates to save the taxpayers' money at first weighed heavily against this reform, and in 1814 a bill to authorize prosecutors failed by nearly two to one. About 40 percent of Republi-

25. *Virginia Argus*, March 24, April 3, 1807; Frederick Hamilton to David Campbell, December 22, 1807, January 16 and 25, 1808, in David Campbell Papers; John C. Hunter to Nathaniel C. Hunter, December 29, 1807, in Charles Simms Papers; letter of Thomas Jones in Winchester *Philanthropist*, September 6, 1808; *Virginia House Journal*, 1807, p. 83.

26. "Argus," in *Virginia Patriot*, May 10, 1811.

27. *Virginia Patriot*, July 30, 1811; letter of Archibald Magill, in *Martinsburg Gazette*, January 24, 1812; *Virginia House Journal*, 1810, p. 79; 1811, p. 90; 1812, p. 146.

can delegates and only 21 percent of Federalists favored the bill. Inexplicably, Federalist opinion shifted completely by 1815 and an attempt to block the prosecutors' bill was turned back overwhelmingly. Republicans remained favorable to prosecutors by more than two to one, and now Federalist members also voted in their favor by a three-to-one margin.[28]

Clearly the history of judicial reform from 1800 to 1815 was not one of party versus party. Federalists sometimes took a more advanced position than Republicans on changing the court system, and at other times they hung back. On this, as on the other large questions of representation and constitutional revision, the Virginia Federalists could not develop a consistent party stand. They were never able to place themselves firmly on the popular side of state issues and thus could not overcome the serious handicaps that kept them a permanently weak minority in Virginia's political system.

28. *Virginia House Journal*, 1814, p. 99; 1815, p. 116.

Chapter 15 THE NORTH CAROLINA FEDERALISTS

AFTER 1800, Federalists enjoyed more success in North Carolina than anywhere else in the South, though one could scarcely have foretold this in the 1790s, when a single intermittent supporter of Hamiltonian programs sat in the first five Congresses. That was a grim decade for the emerging Federalist party. The state's two original senators, elected in 1789 during a temporary spell of nationalism, aligned themselves with the pro-Hamiltonian bloc but were soon replaced by a legislature that grew increasingly suspicious of the national government.[1] Then, in 1798, the sudden appearance of the "French menace" and the refusal of Republicans to support military preparedness changed North Carolina's political attitude. Thousands of voters became temporarily more frightened of Frenchmen than of Federalists; and in both 1798 and 1800 four of the ten congressmen elected were avowed Federalists, while several of the others were no more than marginal Republicans. Presidential electors friendly to John Adams won nearly 45 percent of the votes in 1800, and the state legislature became nearly two-fifths Federalist. In 1798, even the gov-

1. Gilpatrick, *Jeffersonian Democracy*, 38, 55–61, 67; Rose, *Prologue to Democracy*, 79–80; Charles, *Origins of American Party System*, 94 (table).

ernorship was given to a staunch Federalist, William R. Davie; and in 1799, it was given to a quieter one, Benjamin Williams.[2]

As everywhere in the South, this unnaturally high peak of Federalism eroded rapidly during the first Jeffersonian years. Yet even as late as 1808 and 1812, antiadministration men—chiefly Federalists—were able to gather one-third of the presidential vote in North Carolina; and three Federalists went to Congress in both 1808 and 1813. In the legislature, Federalist membership declined but never fell below 25 percent—a percentage that exceeded the highest levels for Virginia, South Carolina, and Georgia after about 1803. During the War of 1812, in fact, Federalists held as much as 40 percent of the house of commons; and even the election of August, 1816, which was held nearly a year and a half after the war's end, gave them a third of the legislature.

North Carolina was unusual not only for its continuing high level of Federalism, but also for the degree to which this strength was spread across the state. The most loyal area was the upper Cape Fear (the Fayetteville congressional district), which gave Federalists 67 percent of its legislative seats from 1800 through 1816; and there were other strong counties in the western Piedmont and on the Atlantic coast. The weakest Federalist showing was in the mountainous west (11 percent of legislative seats) and in the northeastern Albemarle-Pamlico coastal counties (9 percent). This was quite a different pattern from the sectional nature of Federalism in northwestern Virginia and low-country South Carolina.

Analyzing party strength in North Carolina is hazardous because there is no reliable measurement to use. There were no statewide elections; congressmen and presidential electors were chosen by districts, and the Federalists always left some areas uncontested. One cannot be sure how voters throughout the state would have divided at any given election, since many did not have an opportunity to choose between candidates of opposing parties. Legislative elections were therefore the best measure of the locality of party strength, because every county was represented in every year. Even these elections give no indication of the division of votes within a county, and in many cases

2. Gilpatrick, *Jeffersonian Democracy*, Chap. 2; Rose, *Prologue to Democracy*, 172–79, 246–48, 256–61.

there was no party contest at all. However, combining the legislative results with the votes for Congress and president, where available, gives a reasonable indication of party preference from 1800 to 1816.[3]

Three areas of Federalist success are evident: the upper Cape Fear, the central Atlantic coast region around Newbern, and the seven towns that chose their own "borough" representatives to the house of commons. The upper Cape Fear was probably the firmest party stronghold outside New England. Only once in the nine congressional elections from 1800 through 1817 did it fail to elect a Federalist, and several times no Republican even cared to run.[4] People here were more active in producing staple crops for distant markets and thus were more oriented toward commerce than subsistence farmers elsewhere in the state; yet there were other staple-growing areas that were heavily Republican. Nationality, religion, and former Toryism, rather than economics, seemed to produce Federalist sentiment here, for the Fayetteville area had a higher concentration of Scottish Presbyterians than any other and had been a Tory center during the Revolution.[5]

The motives for Federalism in the central coast are more obscure. It is easy to say that men in these counties were tied to commerce, that their proximity to river or ocean transportation for staple exports made them Federalists. But again, the market-oriented planters along the Virginia border were fully as Republican as these coast dwellers were Federalist. The higher than normal concentration of Scots around Newbern could in part account for the region's politics; and since the town of Newbern itself was heavily Federalist, its political influence may have extended to the countryside.[6] Still, there is no obvious explanation for the cast of politics here. People doubtless had their individual reasons for voting Federalist, but demographic and economic statistics do not reveal them. Only in the state's seven borough towns was there a clear association of politics and economics.

3. For the method of identifying legislators by party, see Chap. 20, herein.

4. Gilpatrick, *Jeffersonian Democracy*, 242–43; Raleigh *Minerva*, May 22, 1813; Raleigh *Star*, April 18, 1815; *Raleigh Register*, August 22, 1817.

5. On the Cape Fear district see Leonard L. Richards, "John Adams and the Moderate Federalists: The Cape Fear as a Test Case," *North Carolina Historical Review*, XLIII (1966), 14–30.

6. The southern townsmen may also have influenced the politics of their rural neighbors in a later period: Charles G. Sellers, "Who Were the Southern Whigs?" *American Historical Review*, LIX (1954), 335–46.

Taken together, the towns were second only to the upper Cape Fear as a stronghold of Federalism in North Carolina, despite wide variations in the individual towns' party alignments. During the full seventeen years beginning in 1800, the boroughs elected sixty-six Federalist and only forty-eight Republican representatives. Given the high percentage of commercial and professional men in the towns, this result is quite understandable; but noneconomic motives must also have swayed many voters, for not all the towns were Federalist. Hillsborough, for instance, elected fourteen Republicans and only three Federalists; and Halifax, twelve Republicans and four Federalists.[7]

In spite of persistent Federalist strength across North Carolina, the party did not suffer the rigorous exclusion from state office that it did in Virginia and, to a lesser degree, in South Carolina and Georgia. This is all the more interesting because it seems logical (as V. O. Key has pointed out for the modern South) that the unity and partisanship of the majority party should be greatest where the minority is strongest.[8] In Jeffersonian days this was not always so. While only Republicans were allowed to serve in high capacity in Virginia (even in nonpolitical offices), North Carolina Federalists were being elected judge, speaker, and even governor. Only a seat in the senate was firmly denied them.

Even in 1800, the year of most intense Republican partisanship, the proscription of Federalists was not universal. Benjamin Williams, a quiet but unmistakable Federalist, was reelected governor by an enormous margin, polling 126 votes to 43 against two Republicans.[9] For the governorship, technically the highest state office, to go to a Federalist was by itself enough to mark North Carolina as the least partisan of the southern states. In fact, Williams was a candidate six times beginning in 1800, winning on three occasions. Having already been chosen governor in 1799 and 1800, he was reelected without controversy in 1801 for his third and last permissible consecutive term. He ran once more in 1805, still enjoying an attraction for many Republican legislators. This time, however, Republican leaders balked

7. For a discussion of influences affecting party affiliation in the towns, see Chap. 26, herein.

8. V. O. Key, *Southern Politics in State and Nation* (New York, 1949), 300.

9. Gilpatrick, *Jeffersonian Democracy*, 128; *Alexandria Advertiser*, December 16, 1800.

at letting the office pass out of their hands, and a party caucus, seldom used, put members on firm notice to vote for Nathaniel Alexander, a good Jeffersonian. Even so, about two dozen broke ranks and supported Williams, who, in losing by 108 to 65, far exceeded his party's strength in the assembly. If Williams was a quiet Federalist he certainly was not a mild one, for he privately complained that he had been the victim of the "Demon of Democracy" and that "a party determined on monopolizing all offices have not yet glutted their vengeance" even with his defeat.[10]

But he was not through with the office yet, because Alexander, though reelected without opposition in 1806, ran afoul of legislative pride the next year. The assembly had made great changes in the judiciary and Governor Alexander spoke against the new system in his annual message, offending many legislators. In retaliation, this overwhelmingly Republican body refused Alexander the customary third year in office and turned to Benjamin Williams again. In fact, the disgusted Republicans alone elected Williams because the Federalists, remarkably, are supposed to have voted for Alexander "upon the principle that it was setting a bad example to turn out of office a man with whom the Legislature had found no other fault, than that he had the independence to censure a law passed at a previous session." Since the court reform had particularly angered some leading Federalist members, it is entirely plausible that they may have voted for a Republican over one of their own party in order to show their agreement with Alexander's disapproval of the new judiciary system.[11]

Williams apparently saw no lesson for himself in Alexander's fall because he committed the same error and received the same punishment. The congressional embargo on foreign trade in late 1807 caused great financial hardship in the ensuing year, and the governor received several petitions to call a special legislative session for the relief of debtors. He flatly declined, and when the assembly did meet in regular session, it not only passed a relief law but also denied Williams his

10. Benjamin Williams to Calvin Jones, December 11, 1805, in Calvin Jones Papers, UNC; Joseph Pearson to John Steele, November 24, 1805, in Wagstaff (ed.), *Papers of John Steele*, I, 460–61; Preston Simpson to John Cropper, January 8, 1806, in John Cropper Papers; *Raleigh Register*, December 2, 1805.

11. Raleigh *Minerva*, November 26, 1807, December 1, 1808; Samuel Taggart to John Taylor, December 7, 1807, in Haynes (ed.), "Letters of Taggart," 220–21.

expected reelection. More, perhaps, was involved than this one indiscretion, for Williams was undeniably a Federalist and his being in office at all galled the Republican leadership. A formal party caucus was again held to whip the majority into line, although a score of Republicans still voted for Williams, who made a strong showing even in defeat.[12]

Besides Williams, who was also a token candidate in 1809, only one other Federalist ever made a serious effort to win the governorship. William Polk, a Raleigh financier and active party leader behind the scenes, tried to succeed Williams as chief executive in 1802. Polk, however, was far more obnoxious to Republicans than Williams, who kept his Federalism muted. The 1802 election was not even close; Federalists made up only a third of the legislature, and Polk did not even obtain all their votes.[13] A dozen years later, Polk tried again. The nation was in the midst of a dragging war, and Federalists were stronger than at any time since 1800; victory seemed possible this time because the majority was "completely at Loggerheads—& literally without a leader." Their caucus had been unable to unite behind one candidate, and some rebellious Republicans were ready to support Polk. On the first ballot he had eighty-six votes, twenty more than the total Federalist membership and only one less than the leading Republican. This, however, proved to be his maximum strength and after falling sharply on the next ballot, he withdrew to allow Federalists to swing behind the least partisan Republican. Even this tactic failed, and the Federalist speaker of the house lamented, "We have managed badly. . . . We could have elected a Federalist with all imaginable ease & thereby given a character to the State which it will be very far from obtaining under present circumstances."[14]

Except for these bursts of energy on behalf of Williams and Polk,

12. The vote was Williams 76, David Stone 96. Raleigh *Minerva*, December 1, 1808; Hooker, "Diary," 917; Benjamin Williams to John Haywood, February 22, 1809, in Ernest Haywood Papers.

13. Henry Selby to John G. Blount, November 20, 1802, in Keith and Masterson (eds.), *Papers of John Gray Blount*, III, 559.

14. Frederick Nash to Duncan Cameron, November 25, 1814, Archibald D. Murphey to Duncan Cameron, November 24 and 26, 1814, Archibald McBryde to Duncan Cameron, November 26, 1814, William Polk to Duncan Cameron, September 2, 1814, all in Cameron Family Papers; Archibald D. Murphey to Thomas Ruffin, November 24 and December 1, 1814, in Hoyt (ed.), *Papers of Archibald D. Murphey*, I, 74, 77.

the party showed little interest in gubernatorial elections. Often the Republicans did not even contest the office among themselves, and incumbents could expect to serve three annual terms if they behaved themselves.[15] The choice of senators aroused even less Federalist ambition, since normally there was no chance whatever of winning such a definitely partisan office. Only twice, in 1800 and 1814, when special circumstances offered some hopes of success, were there Federalist candidates for senator. On the first occasion former governor William R. Davie put himself forward, counting upon the wide popularity he enjoyed for his part in the recent negotiation of peace with France. This fame may have won a few Republican legislators to his side, but Davie still lost by a sizable margin of 94 to 72.[16] The result in 1814 was equally unsatisfactory, the defeated candidate then being John Stanly, one-time Federalist congressman from the Newbern district. Republicans were badly split, as many as fifteen or twenty defecting to give Stanly eighty-four votes on the first ballot—twenty-one more than the closest of three Republican opponents. Thereafter he began to slip, as a series of Republicans entered and withdrew. After numerous ballots the majority finally united behind a popular Republican state judge, who easily defeated Stanly, 104 to 75.[17]

For lesser offices, Federalists did better. Although none was ever speaker of the senate, several presided over the house of commons. Republicans could always control this position when they wanted to, and they won, usually by lopsided margins, every contested vote for speaker until 1816.[18] On four occasions, however, Federalists were unanimously chosen speaker at the beginning of the session, and in two other years they were unanimously elected to replace Republican speakers who had moved to higher office. In 1816 James Iredell, a

15. Lists of candidates and their votes are in Gilpatrick, *Jeffersonian Democracy*, 132–35; Raleigh *Minerva*, December 6, 1810, December 11, 1812; *Raleigh Register*, November 26, 1804, December 6, 1811; Raleigh *Star*, December 1, 1815, November 29, 1816.

16. William Blackledge to John G. Blount, November 25, 1800, in Keith and Masterson (eds.), *Papers of John Gray Blount*, III, 453; *Alexandria Advertiser*, December 16, 1800.

17. *Charleston Courier*, January 4, 1815; Murphey to Duncan Cameron, November 22, 1814, in Cameron Family Papers.

18. For the votes, see Schauinger, *William Gaston*, 42; Raleigh *Minerva*, November 23, 1809; *Edenton Gazette*, December 7, 1810; Raleigh *Star*, November 24, 1815; Newbern *Carolina Federal Republican*, November 28, 1812; and Duncan Cameron to Rebecca Cameron, November 17, 1812, in Cameron Family Papers.

confirmed but not blatant Federalist, even achieved the speakership in an open contest against two Republicans—something never accomplished in any other southern state after 1800.[19]

Several Federalists also served as judges of the state's superior court, perhaps partly because of a scarcity of Republican lawyers. The bench was distinctly nonpolitical, and during this period it became involved in only one or two controversial issues, neither of them a party question. Some Republican leaders wanted to reserve all judgeships for their party only, but this feeling was not shared by rank-and-file legislators. In 1800, for instance, former Federalist senator Samuel Johnston was elected to join two others of his party on a unanimously Federalist superior court. Later, the Republican "Warren Junto" tried to block the well-known Federalist lawyer, Duncan Cameron, from a seat on the court in 1814, but they found no one of prominence willing to run against him and gathered only nine protest votes out of nearly two hundred.[20] Altogether, six of the eight superior court judges from 1800 through 1816 were Federalists, and only one was definitely a Republican.

Despite such instances of generosity—far more numerous than in neighboring states—partisanship was not entirely absent from North Carolina politics. Whenever the occasion demanded, Federalism could be humbled, as it was in 1800. That year a bitterly partisan atmosphere enveloped the legislature, which met only a few weeks after the fierce presidential battle between Adams and Jefferson. The national result was still doubtful, and with great stakes depending upon the relative strength of parties in every state, a vigorous Republican majority did everything it could to curb Federalist influence. The speakerships of house and senate, formerly held in a spirit of nonpartisanship by Federalists, were wrenched away; and observers on both sides reported that "party spirit runs [so] high between Federals and Antifederals, that even the doorkeepers are elected upon these princi-

19. Raleigh *Minerva*, December 22, 1808, December 13, 1811; Murphey to Duncan Cameron, November 30, 1814, in Cameron Family Papers; Raleigh *Star*, December 20, 1816; *North Carolina House Journal*, 1805, p. 48; 1806, p. 2; 1807, p. 2.

20. Murphey to Ruffin, November 24, 1814, in Hoyt (ed.), *Papers of Archibald D. Murphey*, I, 74; Montfort Stokes to Duncan Cameron, November 22 and 30, 1814, and Archibald McBryde to Duncan Cameron, November 26, 1814, in Cameron Family Papers.

ples."[21] Once Republicans were securely in charge, their partisanship abated, but they continued to use their ability to assert control when necessary. The Federalist John Steele, for instance, could be allowed to preside over the last days of the 1811 house of commons, but since 1812 was a presidential election year, Steele was turned out when the new session began.[22] As late as 1816, a leading member of the minority felt certain that, regardless of their differences, supporters of rival Republican candidates for senator would unite to defeat any Federalist nominated for that office.[23]

Federalists had ample reason, then, to feel keenly the disadvantages of minority status. Every office that counted in a purely partisan sense was beyond their reach. Even Federalist speakers had to deal with a Republican house; and when the legislature chose a Federalist governor, it was careful to surround him with an entirely Republican council of state. During the entire period from 1800 through 1816, only one or two Federalists ever sat on the council, whose seven members were the governor's official advisors on matters of policy and patronage. When state offices fell vacant, the council made appointments until the next legislative session; and the guiding principle in such cases appears in the *Edenton Gazette*'s report on the selection of the state comptroller in 1808: "We understand that the Council determined that no Federalist should be voted for."[24] Still, Federalists were allowed to share some offices, so that, in the matter of patronage, William Gaston was correct in observing that North Carolina was "not so thoroughly devoted to democracy as some of our sister states."[25]

The North Carolina Federalists enjoyed other advantages over

21. Blackledge to John G. Blount, November 25, 1800, in Keith and Masterson (eds.), *Papers of John Gray Blount*, III, 453; Benjamin Smith to H. W. Harrington, December 20, 1808, in H. M. Wagstaff (ed.), *The Harrington Letters* (Chapel Hill, N.C., 1914), 20; Schauinger, *William Gaston*, 42.

22. Duncan Cameron to Rebecca Cameron, November 17, 1812, in Cameron Family Papers.

23. Duncan Cameron to Murphey, November 27, 1816, in Hoyt (ed.), *Papers of Archibald D. Murphey*, I, 88.

24. *Edenton Gazette*, October 6, 1808.

25. William Gaston to John Rutledge, Jr., January 17, 1809, in Rutledge Papers, UNC.

their brethren elsewhere. Malapportionment in the legislature had much less partisan effect than in Virginia. Every county in North Carolina chose two members of the house of commons and one senator —a system that worked a hardship on the more populous counties, located mainly in the west. However, Federalist strength was not heavily concentrated there. Only when the party happened to sweep the local elections in a number of large counties did it receive less than its due proportion of legislative seats. In the 1800 session, for example, Federalists in the house of commons represented 48 percent of the state's white population,[26] which would have entitled them to fifty-eight members, if the house had been equitably apportioned. They actually had just fifty-two, but the six additional seats would have made no difference on any important vote. Moreover, the situation was sometimes reversed. In 1811, representing counties with 23.5 percent of the white population in the house and 26.5 percent in the senate, Federalists should have had thirty members in the lower house and sixteen in the upper. In fact, they held thirty-six and eighteen respectively, or eight more than a fair apportionment. Again, no major vote would have been reversed by deducting the excess Federalist members. During the entire decade and a half, Federalists were possibly underrepresented by an average of one or two seats per year —hardly a significant disadvantage.

The party was also spared, at least until 1812, the handicap of a statewide presidential election. Because North Carolina chose presidential electors by districts, Federalists were able to win several in 1800, 1804, and 1808, even in the face of statewide Republican majorities.[27] This stimulated two-party competition in those particular districts and in others where the contest was usually close. Not until 1811 did North Carolina Republicans become as zealous as their friends in other southern states in giving a united electoral vote for president. Instead of simply having a statewide ticket like Virginia, they took away the popular vote entirely and had the assembly choose elec-

26. Federalists are credited with representing half the white population of a county if they elected one house member, and the entire white population if they elected both members.

27. In 1800 four Federalist electors won and in 1808, three. One Federalist would have been chosen in 1804, but the sheriff of the most heavily Federalist county in the district failed to make a timely return of votes.

tors.[28] Although an assembly election was as effective as the general ticket in eliminating Federalist electors, it was more difficult to defend publicly, especially for a party that professed to be the people's friend. During its brief life the electoral law of 1811 was a constant target of attack by Federalists and some rebellious Republicans, who sincerely believed that the people should have a direct vote for electors. Late in 1815, Republicans finally realized that the general ticket was quite safe from a partisan viewpoint; and they restored the popular presidential vote after brushing aside a Federalist attempt to revive the district principle.[29]

In congressional elections, the threat of gerrymandered districts always existed, but the minority party was not much abused in practice. After the 1800 census it was commonly expected that district lines would be revised for partisan advantage; therefore, Federalists were especially anxious about the assembly sessions of 1801 and 1802.[30] Republicans were able to adjust boundaries as they pleased and to draw districts for North Carolina's two new seats, yet they showed remarkable restraint. In the entire redistricting process, there was only one instance of gerrymandering, which occurred when two counties were removed from the Salisbury district to reduce its Federalist majority. A Republican won the revised district at the next election, but he would have had a majority even within the old boundaries; so the redistricting had no real effect. In all the elections held under this new map—1803, 1804, 1806, 1808, and 1810—there was not one occasion on which a losing Federalist nominee would have succeeded if the district lines had remained as they were in 1800.[31]

The next redistricting, following the 1810 census, again saw no massive Republican gerrymander. Of the two existing Federalist districts, one was left alone, although the other—the Salisbury district again—was much altered to defeat the incumbent congressman.[32] He

28. For the electoral law and its part in the campaign of 1812, see Chap. 11, herein.

29. *North Carolina House Journal*, 1815, p. 53; *North Carolina Senate Journal*, 1815, p. 40; Gilpatrick, *Jeffersonian Democracy*, 227–28.

30. Archibald Henderson to Walter Alves, March 30, 1801, in Archibald Henderson Collection; Selby to John G. Blount, November 20, 1802, in Keith and Masterson (eds.), *Papers of John Gray Blount*, III, 560.

31. For the election results, see the newspapers each year.

32. William Gaston, then a Federalist senator, attempted to amend the redistricting bill to his party's benefit but was defeated handily: Schauinger, *William Gaston*, 59.

won reelection in 1813, but with a greatly reduced majority; and he lost in 1815, when he would have carried the old district safely. This was the only time in sixteen years when the Federalists lost a seat because of Republican gerrymandering.[33] Aside from the details of district boundaries, the overall distribution of seats by population was also generally fair. In the 1803 redistricting four incumbent Federalists received an average white population of 28,000, and the eight Republican districts averaged 29,000. The 1813 rearrangement gave the two Federalists 36,000 white constituents each and the eleven Republicans an average of only 29,000. The disparity, however, was purely sectional, not partisan; both Federalists happened to be from the west, where there were few Negroes; the Republican districts, chiefly eastern, contained a large number of slaves so that the "federal population" (whites plus three-fifths of slaves) in each party's districts was nearly equal. Thus there was no deliberate Republican attempt to compress the Federalist minority into a few huge districts.

The most serious handicap to Federalist success, in fact, was a self-imposed failure to make political capital from promising state issues. The party might have increased its appeal substantially by taking the "popular" side of certain questions and publicizing its position, while branding the Republicans as indifferent to people's needs. Several such opportunities arose after 1800, but none were taken, partly as the result of lax organization. Before Federalists could establish themselves in the public mind as being on the side of any particular issue, they would require the aid of some institution—a committee, convention, or caucus—capable of taking an official stand. The party could, for instance, have called a standing legislative caucus to draft Federalist resolutions and give them wide circulation.[34] Lacking such a formal decision-making body, Federalist newspapers and pamphleteers might have put forward a consistent party position, as they did on many national issues. However, Federalists themselves were sharply divided on the major state issues of the period, such as more repre-

33. One reason the Federalists were not hurt worse by redistricting is that they were so weak, they could not have won additional seats even with an absolutely fair system.

34. The potential value of a caucus was greater in North Carolina than elsewhere because Federalist legislators came from all parts of the state. In Virginia or South Carolina, a Federalist legislative caucus would have left large sections unrepresented.

sentation for the west, a pay increase for legislators, court reform, and fairer taxation.

The representation question, because of its sectional nature, was the least promising of these from a partisan viewpoint. Sectional animosity was milder in North Carolina than elsewhere but it still existed. The east, containing the port towns, the main navigable rivers, the tobacco plantations, and most of the slaves, was by far the wealthier section. It also had a majority of the state's counties (although a minority of the white population) and dominated politics by controlling the legislature. Western politicians resented this, and elections for state office sometimes had a sectional character.[35] The westerners felt their minority position in the assembly to be unfair. Since every county chose a senator and two commoners, regardless of population, the only way to obtain a larger voice for the west was to create more western counties or to revise the constitution itself to distribute representation more nearly according to white population.

Surprisingly, western voters seemed far less concerned about the problem than their political leaders were. Although proposals to create new counties and to call a constitutional convention were frequently before the assembly, there was very little popular agitation behind them. Since nearly all newspapers were published in the east, they were not likely to editorialize for proposals that would reduce the political power of their section. Western grand juries, which might have protested inequitable representation, did not do so in large numbers, nor were there mass meetings demanding action from the assembly. The Federalists, therefore, were not in a position to capitalize on widespread open resentment among western people. The party would first have to stir up such feelings—a much harder task than merely seizing an already-active issue. Also, the Federalists drew strength almost equally from both parts of the state; if they championed the west, their eastern voters might fall away in large numbers.

Legislative votes indicate the party's confused attitude—or rather, lack of an attitude—on the representation question. One of the pe-

35. On judgeship elections, see Edwin J. Osborn to Gaston, December 14, 1800, in William Gaston Papers; on gubernatorial and senatorial elections, see Edmund Jones to William Lenoir, November 25, 1805, Lenoir Family Papers; and William Polk to Duncan Cameron, September 2, 1814, McBryde to Duncan Cameron, November 26, 1816, in Cameron Family Papers.

rennial sectional bills was a plan to divide Rowan County, the state's largest, giving the west one additional county. The senate voted on this in 1802 and 1807; the house, in 1801, 1807, 1809, and 1815; and usually Federalists were slightly more inclined than Republicans to favor the division. A total of the six roll calls shows that 48 percent of Federalist members and 43 percent of Republicans voted for creating a new county.[36] Four similar votes to divide Buncombe County, the westernmost in the state, showed a different result—only 45 percent of Federalists, but 53 percent of Republicans, favored division.[37] There may be a partisan explanation for the increased Republican willingness to split Buncombe and the slight Federalist preference for Rowan. Buncombe was overwhelmingly Republican, but Rowan was competitive, electing members of both parties. Neither side would gain or lose by dividing Rowan; but if Buncombe were split, there would be three additional Republicans sitting in every future legislature.

On the more general question of a constitutional convention to revise the entire scheme of representation, the Federalists were again reluctant to take a definite party stand. Once more, there was no great popular uproar to give emphasis to the proconvention resolutions of western delegates. From 1801 through 1808, five votes on calling a constitutional convention showed almost no difference in party attitudes; 30 percent of Federalists and 29 percent of Republicans endorsed the idea.[38] After a long silence, the question arose again in 1815, revealing a marked change in party opinions. Federalists had swung toward the idea of a convention and were now nearly equally divided, while Republicans were more strongly opposed than ever.[39] The available evidence yields no apparent explanation for this shift.

Even though the representation issue was not a very promising one for Federalists to use, there were others that they might well have turned to account. The hotly debated North Carolina version of a "salary grab," which occurred in 1803, was just such an opportunity. Leg-

36. *North Carolina Senate Journal*, 1802, p. 50; 1807, p. 25; *North Carolina House Journal*, 1801, p. 23; 1805, p. 30; 1807, p. 28; 1809, p. 40; 1815, p. 47.

37. *North Carolina Senate Journal*, 1808, p. 27; *North Carolina House Journal*, 1805, p. 21; 1807, p. 37; 1808, p. 22.

38. *North Carolina House Journal*, 1801, p. 53; 1802, p. 43; 1803, p. 44; 1807, p. 36; 1808, p. 52.

39. *North Carolina House Journal*, 1815, p. 36. Federalists were only 24–22 against a convention; Republicans were 61–12 against.

islators voted themselves a raise in per diem compensation from 25 to 30 shillings (that is, from $2.50 to $3.00). The house thought it wise not to record votes on this sensitive issue, but senators did commit themselves publicly, showing Republicans 20–14 in favor of the larger salary and Federalists 6–8 against.[40] Given the widespread dislike of anything resembling extravagance, the minority might well have used this issue to advantage. But nothing happened. The Raleigh *Minerva* merely grumbled a bit, calling the pay raise a "wanton waste of publick money" and accusing the house of cowardice in avoiding a record vote. As the election campaign of 1804 began, an anonymous writer, "Sentinel," urged voters to "shew our resentment, and to reject, at our next election, every man who voted in favor of thirty shillings."[41] Now would have been the time for the *Minerva* and the *North Carolina Journal* to fill their pages with diatribes against Republican spending, and for Federalist mass meetings to protest throughout the state, wrapping the party in the attractive mantle of twenty-five shilling economy.

But the "Sentinel's" hint was not taken. There was, indeed, a public reaction against the legislature; thirty-four members of the 1803 senate, including sixteen of the twenty-six who had voted for the pay raise, did not return. This was considerably higher than the normal turnover, but most of the changes involved one Republican replacing another. Only three of the thirty-shilling Republicans were succeeded by Federalists. The salary issue engrossed legislative attention for some years more, but the public outcry quickly subsided. At each session from 1804 through 1806, there were attempts to reduce per diem pay to the old twenty-five shilling figure, but all failed. Various recorded votes on such motions show the Federalist members to be wholly unconcerned with establishing a party record of economy, for they were just as anxious as Republicans to pay themselves thirty shillings.[42]

Just as this controversy faded, a much more acrimonious dispute began. For nearly three decades, North Carolina's county courts met

40. *North Carolina Senate Journal*, 1803, p. 52.

41. Raleigh *Minerva*, January 9, 1804; "Sentinel," *ibid.*, May 7, 1804, and in *Raleigh Register*, May 7, 1804.

42. *North Carolina House Journal*, 1804, pp. 39, 50; 1805, p. 47; 1806, p. 48; *North Carolina Senate Journal*, 1804, pp. 39, 48; 1805, p. 41. Taking all five roll calls together, 64 percent of each party voted in favor of keeping the higher salary.

locally and its superior court met in eight towns throughout the state. Anyone appearing in a case appealed to superior court—principal, witness, or juryman—had to travel to the nearest "court town" at considerable expense and inconvenience. Therefore, a movement began shortly after 1800 to have superior courts meet in each county, greatly reducing the required travel and speeding the administration of justice.

However, an argument against the proposed change was raised, chiefly by lawyers. They doubted whether qualified judges would be willing to serve on the superior courts if so much circuit riding was required. They feared that juries, if chosen wholly from one county instead of from an entire judicial district, would be inclined to render verdicts based on local friendships, not facts. State expenses would rise, since there would be more court officials, more jurymen, and higher travel costs for judges. And of course the lawyers themselves, rather than the common people, would now be put to the trouble of traveling. Instead of attending only the court town in his district, an attorney with many cases to try would have to move from county to county throughout the year.

The issue of court reform was first raised seriously in 1804, when the senate soundly defeated a bill "to advance the administration of justice." Republican senators were strongly against the change, and Federalists were less so; but a majority in both parties evidently agreed with the Federalist leader John Steele that alterations should be made cautiously, if at all.[43] The following year, supporters of the county system[44] were much stronger; their bill passed the house by a heavy majority and only just failed the senate. There was no consistently partisan character to this vote; house Republicans were two to one in favor of the bill, but their comrades in the senate opposed it by the same margin. Federalists were evenly divided in the commons and three to one in favor in the senate.[45]

43. John Steele to Pearson, December 6, 1804, in Wagstaff (ed.), *Papers of John Steele*, I, 442–43; *North Carolina Senate Journal*, 1804, p. 36. Republican senators were 28–10 against the county system; Federalists were only 10–7 against.

44. *County system* refers to the new plan of holding a superior court in each county, and *district system* refers to the old method of holding superior court in only one town per district.

45. *North Carolina House Journal*, 1805, pp. 24, 41; *North Carolina Senate Journal*, 1805, p. 36. The senate vote was on whether to table the bill until after the session ended, that is, to kill it.

Court reform was definitely a controversial issue now, and public interest grew rapidly between sessions. The tide of opinion, as it rose in the newspapers, clearly favored reform. The Raleigh *Minerva* and other sheets printed both sides of the debate as expressed by several pseudonymous writers. "A Poor Soldier," "District Court Suitor," and others attacked the district system and claimed that most people wanted the new county plan. "A Citizen of Hertford" capped his criticism by urging voters to question all candidates and defeat those who opposed court revision. The editors of the two Federalist papers may have had their private opinions, but they stayed entirely out of the controversy, allowing readers to speak for themselves.[46]

The uproar in the press continued through the August elections and had its effect on the 1806 legislature. The house again approved court reform and this time the senate was grudgingly forced to agree. There were still no firm party divisions, Federalists being four to one against reform in the house and two to one in favor in the senate, while Republicans were almost three to one favorable in the commons but evenly split in the senate.[47] The court issue had no connection with party ideologies and, by supporting court reform, the Federalists had every opportunity to label themselves friends of the common people. But the party's legislators were divided and its editors kept silent. Furthermore, those leading Federalists who did express their opinions all opposed superior courts in each county; they fought to retain the district system as though the very existence of human society depended upon it. Duncan Cameron, Joshua G. Wright, Archibald Henderson, John Steele, Frederick Nash—all were nearly frantic against the reform. They were lawyers and viewed the issue from the point of professional convenience. The proposed change seemed to be merely an effort by visionary experimenters to ruin a proven institution.[48]

In the legislature itself, those who led the debate against reform

46. In the *North Carolina Journal*, see "A Poor Soldier," November 11, 1805, and "A Citizen of Hertford," August 28, 1806; in the Raleigh *Minerva*, see "District Court Suitor," June 16, 1806, and "The Old Farmer," June 30, 1806.

47. *North Carolina House Journal*, 1806, pp. 17, 25; *North Carolina Senate Journal*, 1806, pp. 15, 18.

48. M. Tranty to Nash, December 11, 1805, Duncan Cameron to Richard Bennehan, November 30, 1806, Cameron to constituents, December 21, 1806, all in Cameron Family Papers; Joshua G. Wright to Steele, December 18, 1807, Henderson to Steele, December 6, 1807, both in John Steele Papers.

were Federalists, while the loudest advocates of the new county system were generally Republicans. This alignment, although not at all representative of the feelings of either party's legislators, could easily give a public impression of Federalists fighting to preserve the special privileges of a few towns and lawyers against the convenience of the mass of people.[49] Actually, many Republican leaders were also opposed to changing the judiciary, but they usually expressed their sentiments in private. Senators James Turner and Montfort Stokes, Governor Nathaniel Alexander, Congressman Evan Alexander, and former attorney general Blake Baker were just as upset with the new system as any Federalist. Baker even tried to organize a statewide effort to elect legislators who would return to the district courts. He hoped that "if a meeting of 10 or a dozen other sober minded of the friends of the old System could be had this Spring upon the Subject, some general plan of operations might be adopted" for the fall elections.[50] A feeble attempt to abolish the new court system in the 1807 senate session was easily brushed aside and thus the court issue was brought to an end, and with it went one of the few chances Federalists had to popularize their party.[51]

One other controversy also promised the Federalists large political returns at small risk, but this, too, they declined. The problem of how to distribute the state's tax burden vexed nearly every legislature from 1800 to 1816 because, while state expenses were small, money was scarce. A large number of North Carolinians lived outside the money economy, or nearly so, and obtaining even the fraction of a dollar necessary to pay state taxes was sometimes a struggle for them. There were far more small landowners than wealthy plantation magnates, and Federalists were well situated to make use of the tax issue because they had little strength to lose in the prosperous plantation counties and much to gain in the poorest areas.

49. The debates are reported in the *North-Carolina Journal*, December 8, 1806, January 12, 1807, and the Raleigh *Minerva*, December 8, 15, 22, 1806.

50. Blake Baker to Duncan Cameron, January 31, 1807, in Cameron Family Papers; Duncan Cameron to Stokes, October 8, 1807, in Montfort Stokes Papers, NCDAH; Evan Alexander to Steele, December 12, 1806, James Turner to Steele, January 1, 1807, both in Wagstaff (ed.), *Papers of John Steele*, I, 484–85, 491; Raleigh *Minerva*, December 1, 1808.

51. *North Carolina Senate Journal*, 1807, p. 7. Federalists were 8–5 against repealing the county system; Republicans were 29–10 against.

The taxation issue took three forms: reducing or eliminating the poll tax on whites—a tax that was the same for all persons, and thus, bore most heavily on the poor; increasing the poll tax on Negroes, which would tax slaveowners more; and "equalizing" the land tax by levying it on the value of land instead of a flat rate per acre. The most persistently discussed of these was the last. Obviously an acre of rich tobacco land was worth much more than an acre of thin mountain soil or pine barrens, yet all property was assessed at the same rate, forcing the owners of poor land to pay a much higher *ad valorem* tax than plantation owners. From 1802 through 1814 ten separate legislative votes on proposals to graduate the land tax according to value made no headway. Finally in 1815 the equalization bill succeeded and the tax rate was changed from roughly eight cents per one hundred acres to eight cents per $100 value.

Federalists did not play any significant role as a party in the long equalization fight, though they might well have done so without violating their national political principles. Two prominent western Federalists, John Steele and Joseph Pearson, opposed the bill in its early years, but they did it privately and upon grounds of practicality, not principle. Pearson believed that speculators who possessed large quantities of poor land would be the main beneficiaries of the scheme, and Steele thought the land tax was so low anyway that the relief given poor freeholders would not justify the expense and trouble of appraising all the state's lands.[52] These two, however, did not represent the dominant Federalist opinion, which was mildly favorable to equalization. Republicans were slightly hostile to the idea. In the ten roll call votes on this issue, Federalist legislators supported equalization more strongly than Republicans on six occasions and less strongly only once; the remaining three votes showed no difference between the parties. Of the total number of individual votes, 57 percent of Federalist members approved equalization, against only 49 percent of Republicans.[53] This difference in party attitude, if emphasized by newspaper propaganda and caucuses used to produce an even larger

52. Pearson to Steele, November 26, 1804, Steele to Pearson, December 6, 1804, both in Wagstaff (ed.), *Papers of John Steele*, I, 440, 442–43.

53. *North Carolina Senate Journal*, 1802, p. 29; 1809, p. 16; 1810, p. 21; 1811, p. 50; 1812, p. 48; 1814, p. 40; 1815, p. 31; *North Carolina House Journal*, 1812, p. 33; 1813, pp. 35, 39; 1815, p. 43.

Federalist margin for equalization, might have been important in state politics. Federalists could then have campaigned as the champions of the small farmer against the aristocratic Republican planter.

However, nothing was done to exploit any aspect of the tax controversy. Proposals to reduce or abolish the white poll tax (which ranged from 20 to 30 cents) came before the house six times. At first, in 1800 and 1801, Federalists were somewhat more favorable to eliminating the tax than Republicans were. On later votes, from 1805 through 1815, these positions were reversed.[54] Increasing the Negro poll tax was at issue only three times, and neither party took a clear stand on it.[55] In short, the tax question presented several possible avenues to Federalist popularity, but the party declined to travel any of them, even though its voting record on the most important issue—equalization of land taxes—would have justified an effort to court the favor of small landholders.

Overall, Federalism in North Carolina differed in several ways from the pattern of neighboring states. Its long-term strength was greater than anywhere else south or west of Maryland and was not so restricted sectionally as it was in most states. It suffered none of the handicaps, such as malapportionment, gerrymandering, and the general electoral ticket, which afflicted Federalists elsewhere in the South. Its members were even elected to such offices as governor and speaker of the house of commons. But the North Carolina Federalists shared one great shortcoming with their brethren throughout the South. They simply did not choose to act as an organized, professional political party and turn local issues to their advantage, as Federalists and Republicans were doing in some middle and northern states.

54. *North Carolina House Journal*, 1800, p. 51; 1801, p. 57; 1805, p. 50; 1811, p. 58; 1814, p. 38; 1815, p. 50. Totaling the votes, Federalists were only 41 percent in favor of lowering or abolishing white poll taxes, while Republicans were 48 percent in favor.

55. *North Carolina House Journal*, 1813, p. 49; 1815, p. 51; *North Carolina Senate Journal*, 1810, p. 43; 1813, p. 43. Federalists were 45 percent in favor of increasing the Negro poll tax; Republicans were 41 percent in favor.

Chapter 16 THE SOUTH CAROLINA FEDERALISTS

THE considerable strength that South Carolina Federalism showed in the 1790s vanished rapidly after 1800. Although Federalist leaders never had the confidence of more than a small fraction of voters, a remarkable maldistribution of legislative and congressional seats allowed the party to elect at least two of six congressmen and at least one senator throughout the decade of the 1790s. The legislature always had a substantial bloc, sometimes even a majority, of proadministration men. In 1790 and 1791, for instance, the assembly endorsed Hamilton's assumption bill and in 1792 gave John Adams seven out of eight electoral votes for vice-president. The storm over Jay's Treaty temporarily scattered this strength, giving Jefferson's electoral slate a four-to-one victory in 1796; but Federalists quickly recovered and rose to new heights on the strength of the French crisis. In 1798 they won five of six congressional districts (including two in the up-country) and in 1800 still held three, as well as two-fifths or more of the legislature.[1]

Yet within a few years of losing power nationally, this local Feder-

1. Wolfe, *Jeffersonian Democracy*, 95–99, 121–23, 155–60; George C. Rogers, Jr., *Evolution of a Federalist: William Loughton Smith of Charleston, 1758–1812* (Columbia, S.C., 1962), 242–43, 289–94, 344–51; Rose, *Prologue to Democracy*, 51–59, 136–38, 148–52, 181–85; Marvin R. Zahniser, *Charles Cotesworth Pinckney: Founding Father* (Chapel Hill, N.C., 1967), 202–206.

alist strength had all but disappeared. By 1804 the state was sending only Republicans to Congress and most districts never even saw an opposition candidate. Only the Charleston seat was regularly contested, but with no success. The number of Federalists in the legislature dwindled quickly and by 1808 Charleston itself came under Republican rule, leaving only two or three small coastal parishes with a Federalist majority. If there had been a choice of parties in every parish and district, probably no more than 10 or 15 percent of all the people in the state would have voted Federalist, rising perhaps to 20 percent in peak years.[2]

The party's rapid decline was not from want of leadership, for even in defeat Federalism held the loyalty of many eminent and talented Carolinians. These men simply could not induce the common voter to support their party. This handicap might have been overcome, because the planter-merchant aristocracy of the low country cast only a small fraction of the state's popular vote but controlled a majority of the assembly and nearly half the congressional districts. Had the aristocrats themselves been unified in support of Federalism, the party could at least have maintained its strong minority position of the 1790s and occasionally it might have controlled the state.

However, the virtual unanimity with which low-country leaders had ratified the Constitution did not carry over into party politics after 1790, and this doomed the Federalists. The low-country barons had feuded among themselves during the colonial period, and their common support of ratification in 1788 meant nothing for the future. Family connections were supremely important, and when some clans associated themselves with the national administration in the 1790s, their local enemies gravitated to the opposition. Leading men such as Charles Pinckney, Pierce Butler, and other proponents of the Constitution were left out of the distribution of federal patronage, and such personal slights helped push them and their followers into the emerging Republican party. Later in the decade, the Federalist-controlled national Senate dealt an insult to all moderate low-country politi-

2. Technically, the local governmental units in South Carolina were *parishes* in the low country (each originally an actual parish of the Anglican Church) and *districts* in the up-country. For simplicity, the terms *district* or *county* are sometimes used to signify local units throughout the state.

cians, especially to the Rutledge connection; it refused to confirm the nomination of John Rutledge to the Supreme Court because he had condemned the Jay Treaty.[3]

Besides personal considerations, the national Federalists committed several economic sins against the coastal plantation owners and gradually drove a majority of them into opposition. Hamilton's tariff law struck hardest at such men, who probably spent more than any other group in the nation on imported British and European goods. Tariff revenue virtually financed the new American government, and South Carolina planters contributed a disproportionate share. The creation of the national bank, its control by a handful of Hamiltonian politicians, and its refusal to extend credit for agricultural pursuits stirred more resentment. The Jay Treaty, which essentially excluded American trade from the British West Indies while obtaining no compensation for southern slaves carried off during the Revolution, was yet another reason for Carolina planters to align themselves with Madison and Jefferson rather than with Hamilton and Adams. By 1800 the effect of all these events was clear; after that year Federalists never again won so much as half of the low-country assembly seats.[4]

Even so, the coast remained the center of Federalist strength after 1800. Far more than in other southern states, the party was sectional—almost local—in its appeal. The city of Charleston and a few neighboring parishes were most friendly, sometimes even casting Federalist majorities. This was the empire of the merchant, the lawyer, and the planter; and few voters were not influenced by, or related to, some local aristocrat. A prominent man, attached to Federalism for personal reasons, could sometimes hold his parish loyal to the party for many years, while surrounding districts with the same economic and demographic patterns were solidly Republican. For instance, the small parish of St. Thomas and St. Denis was nearly always Federalist, but almost every one of the three dozen voters in its equally small neigh-

3. Wolfe, *Jeffersonian Democracy*, 54–70; Rose, *Prologue to Democracy*, 101–110; Ulrich B. Phillips, "The South Carolina Federalists," *American Historical Review*, XIV (1909), 731–43; George S. Cowan, Jr., "Chief Justice John Rutledge and the Jay Treaty," *South Carolina Historical Magazine*, LXII (1961), 10–23.

4. Wolfe, *Jeffersonian Democracy*, 54–70, 82–91; Rogers, *Evolution of a Federalist*, 276–84; Zahniser, *Pinckney*, 123–28.

bor, Christ Church, was Republican; and flanking Christ Church were two more Federalist parishes.[5] Altogether, the twenty plantation parishes, in a very good Federalist year, might give the party 1,300 votes out of 3,200 cast, or 40 percent. This figure is purely theoretical, for no more than a dozen districts would have Federalist candidates at any given election.

Much more important than these few friendly parishes was Charleston, the only sizable constituency with any real chance of Federalist control. Here were merchants, lawyers, and other professional men with ties of business and friendship to the northeastern Federalist trading community. Here also the upper class lived in close association with the lesser ranks and could appreciate the Federalist argument for an orderly hierarchical society free of "Jacobin" democratic experiments. City elections hinged upon which group could produce the larger turnout—the Federalist elite and their lower-class dependents, or the Republican mechanics and their aristocratic allies.

At the beginning of the century the city was narrowly Federalist but not reliably so; within a few elections after 1800 the Federalist vote dwindled and Republicans achieved a solid dominance. Of the city's fifteen state legislators, Federalists elected thirteen in 1800, ten in 1802, only eight in 1804 and 1806, and none in 1808 or thereafter. Even in defeat the party could produce a substantial minority vote when it wished; Federalist assembly tickets polled 43 percent in 1812 and 39 percent in 1814. In city elections Federalists did somewhat better because there was a smaller turnout, and part of the heavily Republican St. Michael's Parish was outside the city limits. Federalists won the office of intendant in 1800–1802, 1805–1807, and 1813–1816. In that decade and a half, they controlled the local government for nine years, and the Republicans controlled it for six.

In the upper counties of South Carolina a Federalist was looked upon more as a curiosity than as a serious politician. The actual number of up-country Federalists was perhaps two or three thousand, the same as in the lower half of the state, but this represented scarcely 10 percent of the normal up-country vote. A really substantial Federalist

5. Charleston *City Gazette*, May 6, 1801. Rogers, *Evolution of a Federalist*, 265–68, 279–81, Chaps. 7–8, brings out some of the family-group feuds and alliances in low-country politics.

potential existed in less than half a dozen upper districts. Marlborough was carried for Congress in 1800, 1814, and, almost, in 1816; Orange, in 1800 and 1806; Barnwell and St. Matthew's, in 1800; and Darlington, almost, in 1814. In local contests Marlborough, Orange, Kershaw, Chesterfield, Greenville, St. Matthew's, and two or three other districts occasionally sent Federalists to the legislature. Even these few victories owed more to the popularity of some local personality who happened to be a Federalist than to true party loyalty. In nearly all the remaining two dozen up-country districts, there may never have been a Federalist candidate for any office.

Reduced from a vigorous and threatening minority to a small and weak remnant within a few years, the South Carolina Federalists knew it would be ludicrous to put forward candidates for such strictly partisan offices as senator and governor. The last close contest for a high office was in November, 1800, when a Republican was elected senator by only two votes. The next year's election to fill Charles Pinckney's vacant seat in the senate showed the suddenness of the Federalist decline. It was difficult even to find a man who would consent to have his name brought up. C. C. Pinckney, when approached, very wisely pointed out that personal popularity counted for little in such a partisan vote. He told a comrade, "Party has so compleatly drawn the line, that if we could succeed in obtaining . . . [my] election, we can do so in that of any other Federalist." After three others had refused, John Rutledge, Jr., was nominated, only to lose by a shattering 90–47 margin. This was the last attempt to fight the Republican tide. In 1803 there were rumors that Pinckney might offer for governor, but he did not, and from that time on, no Federalist ever received a vote for either of these two offices.[6]

The strict exclusion of Federalists did not always apply to lesser positions. The patronage experience of the South Carolina party fell midway between that of the Virginia Federalists, who were rigorously shut out of all state offices, and of their luckier comrades in North Carolina, who found even the governorship open to them. In the South

6. A. C. Butler to Thomas Sumter, December 9, 1802, in Thomas Sumter Papers, LC; Charleston *Times*, December 9, 1800, December 8, 1801. For accounts of later elections, see *Charleston Courier*, December 13 and 22, 1810, December 12 and 14, 1812, December 3 and 14, 1814, December 10, 1816.

Carolina legislature, Republicans always held the chair of the lower house but allowed John Ward, a prominent low-country Federalist, to serve as speaker of the senate from 1800 through 1805. In the state courts, Federalists were anathema during the early years of the century when they might still be dangerous as a party. Those who were already on the bench retained their seats, but former congressman Abraham Nott lost a judgeship contest by a two-to-one vote in 1801, showing that all vacancies were to be filled by Republicans. Later, the bench was opened to a few qualified Federalists; two of the thirteen judges elected to the law courts after 1800 and one of seven who sat on the court of equity were members of the party. Also, Federalist generals were occasionally in the state militia. The partial lowering of the patronage barrier may simply have reflected the rapidly declining likelihood that Federalists could ever again threaten to win power in South Carolina. As one said, the leaders "make no noise" and in return "are permitted to have some share in the management" of the state.[7]

Federalists were not wholly exempt from partisan harassment, as shown by the astute realignment of congressional districts by the Republican legislature in 1802. Under the old boundaries, which lasted through 1800, Federalists had a clear advantage. Their low-country strongholds dominated three districts while the vastly more populous Republican up-country also had three. The Federalist victors in 1800—Thomas Lowndes, Benjamin Huger, and John Rutledge, Jr.—represented only 22,000 white inhabitants each, while the three Republican congressmen had much larger districts averaging 43,000

7. Peter Freneau to [?], November 25, 1800, photostat in Peter Freneau Papers, USC; Charleston *Carolina Gazette*, December 2, 16, 1802; *South-Carolina State-Gazette*, December 9, 1800, December 8, 1801; *Alexandria Advertiser*, December 10, 1800—all cover the 1800 and 1801 contests for speaker, senator, and judge. On the maneuvering behind the attempt to elect Pinckney to the senate in 1802, see H. W. DeSaussure to John Rutledge, Jr., August 25, September 17, December 19, 1801, January 13, 1802, in Rutledge Papers, UNC, and Rutledge to Otis, September 15, 1801, in Harrison Gray Otis Papers. O'Neall, *Biographical Sketches*, II, 597, lists the state judicial officers after 1800. Federalist lassitude, rewarded by occasional elections of party members to minor offices, is shown in DeSaussure to Josiah Quincy, December 7, 1808, January 21, 1809, in Quincy, *Life of Josiah Quincy*, 189, 191; Washington (Ga.) *Monitor*, March 3, 1815; Willis Wilkinson to John Rutledge, Jr., February 15, 1802, Thomas Lowndes to John Rutledge, Jr., September 16, 1806, both in Rutledge Papers, UNC; and "Mentor" in *Charleston Courier*, September 20, 1804.

whites. With probably less than one-quarter of the total popular vote, the Federalist minority was able to secure half the delegation.

This condition obviously could not last. South Carolina earned two additional seats from the 1800 census and Republicans used the opportunity of redrawing district lines to minimize the chance of future Federalist victories. The surest way to accomplish this was to have all eight congressmen run at large; then the enormous Republican up-country vote would overwhelm the Federalists along the coast. This plan, which one Federalist thought would "annihilate the weight and consequence of the low Country," was nevertheless backed by some leading coastal Republicans who expected to dominate the "junto" that would make nominations for a statewide slate. Federalists fought the idea in the press and in the legislature, complaining that at-large elections would require people to vote for candidates they knew nothing of, whereas nearly everyone knew the candidates in a district election. Members who previously could know the opinion of their one district would now be less responsive, because no congressman would ever learn what the entire state was thinking. Whether these arguments had much effect or not, the general ticket plan was abandoned. Most low-country Republicans apparently concluded that submerging their wealthy minority section in the massive upstate vote was too high a price to pay, even to insure the elimination of Federalists.[8]

The maintenance of single-member districts was not enough, by itself, to allow more than an even chance of a Federalist victory anywhere in the state after 1800. Two of the three existing coastal districts had some up-country Republican counties attached, and these gave every indication of soon being able to outvote the low-country parishes. To avoid this calamity, Federalists drew up their own districting scheme from which two safe seats were possible; one leader thought the plan could have been enacted in 1801, if only the session had lasted longer. This was a mere dream, of course; the Republi-

8. *Charleston Courier*, December 12, 1807; "Socrates," in *South-Carolina State-Gazette*, November 13, 1801; DeSaussure to John Rutledge, Jr., September 17, November 2, December 19, 1801, and C. C. Pinckney to John Rutledge, Jr., January 17, 1803, in Rutledge Papers, UNC; Butler to Sumter, December 9, 1802, in Thomas Sumter Papers; Robert Anderson to John E. Colhoun, November 19, 1801, in Robert Anderson Papers, USC.

can majority had no intention of helping the opposition preserve its strength. There might have been disputes among Republicans about precisely how to carve the districts but there was unanimous agreement that Federalism would be "taken care of."[9]

The actual redistricting law of 1802 gave both new congressmen to the up-country, insuring a Republican gain of two seats. Next, the Beaufort district held by John Rutledge, Jr., was altered to destroy his chances of reelection. Three counties in the middle country southwest of Columbia, which had given Rutledge a 37-vote majority in 1800, were detached and the Edgefield district was added, bringing in 650 new voters, nearly all Republicans. This turned Rutledge's former margin of 275 votes into a probable deficit of over 300. Faced with this prospect, he retired and a Republican gained his seat. The Georgetown district lost its strongest Federalist county, wiping out nearly all of Benjamin Huger's 184-vote margin of 1800. He did manage to win the next election, but only by 17 votes, and that against a very weak Republican candidate. Finally, the Charleston seat lost three of its Federalist parishes, which were placed in a largely Republican up-country district.[10] Gerrymandering thus caused the immediate loss of one Federalist seat, though the party disintegrated so rapidly after 1803 that it probably could not have carried any congressional district in the state, no matter how it was drawn.

More fundamental changes in the political system also helped snuff out the Federalist party. Suffrage extension was the most basic of these. Until 1810, South Carolina required the payment of at least three shillings in taxes to qualify a person for voting. This rule, when enforced (which was not always), eliminated many of the small farmers whose landholdings were not extensive enough to be assessed that much tax. It also, of course, kept out all persons who owned no property at all. In the previous century there had been some rumblings about suffrage reform, but they had accomplished nothing except to familiarize Carolinians with the issue. After 1800, the conquest of American politics by Jeffersonian democracy and the lessening an-

9. Butler to Sumter, December 9, 1802, in Thomas Sumter Papers; DeSaussure to John Rutledge, Jr., December 19, 1801, January 13, 1802, and C. C. Pinckney to John Rutledge, Jr., January 17, 1803, in Rutledge Papers, UNC.

10. *Charleston Courier*, March 24, 1803; Freneau to Thomas Jefferson, June 17, 1803, in Thomas Jefferson Papers.

tagonism between low country and up-country both combined to improve the prospects for reform.

The Federalists were so obviously a class party in South Carolina that they had little chance of attracting votes from the poorest element of the population, and the remaining handful of Federalist legislators fought a hopeless battle against suffrage extension. On half a dozen house and senate votes in 1808, 1809, and 1810, Federalist members stood four to one against reform, while the Republicans voted twelve to one in favor. Table 5 shows the marked partisan split on the suffrage issue.[11] An almost unanimous Republican party gave South Carolina universal white manhood suffrage beginning with the 1812 elections. This caused a large increase in voter turnout; districts from which returns are available for 1806–1810 and 1812–1816 cast almost 50 percent more votes after reform than before. Probably very few of these new electors were inclined to Federalism, and this may help explain why the marked revival of Federalist support after 1810 in Virginia and North Carolina was not duplicated anywhere in South Carolina outside Charleston.

Table 5

South Carolina Assembly Roll Call Votes on Wider Suffrage

	Federalists		*Republicans*	
	For	*Against*	*For*	*Against*
1808, Senate	0	4	27	0
1809, House	5	6	78	15
1809, Senate	0	5	24	1
1809, Senate	0	3	25	1
1810, House	4	8	104	2
1810, Senate	0	4	35	2
1810, Senate	0	4	32	6
	9	34	325	27

Federalist voting power was also eroded by the death of the eighteenth-century custom of allowing a man to vote in each district where

11. Williamson, *American Suffrage*, 151–56; DeSaussure to Ezekiel Pickens, September 12, 1808, in DeSaussure Papers, USC; *South Carolina House Journal*, 1809, p. 115; 1810, pp. 16, 82; *South Carolina Senate Journal*, 1808, p. 117; 1809, pp. 144, 169; 1810, pp. 86, 110.

he had property. The slowness of transportation and the distances to be covered probably did not allow but two, conceivably three, votes to a man with land in several parishes. Still, the electorate was small enough in many places for these multiple votes to be important. The ten smallest parishes cast an average of only seventy votes in a normal election, so an addition of even half a dozen votes by nonresident landowners could tip a close race. Since men of wealth were more likely to be Federalists than poorer voters, plural voting was a clear benefit to the minority party. Attempts to curb this practice began in the 1790s and were soon successful. The house in 1800 and the senate in 1805 both resolved that no person should be entitled to vote in more than one election district. These resolutions did not have the force of law, but since each house was the judge of its members' qualifications, it could nullify the election of anyone who owed his seat to plural votes. Since no such challenges occurred in later years, the threat of unseating those who benefited from multiple voting was apparently effective in ending the practice. Federalists, of course, were hurt most by this change and clearly realized it. They voted 43–1 against outlawing multiple votes in house elections and 5–0 against in the senate, while Republicans were heavily in favor of the reform.[12]

The only aspect of South Carolina's political system that aided Federalists was the gross malapportionment of legislative seats between the sections. Until 1810 the low-country parishes, with 18 percent of the state's white population, elected 56 percent of the house and 54 percent of the senate. There was one legislative seat for every 550 low-country whites but only one seat for every 3,250 in the upcountry. This arrangement was hardly intended to help the Federalists; it was established in colonial days and persisted long after the death of the Federalist party. Still, because of its sectional nature, the party did have a much larger share of legislative seats than of voters in the first years of the century. In the very important session of 1800 the fifty-one Federalist members of the house represented 24,000 whites, while the sixty-five Republican members represented 166,000.

12. DeSaussure to John Rutledge, Jr., January 12, 1801, in Rutledge Papers, UNC; Hooker, "Diary of Edward Hooker," 877–78; William A. Schaper, *Sectionalism and Representation in South Carolina* (Washington, D.C., 1901), 425–26; *South Carolina House Journal*, 1800, pp. 97, 107; *South Carolina Senate Journal*, 1805, p. 155.

After about 1804, when the number of Federalists in the legislature fell toward the vanishing point, overrepresentation meant very little. In the 1808 session, Federalists had 13 percent of the house membership, although they had carried districts containing only 6 percent of the white population. When the assembly was reapportioned in 1810 to give more seats to the Republican up-country, the Federalist advantage dwindled still further. In the 1812 legislature, the last to contain any noticeable number of Federalists, the party had four house members instead of the one member it would have had under a completely equitable apportionment.[13]

The reapportionment of 1810 was the result of long-standing up-country demands for representation more in keeping with its four-fifths majority of white population. Quite naturally, the low-country aristocrats tried to delay any such loss of political power, and the issue had been simmering since the Revolution. The whole question of apportionment was more important here than elsewhere because South Carolina had the most centralized government in the country. Besides making law, choosing the governor and other state officials, and electing United States senators, as other southern legislatures did, the South Carolina assembly also picked presidential electors and all local officeholders such as sheriffs, clerks of court, and justices of the peace. The only popular election in the state, besides that for the legislature itself, was for congressmen, and even there the value of a citizen's vote could be increased or lessened by the assembly's drawing of district lines.

With such vast power residing in the legislature, and with sectionalism the key to state politics, the outcome of the reapportionment battle might decide the control of South Carolina for some time to come. It was most unfortunate for Federalists that they could find no way to turn this all-important issue to their advantage. With their strength concentrated in the low-country, it was naturally to their benefit to keep the existing unbalanced apportionment, which gave the coastal parishes far more than a fair share of the assembly. Any firm Federalist commitment toward increasing up-country representation might cause wholesale desertion by the party's remaining coastal

13. Schaper, *Sectionalism and Representation*, 408–19, shows the Federalist opposition to reapportionment in the 1790s.

voters. Probably no great up-country following could be won to offset coastal losses, since the up-country Republican representatives were themselves strongly in favor of reapportionment.[14] The redistribution of seats was finally carried out in time for the 1810 elections, and it depressed still further the Federalists' already-weak position in state politics. The eleven districts in which Federalists were strongest lost eleven house seats (dropping from forty-five to thirty-four). The twenty-two districts which together elected only a single Federalist in the entire period after 1800 gained fourteen seats (rising from fifty-four to sixty-eight).

Buffeted by this series of adverse changes in the political structure —congressional gerrymandering, broader suffrage, elimination of plural voting, legislative reapportionment—the Federalist party's only hope of securing any influence at all in state affairs was to attach itself to the popular side of some local issue and to work as a united party with publicity geared to offset its national unpopularity. However, no such issues existed at this time. Unlike other states, there was no extended debate over court reform, taxation, general constitutional revision, or other questions. Broadening the franchise and reapportioning the legislature were the only two matters that excited much public heat, and on both of these the Federalists were forced by their geographical and economic concentration among coastal aristocrats to take the unpopular side. Therefore, with the exception of a victory or two in Charleston and Benjamin Huger's brief return to Congress in 1814, the South Carolina Federalists experienced an almost uninterrupted political decline after 1800, and within a very few years they were an essentially negligible force in the state.

14. DeSaussure to John Rutledge, Jr., December 19, 1801, in Rutledge Papers, UNC; DeSaussure to Pickens, September 12, 1808, in DeSaussure Papers, USC; Schaper, *Sectionalism and Representation*, 433–37; Wolfe, *Jeffersonian Democracy*, 218–20.

Chapter 17 THE GEORGIA FEDERALISTS

THE Federalist party in Georgia died as an effective political force even before 1800. Its peak of influence came in 1798–1799 when the trouble with France aroused American patriotic feelings. Caught up in the wave, Georgia's Federalists suddenly found themselves almost popular. Already having the support of Senator James Gunn, they claimed both the state's newly elected congressmen as well. The legislature, though deploring the Alien and Sedition Acts, refused to endorse what it called the "violent" Virginia and Kentucky resolutions. Even most of the state's newspapers were openly friendly or at least benevolently neutral toward the Adams administration. With the end of the French crisis, however, all this evaporated and Georgia returned to the solidly Republican reputation that it had earned after the early 1790s.[1]

Although this exposed frontier state eagerly ratified the Constitution in 1788, a series of irritating events began almost at once, thoroughly alienating Georgians from the national administration and

1. Rose, *Prologue to Democracy*, 170–71, 186–87; Lamplugh, "Politics on the Periphery," 466–75; William O. Foster, *James Jackson: Duellist and Militant Statesman, 1757–1806* (Athens, Ga., 1960), 164–65; Dauer, *Adams Federalists*, 321 (Table 20); Donald H. Stewart, *The Opposition Press of the Federalist Period* (Albany, N.Y., 1969), 872.

from the Federalist party that grew up in support of it. To begin with, the treaties of New York in 1790 and Coleraine in 1796 between the United States and the Creek Indians granted terms far too favorable to the Indians to suit Georgia's land-hungry whites. The Treaty of New York was especially annoying, for it had been made without the slightest consultation between national and state governments, and it asserted the federal government's claim to control Georgia's western lands. Next came the Supreme Court's decision in *Chisholm* v. *Georgia* that the state could be sued by a citizen of another state because it had given up part of its sovereignty by joining the Union. Strong protests from Georgia were eventually satisfied by the Eleventh Amendment to the Constitution, but the *Chisholm* decision drove a further wedge between Georgia voters and the national administration.

Most damaging of all were the Yazoo speculations of 1789 and 1795, in which nearly every prominent Federalist in Georgia took part. In the notorious Yazoo fraud of 1795, the legislature was bribed to sell a huge tract of western land to Federalist speculators for a pittance, causing an immediate popular revulsion. James Jackson, an antiadministration leader in the national Senate, resigned to enter the legislature and force the repeal of the Yazoo sale. By making the affair a party issue he succeeded in disgracing the Federalist leaders and almost destroyed the already small Federalist party in Georgia.[2] With these particular state problems added to the general southern disgust at Hamilton's policies, the Jay Treaty, and other Federalist measures, the party was lucky to win something like 25 percent of Georgia's popular vote for John Adams in the 1796 election.[3]

Against such a dismal background, the sudden rise in party fortunes during the French crisis was obviously no more than a temporary emotional response to danger from abroad. By the year 1800 Georgia's Republican sympathies reasserted themselves. Congress-

2. Ulrich B. Phillips, *Georgia and State Rights* (Washington, D.C., 1902), 24–28, 30–32, 42–43; Foster, *James Jackson*, 46–48, 52–55, Chap. 7; Rose, *Prologue to Democracy*, 15–16, 61–64, 90–98; Lamplugh, "Politics on the Periphery," Chaps. 5, 7–8; C. Peter Magrath, *Yazoo: Law and Politics in the New Republic: The Case of Fletcher v. Peck* (Providence, R.I., 1966), Chap. 1.

3. Incomplete returns for the 1796 election are in the Savannah *Columbian Museum*, December 6, 1796. The total vote for nine Republican electors was 22,084; the total for two Federalists was 5,001 (18.5 percent). The highest vote for a Republican was 6,200; the highest for a Federalist was 2,644 (30 percent).

men Benjamin Taliaferro and James Jones, elected as supposed Federalists in 1798, quickly produced Republican voting records. The legislature of 1800 contained only a half-dozen Federalist members out of forty-eight. Only three areas of the state harbored many survivors of Federalism after 1800: the towns of Savannah and Augusta and their counties, Chatham and Richmond; the rich plantation fringe along the Atlantic coast; and a cluster of former frontier counties in northern Georgia.[4]

The merchant communities of Savannah and Augusta, with their allies in the law and other professions, made up the key element of Georgia Federalism. Here were the only active party organizations, the only party newspapers, and the only men with ties to the Federalists of other states. In Savannah, Georgia's only significant port, most merchants were probably Federalists. There was at least as much mercantile advertising in the *Columbian Museum*, the mild but consistent voice of Federalism, as in the Republican newspapers. If one can believe the Republican postmaster of Savannah, the "major part" of the Chamber of Commerce, which had complained of his mail service, was Federalist. When the collector of customs, a Federalist holdover from the Adams years, was ousted in 1801, no less than forty-seven commercial firms or individuals consoled him in a public letter loaded with criticism of Jeffersonian government. There is no direct evidence for Augusta; but, like Savannah, it had a large commercial element and a sizable Federalist vote, and very likely the connection between the two factors in Savannah extended also to Augusta.[5]

These well-to-do Federalists in mercantile and professional occupations were able to afford membership in the local military companies such as the Augusta Volunteer Artillery and the Savannah Volunteer Guards. They met either in these organizations or at public dinners on the Fourth of July and Washington's Birthday to reaffirm their partisan allegiance by drinking toasts to Washington, the navy,

4. Dauer, *Adams Federalists*, 323 (Chart 7); James Jackson to Abraham Baldwin, November 26, 1800, in Foster, *James Jackson*, 146; Lamplugh, "Politics on the Periphery," 475–82.

5. Savannah *Columbian Museum*, July 30, 1803; "A Friend to Virtue," *ibid.*, August 24, 1803; letter of support for the collector, *ibid.*, October 20, 1803; *Georgia Gazette*, October 22, 1801; Philip Box to [?], August 8, 1807, in Philip Box Letterbook, Georgia Historical Society.

the minority in Congress, and other objects of Federalist praise. In Savannah, particularly, the local party leaders made a point of such occasions, and they also gathered to honor visiting Federalist dignitaries and even—when he was being wooed by their party—Vice-President Aaron Burr.[6]

Federalist strength spread far enough beyond this small group of merchants and lawyers to give Republicans in both towns considerable fear on election day. In Savannah, Federalists dominated the city government during five of the eight years from 1800 through 1807. Only after the legislature replaced the ward system of electing councilmen with an at-large ticket, did Republicans achieve uniform control. Even then, they constantly warned each other to be on guard against "Federalist strategems." Augusta also had some party contests for office, but there is little indication that city elections were taken as seriously as in Savannah. At least two known Federalists served as intendant—William J. Hobby in 1805 and Seaborn Jones in 1813—indicating that the city council, which chose intendants, had a Federalist majority in those years. A prominent Republican was intendant in 1815 and 1816, but in all the remaining years it is impossible to determine the party affiliation of the intendants.[7]

Even in Chatham and Richmond counties, where the mercantile influence of Savannah and Augusta would be diluted, Federalists were able to force sharp contests on occasion. Usually they contented themselves with supporting maverick Republicans who ran without the endorsement of the official Republican organization, but sometimes they were bolder. In 1806 two outright Federalists polled 40 percent of the vote for the state house and senate in Chatham, and in 1809 another Federalist received 30 percent for the house. Two years later

6. For examples of Federalist toasts and resolutions, see *Augusta Herald*, July 7, 1802; Savannah *Columbian Museum*, July 6, 1803; and Thomas Gibbons to John Rutledge, Jr., May 11, 1802, in Rutledge Papers, UNC.

7. Lists of mayors and city councilmen in Savannah may be found in the newspapers during July, 1800–1807, and September, 1807–1816. The Federalist mayors, elected by the city council each year, were Thomas Gibbons (1800) and John Y. Noel (1804–1807). For Republican efforts to win or maintain control of the city, see *Georgia Republican*: July 7, 1803; "An Inhabitant," July 21, 1805; "A Voter," July 4, 1806; and "Breakers A-Head!" and "Democritus," September 3, 1808. See also "A Republican Voter," in Savannah *Public Intelligencer*, August 25, 1807; and Savannah *Columbian Museum*, October 27, 1804. Lists of mayors of Augusta may be found in *Augusta Herald*, April, 1800–16, and the *Augusta Yearbook* (Augusta, Ga., 1966).

James Johnston, a Federalist judge, was actually elected to the state senate from Chatham county.[8]

Evidence of partisan contests in Richmond County is scarce, and the absence of frantic Republican effort indicates less concern about possible Federalist victories. Nevertheless, an Augusta Federalist boasted of his party's clean sweep in the legislative contest of 1802, claiming that two Federalist representatives and a state senator had been elected. Faced with this coup, Republicans made an unusually vigorous effort the next year and succeeded in defeating the senator and one of the representatives. Voter turnout was up one-sixth from the preceding year, and the *Augusta Herald* remarked that "there seemed to be more *anxiety* for the event, than we ever before witnessed." The remaining Federalist retired in 1804 after two years in the legislature. Even in defeat, the party's candidate for state senator polled 38 percent of the vote in 1803 and 32 percent in 1804. As late as 1810 another probable Federalist, the son of the late party leader Thomas Glascock, was elected to the house, outpolling all other candidates.[9]

Other Federalist votes came from the string of wealthy rice and Sea Island cotton plantation counties along the Atlantic coast. There, as everywhere, Republicans were in a clear majority; but the Federalist fraction was greater than in the state at large, and it increased when candidates could appeal to local interests. John Elliott, a planter who had once represented coastal Liberty County in the legislature, was the Federalist candidate for Congress in 1810. While he ran far behind in the race, he did very well in the half-dozen seaboard counties. The two other Federalist congressional candidates (in 1802 and 1808) were from up-country and could hardly match Elliott's show-

8. The contested legislative elections in Chatham County caused much newspaper controversy: *Georgia Republican*, October 7, 1806, October 3, 1809, October 8, 1811; Savannah *Columbian Museum*, October 2, 1809, September 16, 1811. Republican fears of open or secret Federalist campaigning appear in Savannah *Southern Patriot*, September 1, October 6, 1806; and Savannah *Republican*, September 22, 1807, "Publicola," September 28, 1809, and "Paulding," September 22, 1810. Savannah *Evening Ledger*, September 24, 1808.

9. Richmond County contests are reported in a letter from Augusta, in *Alexandria Advertiser*, November 15, 1802; *Augusta Chronicle*, October 9, 1802; *Augusta Herald*, October 5, 1803; Savannah *Columbian Museum*, October 10, 1804; and Augusta *Mirror of the Times*, October 19, 1812.

ing on the coast, but they did do relatively well there compared to their statewide vote.[10]

The third remnant of Federalism in Georgia existed in a group of counties north of Augusta, between the Savannah and Oconee rivers. This area was near, but not actually on, the frontier. It was a land of small farms, but it had the fertile soil and access to transportation that allowed the creation of a well-to-do class of staple planters. Three of the most notable Federalist judges in Georgia lived here: Augustin S. Clayton in Clarke County, John M. Dooly in Lincoln, and Thomas P. Carnes in Franklin. In the 1796 election, John Adams did better in this region than anywhere else in the state. He carried Wilkes County, nearly took Greene, and polled about 40 percent in Lincoln and Franklin. In legislative elections, Lincoln County sent a Federalist to the state house four times; Clarke, three times; and Franklin, twice. Given the highly personal nature of Georgia politics, the Federalist showing there may simply reflect the deferential voting of small farmers, who supported local worthies like Dooly, Clayton, and Carnes in spite of their taint of Federalism. Possibly, too, this region was showing its objection to the aristocratic low-country dominance of Georgia's Republican party by voting occasionally for those few men who were either Federalists or were reputed not to be good Republicans.[11]

The great influence of personality in winning votes for Federalist candidates demonstrated Georgia's tradition of personal politics—a characteristic that may have derived from the state's small population and recent experience as a frontier area. There was little to suppress the common tendency of voters to rally around colorful or forceful candidates. Everywhere in the state, party organizations were rudimentary if present at all. The Federalists were too weak to threaten Republican supremacy, and sectionalism was rarely a divisive question between coast and up-country. Therefore, the dominant political group in Georgia was not so much the Republican party as the "Jackson party," built around Senator James Jackson, the hero of the popular anti-Yazoo movement of 1795–1796. The only worthwhile opposition to this faction was another personality group, the "Clark party,"

10. *Augusta Chronicle*, August 16, 23, 30, 1802; Savannah *Columbian Museum*, October 7, 11, 14, 18, 1808, October 4, 8, 1810; *Georgia Express*, October 6, 1810.

11. Savannah *Columbian Museum*, December 6, 1796.

adherents of up-country leader John Clark. After Jackson's death in 1806, his majority group found a new chief and as the "Troup party" continued its successful battle with the underdog Clark faction.[12]

Since Federalists were so obviously incapable of competing seriously for control of the state, they were not rigidly excluded from nonpartisan offices in Georgia. Federal positions, however, were turned over to Republicans early in Jefferson's administration. James Jackson was determined to force this, and in September, 1801, he reminded the president that the federal district attorney, the marshall, and the revenue supervisor for Georgia were all lame-duck Federalists. What especially incensed Jackson was President Adams' "midnight" appointment of Thomas Gibbons ("Impudent—Arrogant—An Old Tory") as district judge. Gibbons was soon replaced by a Republican, William Stephens, who the Federalists in their turn branded a Tory. They said that he had actually defected to the British during the Revolution and that his name appeared on the banishment and property-confiscation lists drawn up by the Georgia patriots. The Federalist collector of customs at Savannah was also ousted, and the district attorney and other holdovers followed him into forced retirement in 1802, bringing forth the usual Federalist protests. In the same year William J. Hobby, editor of the Federalist *Augusta Herald*, lost his postmaster's job. To finish the business properly, the only high national office held by a Georgia Federalist was also vacated when Joseph Habersham resigned as postmaster general on a hint that his departure was desired.[13]

At the state level there was no proscription of Federalists. They were not allowed in the governorship or the national Senate seats (and after 1802 none even ran for these offices), but judicial positions were remarkably open to them. Federalists held two of three judgeships in

12. Lamplugh, "Politics on the Periphery," shows the basically personal, rather than formally partisan, nature of Georgia politics in this period.

13. James Jackson to John Milledge, September 1, 1801, in Harriet M. Salley (ed.), *Correspondence (1785–1818) of John Milledge, Governor of Georgia, 1802–1806* (Columbia, S.C., 1949), 75; James Jackson to James Madison, May 15, 1801, in Madison Papers, LC; *Augusta Herald*, February 3, March 24, 1802, and "A Citizen," February 10, 1801; Thomas Gibbons to John Rutledge, Jr., April 15, 1802, in Rutledge Papers, UNC; *Georgia Gazette*, October 22, 1801; Savannah *Columbian Museum*, October 20, 1801; Joseph Habersham to Baldwin, March 15, 1802, in Abraham Baldwin Papers, University of Georgia.

1800–1803 and two of four in 1810. At least half a dozen prominent party leaders were appointed or elected judges or solicitors of the state district courts: John M. Berrien, John M. Dooly, Thomas P. Carnes, George Walton, Matthew McAllister, John Y. Noel, and Peter L. Van Alen.[14] This surprisingly wide admittance to nonpolitical offices was partly gained by capitalizing on personal and sectional divisions within the Republican majority. Federalists were unable to find any state issue that would win their party a large following; to elect a few individual state officers, they had more luck making temporary alliances with up-country and anti-Jackson legislators. Such unions allowed Federalist candidates to make a showing that was out of all proportion to their actual party strength, which was always very small.

The persistent candidacy of Thomas P. Carnes illustrates this. Carnes was an up-country judge, a popular man who happened to be a Federalist. So strong was his "friends-and-neighbors" appeal to Republicans from neighboring counties, that he seemed actually to have a serious chance of election to the United States Senate in 1800. As James Jackson reported, "the aristocratic set" of Augusta Federalists "persuaded the Western members a back countryman ought to be the person" chosen senator. Carnes seemed likely to pick up a few coastal votes also, and to prevent his victory the fragmented Republicans finally agreed to unite behind Jackson himself, giving him fifty-eight votes out of sixty-seven. Even the nine holdouts may have been an exaggeration of the actual Federalist membership. In 1801 Carnes was again a candidate, this time for governor. Although there were not half a dozen members of his party in the assembly, he polled 21 of 69 votes on joint ballot, evidently winning his home section in northwest Georgia. The next year he repeated the feat, drawing 22 of 70 votes for governor. Years later, in the spring of 1810, there was a concerted effort to put together a slate for the election of district judges

14. For the gubernatorial contests see Sparta *Farmers Gazette*, November 25, 1803, November 16, 1805; *Augusta Chronicle*, November 14, 1807, November 18, 1809, November 15, 1811; Washington (Ga.) *Monitor*, November 13, 1813; and *Augusta Herald*, November 15, 1815. For the senatorial elections see Peter Crawford to Baldwin, December 2, 1804, in Abraham Baldwin Papers; *Georgia Republican*, June 27, 1806; letter from Louisville (Ga.) in Savannah *Columbian Museum*, June 25, 1806; *Augusta Chronicle*, November 14, 1807; *Augusta Herald*, November 30, 1809; and *Georgia Journal*, November 13, 1816. Judicial officers are listed in the *Georgia Official and Statistical Register, 1971–1972* (Atlanta, 1972).

and solicitors. Two Federalists, Carnes and John M. Berrien, were among the three judgeship candidates, and at the fall session Carnes was easily elected judge of the western circuit, 55–36, almost entirely by Republican votes. In 1816 another Federalist was chosen to fill the eastern district judgeship, probably as a package deal with a minority of the Republican members.[15]

While this sort of effort within the legislature itself could occasionally elect Federalists to relatively harmless offices, the party never generated such sectional or personal alliances among the mass of voters. Lacking any organization that could speak as the voice of a united party, and limited to two newspapers along the Savannah River for broadcasting arguments, Federalists had a difficult time making any impression upon the public. The most that could be done was to strike out occasionally on some issue of temporary importance, as in 1800, when the party tried to portray James Jackson as a dictator over the state Republican party. The two newspapers and their anonymous contributors complained that Jackson "has never suffered any of his adherents to have any opinion of their own; nor will he allow them or other citizens, to express their opinions of public measures freely or at all, if he can prevent." Jackson was accused of heaping abuse on those who disagreed with him and of having a much overblown opinion of himself. Such charges were of doubtful use, coming from a party that had recently enacted the Sedition Law and that was even then defending several well-publicized prosecutions under it. Besides, the *Columbian Museum* in Savannah reduced the effectiveness of the anti-Jackson drive by opening its columns to letters in favor of the Republican leader.[16]

A few years later the other Federalist paper, the *Augusta Herald*, tried to launch a crusade against the legislature's decision to distribute by lottery all the land obtained from the Creek Indians. The *Herald* wanted the land sold for cash and the money to be used for retiring the outstanding state debt and the bounty warrants issued to Revolu-

15. James Jackson to Baldwin, November 26, 1800, in Abraham Baldwin Papers; *Louisville* (Ga.) *Gazette*, November 17, 1801, November 6, 1802; T. Fitch to Daniel Mulford, April 5, 1810, in Mulford Papers, Georgia Historical Society; *Georgia Journal*, December 12, 1810, November 13, 1816.

16. Among examples in the Savannah *Columbian Museum* are: "Super-Dictator," December 2, 1800; "A," December 5 and 23, 1800; and "Z," December 9 and 20, 1800.

tionary troops. Editor William Hobby protested that "were an individual to *give* away a valuable property, while he refused to pay his just debts, his conduct would not be considered either honest or proper." There was some criticism of the lottery, too, in the *Columbian Museum*, but nothing ever came of the issue. Everyone in the state had a chance to win free land in the giveaway, and the public would naturally think it was irksome to give up this privilege in order to benefit the few holders of bounty certificates and other forms of state debt.[17]

Except for these minor rumblings, Federalists in Georgia let the years go by without ever attempting to organize themselves around popular state issues. Suffering a poor national image for their party and facing in James Jackson and his successors a series of very forceful Republican leaders, the Georgia Federalists never recovered from the depressed position they held in 1800. A few individuals might form temporary personal alliances and win election to nonpolitical offices in the court system, but the Federalist party itself was never effective.

17. *Augusta Herald*, August 1, 1805; "Protest," *ibid.*, June 12, 1806; letter from Louisville, Ga., in Savannah *Columbian Museum*, June 18, 1806.

Chapter 18 FEDERALIST PARTY ORGANIZATION IN THE SOUTH

THE southern Federalists' greatest failing as politicians was their inability to develop a party organization after 1800. Victory in any state was probably impossible, but closer attention to organization would surely have increased the Federalist minority in Congress and the legislatures. The Federalist problem was not simply a distaste for the "democratic" style of campaigning. Many individual Federalists ran for office using every possible method of winning votes, although some prominent leaders did hold themselves aloof from what they considered degrading activity. Far more serious was the lack of *organized* effort, of any attempt to coordinate the campaigns of individual candidates. Federalists could have managed without a year-round organization; indeed, there was little for a permanent body to do, and neither party ever created one except perhaps in one or two northern states.[1] Only in the crucial months before an election was a certain amount of well-directed centralized activity essential to the success of a minority party.

1. The closest either party came to having a permanent state organization was the Republicans' "Richmond junto" in Virginia, and even it did little except during legislative sessions and election campaigns: Harry M. Ammon, "The Richmond Junto, 1800–1824," *Virginia Magazine of History and Biography*, LXI (1953), 394–418.

Southern Republicans were not highly organized either, except in Virginia, but they had the advantage of overwhelming numbers. A majority that could count on receiving upwards of two-thirds of the votes in any contest could continue to win office indefinitely without much disciplined effort. Such a party did not need to propagandize heavily in order to change voters' minds, for it already had a sure majority. It did not need to drum up a large turnout of the faithful, for if all the Federalists and only half the Republicans had voted, the Republican party would still have won nearly every southern election. Republicans did not need to seek out especially able and energetic candidates, for an empty name could win office with the party label as its only asset. They did not even need to restrict the number of candidates, because a Republican vote divided among two or three men could still shut out a single Federalist in most districts.

Only where the opposition demonstrated a real threat by closely contesting or even winning offices was there a vital need for the majority to organize in order to maintain itself in power. In most areas where Federalists might reasonably hope for victory—Richmond, Norfolk, the upper Potomac, the Shenandoah Valley, and the Alleghenies in Virginia; Charleston and environs in South Carolina; and Savannah and Augusta in Georgia—the Republicans responded with their own well-developed organization. Only in parts of North Carolina and in the heavily Federalist Eastern Shore of Virginia were Republicans lax in organizing themselves when there was real danger of defeat.

The situation of the Federalists was vastly different. If a minority party expects to win at all, it must have every possible advantage. It must encourage candidates who are more capable, or at least more popular, than the majority nominees; it must avoid at all costs splitting its votes among two or more men; it must cover the constituency with speeches and literature to sway undecided voters and reinforce the faithful; and it must excite the loyal minority to turn out on election day. Nevertheless, southern Federalists ignored political realities and were very slow to create the organization that their minority position required. Of course, the party system was only rudimentary in the early nineteenth century, but both parties in several other states had adopted a rather complex organization that selected candidates, distributed propaganda, and brought voters to the polls.[2]

Southern Federalists were defective at every level of party effort—national, state, and local. The most visible shortcoming was the weak and intermittent tie between southerners and the northern Federalists, who directed the fortunes of the national party. While Republicans maintained a lively coordination through correspondence and caucuses, Federalists north of the Potomac had little to do with the withered southern remnant of their party after 1800. Of all the southern leaders only John Rutledge, Jr., of South Carolina kept up anything like an active correspondence with the New England or middle-state Federalists. A few others, such as H. W. DeSaussure, William Gaston, and Joseph Pearson, exchanged an occasional letter with northern comrades, but otherwise there was an amazing shortage of intersectional contact, especially when compared to the work Republicans did before 1800 in drawing together their minority forces throughout the Union.[3]

Presumably, the large southern contingent in the Sixth Congress joined the 1800 congressional caucus at Philadelphia, which nominated Adams and Pinckney; but this is the only known full-scale intersectional party meeting. Soon after Jefferson's victory, there were several attempts to hold a national Federalist conclave, but all were abortive. In May, 1801, for instance, Republican congressman Nathaniel Macon was "pretty well assured, that a systematic opposition . . . was probably organized at Washington last winter." No permanent national committee emerged from that meeting, but the participants decided to work out a system for Federalist congressmen to send reg-

2. On the electioneering organizations of both parties in New Jersey, Delaware, and Massachusetts, see Carl E. Prince, *New Jersey's Jeffersonian Republicans: The Genesis of an Early Party Machine, 1789–1817* (Chapel Hill, N.C., 1967), Chaps. 3–4; Rudolph J. Pasler and Margaret C. Pasler, *The New Jersey Federalists* (Rutherford, N.J., 1975), Chaps. 3, 5; John A. Munroe, *Federalist Delaware, 1775–1815* (New Brunswick, 1954), 228–38; Paul Goodman, *The Democratic-Republicans of Massachusetts: Politics in a Young Republic* (Cambridge, Mass., 1964), Chap. 6; James M. Banner, Jr., *To the Hartford Convention: The Federalists and the Origins of Party Politics in Massachusetts, 1789–1815* (New York, 1970), Chaps. 6–7.

3. On the Republican effort in the 1790s, see Cunningham, *Jeffersonian Republicans, passim*.

ular letters to prominent men throughout their states. In this way the Federalist side of public issues could be brought home to voters who might be beyond the reach of party newspapers and who would give more weight to the opinion of a local worthy than to an impersonal editorial. The idea had merit, but it never got beyond the initial stage of collecting names of prospective recipients of the letters. A year later, when Alexander Hamilton tried to assemble another interstate leadership meeting at Washington for which he solicited the presence of Charles Cotesworth Pinckney, William R. Davie, and possibly other southerners, there was no response.[4]

By this time party fortunes were in a steep decline, and there is no evidence of another national caucus until 1808, when Federalist hopes for presidential victory rose with the mounting public outcry against the embargo. In the summer of that year Elias B. Caldwell, editor of the Washington *Federalist*, wrote to North Carolina and possibly to other southern states, asking who the local Federalists would prefer for president, how many votes the party could expect, and other information. Shortly after, a more ambitious project was put on foot—the calling of an informal Federalist convention in New York City to choose a presidential candidate and to form campaign strategy.

This was almost entirely a northern affair, and there was no particular effort to involve the southern leaders. John Rutledge, Jr., who happened to be in the vicinity of New York, was the only person attending from any southern state, and there is no indication that opinions from Virginia or Georgia were even sought. The meeting settled upon Charles Cotesworth Pinckney and Rufus King as nominees, but this decision did not prevent a division of southern support among Pinckney, James Monroe, and George Clinton. Being virtually ignored in the choice of a candidate irked the southern leadership and they made their grievance known. One of their northern colleagues admitted, "I do not think there is communication enough with the Southern Federalists. . . . They feel mortified, that they are so often passed over by their Eastern friends. This was particularly the case with re-

4. Dauer, *Adams Federalists*, 249–50; Nathaniel Macon to Thomas Jefferson, May 24, 1801, in McPherson (ed.), "Unpublished Letters," 272; Charles W. Harris to Duncan Cameron, January 9, 1801, in Cameron Family Papers; C. C. Pinckney to Alexander Hamilton, May 3, 1802, in Hamilton (ed.), *Hamilton*, VI, 545.

spect to the consultations about the late Presidential election."[5] Perhaps because of this grumbling, when another "national convention" gathered in New York four years later, there was a real effort to consult southern opinion. Results were disappointing. Four delegates represented South Carolina, but there were only a few letters from individual Federalists in Virginia and North Carolina, and nothing came from Georgia. The southerners were divided as to a candidate but agreed to support the convention's choice of DeWitt Clinton as the strongest anti-Madisonian. Presumably South Carolina's delegates carried the news back to their state, and North Carolina was notified by letter. Virginia newspapers publicized the decision in approving terms, but Federalists there ultimately ignored Clinton and held their own state convention to nominate a "pure" ticket of Rufus King and William R. Davie.[6]

Such were the infrequent and unsatisfactory ties between the southern and northern wings of the party. There were, in addition, some informal occasions for an exchange of views, as when Rutledge, DeSaussure, and others vacationed extensively in the North; but these could hardly serve as regular or dependable channels of party organization. Sessions of Congress gave southern members opportunity to meet frequently with their colleagues from New England and elsewhere, but this type of consultation, even when it transcended a mere discussion of legislative tactics, was not an effective means of forming national party policy. There never were enough southern Federalist congressmen to be properly representative of party opinion in the whole section. Georgia did not elect any Federalists after 1800, and South Carolina elected only one after 1803. During the Ninth Con-

5. Elias B. Caldwell to William Gaston, June 1, 1808, in William Gaston Papers; Harrison Gray Otis to John Rutledge, Jr., July 3, 1808, and letter to the "Federal Republican Committee, Charleston, South Carolina," September, 1808, in Morison (ed.), *Otis*, I, 314–15; William Barry Grove to Walter Alves, September 19, 1808, in Walter Alves Papers; Jacob Wagner to Timothy Pickering, January 21, 1809, in Timothy Pickering Papers; Fischer, *Revolution of American Conservatism*, 85–87.

6. C. C. Pinckney to James Milnor *et al.*, August 24, 1812, in Pinckney Family Papers; Milnor *et al.* to Joseph Pearson, August 10, 1812, and to John Stanly and Gaston, August 13, 1812, Jacob Radcliffe *et al.* to Gaston, August 25, 1812, and David B. Ogden to Gaston, September 21, 1812, all in William Gaston Papers; Benjamin Stoddert to James McHenry, July 15, 1812, in Steiner, *McHenry*, 581–82; Pearson to Otis, November 9, 1812, in Harrison Gray Otis Papers; Rufus King's account of the convention, in King (ed.), *King*, V, 226; Fischer, *Revolution of American Conservatism*, 87–90.

gress there was only one party member from the entire South, and only two appeared in the Tenth. Even when a half-dozen Federalists from Virginia and North Carolina were present, their participation in congressional meetings was not of much use in improving party organization. They neither gathered opinion from within their states to present to northern colleagues nor attempted to report their Washington conversations to correspondents at home.

All this is not to say that southern Federalist congressmen were not fully a part of the national party. While in Washington they faithfully aligned themselves with most other Federalists on nearly every partisan issue. As far as votes on public policy are concerned, no distinctive southern wing of the Federalist party existed. Harry Fritz's recent study of party cohesion in the House from 1807 to 1817 shows Federalists from the South only slightly less firm in support of the party's position than northern Federalists. The trouble was that such cooperation on the floor of Congress did not extend outside the House, and except on very rare occasions southern Federalists had little influence on, or knowledge of, the decision-making process in the national party.[7]

Interstate contacts among the southerners were scarcely more frequent or satisfactory. No formal groups existed to exchange ideas among the various states, and individual leaders rarely corresponded with each other. The John Rutledge Papers in the University of North Carolina, for example, are the largest single collection of southern Federalist political manuscripts; they contain probably two letters from northern leaders for every one from the South. The William Gaston Papers, also at the University of North Carolina, likewise show more contact with northern men than with out-of-state southerners, although there is little with either. The only information that most Federalist leaders received about their brothers in other southern states came from the weekly newspapers.

Organization on the state level varied widely, but nowhere was it

7. Harry W. Fritz, "The Collapse of Party: President, Congress, and the Decline of Party Action, 1807–1817" (Ph.D. dissertation, Washington University of St. Louis, 1971), Chap. 5. See also Ronald L. Hatzenbuehler, "Foreign Policy Voting in the United States Congress, 1808–1812" (Ph.D. dissertation, Kent State University, 1972), 64–69, 87–90, 174–80, 193–98, 227–30, 234–38.

very advanced except in Virginia during 1800 and 1812. This backwardness was partly a by-product of the election system, because there were no statewide elections for governor in the South and none for president outside of Virginia. Since all candidates were elected locally, one of the chief incentives for a statewide organization was removed. In Virginia, however, the General Ticket Law required presidential electors to be chosen by the voters of the whole state, so that each party had to pick a slate of nominees, one from each district. Republicans solved this problem by holding a caucus of legislators every four years. The caucus drew up an electoral ticket, selected a state central committee, and designated a few men in each county to form local campaign committees.

There being only two or three dozen Federalists in the General Assembly, the caucus system was ill-suited to party needs, and several alternative methods were tried. In 1800 it was still possible to hold an official legislative caucus, since there were more than fifty Federalist delegates and senators from every section of the state. The caucus met in Richmond, certified a slate of electors for Adams and Pinckney, drew up a party manifesto to the voters, and named William Austin of Richmond as corresponding secretary. Austin sent copies of the ticket and address to each county, and, to spread information and opinion even more widely throughout the state, a party newspaper was established. From its lack of advertisements, this was patently a political sheet intended only for election-year duty.[8]

After 1800, Federalists abandoned the caucus as their legislative membership steadily shrank, and their search for a substitute was not at first very fruitful. In 1804 party fortunes had sunk so low that no electors were even nominated, and except for one or two local write-in efforts, the Jeffersonian ticket had no opposition. Much brighter prospects appeared in 1808, when James Monroe came forth as an antiadministration candidate in Virginia. There were two attempts to galvanize and direct the state's Federalist voters, although neither had much success. Eastern leaders met in Richmond to support Monroe, and although they created no formal organization, election returns

8. On the 1800 campaign in Virginia, see Chap. 2, herein.

indicate that most Federalist voters followed their lead. In answer to the pro-Monroe group a number of western Federalists gathered at Staunton to support the "regular" nominee, Charles Cotesworth Pinckney. They set up a central committee and hoped to extend their organization downward into the counties, but they were unable to make headway. The Pinckney electoral ticket was not widely distributed and it won a substantial vote in only ten counties. Elsewhere, local Federalists cast their ballots for Monroe or else stayed home, ignoring the plea of the Staunton organizers.[9]

By 1812 the party was better prepared, and after a few weeks of feverish work, it held the most nearly modern political convention in any southern state before the days of Jackson. Mass meetings of Federalists in each county were to elect two delegates to a state presidential nominating convention at Staunton. For participating counties, this was a tremendous advance in party organization and was far more representative of the voters' choice than the legislative caucus that Republicans used. However, fewer than twenty counties chose delegates, and some of the strongest Federalist areas in the state were unrepresented. In concept, therefore, the 1812 Staunton convention was remarkable, but in execution it was quite incomplete. Still, the three dozen delegates who assembled did make nominations, publish a bold antiwar address, and name a state executive committee. This committee was supposed to correspond with county organizations, of which there were probably very few, since the time remaining before the election was so short. As a result, Virginia Federalists never did achieve the network of central and county committees that worked so well for Republicans.[10]

Below the statewide level Federalists were better organized in Virginia than anywhere else, but their effectiveness varied from place to place. In the first years after 1800 they did little anywhere in the state to perform the most basic party functions—concentrating upon one official candidate, coordinating the efforts of various counties in a congressional district, and turning out the maximum vote on election day. It was possible for a Loudoun County leader to say in 1801, for instance, that "we have three Federalist candidates [for two seats] for

9. See Chap. 8, herein.
10. For the 1812 election in Virginia, see Chap. 11, herein.

the State Legislature. I do not regret this circumstance."[11] Later, the party began to realize the need for more organization, and by the wartime years Federalists in several parts of Virginia were capable of acting in close cooperation through a well-established formal party system. Elsewhere there were some rather effective informal consultations between local leadership groups. In most of the state, however, the sheer lack of Federalist numbers prevented any attempt at organization.

The first efficient party organization in a congressional race appeared in the very competitive Eastern Shore district in 1803. This was the only seat to remain in Federalist hands after the 1801 election, and the party was eager to retain it. In good years and with a strong campaign, victory was possible; but proper coordination between the two stalwart Eastern Shore counties and the less friendly western shore was vital. Two candidates threatened to split the vote in 1803, with disastrous consequences. Thomas Griffin claimed precedence because he had announced first; but his competitor, a Major Smith, refused to bow out because Griffin had come forward "without making himself acquainted with the Federal Will." Party leaders desperately tried to induce one to withdraw and finally were able to pressure Smith into doing so just days before the election. Griffin won a narrow victory and surely would have lost without the mobilization of an intercounty consensus of leaders in his favor and without Smith's willingness to abide by that consensus.[12]

In the marginal Botetourt district of the middle valley another Federalist organization was created somewhat later. James Breckinridge became the party's candidate in 1807 after a simple communication from a friend who had "been requested by a number of federalists to write you and solicit you to appear as a Candidate." This makeshift procedure was not very successful, since Breckinridge lost the race. Perhaps learning from experience, Federalists followed a more formal process in 1809. County meetings across the district tested the sentiment of local workers and, after giving Breckinridge a public

11. Thomas Simms to Leven Powell, February 20, 1801, in "Correspondence of Col. Leven Powell," 61.

12. Thomas Griffin to John Cropper, February 7 and May 7, 1803, and John Patterson to Cropper, March 12, 1803, in John Cropper Papers; John Stratton to [?], April 6, 1803, in Stratton Letter.

nomination, appointed committees of correspondence to work out a districtwide campaign. This time success rewarded the improved organization.[13]

The most elaborate and successful Federalist network grew up in the Berkeley-Jefferson district on Virginia's northern border. After defeats in 1801, 1805, and 1807, the party created a strict system of intercounty consultation on nominations and campaign activity. The search for a suitable candidate began well in advance of the 1809 election, and before the beginning of the year, county mass meetings in Berkeley, Jefferson, and Hampshire had agreed to support James Stephenson, a former congressman, for the April balloting. Corresponding committees were chosen to avoid any misstep in uniting the entire Federalist vote of the district behind Stephenson. In 1811 the same process was followed, with John Baker chosen to replace Stephenson, who retired after one term. Again the activity began very early, the first meetings being held in October, 1810, and the final nomination occurring in December. This was far earlier than the usual Federalist practice of scraping together a campaign for a last-minute candidate a few weeks before election day. In 1813 the system functioned well again; each county chose delegates to a single districtwide convention that nominated Francis White, Baker having followed Stephenson's example of retiring after one term.[14] The mass meeting and convention method of picking a Federalist candidate had become so firmly established in the district that in 1815 Magnus Tate, running against White, felt compelled to issue a public statement to the freeholders explaining "why I have become a candidate without the sanction of a committee." He attacked the concept of organized nominations and upheld the old system of each candidate running on his own. Since he won the election against the regularly designated Federalist, there must have been many voters who disliked the advent of official party nominations.[15]

13. John McCampbell to James Breckinridge, February 27, 1807, in Breckinridge Papers, UVa; *Norfolk Gazette*, March 3, 1809; Staunton *Political Censor*, February 22, 1809.

14. Martinsburg *Berkeley & Jefferson Intelligencer*, July 28, October 14, December 2, 23, 1808; *Alexandria Advertiser*, September 20, 1808; Charlestown *Farmer's Repository*, October 5, December 14, 1810; *Martinsburg Gazette*, February 19, March 19, 1813; *Virginia Patriot*, March 30, 1813.

15. *Martinsburg Gazette*, January 19, 1815.

The vigor of organized Federalism in the Berkeley district was hardly typical of Virginia. Even the more casual arrangements described in the Eastern Shore and Botetourt campaigns were unusual. Most districts had no Federalist candidates at all, and most of those that did got along without anything that could be called an organization. The Norfolk district is an example. Though difficult to win, it was not hopeless, and in 1809 a Federalist candidate appeared for the first time in years. In spite of the opportunity, little was done to help him. The party newspaper complained that "while their opponents were organized by various meetings and associations, the friends of Mr. Taylor [the Federalist] seemed to think it was enough to vote." Only one Federalist meeting was held, just a day or two before the election. After the inevitable defeat, the same editor hoped that the local Federalists "have been instructed that industry and management are necessary in conducting elections." Instead, the Norfolk Federalists lapsed into even deeper apathy. The same problem afflicted the party in the Richmond area that year. Like Norfolk, this district was Republican but not impossibly so, and a prominent Hanover County Federalist entered the race. Yet in Richmond itself a party leader admitted on election day that "it was not known until this morning that a poll would be taken for him."[16]

Despite, or perhaps because of, such unpromising experiences, Federalists became more adept at organizing themselves in later years. In the wartime election of 1813 several districts exhibited the workings of a formal nominating and canvassing system. In the Richmond area conditions were far different from those of 1809. A public meeting nominated the party's candidate and appointed the usual committee of correspondence and also a committee of vigilance, which was to purchase and distribute speeches and political essays setting forth the Federalist view of public affairs. In the Augusta district centered around Staunton, the congressional nomination was made by a central committee appointed by "the Friends of Peace, Commerce, and No Foreign Alliances." Its members were probably chosen by mass meetings of Federalists in the individual counties, the first time such a technique was used in this part of the valley. Perhaps the Vir-

16. *Norfolk Gazette*, March 20, April 12, 24, 26, 1809; *Alexandria Gazette*, May 1, 1809; Robert Gamble, Jr., to James McDowell, April 3, 1809, in James McDowell Papers.

ginia party was heading toward a more organized existence, at least in western districts; but this tendency was cut short by the rapid disintegration of both parties after the war.[17]

In contrast to Virginia, North Carolina had the loosest Federalist party of any in the South. There was no statewide election at all and, hence, no institutional need for a centrally selected slate of candidates. Within the legislature, Federalist members held an occasional caucus, but these always related to legislative business rather than to state party organization. In fact, neither party took advantage of the annual legislative sessions to hold a broader caucus dealing with state issues or nominations.[18] Even in the congressional and electoral districts, the largest voting units, there was no formal party structure and rarely even a meeting of political leaders. The closest thing to continuous Federalist consultation was among the lawyers, many of whom were politicians, who traveled from town to town to try superior court cases. On the county level Federalists presumably did gather informally at times, especially in the few towns; but there were no mass meetings or formal county conventions as in Virginia. Consequently, no uniformity existed in Federalist campaign efforts, and two or three active newspapers provided the only permanent voice for the state party.

In the absence of a caucus or central committee, individual leaders with a wide range of correspondents tried their best to act as informal state chairmen. Archibald Henderson, a Salisbury lawyer and sometime congressman, filled this role in the 1800 and 1808 campaigns. He received information from the national party, passed it on to his correspondents across the state, urged local people to run for office, and gave hints on campaign strategy.[19] In the 1812 presiden-

17. *Virginia Patriot*, November 10, 1812; Staunton *Republican Farmer*, March 18, 1813. For organizing in other districts, see Allen Taylor to James Breckinridge, January 20, 1813, in Breckinridge Papers, UVa; Staunton *Republican Farmer*, March 4, 25, 1813 (Greenbrier district); *Virginia Patriot*, April 2, 1813 (Eastern Shore); and *Virginia Herald*, December 2, 1812 (Culpepper district).

18. For information on caucuses, see Chap. 20*n*12, herein.

19. Archibald Henderson to Walter Alves, July 28, 1800, in Henderson, "Federalist of the Old School," 18; Henderson to Walter Alves, March 3, 1801, in Archibald Henderson Collection; Henderson to John Rutledge, Jr., September 9, 1808, in Rutledge Papers, UNC.

tial race and the 1813 congressional campaign, Raleigh banker William Polk served the same function. Located at the state capital, he was familiar with the party's legislators, who met there annually, and he worked closely with William Boylan, editor of the chief Federalist newspaper, the *Minerva*. Polk was deeply involved with forming the 1812 and 1813 campaigns around a "peace ticket," which included both regular Federalists and antiwar Republicans such as Archibald Murphey and Congressmen Richard Stanford and William Kennedy.[20] Neither Henderson nor Polk ever held an official party position; both undertook the work of statewide organization on their own simply because no one else would do so. Boylan also served in this capacity throughout the entire period after 1800, using his paper to urge stronger Federalist efforts in election after election.

In fact, Boylan was involved in an ambitious plan for strengthening the Federalist party throughout North Carolina by distributing the *Minerva* free of charge to prominent men in each county. The free subscriptions were to be paid for in bulk by loyal party contributors, in hopes that those who received their news through a Federalist filter would in time become bulwarks of party strength in their neighborhoods. First set up in 1802, this scheme was in operation possibly as late as 1810. Its effect is unknown, but it was certainly an imaginative effort that took some degree of organization and finance to carry out.[21] Boylan may also have worked with Polk to coordinate an electoral ticket in 1812. After state legislators were chosen in August, the party had to decide whether to support DeWitt Clinton, as the national Federalist caucus had recommended, or to take a "pure" but losing ticket as the Virginia party had done. There is no indication of how the final Federalist slate was drawn up or how its decision to favor Clinton was made—whether by Polk, Boylan, and other activists or by a caucus of legislators. Whatever the decision-making process

20. William Boylan to John Steele, September 5, 1812, and William Polk to Steele, March 27, 1813, in Wagstaff (ed.), *Papers of John Steele*, II, 686–87, 706–08; Polk to Gaston, March 23, 1813, in William Gaston Papers; Boylan to Duncan Cameron, April 25, May 13, in Cameron Family Papers; Pearson to Otis, November 9, 1812, in Harrison Gray Otis Papers.

21. Duncan Cameron to John Moore, September 1, 1802, in *Branch Historical Papers*, III (1909), 36–38; Boylan to Duncan Cameron, November 7, 1803, in Cameron Family Papers; *Raleigh Register*, July 19, 1810; Raleigh *Minerva*, July 26, 1810.

was in the fall of 1812, it left behind no permanent organizing body for the North Carolina Federalists.

Within each congressional and electoral district, party activity was even less coordinated. In no known instance was a nomination made by mass meeting or formal convention, even within a single county. The usual method of candidacy was for a person to announce himself either by a brief "card" in the newspapers or by a printed form letter to leading men in the area. Duncan Cameron's announcement for the legislature in 1809 was typical of many:

> Dear Sir!
>
> Permit me to inform you, that I am a candidate to represent my fellow Citizens of this County in the Commons of the next assembly.
>
> Having always endeavored to merit the Confidence of my countrymen, I shall continue to do so in future. Your friendly support & Interest will be duly esteemed by
>
> Dear Sir!
> Yr. Hum: Sert.
> Dun. Cameron

Even though candidates might put themselves forward, they did so sometimes as a result of talks with local Federalist leaders. However, the lack of written evidence makes it very difficult to know the extent of such silent party networks.[22]

The absence of a formal organization to which intraparty disputes could be referred made it difficult to resolve the problem of dual candidacies. In 1800 two electoral districts each had two Federalists running, and it was necessary to induce one to withdraw in order to concentrate the party's vote. In both cases the task was accomplished, implying some degree of consultation among district Federalists and a willingness by the contending candidates to bow to the party consensus. The same problem arose in 1808; both the Fayetteville and Salisbury districts had two anti-Madison candidates for elector, and

22. Cameron's circular, July 12, 1809, in Cameron Family Papers. For evidence of consultation on local candidates, see Peter Browne to Archibald D. Murphey, August 11, 1815, in Hoyt (ed.), *Papers of Archibald D. Murphey*, I, 81; Henderson to Duncan Cameron, December 21, 1802, and Duncan Cameron to Richard Bennehan, January 8, 1803, in Cameron Family Papers; and Edmund Jones to Walter Alves, February 1, 1800, in Archibald Henderson Collection.

in each district one did finally withdraw before the end of the campaign.[23] In several other races the party was unable to unite its vote behind a single nominee, but none of them caused a Republican victory. The Fayetteville district, for instance, often had intraparty contests for Congress, but usually no Republican even ran for the office. Two Federalists competed for the Salisbury congressional seat in 1800 against a single Republican, and neither would agree to step aside, but the Republican was so weak that both Federalists outpolled him.

In the two more southerly states the Federalist party shriveled so rapidly after 1800 that a coherent organization had little time to emerge outside the vicinities of Charleston, Savannah, and Augusta. Within these urban areas, however, the remnant of Federalism was so concentrated geographically that consultation among the leadership was easier than in other states. Charleston, in fact, had the best organization in the entire South. A party mass meeting or leadership caucus usually nominated the city's legislative ticket (fifteen or sixteen representatives and two senators). When there were no formal Federalist nominations, as in 1810, it was remarked upon as unusual. Anywhere else, such lack of effort would have been accepted as a matter of course.[24]

Following their selection, the nominees were widely publicized in the *Charleston Courier*, the only Federalist daily newspaper south of the Potomac. In particularly heated campaigns the city was canvassed house-to-house by ward committees of the party faithful. By these methods, Federalists continued to win elections in Charleston through 1806, long after they had lost nearly every other parish and district in the state. As late as 1811 and 1813 it was possible, by great exertion, to elect an occasional member to fill a legislative vacancy. The city government, too, showed the effect of a strong Federalist organization. Charleston's intendant, elected at first by the city council and

23. John Hamilton to Duncan Cameron, June 18, 1800, in Cameron Family Papers; *Raleigh Register*, May 20, 1800; *Newbern Gazette*, May 23, 1800; Raleigh *Minerva*, May 6, July 1, 8, September 20, 1800, June 2, September 15, 29, November 3, 1808; Raleigh *Star*, November 3, 1808; John B. Masters to Lewis Beard, October 24, 1808, in Wagstaff (ed.), *Papers of John Steele*, II, 569.

24. *Charleston Courier*, October 12, 1810; Charleston *City Gazette*, September, 1812; Charleston *Southern Patriot*, September 28, 1814.

later by popular vote, was the chief officer in town, and both parties strove to win the position. Over the years, Federalists held the intendancy more often than Republicans did, even after the city's legislative delegation became unanimously Republican.[25]

A similar network of party activists worked in Charleston's congressional contests. Besides the city itself, the district included more than half a dozen coastal plantation parishes, with a slight majority of the popular votes being cast inside Charleston. Although never victorious after 1803, Federalists sometimes put up a strong candidate and supported him by a vigorous effort. In 1812, a year of greater party activity than usual, delegates from each ward in Charleston met to nominate John Rutledge, Jr., for Congress. They addressed a printed circular to Federalist leaders in the rural parishes, requesting them to "announce his name at the usual places of Election in your Parish; and to use your best endeavours to cooperate with us in promoting his Election."[26] At other times, the organization failed to work so smoothly. In 1804 the incumbent, Thomas Lowndes, waited until six weeks before the election to announce his retirement. Two other Federalists offered themselves, apparently without any formal nomination; and it was not until a month later, barely two weeks before the balloting, that one of them could be persuaded to withdraw. Not surprisingly, a Republican captured the seat. Similar confusion crippled the party in 1806. The *Courier* proclaimed on October 6 that James Lowndes was to be the Federalist candidate and that William Loughton Smith, a former congressman who had considered making the race, was not running. Three days later, with the election only a week away, Lowndes withdrew and Smith became the party's last-minute nominee. Of course he lost.[27]

Beyond Charleston and its outlying parishes, there was nothing

25. *South-Carolina State-Gazette*, October 21, 1800; *Charleston Courier*, October 15, 1806, October 14, 1812; Thomas Lehre to Jefferson, August 1, 1812, in Thomas Jefferson Papers.

26. C. C. Pinckney to John Rutledge, Jr., August 24, 1808, in Rutledge Papers, UNC; "A Republican Planter," in Charleston *Investigator*, November 17, 1812; circular Federalist committee of correspondence to William Sinclair, September 24, 1812, in Rutledge Papers, USC.

27. *Charleston Courier*, August 23, 30, September 21, October 8, 1804, October 6, 9, 11, 1806.

that could be called a Federalist organization, except perhaps in the first few years of the century. H. W. DeSaussure and other leaders of the Charleston group briefly tried to rally Federalist legislators in coordinated drives to reelect Senator Jacob Read in 1800 and to make C. C. Pinckney governor in 1802, but they were unsuccessful. Even though Federalists voted solidly as desired, Republicans held their own members in line and prevailed. Pinckney was so sure of defeat that he finally refused to have his name put forward. After such an unpromising start, and in the wake of the disastrous legislative losses after 1800, this halfhearted organizing activity ceased.[28]

In Georgia, even before 1800, a substantial minority of citizens was willing to vote for an occasional Federalist candidate, but no organized party could be found anywhere outside Savannah and Augusta. The party leadership kept up some contact with northern Federalists and at times put together a slate of nominees for municipal or legislative office. Beyond this, there was nothing. Politics in Georgia had always been much more personal than partisan, and Federalist leaders could hope for some influence in local affairs if they did not call undue attention to their national affiliations. When William J. Hobby, the aggressively Federalist editor of the *Augusta Herald*, tried from time to time to stir the faithful to action, he encountered only indifference. There were Federalists in Georgia, but there was no Federalist party.[29]

David H. Fischer has proposed that Federalist organizing and electioneering techniques benefited greatly from the efforts of a new breed of young Federalists in the years after 1800. He has presented convincing evidence for such a transformation north of the Potomac, where nearly all Federalist activists lived. Fischer has shown that there was a great improvement in Federalist vote-getting methods after the first shock of defeat had worn off in the early Jeffersonian

28. Charleston *Times*, December 9, 1800, December 8, 1801; A. C. Butler to Thomas Sumter, December 9, 1802, in Thomas Sumter Papers; H. W. DeSaussure to John Rutledge, Jr., August 25, September 17, December 19, 1801, January 13, 1802, in Rutledge Papers, UNC; John Rutledge, Jr., to Otis, September 15, 1801, in Harrison Gray Otis Papers; DeSaussure to Josiah Quincy, January 21, 1809, in Quincy, *Life of Josiah Quincy*, 191.

29. See Chap. 17, herein, and Lamplugh, "Politics on the Periphery," for a further discussion of Georgia's chaotic politics.

years, and that this improvement was largely wrought by new and younger men while the old, crusty leaders of the 1790s remained muttering and inactive in the background.[30] In testing the application of this theory to the South, one must ask two questions: Was there a gradual shift of leadership from older to younger men in these states, and were Federalist campaign efforts modernized and improved by 1815?

There was, of course, a slow and constant attrition among older men from death or retirement, and a constant influx of younger men into positions of responsibility. This occurs in every generation and in every organization. The failure of any political group to attract new young leaders over any extended period of time would be unusual, indeed, and fatal. If this normal replacement of one generation by another is all that Fischer means to claim, then the evidence clearly supports him. By 1815, the men who led the Federalist party in the South had been born, on the average, about ten years later than the leaders of 1800. The same thing, of course, applied to southern Republicans.

However, the rate at which young Federalists entered the party was *less*, not greater, than the normal change of generations. The average age of southern Federalist leaders was rising over the years, clearly indicating that fewer young men were becoming active workers after 1800. In the first elections of the new century (1800–1803) the southern party leadership averaged forty-one years old; by the middle of the period (1806–1809) the average had risen to forty-four years, and it remained at this level in the wartime elections (1812–1815). Thus, the young Federalists did not take over direction of the southern party as they did in the North. Certainly some new candidates and organizers emerged, but they were outnumbered by the older Federalists who joined or remained in the party hierarchy after 1800. During this decade and a half, the number of Federalist leaders under age thirty *dropped* by one-third, while the number over age fifty *increased* by more than a third. Table 6 shows the progressive aging of the southern party leadership.[31]

30. Fischer, *Revolution of American Conservatism*, especially Chaps. 5–7, 9.

31. Federalist leaders are those who ran for Congress or high state office, served long terms in the legislature, edited important newspapers, or were key organizers. A Federalist who is prominent but not active in electioneering is not counted; if this group were included, the average age would be higher still. The percentages are based on approximately forty-five men in each of the three periods.

Table 6 **Age of Southern Federalist Leaders, 1800–1815**

Years	*Percentage of Leaders in Each Age Group*			
	Under 30	*30 to 40*	*40 to 50*	*Over 50*
1800–1803	19%	30%	30%	21%
1806–1809	7%	29%	42%	22%
1812–1815	13%	27%	31%	29%

The second of Fischer's observations—that Federalist campaign efforts were superior after 1800—is more difficult to test in the South. At its best the party was never as organized or efficient as it was in any northern state. If one judges party effectiveness by the number of candidates, there was a measurable decline, not an increase, in Federalist vigor between 1800–1803 and 1806–1809, followed by a rebirth of competition in 1812–1815. During the first years, Federalist candidates contested 36 percent of all southern congressional elections; by 1806–1809 this percentage had fallen to 22, and during the war it rose again to 37 percent. Legislative elections showed a less favorable pattern. In South Carolina the Federalist party collapsed very quickly and by 1806 existed hardly anywhere outside Charleston. By 1812 there were only nine Federalists in the legislature, compared to sixty-six in 1800 and nineteen in 1808. The Virginia party lost ground quickly after 1800, soon reaching an irreducible minimum of about 16 percent of legislative seats, and it experienced only a mild revival during the war. Only North Carolina showed continual Federalist vigor; from having 39 percent of the legislature in 1800, the party fell to an average of 29 percent between 1804 and 1812 but rose sharply to 37 percent in 1813–1816.

Other measures of Federalist organization reveal little sign of any massive accommodation to new and better campaign methods such as Fischer shows for the North. The number of party newspapers, for instance, remained fairly constant after 1800, while the number of Republican papers increased substantially. In the legislatures, Federalists never did use the machinery of a party caucus in an effective way, whereas Republicans did so on several occasions. No statewide standing Federalist organization existed anywhere, though Republicans had one in Virginia. There is some evidence of increased local organizing ability in Virginia, at least in a few congressional districts; and the Federalist state convention of 1812 was a step more advanced than any taken by southern Republicans. These, however, are minor points; after 1800, the southern Federalists remained what they always had been—a collection of individuals with definite political opinions but little in the way of a determined party organization.

Chapter 19 THE SOUTHERN FEDERALIST PRESS

IN THE early Republic, the press was by far the most important means of communicating ideas. Its influence on public opinion was tremendous and was usually exerted in a deliberately partisan style. Although the actual subscription lists of the several dozen southern newspapers were not large—almost none exceeded a few hundred customers—the political impact of the press was far greater than the small circle of subscribers indicated. Newspapers had a virtual monopoly of the written word, except for pamphlets or handbills at election time and an occasional letter from a friend. Often, correspondents merely passed on in their letters what they had seen in their own local papers. There was no competition for the citizen's attention from the host of magazines, books, and advertising leaflets that saturate the modern reader; even the number of personal letters was much smaller. If the ordinary voter of 1810 wanted to read anything at all, he read a newspaper.

The information contained in any one issue circulated far beyond the individual subscriber. The newspaper itself was often passed around from hand to hand, and its content also entered the word-of-mouth network and was spread among neighbors during casual conversations. Several recent issues were usually posted in the local tavern or store, or in front of the courthouse; they were also brought to church and to militia musters. The average person's deadening isolation from the outside world impelled him to seek news whenever he had the opportunity. His infrequent trips off the farm or plantation would be used partly to catch up on events of the past few months by reading a paper or asking a friend who had himself read one. In every county and town a few men—the local merchant, lawyer, teacher, sheriff, preacher, postmaster, legislator, peace justice, or affluent planter—kept up with current events by subscribing to a newspaper. One or more of these "opinion leaders" was likely to be present on nearly every occasion when the plain farmer left his land, and nothing was more natural than the farmer's asking them what the world was about lately. Depending on the politics of the informant and his newspaper, the inquirer would then receive a partisan summary of the national and international news.

Such information and opinion as the voter gleaned from this process was likely to be heavily weighted toward politics and public affairs, simply because the average newspaper was overwhelmingly political. Of the paper's four pages, about half was advertising and the rest was almost completely devoted to national and international politics. Speeches and official documents, both domestic and foreign, would be printed verbatim; long articles were copied from the major northern papers, and an occasional original editorial or anonymous letter made up the balance. During the sessions of Congress, proceedings, speeches, and executive documents might fill two entire pages of each issue; and at the end of each session long circular letters from the local congressmen would appear. Naturally this information was heavily partisan. Unless a voter had access to newspapers of opposite views (an unusual circumstance), he would always see the world through this highly colored journalistic looking glass. In distilling the paper's contents for verbal transmission to neighbors and subordinates, the subscriber would add his own prejudices to those of the editor, reinforcing the already strong bias.[1]

This broad dissemination of newspaper content by direct reading

1. On the role and content of early nineteenth-century newspapers, see Milton W. Hamilton, *The Country Printer: New York State, 1785–1830* (New York, 1936), and William H. Lyon, *The Pioneer Editor in Missouri, 1808–1860* (Columbia, Mo., 1965).

and word of mouth made the press a key element in any effective election campaign. Besides distributing party viewpoints, the papers were also useful simply in telling voters that Federalist nominees were in the field. Since there were no official ballots, each citizen had to write out the names of the persons for whom he wished to vote. Unless he knew that a Federalist candidate existed, he would be unable to cast a Federalist vote. In those many counties with no party organization to spread the word, a simple statement in the weekly paper ("We are authorized to state that John Smith, Esq., is put forward as a candidate.") would be sufficient notice to all. Party affiliation was almost never included in such announcements, except those for Congress, presumably because local readers were expected to know the candidate's politics already.

The press was also important as a tool of party organization. Since personal contact was difficult in the vast and thinly populated South, newspapers were of special assistance in holding a party together. Wherever a Federalist or neutral paper existed, party leaders had a regular and fairly rapid means of widespread publicity. News of mass meetings or local committee sessions could be reprinted in other party sheets across the state and might stimulate increased organizing activity elsewhere. The press also provided a partisan commentary by leading editors and writers on international and national events; their ideas could be extracted to guide Federalists everywhere toward a unified set of beliefs. When Congress met, newspaper coverage allowed partisans to keep up with Federalist arguments and tactics in Washington. Federalist activities in the northern states—mass meetings, campaign addresses, election returns—also received good coverage. If a local Federalist in the most isolated part of the South had even secondhand access to a friendly newspaper, he would never be out of touch with what his party was doing and saying in the capital and in the North.

Considering the political usefulness of the press, it is not surprising to find close ties between the newspapers and the parties. Federalist editors, even while they denounced "party spirit" as a dangerous evil gnawing at American society, openly proclaimed their own attachment to party. The editors of the *Alexandria Advertiser* (published in the District of Columbia but circulated widely in northern Virginia) promised in 1800 that their principles would be "correct and strictly Federal." And when the *Norfolk Gazette* began in 1804 its editors declared themselves "attached to the political, or constitutional principles of that sect, or party, denominated, with strict propriety, FEDERAL." Similar professions of faith can be found in other papers, especially in new ones beginning after 1800.[2] Party journalism was so much expected that those newspapers endeavoring to be impartial usually made specific announcements to that effect. The Lexington *Virginia Telegraphe*, for instance, said it would not "be exclusively devoted to the views of any political party"; and the Staunton *Candid Review* went still further in pledging that not even "a *letter* shall ever be found in its columns that will enable any person to say it is bordering either on the one side or the other."[3] Such neutrality was unusual in the South, however, and most editors enlisted either blatantly or discreetly in the cause of one party. The Federalist newspapers below the Potomac are listed in Table 7.

Competition between Federalist and Republican newspapers degenerated easily into feuding, especially if opposing papers shared the same town. In Norfolk the Federalist editor of the *Gazette* made a great show of disregarding the "numerous attacks" on him by the Republican *Herald* because they "were dictated by the meanest and basest motives," and "truth or decency had no restraints on the authors." A similar running battle was fought in Newbern by the *Carolina Federal Republican* and the proadministration *Herald* (an "inert mass of stupidity and vulgarity"). In Georgia the Federalist *Augusta Herald* and Savannah *Columbian Museum* levied frequent blasts at their competitors, the *Chronicle* and the *Georgia Republican*, whose editor was described as the "jacobin bellows-blower to the forge of falsehood."[4]

William Boylan of the Raleigh *Minerva* periodically heaped abuse

2. *Alexandria Advertiser*, December 2, 1800; *Norfolk Gazette*, July 17, 1804.

3. *Virginia Telegraphe*, August 30, 1806; Staunton *Candid Review*, May 17, 1805; Pendleton (S.C.) *Miller's Weekly Messenger*, June 11, 1808.

4. *Norfolk Gazette*, February 19, 1812; Newbern *Carolina Federal Republican*, September 1, 1810; *Newbern Herald*, September 9, 1809; *Augusta Herald*, September 14, 1803; *Augusta Chronicle*, September 10, 1803; Savannah *Columbian Museum*, January 11, July 30, 1803; Louis T. Griffith and John E. Talmadge, *Georgia Journalism, 1763–1950* (Athens, Ga., 1951), 22–24.

Table 7 **Southern Federalist Newspapers, 1800–1816**
(excluding papers of only a few weeks' duration)

DC:	Alexandria *Columbian Mirror, Alexandria Advertiser,* and *Alexandria Gazette* 1800–1816
Va:	*Fincastle Weekly Advertiser & Herald*, 1800–1801
	Fredericksburg *Virginia Herald*, 1800–1816
	Leesburg *Washingtonian*, 1808–1816
	Lexington *Virginia Telegraphe*, 1803–1804 (later neutral)
	Lynchburg *Weekly Gazette*, 1800–1801 (mildly Federalist)
	Martinsburg *Berkeley & Jefferson Intelligencer*, 1800–1809
	Martinsburg Gazette, 1810–1816
	Norfolk Gazette and Publick Ledger, 1804–1816
	Richmond *Virginia Federalist*, 1800
	Richmond *Virginia Gazette* and Richmond *Virginia Patriot*, 1800–1816
	Staunton *Candid Review*, 1804–1805 (later neutral)
	Staunton *Political Censor*, 1808–1809
	Staunton *Republican Farmer*, 1809–1816
	Winchester *Centinel* and *Winchester Gazette*, 1800–1816
NC:	*Edenton Gazette*, 1800–1801
	Halifax *North-Carolina Journal*, 1800–1807 (later Republican)
	Newbern *Carolina Federal Republican*, 1808–1816
	Newbern Gazette, 1800–1804
	Raleigh *North-Carolina Minerva* and Raleigh *Minerva*, 1800–1816
	Wilmington *Cape-Fear Herald*, 1802–1803
	Wilmington Gazette, 1800, 1808–1812 (Republican between 1800 and 1808)
SC:	Charleston *Carolina Weekly Messenger*, 1806–1810
	Charleston Courier, 1803–1816
	Charleston *Federal Carolina Gazette*, 1800
	Charleston *South-Carolina State-Gazette*, 1800–1802
	Georgetown Gazette, 1800–1816
Ga:	*Augusta Herald*, 1800–1816
	Savannah *Columbian Museum*, 1800–1816

on the editor of the strongly Republican Warrenton *Messenger*, calling him the "Warrenton Scape Gallows," the "stupid creature at Warrenton," and the "sub-editor and toad-eater" to Joseph Gales, who put out the *Raleigh Register*.[5] The most serious feud, in fact, was between Boylan and Gales, who published the leading Federalist and Republican newspapers in North Carolina. Harsh words were exchanged several times, and aspersions on each other's intelligence and hon-

5. Raleigh *Minerva*, November 5, 12, 1804; Robert N. Elliott, Jr., *The Raleigh Register, 1799–1863* (Chapel Hill, N.C., 1955), 21.

esty were not uncommon. The *Minerva* eventually went too far and actually libeled Gales, who hired a Federalist attorney and collected $200 damages from Boylan. Once there was even a physical encounter between the two men. Despite all this antagonism, when the *Register*'s printing shop burned down, Boylan obligingly allowed Gales to turn out his rabidly Republican sheet on the *Minerva*'s own press.[6]

As these experiences show, the most partisan editors took their politics seriously. Yet the existence of a Federalist newspaper was no guarantee that it would serve the party as an effective instrument. Some editors kept their opinions so closely concealed that it was difficult to tell, for months or even years at a time, what their affiliation really was. The *Virginia Herald* of Fredericksburg willingly spread the Federalist doctrine in major election years (1800, 1808, and 1812) but during the long stretches between, it was virtually neutral. The Georgetown, South Carolina, *Gazette* operated on similar principles, except that it did not always revert dependably to active Federalism, even during some of the hard-fought campaigns. In Savannah the *Columbian Museum* behaved the same way, although it did run an occasional Federalist article in the off years.

Some Federalist newspapers deserted the cause entirely; the editor might change parties or the paper might change editors. The striking example of the first situation is the case of the *Wilmington Gazette*. Its editor, Allmand Hall, evidently took the election returns greatly to heart, or else he experienced an honest conversion of faith. In 1798, 1799, and 1800, almost 75 percent of the political matter in his *Gazette* was Federalist-oriented; in 1801 and later, almost 100 percent was Republican. Two Virginia papers made a partial transformation by going from Federalist to neutral—the Lexington *Virginia Telegraphe* in 1804 and the Staunton *Candid Review* a year later. The Halifax *North-Carolina Journal* remained staunchly Federalist while its old editor, Abraham Hodge, lived, but on his death it went through several changes of ownership and finally emerged in 1808 as a Republican sheet. This loss was balanced by the reverse process in Wilmington,

6. Raleigh *Minerva*, December 17, 1804; *Raleigh Register*, December 10, 1804, April 22, October 14, 1805; Duncan Cameron to Joseph Gales, January 21, 1805, in Cameron Family Papers; *North-Carolina Journal*, February 6, 1804.

where an ardent Federalist, William Hassell, bought out the Republican publisher of the *Gazette* and turned the newspaper back to its old Federalist views. Table 8 shows the year-by-year party division for the southern press as a whole.

Table 8 **The Southern Party Press, 1800–1816**
Newspapers in Existence January 1 Each Year

Politics	*1800*	*1801*	*1802*	*1803*	*1804*	*1805*	*1806*	*1807*	*1808*
Federalist	16	15	12	13	13	13	12	13	12
Republican	13	16	18	17	18	19	18	20	23
Neutral/Unknown	7	6	6	5	7	7	10	12	12
Federalist %	44%	41%	33%	37%	34%	33%	30%	29%	26%

	1809	*1810*	*1811*	*1812*	*1813*	*1814*	*1815*	*1816*	*Average*
Federalist	16	15	16	17	15	15	15	15	14
Republican	25	26	24	23	24	21	19	16	20
Neutral/Unknown	12	13	8	6	8	10	15	15	9
Federalist %	30%	28%	33%	37%	32%	32%	31%	33%	33%

When a reliable paper could be obtained in no other way, local Federalists sometimes made extraordinary efforts to bring in outside talent and found a new publication. The prime example of this was Charleston. The South's largest city began the new century with two vigorous Federalist papers, but the *Federal Carolina Gazette* ceased operations during 1800 and the *South-Carolina State-Gazette* was not capable enough for the party leadership. A search was begun for "an able, sensible, virtuous, well informed man" from the North who would revitalize Federalist journalism with the "great & decisive support" of the local party. When the *State-Gazette* expired entirely in 1802, this project became even more essential. Negotiating through William Coleman of the New York *Evening Post*, H. W. DeSaussure tried to induce a well-recommended upstate New York printer to move to Charleston. This fell through, but finally another printer from along the Hudson River, Loring Andrews, was secured early in 1803.[7]

Andrews established the *Charleston Courier* as the major southern

7. H. W. DeSaussure to John Rutledge, Jr., September 17, 1801, September 10, 1802, January, 1803, in Rutledge Papers, UNC.

voice of Federalism, and every effort was made to drum up subscriptions for it in up-country South Carolina and in neighboring states. This was quite difficult at first because the *Courier* was a daily and thus cost several times as much as the usual weekly newspapers. In little more than a year Andrews had to confess, "My hopes in this quarter have been most mortifyingly disapointed—I meet with no success equal to my expectations—indeed not with that kind of support which can enable me even to publish the paper much longer, unless a change takes place."[8] Even as the editor despaired, the fortunes of the *Courier* were improving, and by April of 1805 it claimed seven hundred subscribers in Charleston, three hundred to four hundred elsewhere in the Carolinas and Georgia, and still more in other states. The paper not only survived but prospered, partly from government patronage. When Federalists controlled the Charleston city administration, Andrews was made public printer to the city—a position that brought in very welcome revenue. Over the years the *Courier* had several changes of ownership, but the successive editors all pledged themselves "to maintain the Federal Constitution inviolate, pure and uncorrupted; generally to defend, as far as they can, the cause of Christianity, order, and good government." Eventually, to overcome the objection of high price made by rural readers, the *Courier* put out a weekly country edition entitled the *Carolina Weekly Messenger*, which met with considerable success.[9]

The chronic problems Andrews had in keeping his enterprise afloat were common to every editor. Technical difficulties alone were enough to drive a man from the business. Keeping a sufficient supply of paper was never easy, particularly for inland publishers who had to cope with erratic deliveries from distant suppliers. The editor alone could

8. John Rutledge, Jr., to Harrison Gray Otis, April 3, 1803, in Harrison Gray Otis Papers; John Stanly to John Rutledge, Jr., April 23, 1803, Abraham Nott to John Rutledge, Jr., June 26, 1803, both in Rutledge Papers, UNC; Peter Freneau to Thomas Jefferson, June 17, 1803, in Thomas Jefferson Papers; Eldred Simkins to Creed Taylor, April 30, 1805, in Creed Taylor Papers, UVa; Loring Andrews to Samuel Norton, November 5, 1804, in Loring Andrews Papers, Harvard University.

9. *Charleston Courier*, April 19, May 18, 1805, January 10, 1806, January 10, 1807; C. C. Pinckney to Rufus King, July 18, 1806, in Rufus King Papers, New-York Historical Society; William L. King, *The Newspaper Press of Charleston, South Carolina* (Charleston, S.C., 1872), Chap. 9, deals in a cursory way with the early years of the *Courier*.

not fill the columns of his four large pages, and he depended heavily on copy from other papers and on local writers. Often the out-of-town papers were late in the mails, and even the leading Federalist organs sometimes had to plead for articles from the party faithful, as the *Virginia Patriot* did in 1810: "We feel strongly disposed to complain of our federal friends for not favoring us with more of their communications," especially those who "can wield the pen of a master." Delivery of the newspaper was in the hands of either regular postriders or hired private agents, and both sometimes proved unreliable. Federalists were particularly suspicious that Republican postmasters neglected to give speedy treatment to bundles of opposition newspapers.[10]

The greatest danger to the life of every paper was the failure of subscribers to pay their bills, amounting to several dollars a year for a weekly. Editors commonly sent their papers out for months or even a year in advance of payment rather than collect before delivery. Once a subscriber was in arrears, it was difficult to decide whether to continue the paper in hopes he would eventually pay, or to stop delivery and risk his refusal to settle the bill. Sometimes the editor persisted beyond all reason in keeping a deadbeat on the rolls; having received the *Edenton Gazette* this way for seven years, one North Carolina congressman took offense at the paper's politics, canceled his subscription, and declined to pay a penny for his long "free ride." At one point in 1806 the *Norfolk Gazette* carried over eight thousand dollars in unpaid bills on its books because more than half the subscribers were overdue. To encourage readers to keep their accounts current, some editors were willing to take any form of marketable produce in place of money, while others resorted to hyperbole. Augustine Davis of Richmond complained that "every six months the printer sends out his bills; he expects a shower: a few 'strained' drops only fall. He opens his mouth to catch enough to allay thirst; his wife does the same, and his children; his editor (if he is not his own), his foreman (if not too poor to have one), his pressmen, his clerk, (if not his own), his journeymen; his boys, and carriers; and wider than all, HORRIBLE VISU!

10. *Virginia Patriot*, May 29, 1810, June 11, 1811; Pendleton *Miller's Weekly Messenger*, November 26, 1808; Samuel J. Donaldson to Augustine Davis, May 31, 1810, Davis to Harry Heth, September 5, 1810, both in Harry Heth Papers.

his *paper maker*. . . . It is one of the most distressing scenes in the world."[11]

So strait were the circumstances of the average newspaper that any additional income was a godsend. Most enterprises carried on job printing, sold books and blank forms, and hoped for government patronage in the form of public printing. On this last point Federalists were usually disappointed; the national Republican administration was careful to reward only loyal editors with the lucrative business of printing federal laws. State governments also patronized the Republican presses, but not always without a struggle. Even when Federalists saw no chance of obtaining the public printing themselves, they might try to reduce the compensation of the Republican printer in order to damage the financial health of his paper. Although every southern legislature after 1800 was thoroughly Republican, the cry of economy in government was occasionally effective in splintering the majority.

The Virginia assembly saw a heated debate over public printing in 1802 and 1803, in which the Federalists rallied a group of economy-minded Republicans to their cause. During the late 1790s the printer had been Augustine Davis, publisher of the Richmond Federalist newspaper, but in the bitterly partisan atmosphere of 1800 Davis was deprived of the contract and obviously had no chance to regain it. The new printer, Meriwether Jones of the Richmond *Examiner*, was asking $2,700 yearly for his services, but in December of 1802 the firm of Pace and Nicholson, which was Republican though not so partisan, submitted a bid of $1,200. After some debate, Republican legislators rejected the lower offer as unrealistic and chose Jones again by a vote of 117 to 54. This brought cries of rage from Federalists as "the most glaring piece of robbery of the kind ever committed. By partiality to a worthless favorite, the public are robbed of one thousand five hun-

11. *Augusta Herald*, July 10, 1806; *Virginia Telegraphe*, February 21, 1807; Lexington *Rockbridge Repository*, August 6, 1805; *Edenton Gazette*, February 23, 1813; *Norfolk Gazette*, June 16, 1806; *Virginia Patriot*, November 2, 1810; Elias B. Caldwell to John Rutledge, Jr., August 7, 1802, in Rutledge Papers, UNC; Otis K. Rice, "West Virginia Printers and Their Work, 1790–1830," *West Virginia History*, XIV (1953), 335–36; Daniel M. McFarland, "North Carolina Newspapers, Editors, and Journalistic Politics, 1815–1835," *North Carolina Historical Review*, XXX (1953), 376–77.

dred dollars, to lavish away on him, and without any other pretext than that he is a democrat" and "an outrageous bawler for Mr. Jefferson." The vote became a major issue in some legislative races in the spring of 1803, as incumbent Republicans were forced to defend their action.[12]

Heartened by the controversy, Federalists resumed their attack in the 1803 session, pressing for a reduction of Jones's fee. Although some Republicans tried to make the contest a party question, others admitted that a salary cut was in order. After the sum of $2,000 was rejected as too low, the economy coalition finally won a close 87–84 vote to set the figure at $2,500, and Jones was again chosen printer. This was the last major Federalist effort to influence the award of public printing in Virginia, although in 1804 and 1805 the minority united with moderate Republican members to elect the least obnoxious of two Republican editors.[13]

The most vigorous battle over printing was in North Carolina, where the issue was a lively one for a decade and a half and was sometimes the most prominent controversy in state politics. The simple question of whether to award the state's printing business to a Federalist or a Republican had an easy partisan answer; but the minority, especially William Boylan of the Raleigh *Minerva*, fought the issue on the same grounds as the Virginia Federalists did. Their motive was partisan, but their rhetoric emphasized economy in government. Throughout the 1790s the state printer had been Abraham Hodge, who increasingly became a supporter of the Washington and Adams administrations. Although North Carolina was heavily Republican, there was no first-rate opposition editor to challenge Hodge for legislative favor. Hoping to end the spectacle of a Republican assembly subsidizing an arch-Federalist printer, several Jeffersonian leaders induced Joseph Gales, a fugitive from England, to open a newspaper at

12. Thomas H. Wooding to voters of Pittsylvania County, and "A Loudoun customer," in *Alexandria Advertiser*, February 12, 1803; "A True Republican" and Osborne Sprigg's letter to the people, March 25, 1803, and James Stephenson "To the Citizens of Berkeley, Jefferson, & Hampshire Counties," April 8, 1803, all in Martinsburg *Berkeley & Jefferson Intelligencer*; Richmond *Examiner*, December 11, 1802.

13. Andrew Russell to David Campbell, December 17, 1803, in David Campbell Papers; Richmond *Enquirer*, December 20, 1804; Charles H. Ambler, *Thomas Ritchie: A Study in Virginia Politics* (Richmond, Va., 1913), 32.

Raleigh in 1799. They promised him assistance in making his *Raleigh Register* a financial success, chiefly by settling on him the annual stipend for state printing.[14]

A hasty effort to do this in 1799 failed, so one of the chief Republican goals in the 1800 session was to transfer the public printing from Hodge (and Boylan, his nephew and now his partner) to Gales. An intensive campaign, and the fact that the legislature was safely Republican, made the outcome certain. Gales received ninety-five votes to seventy-one for Hodge and Boylan. In 1801 Gales was reelected without opposition, but the next year Boylan, now the sole Federalist candidate for printer, introduced the question of economy.[15] He accused Gales of wasting money and of lateness in finishing work, and he offered to do the printing for a lower price. At the very least, Boylan said, the business should be split between the two of them. The house of commons, overwhelmingly Republican but attracted by the possibility of saving money, thought a division of the printing was reasonable; but the senate refused and Gales again got the entire contract. At this, Boylan struck off such a bitter attack against the obdurate senators that some of them considered punishing him for contempt.[16]

Two years later he returned with a more calmly worded proposal, again requesting either a division of the printing or an award of the whole contract for less money. Some Federalists hoped that Boylan's "modest" and "just" memorial would impress legislators far more than Gales's "arrogant and dictatorial" reply, but the "sensibility of party" was still too great for many Republicans to desert Gales, even to save money. After this rebuff to Boylan the issue subsided, and in some sessions Gales was reelected almost without opposition.[17] The

14. Elliott, *Raleigh Register*, 16–18; Mary Lindsay Thornton, "Public Printing in North Carolina, 1749–1815," *North Carolina Historical Review*, XXI (1944), 188–202.

15. Thomas Blount to John G. Blount, November 29, 1800, in Keith and Masterson (eds.), *Papers of John Gray Blount*, III, 457; William Polk to John Steele, November 28, 1800, in Wagstaff (ed.), *Papers of John Steele*, I, 191–92; Charles W. Harris to Robert W. Harris, August 29 and September 18, 1800, in Wagstaff (ed.), *Harris Letters*, 81, 83; *Wilmington Gazette*, December 4, 1800.

16. Gilpatrick, *Jeffersonian Democracy*, 136–37; John Haywood to Steele, November 19, 1802, in Wagstaff (ed.), *Papers of John Steele*, I, 330–31; Duncan Cameron to Richard Bennehan, November 24, 1802, in Cameron Family Papers; Thornton, "Public Printing," 197–98.

17. On the straight issue of electing a printer in 1804, Joseph Gales won by 123 to 54, showing that a few Republicans did vote for Boylan: Joseph Pearson to Steele,

minority still sniped at him, charging him with extravagance and inattention to duty. They finally suggested that the printing should be let by competitive bidding to secure the lowest possible price to the taxpayers. This proved to be a powerful argument, especially in a legislature dominated by those who prided themselves upon "Jeffersonian economy" in government. An increasing number of Republicans were willing to endorse the idea, though a majority always preferred an expensive Gales to a cheap Boylan.[18]

The constant criticism of Gales eventually began to have a cumulative effect. If only the alternative had not been the offensively Federalist Boylan, the printing dispute would not always have had the same ending. In 1808, a third newspaper was founded at Raleigh, and the situation suddenly altered. The *Star* was edited by mild Federalists but was almost perfectly impartial in its columns. Boylan immediately dropped out of the printing contest, allowing Thomas Henderson of the *Star* to come forward as an attractive substitute for Gales. Henderson was rejected in 1809 but applied again the next year, touching off the most extended debate yet. Gales won the actual vote, but only by 98 to 84, and other events confirmed that his tenure was now very shaky. A member of his own party introduced a resolution to reduce the printer's compensation as an economy measure. Federalists were gleeful; one said that "coming from the Quarter it did, this Resolution was a thunder bolt to Gales & his friends." By a large majority the house sent the proposal to the senate, where Republican leaders drew the party line and denounced all who strayed from it. But the economy flame, eagerly fed by the Federalists, was burning too strongly to be quenched, and the printer's contract was cut to nine hundred dollars. This did not go far enough to please some enemies of Gales, but it satisfied most Federalists and those Republicans who were interested in saving money. Gales himself took the reduction as

November 26, 1804, in Wagstaff (ed.), *Papers of John Steele*, I, 441; Gilpatrick, *Jeffersonian Democracy*, 137–38; Raleigh *Minerva*, December 3, 10, 1804; and *Wilmington Gazette*, December 25, 1804. On succeeding years, see *Raleigh Register*, November 25, 1805, November 24, 1806, November 26, 1807, and Raleigh *Minerva*, December 1, 1808.

18. Raleigh *Minerva*, December 29, 1806. In the senate a motion for competitive printing bids lost by 29–18 in 1806: *North Carolina Senate Journal*, 1806, p. 48. A Federalist motion to require bids for printing additional copies of state militia laws failed the next year: *North Carolina House Journal*, 1807, p. 54; Gilpatrick, *Jeffersonian Democracy*, 139.

a personal affront and was further insulted when the legislature sent inquiries to other states asking what their printing cost each year.[19]

In 1811, after a full decade of intermittent battling, the Federalists at last achieved their goal of entirely denying Gales the public printing. When the legislature convened in November, Republicans sought to repeal the previous year's reduction in pay. Despite an aggressive campaign, the "shameful prostitution of principles to party" failed by the casting vote of the speaker of the house. Announcing that the nine hundred dollar figure was too low to give him a profit, Gales then declined to enter his name, and Henderson of the *Star* was the only candidate for printer. Even so, Republican diehards prevented Henderson from winning by a majority of votes until the third ballot, in which nearly half the members still cast blank votes or scrawled defiant slogans on their tickets, such as "No Federalist"; "No pay, no printer"; or "Republican printer or none." Once installed as North Carolina's public printer, Thomas Henderson kept the position for many years, turning back strong competition from Gales in 1815 and 1816 but otherwise facing no serious challenge.[20]

Deprived of the chance to obtain much public printing business, Federalist editors and publishers had to scramble for revenue elsewhere. Since their main expedient was to attract more advertisers by increasing the paper's circulation, there were frequent attempts to drum up new subscribers. When the *Charleston Courier* was riding out its difficult early months, for example, men such as Congressman John Stanly in Newbern sent in names and subscription money from out of state. This was done to such an extent that within two years,

19. Debates are in Raleigh *Minerva*, November 29, December 6, 20, 1810; and Raleigh *Star*, November 29, December 13, 1810. *Raleigh Register*, January 3, 1811, has an editorial by Gales upholding his side of the dispute; Raleigh *Star*, December 20, 1810, has the record vote in the assembly. See also John A. Cameron to Duncan Cameron, November 24, December 6, 1810, in Cameron Family Papers; William E. Webb to constituents, December 24, 1810, copy in Wood Jones Hamlin Papers, NCDAH; Gilpatrick, *Jeffersonian Democracy*, 140–41; *North Carolina House Journal*, 1810, pp. 7, 20, 35; *North Carolina Senate Journal*, 1810, pp. 7, 33; Raleigh *Minerva*, December 6, 20, 27, 1810; *Edenton Gazette*, December 28, 1810; and Thornton, "Public Printing," 200.

20. Polk to Duncan Cameron, December 20, 1811, and John A. Cameron to Duncan Cameron, December 24, 1811, in Cameron Family Papers; *Raleigh Register*, December 27, 1811. Gilpatrick, *Jeffersonian Democracy*, 141, says Henderson won without a partisan contest from 1812 through 1816; but, according to the Raleigh *Star*, December 24, 1815, and November 29, 1816, the vote in 1815 was Henderson 93 and Gales 68, and in 1816 it was Henderson 97 and Gales 82.

over a third of the *Courier's* circulation was in backcountry South Carolina and in neighboring states—a remarkable achievement for a daily newspaper that chiefly covered events in Charleston itself.[21]

A common practice was to have permanent agents in many towns to solicit new subscriptions and advertising; at one point the *Augusta Herald*, far from the largest southern paper, listed twenty-one agents in fifteen places throughout Georgia. Even northern Federalist papers benefited from these circulation drives; in 1801 John Rutledge, Jr., was rounding up South Carolina readers for the *New England Palladium* of Boston, and his colleague Thomas Evans was performing the same service on Virginia's Eastern Shore for the *Washington Federalist*. The result of such efforts was sometimes very gratifying, and numerous papers claimed that they had added a hundred or more subscribers within the space of a few months. Since the average southern newspaper probably did not sell more than about five hundred copies, an increase of this magnitude, if true, was bound to be heartening.[22]

It is apparent, then, that southern Federalists depended greatly on their party press to play a large role in politics. Editors were often men of some prominence in party councils; William Boylan of the Raleigh *Minerva* acted as the virtual leader of North Carolina Federalism on several occasions. Where dependable papers did not exist, attempts were made to establish them; where newspapers already operated, the leadership tried to support them by financial and literary contributions. It would not be an exaggeration to say that without its vigorous partisan editors, the southern Federalist party would scarcely have existed at all.

21. Stanly to John Rutledge, Jr., April 23, 1803, Nott to John Rutledge, Jr., June 26, 1803, both in Rutledge Papers, UNC; *Charleston Courier*, April 19, 1805.

22. *Augusta Herald*, July 31, 1806; John Rutledge, Jr., to Theodore Sedgwick, September 24, 1801, in Theodore Sedgwick Papers; Thomas Evans to John Cropper, December 15, 1800, in John Cropper Papers. Reports of subscription drives are in *Augusta Herald*, July 11, 1805, January 1, 1807; Raleigh *Minerva*, July 18, 1803; *Charleston Courier*, July 10, 1805; *Norfolk Gazette*, March 28, 1808; and *Alexandria Advertiser*, December 26, 1807.

Chapter 20 FEDERALISTS IN THE SOUTHERN LEGISLATURES

ONE of the most rewarding ways to study the Federalist party in the South is to examine the role its members played in the proceedings of the state legislatures. Such a study must begin by overcoming a serious problem. In this period of southern history neither the official membership lists printed in the assembly journals nor the various unofficial newspaper lists mention party affiliation. Therefore, one cannot say that any particular legislator was a Federalist or a Republican unless his party is known from some other source. Unfortunately, only a few legislators can be identified in this way. Congressional candidates were usually labeled by party, and many of them sat at one time or another in the assemblies. Private correspondence and an occasional newspaper item identify a handful of other men. But most members must be classified solely on the basis of their votes on key legislative issues.

All roll call votes in both houses of the Virginia, North Carolina and South Carolina legislatures for the period 1800 through 1816 were examined, and the most important ones were selected for analysis.[1] The important roll calls in any given session included at least one for

1. The journals of both houses of the southern legislatures are readily available on microfilm. Occasionally a part of one year's proceedings is missing. The journals do not include any debates, but sometimes the newspapers will carry important speeches.

each substantive issue voted upon; private bills and motions for adjournment were excluded. If there was more than one roll call on an issue, the vote on final passage of bills and resolutions was usually chosen; but sometimes, when substantially more members voted at some preliminary stage, or when the issue was more clearly put than on final passage, the earlier roll call was used.

The roll calls on which two-thirds or more of the known Federalists voted in opposition to two-thirds or more of the known Republicans were taken as key party votes. Those few occasions when nine-tenths of the known Federalists opposed nine-tenths of the known Republicans were further assumed to be almost certain indicators of party allegiance. Each member of the legislatures during these years was then classified according to the number of times he voted for or against the position of the known Federalists on these key notes. All those voting pro-Federalist on two-thirds or more of the votes in which they participated were counted as Federalist. Those who voted pro-Federalist more than half but less than two-thirds of the time were recorded as probable Federalists. The reverse procedure served to identify Republicans and probable Republicans. A few members remained who either were not recorded on any key vote or voted almost exactly half the time with each party. These men were listed as "doubtful" unless their party affiliation was clear from other sources.

Table 9 shows the approximate strength of parties in the three legislatures, as derived from this process of roll call analysis. While some persons are no doubt incorrectly placed—there are certain to be a few who considered themselves members of one party but who voted most of the time with the other party—these figures probably do not vary much from the actual party totals.[2] Of particular interest is the small number of doubtful or independent members in most of

2. Various private estimates give roughly the same figure as the table, and sometimes the votes for speaker, senator, or judges also reveal the strength of parties. Thus, for a few years the roll call analysis can be checked against other sources. For Virginia, see: Richmond *Examiner*, April 29, 1800; Norfolk *Commercial Register*, December 15, 1802; Allen Taylor to James Breckinridge, January 23, 1811, in Breckinridge Papers, LC. For North Carolina, see: Thomas Blount to John G. Blount, November 29, 1800, in Keith and Masterson (eds.), *Papers of John Gray Blount*, III, 457; Raleigh *Minerva*, December 24, 1804, November 23, 1809; *Wilmington Gazette*, December 25, 1800; *Raleigh Register*, November 25, 1805, November 27, 1812; William Gaston to Judge Taylor, December 13, 1807, in William Gaston Papers; Newbern *True Republican*, November 28,

Table 9 **Approximate Party Strength in Southern Legislatures, 1800–1816**

VIRGINIA

	Senate			House			Fed. % of Seats	
Year	*Fed.*	*Rep.*	*Doubtful**	*Fed.*	*Rep.*	*Doubtful**	*Senate*	*House*
1800	6	18	0	49	130	4	25%	27%
1801	5	19	0	27	150	8	21%	15%
1802	4	20	0	33	151	3	17%	18%
1803	4	20	0	31	152	4	17%	17%
1804	4	20	0	28	147	12	17%	16%
1805	4	20	0	27	144	18	17%	16%
1806	4	20	0	26	157	6	17%	14%
1807	4	20	0	25	165	3	17%	13%
1808	4	19	1	28	161	8	17%	15%
1809	5	19	0	37	153	5	21%	20%
1810	5	19	0	36	153	6	21%	19%
1811	5	19	0	32	159	4	21%	17%
1812	5	19	0	31	154	10	21%	17%
1813	5	18	1	39	152	4	22%	20%
1814	5	18	1	41	146	8	22%	22%
1815	4	16	4	35	141	23	20%	20%
1816	3	16	5	30	132	38	16%	19%

these years. This does not indicate that party lines were drawn on a large percentage of roll calls; it merely shows that on those few occasions when Federalist and Republican leaders were in strong conflict, legislators supported one side or the other quite consistently, with very few members switching from side to side.[3]

As the tables indicate, Federalists were never a serious threat to Republican ascendancy except for the single year of 1800 in the lower houses of North and South Carolina. For the full period from 1800 through 1816, the minority averaged about 33 representatives (18 percent) and 4.5 senators (19 percent) in Virginia, 41 representatives (33

1810. For South Carolina, see: *Georgetown Gazette*, December 3, 1800; *South-Carolina State-Gazette*, December 9, 1800, December 8, 1801; A. C. Butler to Thomas Sumter, December 9, 1802, in Thomas Sumter Papers; Richmond *Examiner*, January 1, 1803; *North-Carolina Journal*, June 4, 1804; Charleston *City Gazette*, September 22, 1812.

3. Very few of the doubtful members were independents who voted some of the time with each party. Most of the doubtfuls either did not attend the sessions or were never present when a party-determining vote was taken. In each state periods of several years passed without a single party-line vote, and a member who served only during these years would never have an opportunity to be recorded for either side, although he might be a fervent Republican or Federalist.

(Table 9 cont.)

NORTH CAROLINA

	Senate			House			Fed. % of Seats	
Year	Fed.	Rep.	Doubtful*	Fed.	Rep.	Doubtful*	Senate	House
1800	17	40	3	52	70	5	30%	43%
1801	17	43	0	46	77	4	28%	37%
1802	20	39	1	41	78	8	34%	34%
1803	15	41	4	40	82	5	27%	33%
1804	17	41	2	30	93	4	29%	24%
1805	17	38	5	28	93	6	31%	23%
1806	14	42	4	36	87	4	25%	29%
1807	13	46	1	39	85	3	22%	31%
1808	17	42	1	41	84	2	29%	33%
1809	17	43	2	32	99	0	28%	24%
1810	22	40	0	42	89	0	35%	32%
1811	18	41	3	36	93	2	31%	28%
1812	20	42	0	46	85	0	32%	35%
1813	18	44	0	47	80	4	29%	37%
1814	18	43	1	48	70	13	30%	41%
1815	19	42	1	52	76	3	31%	41%
1816	19	35	8	47	73	11	35%	39%

SOUTH CAROLINA

	Senate			House			Fed. % of Seats	
Year	Fed.	Rep.	Doubtful*	Fed.	Rep.	Doubtful*	Senate	House
1800	15	21	1	51	65	8	42%	44%
1801	14	22	1	50	70	4	39%	42%
1802	12	24	1	29	86	9	33%	25%
1803	12	23	2	29	88	7	34%	25%
1804	6	29	2	23	85	16	17%	21%
1805	6	30	1	21	88	15	17%	19%
1806	6	30	1	21	97	6	17%	18%
1807	6	31	0	20	98	6	16%	17%
1808	5	32	0	16	105	3	14%	13%
1809	5	32	0	15	104	5	14%	13%
1810	5	40	0	13	106	5	11%	11%
1811	5	40	0	16	104	4	11%	13%
1812	5	37	3	4	116	4	12%	3%
1813	5	39	1	5	115	4	11%	4%
1814	2	40	3	6	115	3	5%	5%
1815	3	41	1	7	112	5	7%	6%
1816	6	35	4	3	73	48	15%	4%

*Doubtful members include those who never attended, never voted on a party issue, or voted an equal number of times with each party. Doubtful members are excluded in calculating Federalist percentage of seats in each year.

percent) and 17 senators (30 percent) in North Carolina, and 19 representatives (17 percent) and 7 senators (18 percent) in South Carolina. The figures for Georgia cannot be accurately determined, but very likely the Federalists averaged less than 5 percent of the seats in each house. In 1800, probably their strongest year, they seated half a dozen in the entire Georgia legislature.[4]

With their numbers consistently so small in all the southern states, Federalists usually made no serious attempt to control legislative proceedings. This lack of effort by the minority may help account for the low degree of partisanship often shown in the state assemblies, which was in striking contrast to the extreme bitterness of party warfare on national issues. The strict party lines that formed in presidential and congressional politics usually dissolved when state issues were involved. One indication of this low level of partisanship in the legislatures is the lack of any recorded affiliation even in unofficial newspaper rosters and almanacs.[5]

Another indication is the lack of a formal party contest for the speakership at the opening of each session. In Virginia and Georgia, during the entire seventeen years from 1800 through 1816, no such contest occurred in either house. Only once in the North Carolina senate (in 1800) and on only five occasions in the house (1800, 1809, 1810, 1812, 1815) were there rival Federalist and Republican candidates for speaker. South Carolina had a partisan ballot for speaker of the house in 1800 and 1802 but never thereafter and never in the senate. Usually the presiding officers were elected unanimously (except in Virginia), and not infrequently they were nominated by members of the opposite party. The absence of a routine partisan battle over this prestigious post hints that party feeling was not the overriding influence in the legislatures. Indeed, in a few cases Federalists were actually chosen to preside over sessions. For three years in succession (1806–1808) the North Carolina house unanimously elected Federalist speakers, and the South Carolina senate, with Republicans in the majority, allowed Federalist speaker John Ward to retain his office

4. James Jackson to Abraham Baldwin, November 26, 1800, in Foster, *James Jackson*, 146.

5. In these same years, unofficial newspaper lists of members of Congress usually did give party affiliation; see, for example, *Raleigh Register*, October 6, 1801.

from 1800 through 1802, and they elected him again in 1804–1805.[6]

The same casual attitude toward party is evident in the selection of standing committees. Then, as now, much of the work of the legislature was done in committee, where petitions, claims, and executive messages were considered and bills were drafted. The proportion of seats that the Federalist minority held on important committees is therefore a rough indication of the degree to which it participated in helping to mold legislation and to right the grievances and fulfill the requests of citizens. In the South from 1800 through 1816, the minority generally received fair treatment in the allotment of committee seats. The average percentage of Federalists on the major standing committees (16 percent in Virginia, 32 percent in North Carolina, and 16 percent in South Carolina) was nearly the same as the average Federalist share of assembly seats (18, 31, and 17 percent.)[7]

This generally close correspondence between the proportion of places on committees and seats in the house may indicate either that party affiliation was virtually ignored in committee assignments or that it was scrupulously consulted. In most legislative bodies today, even those in which the degree of partisanship in voting is low, each party is assigned roughly the same percentage of seats on committees as it has in the entire house. The minority receives, if anything, less than its due in the composition of important committees because, in this strictly partisan practice, assignments are made with specific

6. The absence of partisan contests for speaker is not, standing alone, proof of a low level of partisanship. In Congress the Federalists sometimes failed to set up a ceremonial candidate for speaker, yet there was still a highly partisan atmosphere in congressional deliberations. Information on the elections for speaker may be found in the journal of each house, usually on the first day of a session. Newspaper reports are often more helpful, providing the vote for speaker and the names and parties of candidates. Consult the *Virginia Argus*, Richmond *Enquirer*, *Virginia Gazette*, *Raleigh Register*, Raleigh *Minerva*, *Charleston Courier*, Charleston *City Gazette*, *Augusta Herald*, Savannah *Columbian Museum*, and *Georgia Argus* for the first week of each legislative session. For the North Carolina contested elections, see *North Carolina Senate Journal*, 1800, p. 1; *North Carolina House Journal*, 1800, p. 2; 1809, p. 2; 1810, p. 2; 1812, p. 2. For South Carolina, Peter Freneau to [?], November 25, 1800, photostat in Freneau Papers, and *Carolina Gazette*, December 2, 1802. Federalist speakers are listed in *North Carolina House Journal*, 1806, p. 2; 1807, p. 2; 1808, p. 2; and *South Carolina Senate Journal*, 1800, p. 2; 1801, p. 2; 1802, p. 2.

7. The membership of standing committees is listed in the legislative journals in the first few days of each session. In South Carolina, which had legislative elections every two years, only the changes in committee membership are listed in the odd-numbered years.

regard to the members' party affiliations. Either all committees are divided between the parties in the same proportion that the house is divided, or the minority is perhaps underrepresented on the most vital committees and overrepresented on the unimportant ones.

In the Jeffersonian South this partisan custom did not prevail—another indication that parties had not become a very strong influence in state legislative proceedings. The division of Federalists and Republicans on any given committee had no relation to party strength in the assembly. It appears, in fact, that committee members were selected on an almost random basis, for in any one year a wide variation exists in the Federalist proportion of seats on committees. Furthermore, the minority sometimes was in a stronger position on the important committees than on the unimportant ones. Apparently, the Republican majority was not especially concerned with dominating committee proceedings, an attitude that certainly would not have prevailed if parties had been of much consequence in the legislature.

In 1808, for example, North Carolina's vital house committee of privileges and elections had eight members of each party, while of the less important committees, claims had nineteen Republicans and only four Federalists, and divorce and alimony had eighteen Republicans and six Federalists. In 1810 in the same state, Federalists actually held a majority of the senate committee of privileges and elections but were a 16–8 minority on the less consequential joint committee of propositions and grievances. In the Virginia legislature Federalists were never a majority on any committee, but sometimes they held more than their share of places on the important ones.The Virginia senate had two standing committees, both important—privileges and elections, and executive expenses. At least once on the former committee and at least four times on the latter, Federalists filled two of the five seats, which was double their proportion of the whole senate. In 1806, the house of delegates gave Federalists one-third of the seats on the finance committee and one-fourth on privileges and elections, but only one-fifth and one-ninth of the places on two lesser committees (claims, and propositions and grievances). In 1800 and 1801, Federalists in the South Carolina senate were entirely unrepresented on the two routine committees of religion and grievances, yet they were a majority in both years on the most vital committee of all, privileges and elections. Taking the entire period from 1800 to 1816, twice the proportion of Federalists served on this key committee as on any of the less important ones.

Besides these variations among committees at any one session, each committee showed a fluctuation in party strength from year to year, even when the division of the entire house remained fairly constant. This tendency was most marked in North Carolina, where the joint committee of propositions and grievances had the following composition from 1807 to 1810:

1807: 16 Republicans, 8 Federalists
1808: 13 Republicans, 11 Federalists
1809: 21 Republicans, 3 Federalists
1810: 16 Republicans, 8 Federalists

Variations were not so wide in South Carolina because of the small number of places on each committee. The most extreme example for this state is the senate committee on high roads, which showed the following variations in a period when the party division in the whole senate was almost unchanging:

1806: 5 Republicans, 0 Federalists
1807: 4 Republicans, 1 Federalist
1808: 7 Republicans, 0 Federalists
1809: 5 Republicans, 2 Federalists
1810: 6 Republicans, 1 Federalist.

The composition of Virginia's committees was also usually less erratic than North Carolina's, but the house committee on courts showed this fluctuation from 1801 through 1803:

1801: 40 Republicans, 4 Federalists
1802: 14 Republicans, 0 Federalists
1803: 29 Republicans, 7 Federalists

An examination of the roll call votes in all three legislatures also reveals a lack of partisanship. On the few occasions when Federalists and Republicans did cluster on opposite sides of a vote, issues directly affecting the parties themselves rather than the state as a whole were at stake. Seldom were such purely state issues as slavery, internal improvements, taxation, and public morals the subjects of party-line voting.[8]

A useful measure of party unity on roll call votes is the *index of cohesion* developed by Stuart Arthur Rice.[9] On any given vote the percentage of party members voting on one side is subtracted from the percentage voting on the other side, and the resulting figure is the index of cohesion. For instance, if the Federalist members divided 50 percent on each side of an issue, the party's index of cohesion would be zero. If the Federalists split 70 percent to 30 percent, the index of cohesion would be 40; and if the members were 95 percent on one side and 5 percent on the other, the index would be 90. Table 10 gives, for every third year in the period, the Federalist and Republican indexes of cohesion on all important roll calls not involving national party politics or patronage.

Table 10 **Level of Party Unity in South Atlantic Legislatures, 1800–1815: Indexes of Cohesion on Important Roll Calls in Lower Houses in Selected Years**

	Virginia		*North Carolina*		*South Carolina*	
Year	*Fed.*	*Rep.*	*Fed.*	*Rep.*	*Fed.*	*Rep.*
1800	48	30	34	30	60	22
1803	36	20	21	22	61	15
1806	40	26	37	40	61	25
1809	34	25	21	38	80	34
1812*	42	33	27	30	79	21
1815	47	28	29	33	—	—
Average	41	27	28	32	68	25

*In South Carolina, 1811 session is indicated; there were too few Federalists in 1812 to provide a meaningful index.

8. Two-thirds or more of the Federalists opposed two-thirds or more of the Republicans on only 19 percent of the roll calls studied, and two-thirds of the 19 percent were generally concerned with direct party matters (national politics, patronage, election laws, redistricting) rather than with state problems.

9. See Stuart A. Rice, *Quantitative Methods in Politics* (New York, 1928), and on legislative voting analysis in general, Lee F. Anderson *et al.*, *Legislative Roll-Call Analysis* (Evanston, Ill., 1966).

In every year, the Federalist members in Virginia and South Carolina were more united than the Republicans on these purely state issues, but in North Carolina, Republicans showed more unity than Federalists in every session but one. Republican legislators displayed almost the same degree of party cohesion in all three states; their average index ranges from 25 (meaning a 62.5 percent to 37.5 percent division) in South Carolina up to 32 (or a 66 percent to 34 percent division) in North Carolina. The Federalists, by contrast, have a very strong cohesion index of 68 in South Carolina (the average vote being 84 percent to 16 percent), but they fall to 41 in Virginia and are more divided still in North Carolina, with an index of only 28 (or 64 percent to 36 percent).[10]

The wide variation in Federalist legislative unity was probably caused by the different patterns of party strength in each state. In South Carolina, within one or two elections after 1800, Federalist victories were restricted almost entirely to a small number of coastal parishes on either side of Charleston. Legislators chosen by these staple-growing planters and their merchant and professional allies would be likely to have mutual economic, social, moral, and regional interests and would therefore tend to vote as a bloc on state issues. In Virginia the situation was similar but not so marked. Except for 1800 and 1801, most Federalist legislators were elected from western Virginia—the Shenandoah Valley and the Appalachian counties. Although the valley and the mountains would not always have the same position on state problems, these two neighboring regions west of the Blue Ridge had far more in common with each other than either of them had with eastern Virginia. Republicans, who were well represented on both sides of the Blue Ridge, would speak for more con-

10. The index of cohesion is not a very sophisticated analytical tool, and in a book-length study of legislative operations in these states a number of other methods should be used as well. For one critique of the index of cohesion, see John G. Grumm, "The Means of Measuring Conflict and Cohesion in the Legislature," *Southwestern Social Science Quarterly*, XLIV (1964), 377–88; and also Wilder Crane, Jr., "A Caveat on Roll-Call Studies of Party Voting," *Midwest Journal of Political Science*, IV (1960), 237–49. Techniques such as Guttman scaling, which a number of analysts use, would probably be impossible to use effectively in the South in these years because there are very few issues on which a scalable series of votes was taken in any given year, and membership turnover was very great from year to year.

flicting interests than would the Federalist members, of whom perhaps 80 percent came from the valley and the mountains. In North Carolina the distribution of party strength was quite different. Federalists were strongest in the Scottish and Scotch-Irish counties of south central North Carolina, but they also elected many members from the central coast around Newbern and a sprinkling from the north central plantation counties and the western frontier. In addition, the seven major towns sent their own representatives to the legislature, and most of these "urban" members were Federalists. Therefore, in North Carolina the Federalist legislators represented a much more varied base than in either Virginia or South Carolina. The towns, the coast, the south central region, and the mountains might all have differing views on state matters, and Federalists would show much less unity as a party than in the states where their counties' interests were more closely knit.[11]

Influences that might have produced stricter cohesion within both parties, had they been used sufficiently, were the caucus system and the appointment of at least unofficial floor leaders and whips. The failure to use these methods of bringing members into line is still another clue that party counted for little in legislative proceedings. In this matter of discipline Federalists were considerably more lax than Republicans, who did occasionally caucus to thrash out issues and develop a solid party position. The minority generally expressed disdain for the caucus system and almost never used it. The Federalist Raleigh *Minerva*, for example, scoffed at the "grand caucus of the republican, or more properly speaking, Jacobinic club," which marshaled a nearly solid Republican vote for governor in the North Carolina assembly of 1808. Apparently, Federalists did caucus in the South Carolina legislature in 1801 to choose a senate candidate and in Virginia in 1805 to fight the election of Republican directors for the Bank of Virginia. No doubt there were a few other caucuses not mentioned in newspaper or manuscript accounts, but on the whole Federalists held fewer such meetings than Republicans did.[12]

All these negative facts—no party affiliation in routine newspaper

11. See a detailed discussion of Federalist strength in each state in Chaps. 14–17, herein.

12. Raleigh *Minerva*, December 1, 1808. For evidence of Federalist caucuses see

lists of assembly members, no ceremonial party clash over the speakership, no systematic allocation of committee seats by party, no high degree of partisan cohesion in voting on state issues, and no regular use of the caucus—lead to the conclusion that party, by itself, was not a very important influence upon legislative decision-making in the South. Two positive indicators—the willingness of the Republican majority to allow an occasional Federalist to be speaker and the unconcern about minority party control of important committees—reinforce this impression. Party affiliation was indeed well marked; almost every member considered himself a Federalist or a Republican when national issues were at stake. However, this strong partisanship rarely filtered down to state questions, and since the legislatures were primarily concerned with state rather than national issues, the Federalist minority was allowed a full and fair share in all proceedings.

H. W. DeSaussure to John Rutledge, Jr., December 19, 1801, in Rutledge Papers, UNC; Robert Saunders to Joseph Prentis, Jr., January 2, 1805, in Prentis Transcripts, UVa. Joseph Pearson to John Steele, November 24, 1805, in Wagstaff (ed.), *Papers of John Steele*, I, 460–61; Archibald D. Murphey to Thomas Ruffin, November 24, 1814, in Hoyt (ed.), *Papers of Archibald D. Murphey*, I, 74; Frederick Nash to Duncan Cameron, November 25, 1814, in Cameron Family Papers; and Preston Simpson to John Cropper, January 6, 1806, in John Cropper Papers. Among the mentions of Republican caucuses are John Campbell to John Campbell, Sr., December 30, 1810, in David Campbell Papers and circular of Azariah Graves *et al.* to "The Citizens of Caswell County [North Carolina]," December 21, 1810, in Cameron Family Papers; and Raleigh *Minerva*, December 4, 1812.

FIVE Federalists and Southern Society

Chapter 21 FEDERALISM, DEMOCRACY, AND SLAVERY

THE southern Federalists, like their northern friends, were a sour and disgruntled lot after 1800; they shared little of the buoyant optimism of the Jeffersonian American. They prized social stability and deference, rule by the qualified elite, and restraints on the passions of the majority, but all these essential props to sound republican government seemed in decay; the future was full of danger. Abroad, Napoleonic tyranny was spreading over Europe, and even Britain, the citadel of order and sensible liberty, appeared to be in danger. In American diplomacy, a pro-French outlook seemed now to replace the neutral policy of the 1790s, which had distrusted France more than Britain. In the capital, conservative and commercially oriented government had given way to unsettling Jeffersonian "mobocracy" and an anticommercial attitude. The eastern cities yearly received frightening hordes of new immigrants soaked in the liquor of European Jacobinism. To the west, the ever-growing boisterous frontier steadily reduced the national influence of older Federalist areas. At home in the South, the democratic enthusiasm of Baptists and Methodists was rapidly dominating religious life and eclipsing the social influence of the more conservative, hierarchical churches. And there was no realistic hope of reversing these processes. No wonder so many Federalists found the world vile to look upon.[1]

It is difficult to analyze the political thought of these men properly because their political writings were infrequent and usually appeared within a polemical context. Philosophical comments made under such circumstances may display more bitterness and pessimism than a long theoretical discourse written apart from an immediate attack on the Republican administration. Nevertheless, it is impossible to escape the impression that southern Federalists, like their northern comrades who were more prolific writers, held a dismal view of human nature, a low opinion of the common man's intelligence, and little hope for the future of America.

The Federalist idea of the good society was a rather British one. Social order, respect by the lower classes for their betters, stability of position, a good moral character in the general population—these were the attributes of a truly republican nation. Reason rather than emotion ought to guide the people in their attitude toward public men and policies. The wise, virtuous, and talented should occupy the seats of power, and the mass of citizens, if they truly desired good government and "rational" liberty, should be content to choose their rulers from among the rich and socially prominent. Some Federalists went so far as to declare the British system of government superior to the American, to ridicule the idea that men were born free or equal, and to address political campaign pamphlets to "the *substantial* (not *the people*) citizens" of a congressional district.[2]

To rule their ideal society, Federalists desired a "mixed" government containing some aspects of democracy, aristocracy, and monarchy. They viewed the Constitution as establishing just such a system, with the people directly electing their congressmen and, in some states, the presidential electors. At this point, the direct popular voice would be muted and the aristocratic element would enter with the in-

1. For Federalist objections to nearly every facet of American life after 1800, see Linda K. Kerber, *The Federalists in Dissent* (Ithaca, N.Y., 1970), which touches lightly upon southern Federalists; see especially Chap. 6.

2. H. W. DeSaussure to Joseph Dennie, April 4, 1803, in Joseph Dennie Papers, Harvard University; "Ames," in Savannah *Columbian Museum*, August 1, 1814; James C. Johnston to James Iredell, Jr., August 24, 1804, in Charles E. Johnson Papers; "A Ploughman," in *Virginia Gazette*, August 11, 1802.

direct election of senators (by the legislatures) and of the president (by the electoral college). The chief executive himself was to supply the tinge of monarchy. This mixture of forms, the Federalists believed, was essential to good government. The people should select their rulers, yes; but once chosen, the rulers would be above the people and not bound to consult them on every policy decision, much less to follow their wishes. The wisdom and integrity of those in power would guarantee that the nation would be run in the true interests of the people.

Above all, America ought to avoid an unmixed democracy, in which the whim of the masses ruled and the government shifted its mighty bulk with every change in public opinion. Ordinary people were incapable of deciding wisely on involved matters of policy; therefore, a democracy—a pure rule by the people—would produce irrational and wrongheaded government, frequent changes of course, and eventual chaos. Constant innovation was dangerous and confusing. Built on an unsteady foundation, a pure domocracy would quickly fall, and the ensuing disorder would produce a dictator. Indeed, this last development might not be accidental; the Raleigh *Minerva* warned that "a zealous and active democrat by profession, is in fact always a despotic tyrant, if ever an opportunity offers that he dare embrace." What better proof than Napoleon, the archdemocrat turned archtyrant? Democracy was not only bad, the Federalists said, it was the worst of all forms of government; or, as the editor of the *Charleston Courier* more delicately stated, "Simple monarchy we abhor as much, or at least almost as much as simple democracy."[3]

What gave southern Federalists long faces and sour dispositions was their belief that America had quite fallen off from the ideal of a deferential society and a balanced government. They drew back in alarm at "the hasty and tremendous strides which, under the influence of the party in power, unmixed democracy is making in America." They even denied the other party the respectable name of Republican and insisted on calling it democratic, which was to Federalists an epi-

3. *Charleston Courier*, July 30, 1804; Raleigh *Minerva*, June 27, 1803; a reader, in *Virginia Telegraphe*, May 12, 1804; *Norfolk Gazette*, August 9–October 9, 1805 (reprinting a long series of essays); John Rutledge, Jr., to Theodore Sedgwick, May 10, 1801, in Theodore Sedgwick Papers.

thet. They attributed the current Republican ascendancy to constant demagogic flattery of the people. Used at first as a mere electioneering tactic, this Republican practice soon produced, in the Federalist view, a fundamental change in American political society.[4]

The change, they believed, was caused by two flaws in the American people—the gullibility of the lower classes and their hostility toward the upper class. It seemed obvious to Federalists that the ordinary voter was pitifully credulous. When forming his political opinions he allowed emotion and prejudice to banish reason, making him easy prey for demagogues. How else could one explain why Federalists lost election after election? Surely a party that had provided sober, honest government under Washington and Adams should be preferred to a batch of unstable democrats. But successive elections made painfully clear that a substantial majority in most states consisted of irrational persons who believed the Republicans were entitled to rule.

Since logic had not made people Republicans to begin with, it was impossible to reason them out of their imbecile attachment. Unfortunately for the country, Republican politicians had found the key to power in an inevitable characteristic of human nature—the jealousy of the lower orders toward the upper. This was the greatest danger in a republic, because designing men could play upon the common people's ungenerous suspicion of virtue, talent, and character and could sweep into power by raising a false clamor about the menace of aristocracy. Those without intelligence or ability naturally desired to humble their betters; and since the lower ranks were always a majority, there seemed scant prospect of reversing the trend toward a dissolute democracy. Viewed from this sour Federalist perspective, the very use of popular elections was unfair because they would always be manipulated by Republican incendiaries. To be known as a man of ability was a burden rather than an advantage at the polls. The American system appeared, therefore, almost to guarantee the future perpetual rule of the Republican party.[5]

4. A reader, in *Charleston Courier*, April 6, 1804; Raleigh *Minerva*, June 27, 1803; *Virginia Gazette*, September 7, 1803.

5. William R. Davie to John Haywood, May 14, 1816, in Ernest Haywood Papers; John Cameron to Duncan Cameron, September 21, 1800, in Cameron Family Papers; Loring Andrews to Samuel Norton, April 3, 1804, in Loring Andrews Papers; *North-Carolina Journal*, March 11, 1805; *Virginia Patriot*, July 19, 1811.

Having such a low view of the common people and of their attachment to unwholesome democracy, Federalists opposed any extension of the suffrage, for this would debase still further the quality of the electorate. The issue did not arise in Georgia or North Carolina, where all taxpayers could already vote; since both states levied a poll tax, they had virtually universal manhood suffrage. The North Carolina senate, however, was elected by fifty-acre freeholders. In the other two states the ballot issue was of some consequence, and nearly all Federalists who took a public position firmly defended the freehold property qualification. In both Virginia and South Carolina the agitation for expanded suffrage was more a sectional than a party question; low-country Republicans and most Federalists opposed reform while the up-country Republicans and a few Federalists insisted upon it.

When the suffrage question was raised in Virginia, a small number of western Federalists protested the existing disfranchisement of nonfreeholders. However, the general party attitude was quite different, as summarized in a letter to the Richmond *Virginia Patriot*: "Property gives interest, and generally promotes information: these are the two most important attributes of freedom. Poverty then being most commonly without risk in society, feels indifferent about convulsions and hazards, and is too much without the proper means of information to guard it sufficiently against the ambitious views of demagogues, partizans and place-hunters." The South Carolina lawyer H. W. DeSaussure opposed the leveling effects of universal suffrage in his state, especially where "there is a floating population not attached to the soil," and nearly all the small Federalist remnant in the legislature of South Carolina voted against bills to extend the vote outside the ranks of freeholders.[6]

As if American society were not endangered enough by these democratic tendencies within itself, there was the added menace of an un-

6. "Philemon," in *Virginia Patriot*, May 3, 1811; DeSaussure to Ezekiel Pickens, September 12, 1808, in DeSaussure Papers, USC; "Publius," in *Charleston Courier*, July 19, 1814; Heaney, "Letters of Bushrod Washington," 165. John Marshall's views on broader suffrage are the subject of some conflict: Robert K. Faulkner, *The Jurisprudence of John Marshall* (Princeton, N.J., 1968), 122–23; Saul K. Padover, "The Political Ideas of John Marshall," *Social Research*, XXVI (1959), 56–58. The votes in Virginia are in the *House Journal*, 1806, p. 68; 1807, p. 100; 1812, p. 125; 1816, pp. 166, 168, and show Federalists (nearly all from the west) evenly divided on extending voting rights, while Republicans (mostly from the east) are almost two to one against.

settling foreign immigration. Southern Federalists seldom commented upon the subject, perhaps because most foreigners chose to settle in the North. One must therefore be cautious in speaking of a "Federalist attitude" toward immigration, since the only available evidence for the entire South is limited to a few newspaper stories, letters, and votes in Congress. However, nearly every mention of the issue is derogatory to aliens, and this unanimity of opinion adds weight to the scanty evidence. The *Charleston Courier's* admission that America owed much to such foreigners as Paul Jones, Casimir Pulaski, and Baron DeKalb, was rare indeed. The more general Federalist view opposed immigration and questioned whether immigrants should ever be allowed the same rights as native Americans.[7]

Those few Federalists who made their views public opposed every attempt to incorporate aliens more readily into American society. When Jefferson urged Congress to shorten the residence requirement for naturalization, reaction was entirely hostile. If foreigners were allowed to vote and hold office at all, they ought to undergo a long period of residence in the United States first. Only thus could they absorb American political beliefs, acquire a stake in the country, and develop an attachment to their new homeland. It was all very well to provide a hospitable asylum to aliens, but granting them full citizenship too quickly was unwise and dangerous.[8]

Federalist hostility to aliens stemmed from fear of foreign ideas and foreign influence at the polls. "Renegades" from revolutionary Europe might infect Americans with dangerous doctrines. If voters were gullible enough to install "domestic Jacobins" such as Jefferson in power, they could easily fall prey to European subversion. Some immigrants might be actual foreign agents plotting the downfall of the United States. If nothing else, immigrants might arrive in such hordes that they could outnumber native voters in some areas and dominate local politics. Indeed, the *Charleston Courier* thought foreigners were already trying to control elections in New York City.

7. *Charleston Courier*, April 29, 1805; "Camillus," in *Virginia Patriot*, June 28, July 2, 23, 1811.

8. "Recantor," in *Virginia Gazette*, May 29, 1802; *South-Carolina State-Gazette*, January 22, 1802.

Alien influence in politics was undesirable chiefly because immigrants drifted so strongly toward the Republican party; and some Federalists saw Jefferson's Naturalization Act as a mere partisan scheme to entice aliens to America and add more Republican votes on election day. Immigrants served the Republican cause in other ways, too; editor William Boylan claimed that all the Federalist papers in the United States were managed by native citizens, but at least half the Republican newspapers of any consequence were said to be run by foreigners.[9]

Actually, southern Federalists did not despise all immigrants alike; they chiefly feared the French and the Irish (who were largely pro-French). It was the belief that immigrants were tainted with French influence and would join the friends of France in America that caused the party to oppose immigration and easy naturalization. A backwoods Virginia paper, the Staunton *Political Censor*, gave perhaps the clearest statement of the Federalist position, if one substitutes the word *alien* for *Irish*: "The respectable Irish emigrants who have been in this country for several years, and who have, by their industry and enterprise, acquired a property and standing here, are, almost to a man, *Federalists*—while, on the other hand, the thousands and tens of thousands, who have been pouring in upon us from Ireland, since that country became distracted by French doctrines and French conspiracies, are generally democrats, and support by their votes, often illegally obtained, and illegally given, the present ruling party."[10]

To most southerners, of course, immigration was not nearly so important a social question as slavery. On this much more delicate issue the Federalist position was ambivalent. Party leaders considered themselves to be members of an elite class whose natural right to govern carried a corresponding obligation to improve the condition of less fortunate persons. This feeling of stewardship generally in-

9. *Virginia Gazette*, May 29, 1802; *Charleston Courier*, March 10, 1803, April 23, 1807; Raleigh *Minerva*, February 1, 1810.

10. Staunton *Political Censor*, June 22, 1808; Stanly, *Letter to His Constituents*, 19–20. Edward C. Carter II, "A 'Wild Irishman' Under Every Federalist's Bed: Naturalization in Philadelphia, 1789–1806," *Pennsylvania Magazine of History and Biography*, XCIV (1970), 331–46, shows clearly the political threat that heavy local immigration posed to the Federalist party.

clined them to mitigate the severities of the slave system by opposing the slave trade, encouraging voluntary manumission, and reducing discrimination against both slaves and free Negroes. Except in South Carolina, Federalism was not closely associated with plantation agriculture, and few of its leaders exhibited the "siege mentality" that afflicted many people in regions where slaves far outnumbered whites. Still, southern Federalist politicians *were* attempting to build a party in a section increasingly distinguished by its slave labor system, and their policy was bound to be affected by the growing southern feeling that the preservation of slavery and of white supremacy was an absolute necessity.

The foreign slave trade, however, was rather easy for the party to oppose because humanitarian concern for the wretched condition of Negroes in the slave ships could be expressed at a very low political risk. This was the aspect of slavery most easily dispensed with, for it did not touch the heart of the system at all, and there were strong economic arguments against a large influx of new slaves. A man could believe strongly in the necessity for slavery and still find the importation of Africans morally repugnant. He would also doubtless be aware that the smaller the supply of Negroes from outside, the greater the probable rise in value of his existing slaveholdings.

On the national level, the Constitution prevented any outright ban on the slave trade until 1808, but there were several attempts to restrict or curtail it. In 1803, Congress passed by a large margin a bill to forbid importing foreign slaves into states having local laws against the practice; this included every state in the Union at that time. All three southern Federalists who voted were in favor of this disguised prohibition. Soon afterward, South Carolina repealed her local ban on importing Africans, and some congressmen were impelled to retaliate by seeking a tax of ten dollars per head on all such imports. Two votes were taken on postponing consideration of the tax, which would effectively have killed it. The southern Federalist members voted three to one and then four to two in favor of postponement, and two of them (Lowndes and Huger of South Carolina) made speeches against the tax. Neither they nor any other southerner actually favored the foreign slave trade; both Huger and Lowndes publicly declared themselves hostile to it. What they objected to was a federal tax that only South Carolinians would pay; this seemed to be gross discrimination. They scoffed at the idea that any planter would be deterred from importing a slave by a mere ten dollar increase in the price. Another tax bill came before the next Congress, and the only southern Federalist in the House, Joseph Lewis, Jr., of Virginia, supported it. He also voted with the overwhelming majority of members for a bill totally outlawing the importation of slaves, to go into effect January 1, 1808, the earliest date the Constitution permitted.[11]

Outside Congress, other Federalists also opposed the foreign slave trade. The Halifax *North-Carolina Journal* praised as "salutary and very necessary" a constitutional amendment to end slave imports even before 1808, and a number of Federalist newspapers criticized South Carolina for reopening her slave trade. Not all opposed the trade on humane grounds; the *Charleston Courier* condemned the state's action purely from an economic view, because it would glut the slave market and drain money from the planters' pockets. One of the *Courier*'s editors took a partisan tack, blasting the hypocrisy of the "liberty and equality folks" whereby a Republican planter "buys his fellow with as little ceremony as you purchase a bullock."[12]

In the South Carolina legislature Federalists indicated strong opposition to the foreign slave trade, though Republicans tended slightly to favor it. In 1802, when the state house took up the matter, a motion to allow slave imports from anywhere except the French West Indies (contaminated by Negro revolts) received one Federalist vote and nine Republican votes. An attempt to crack down on widespread evasion of antiimportation laws by making slave traders ineligible to hold public office for seven years was endorsed 16–3 by Federalists and opposed 52–11 by Republicans. Two years later, 85 percent of the

11. *Annals of Congress*, 7th Cong., 2nd Sess., 534; 8th Cong., 1st Sess., 991–93, 1004–1007, 1024–27; 9th Cong., 1st Sess., 375, 443–44, 515–16; 9th Cong., 2nd Sess., 243–44, 264–67, 273–74, 483–87, 627, 637–38; Winthrop D. Jordan, *White Over Black: American Attitudes Toward the Negro, 1550–1812* (Chapel Hill, N.C., 1968), 330–31; Howard H. Ohline, "Politics and Slavery: The Issue of Slavery in National Politics, 1787–1815" (Ph.D. dissertation, University of Missouri, 1969), Chap. 9.

12. *North-Carolina Journal*, March 25, 1805; *Norfolk Gazette*, January 4, 1805; *Charleston Courier*, August 11, 1804; Andrews to Norton, April 30, 1804, in Loring Andrews Papers.

Federalist representatives and only 43 percent of the Republicans voted to outlaw absolutely all slave imports. The same year senate Republicans voted to open the slave trade anew, but Federalists were unanimously against; and on a series of roll calls in 1805, Federalist senators were almost three to one against the slave trade, though Republicans were slightly in favor of it. North Carolina also faced the problem of traders illegally slipping Negroes into the state, and again Federalists were more diligent than their opponents in seeking to close this illicit traffic. A fruitless attempt to enforce the penalties of a 1794 state law against the slave trade received a 10–9 majority of Federalist votes in the North Carolina senate; Republicans voted 25–7 against enforcement.[13]

The purely interstate slave trade was another item of concern. Reasons of security argued against allowing Negroes to be brought into a state from any source, because whites feared a high ratio of blacks in their midst. However, a ban on importing slaves from other states might seriously interfere with the ordinary conduct of plantation agriculture. A planter could not move readily from one state to another if he had to leave his slaves behind and purchase new ones; a man who married an out-of-state woman could not merge the combined slaveholdings and move them to his plantation, nor could an heir bring in slaves inherited in another state. With strong arguments on both sides, legislative votes on the question followed no explicable pattern from place to place. Some Federalists in Virginia spoke up for barring every avenue to the introduction of Negroes, whether from other states or from abroad. Federalists in the legislature revealed exactly contrary sentiments; they voted on almost every possible occasion against restricting the interstate trade, while the Republican majority took the opposite view. In South Carolina, on the other hand, Federalists were much more hostile than Republicans to the interstate slave trade in legislative votes from 1800 to 1803, even wanting

13. *South Carolina House Journal*, 1802, pp. 134, 135; 1804, p. 194; *South Carolina Senate Journal*, 1804, p. 94; 1805, pp. 158, 172, 173, 176, 177, 178; *North Carolina Senate Journal*, 1802, p. 38. In the North Carolina house, both parties were equally interested in enforcing the law: *North Carolina House Journal*, 1802, p. 41. See also Patrick S. Brady, "The Slave Trade and Sectionalism in South Carolina, 1787–1808," *Journal of Southern History*, XXXVIII (1972), 601–20.

to prevent South Carolina residents from bringing in their own slaves acquired elsewhere.[14]

Chipping away at the slave trade in its various forms was all well enough, but this by no means indicated Federalist hostility toward slavery itself. Some southerners might have branded the institution an economic and moral burden, but very few took any positive steps to eliminate it, even gradually. Federalists were no exception. A few North Carolina party leaders probably opposed slavery, and the *Berkeley and Jefferson Intelligencer* in western Virginia once published an address by northern abolitionists; but these were aberrations. The general party attitude was more correctly revealed when the Eighth Congress considered a resolution to free all slaves in the District of Columbia. On a strongly sectional vote, all five southern Federalists who were present stood with their Republican neighbors in soundly rejecting the idea.[15]

The sporadic voluntary emancipation of individual slaves by their masters was not so dangerous, however, and this practice met some degree of approval. Legislative votes on restricting or easing emancipation and on manumitting Negroes at their owners' request gave hundreds of local leaders in both parties an opportunity to record their feelings. There were ten such votes in North Carolina, four in Virginia, and one in South Carolina; and on two-thirds of these the Federalist members were more anxious than Republicans to allow small-scale emancipation. Five of the votes concerned bills to restrict or prevent altogether the manumission of even one slave by his willing owner. On four of these roll calls Federalists were the more "liberal" party, giving 70 percent of their ballots in favor of easy manu-

14. Martinsburg *Berkeley & Jefferson Intelligencer*, January 25, 1805; *Virginia House Journal*, 1804, p. 64; 1805, p. 78; 1806, p. 51; 1807, p. 17; *Virginia Senate Journal*, 1805, p. 67; 1806, p. 48. The total of individual votes on the six Virginia roll calls shows Federalists almost three to one in favor of allowing Negro imports from other states and Republicans almost two to one against. On South Carolina, see votes in *South Carolina House Journal*, 1800, p. 38; 1801, p. 64; 1802, p. 136; 1803, p. 125.

15. *Annals of Congress*, 8th Cong., 2nd Sess., 995–96; Martinsburg *Berkeley & Jefferson Intelligencer*, February 24, 1804. Henderson, "Federalist of the Old School," 72–73, and William K. Boyd, "Currency and Banking in North Carolina, 1790–1836," *Trinity College Historical Society Papers*, X (1914), 54, both say that Archibald Henderson and William Gaston both condemned slavery.

mission—substantially more than the Republicans.[16] There were five other proposals, all in North Carolina, whose object was to expedite emancipation. On these there was not much party contrast; Federalists were more favorable twice and Republicans once, and on the remaining two votes there was no difference between the parties. Four additional roll calls in North Carolina and one in Virginia, on freeing particular Negroes at the request of their owners, again showed no partisan conflict.[17]

The slight tendency for Federalists to be more friendly to emancipation may have something to do with partisan geography. In both Virginia and North Carolina, Republicans dominated the plantation counties where slaves were plentiful. Federalist legislators, living in areas with fewer slaves, would feel less direct personal concern about undermining the slave system through manumissions. However, even in South Carolina, where Federalist legislators were limited to the slave-laden coastal parishes, the party was distinctly more willing than the up-country Republicans to allow emancipation.

Perhaps another reason for this Federalist attitude lay in the deep concern that party leaders felt for property rights. As one Virginian asked in opposing a bill to prohibit all emancipations, "Will not Sir such a law infringe upon the liberty of individuals to do with their property as they shall think proper?" If a man wished to give away a cow or free a slave, that was his right; no legislature should restrict a person's control of his own property. Too, Federalist thinking was shaped by the stewardship that they claimed as their proper role in society. They tried to promote the good of the whole community by holding out some promise of improvement for the lowest orders of society. Restricting or prohibiting manumission would do away with the hope of freedom for slaves, "the great Reward which probably promotes them to the faithful discharge of their duty" and "proves

16. *Virginia House Journal*, 1804, p. 76; 1805, p. 77; *Virginia Senate Journal*, 1801, p. 68; *North Carolina House Journal*, 1803, p. 32; *South Carolina House Journal*, 1803, p. 24; Howell M. Henry, *The Police Control of the Slave in South Carolina* (Nashville, Tenn., 1914), 168.

17. *North Carolina House Journal*, 1809, p. 26; 1810, p. 26; and *North Carolina Senate Journal*, 1801, p. 58; 1808, p. 28; 1811, p. 28, for the votes on emancipation; *Virginia House Journal*, 1808, p. 46; *North Carolina Senate Journal*, 1802, p. 29; 1804, pp. 33, 50; 1809, p. 38, for the votes on freeing individual slaves.

a security for the peace of Families." Removing this hope would be cruel to the slaves and dangerous to whites, for it would increase the chance of bloody uprisings.[18]

On yet another aspect of the slave system—the restrictions and disabilities imposed upon Negroes—Federalists were once again the more lenient party. Although no roll calls were taken in the South Carolina legislature, both Virginia and North Carolina voted several times on whether to make the institution of slavery still more restrictive. Alarm over the Gabriel conspiracy in 1800 led both states to consider outlawing certain types of slave gatherings. In Virginia, the legislature voted a number of times on bills to force emancipated slaves to leave the state; and both there and in North Carolina a variety of other burdens placed on free Negroes forbade them to sell liquor, serve

Table 11 **Legislative Votes on Bills Restricting Slaves and Free Negroes**

State, Year and House	*Subject of Roll Call Vote*	*Federalists* Yea	*Federalists* Nay	*Republicans* Yea	*Republicans* Nay
VA–1803 (h)	Declare certain meetings of slaves unlawful	7	14	54	32
VA–1805 (h)	Require freed slaves to leave the state within a year	6	18	82	42
VA–1805 (s)	Require freed slaves to leave the state within a year	0	2	8	4
VA–1810 (h)	Refuse to allow one male Negro to remain within the state	12	16	64	56
VA–1813 (h)	Forbid Negroes to sell liquor and provisions	12	19	59	46
NC–1802 (s)	Prevent conspiracies and rebellions among slaves	17	3	28	6
NC–1806 (s)	Forbid free Negroes to move out of county without certificate	5	6	20	16
NC–1814 (h)	Forbid free Negroes to serve in state militia	27	13	15	40
Total on All Eight Votes		86	91	330	242
		(49% to 51%)		(58% to 42%)	

18. Richard Drummond Bayly to John Cropper, January 6, 1805, in John Cropper Papers; for another criticism of the same law, see H. Brooke to Leven Powell, December 22, 1800, in Leven Powell Papers.

in the militia, or move from their native county without carrying freedom certificates. As Table 11 shows, Federalists were usually less willing than Republicans to vote for such restrictive measures.[19]

If any conclusion is drawn from the rather scanty evidence of votes, speeches, and editorials on the slavery question, it would be a cautious claim that southern Federalists were somewhat more liberal than southern Republicans. Whether their social philosophy, their economic interests, or their residence in areas less populated with slaves is responsible for this attitude, one cannot say. Furthermore, the difference between parties was only a marginal one; southern Federalist leaders and legislators were still southerners, and none of them took nearly so advanced a position on the slavery issue as some of their northern colleagues.

19. The overall vote on eight such bills shows Republicans almost three to two for imposing more restrictions on Negroes whereas Federalists were evenly split: *North Carolina House Journal*, 1814, p. 36; *North Carolina Senate Journal*, 1802, p. 40; 1806, p. 42; *Virginia House Journal*, 1803, p. 85; 1805, p. 87; 1810, p. 81; 1813, p. 153; *Virginia Senate Journal*, 1805, p. 67. The only congressional vote of this nature, on an amendment to exclude free Negroes from the suffrage in Louisiana, saw the half-dozen southern Federalists stand unanimously against allowing Negroes to vote: *Annals of Congress*, 11th Cong., 3rd Sess., 937–38. See also Henry, *Police Control*, 134–35, 150; and Jordan, *White Over Black*, 391–402, 408–11.

Chapter 22 SOUTHERN FEDERALISTS AND EDUCATION

AMONG the foremost Federalist contributions to southern development was a lively interest in education. The first two decades of the nineteenth century saw the early growth of state universities, the spread of local academies for secondary schooling, and the beginnings of a movement toward state-supported public education. To all these educational advances Federalists gave their blessings and their active participation.[1]

No clear statement of their educational philosophy exists, but the southern Federalist party chiefs considered themselves the natural leaders and moral stewards of society. The outlook of such men has been well summarized by Rush Welter and others. Believing that government should be the province of rational, able, and morally upright men, Federalists thought wider education would produce better public servants and reduce the likelihood of "Jacobin excesses" by those in office. A better-educated voting population might also re-

1. The best collection of source material is Edgar W. Knight (ed.), *A Documentary History of Education in the South Before 1860* (5 vols.; Chapel Hill, N.C., 1949–53), II, III. There is no thorough modern secondary study of southern education in this period, although several good histories of individual colleges and states exist.

strain the Republican desire for "visionary innovation" in government, because the wisdom of the traditional social and political order would be more widely understood. America was showing less and less deference to men of talent and breeding, and a sound educational system could replenish that diminishing virtue.

Aside from any political motive, Federalists may simply have been convinced that education was a national necessity. It broadened the mind, sharpened the intellect, and increased the value of America's greatest resource, her people. The southern party leaders were themselves very well educated by the standards of the time; most of them had at least attended college. They cannot have overlooked the country's need for professional men of every sort. Trained lawyers, doctors, ministers, and teachers were all in short supply, especially in the South. Increasing the number and ability of this important professional class was essential to American cultural advancement.[2]

Although precise motives must be conjectured, active Federalist involvement in advancing southern education is well established. Higher education was a special object of concern, particularly in North Carolina, but also in South Carolina and Virginia. The handful of Federalists in Georgia had little part in building Franklin College, as that state's university was first called, although party activist John Macpherson Berrien did serve on the college's board of trustees for three decades. Elsewhere the Federalist role was much larger. North Carolina's most famous Federalist, William R. Davie, earned the title Father of the University for his efforts in establishing and nurturing the University of North Carolina in the 1790s. Such well-known Federalists as Senator Samuel Johnston, Judge John Louis Taylor, Congressmen William Barry Grove and William Gaston, and banker William Polk, along with Davie himself, served as trustees in the early years of the century. Also on the board from time to time were several locally

2. Rush Welter, *Popular Education and Democratic Thought in America* (New York, 1962), 27–28, 36. Among the very few lengthy Federalist comments on the value of education (both published after 1816) are Charles Fenton Mercer, "A Discourse on Popular Education," and Joseph Caldwell, "Letters on Popular Education, Addressed to the People of North Carolina," both in Knight (ed.), *Documentary History*, II, 297–356 and 397–405. See also Faulkner, *Jurisprudence of Marshall*, 141–44, and Wiley E. Hodges, "Pro-Governmentalism in Virginia, 1789–1836: A Pragmatic Liberal Pattern in the Political Heritage," *Journal of Politics*, XXV (1963), 334–36.

prominent Federalists, and in the faculty Federalism was very strong, possibly even dominant.[3]

So marked was the party's presence in university affairs that many Republicans became angry enough to turn against the school itself. Reasons other than partisan jealousy may have been important, but it was obvious when the North Carolina legislature met in November, 1800, that the Republican majority was hostile to the university. A previous assembly had given the school's trustees the use of all escheated and confiscated lands, thus supplying indirect financial aid to the young institution. Soon after the 1800 assembly convened, a motion was on the floor of each house seeking not only to prevent any further grants, but also to take back from the university any escheated property that had not already been put to use. This bill outraged the state's Federalist leaders. Congressman Archibald Henderson moaned, "Alas! Alas! the Legislature of No. Carolina about to wage war against the arts and sciences. I blush for my native State!"[4]

In the legislature itself, however, the antiuniversity attack was not strictly a partisan matter. Heavy majorities of Republicans favored the bill in both houses, but Federalist members of the lower house also approved it. Taking the house and senate combined, 71 percent of the Republicans and 57 percent of the Federalists supported the bill. The Federalist minority could have defeated the antiuniversity law in either house by voting as a bloc against it; instead, an actual majority lent active consent to the Republican attack. Only in a negative sense could the party be called friendly to the university on this occasion, in that a larger minority of Federalists than of Republicans stood by the school.[5]

3. Dorothy Orr, *A History of Education in Georgia* (Chapel Hill, N.C., 1950), 384; Robinson, *Davie*, Chap. 8; Hooker, "Diary," 916; Schauinger, *William Gaston*, 43–44. Knight (ed.), *Documentary History*, III, 6, 9, lists the original trustees of the Universities of Georgia and North Carolina; Kemp P. Battle, *History of the University of North Carolina* (2 vols.; Raleigh, N.C., 1907–12), II, 821–23, lists all North Carolina trustees for the whole period.

4. William Polk to John Steele, November 28, 1800, in Wagstaff (ed.), *Papers of John Steele*, I, 192; Archibald Henderson to Walter Alves, January 2, 1801, in Henderson, "Federalist of the Old School," 21.

5. *North Carolina House Journal*, 1800, p. 32; *North Carolina Senate Journal*, 1800, p. 49.

After its passage, the antiuniversity law continued to be a subject of controversy in the assembly, if not in the state at large. There was never an outpouring of public sentiment, either for or against the law; the mass meetings, letters to the editor, and newspaper articles that other legislative issues sometimes evoked were absent. Within the assembly, though, the battle continued at the very next session. A motion to repeal the law came before the senate in December, 1801, and was rebuffed, but the school's supporters were not entirely discouraged. Davie confessed that he had not expected the repeal to succeed, but he "considered the support it received as a proof of the condition of the public mind and the progress of reason." His optimism was premature; actually, fewer senators voted to repeal the law than had voted against its passage a year earlier. Again, Federalist members were less hostile to the school than were Republicans, but neither party cast a majority in favor of repeal. For several years thereafter the university issue was presented, argued, and rejected in one chamber or the other. The repealing bill died in the house of commons in 1802, passed the next year only to lose in the senate, and failed again to clear the house in 1804. These continued disappointments sapped the early optimism of the school's friends and drew even from Davie himself a disconsolate note. "The situation of the University," he said, "is a distressing one, and the more so, as it is not likely to be soon capable of any Remedy, being the necessary consequence of Legislative hostility to the Institution. The friends of science in other States regard the people of North Carolina as a sort of Semi-Barbarians. . . . The conduct of the Legislature for several years past has stamped this character on the State."[6]

Gradually, however, the assembly was having second thoughts, and by December, 1805, its attitude had changed. A compromise was proposed to restore the escheated lands for the school's use but to allow the legislature to appoint additional trustees and to fill all future vacancies on the board. This plan provided the university with funds

6. William R. Davie to John R. Eaton, December 27, 1801, William R. Davie to John Haywood, June 9, 1805, both in Hamilton (ed.), *William R. Davie*, 48–49, 57; *North Carolina Senate Journal*, 1801, p. 39; 1803, p. 37; *North Carolina House Journal*, 1802, p. 26; 1803, p. 33; 1804, p. 27.

while clearly bringing it under state control and presumably eliminating any undue Federalist influence in its affairs. The compromise quickly won general approval in both chambers, at last ending the long controversy. In the six legislative sessions that had debated the matter, Federalists had not always given majority support to the school's position, but on nearly every vote they had been more friendly than the Republicans. Table 12 illustrates this point; altogether, Federalist senators cast 39 votes for and 22 against the university; Republicans gave 60 votes for and 86 against. In the commons, Federalists voted 91 to 81 for the school, while Republicans were 180 for and 196 against.[7]

Table 12 **North Carolina Legislative Votes on the Antiuniversity Bill**

	Federalist Members			*Republican Members*		
Year & House	*Pro-UNC*	*Anti-UNC*	*% Pro*	*Pro-UNC*	*Anti-UNC*	*% Pro*
1800 House	17	30	36%	18	48	27%
1800 Senate	10	6	63%	12	25	32%
1801 Senate	7	8	47%	11	25	31%
1802 House	23	15	61%	23	50	32%
1803 House	20	15	57%	33	35	49%
1803 Senate	11	3	79%	16	23	41%
1804 House	12	16	43%	43	45	49%
1805 House	19	5	79%	63	18	78%
1805 Senate	11	5	69%	21	13	62%

There were other, less controversial, votes concerning the University of North Carolina in the decade after 1800, all involving some form of financial aid to the institution. Federalists, if not always willing to help, were at least less inclined than Republicans to deny such requests. In 1802, for example, the senate refused to buy 350 tickets in a lottery for the university's benefit; one-third of the Federalist senators and only one-fifth of the Republicans favored the purchase.

7. *Raleigh Register*, January 7, 1805; *North Carolina House Journal*, 1805, p. 42; *North Carolina Senate Journal*, 1805, p. 40; and the votes cited in the two preceding notes.

Three years later, the lower house declined to give the university all the state's interest in unpaid installments on public land sales. Federalists were only narrowly against the proposal, 8 to 6, but Republicans scorned it by 45 to 16. In 1809, another bill to aid the school actually passed the house with a 20–8 margin among Federalist members and a narrow 46–42 approval by Republicans.[8]

The end of the escheated lands dispute in 1805 neither solved the university's problems nor ended the Federalists' association with it. Some of them continued to serve as trustees and others took an active concern in the school's health. In 1809 the university's Federalist treasurer, Gavin Alves, was much distressed by the "truly deplorable situation of the University Coffers"; and when this penniless condition forced a public fund-raising drive to complete a college building, the leading Federalist newspaper lent its full support. Matters still did not improve. A half-dozen years later, after the legislature had been electing trustees for a decade, the university president was a lone Federalist in a sea of Republican trustees. He bemoaned his isolated position, "thwarted and defeated in all proposed measures for the benefit of the seminary." He grieved at being "the head of a seminary where with a majority the mean consideration of party politics is the main director in the choice of men and measures. Witness the late choice of Trustees. . . . For my part I despise the idea of being a party man in my station & I defy any man any student to produce an instance where as President I have said one word or done one action to promote Federal principles or Federal measures among the students."[9]

In South Carolina, Federalist participation in the growth of higher education was less complicated and more satisfying; the struggle to build an adequate university faced financial and intellectual obstacles but not political controversy. By the beginning of the nineteenth century a half-dozen "colleges" had been established, but most of them were primitive affairs. Only the College of Charleston resembled a proper institution, and it was a small and faltering school struggling

8. *North Carolina Senate Journal*, 1802, p. 27; *North Carolina House Journal*, 1805, p. 55; 1809, p. 38.

9. Gavin Alves to Archibald D. Murphey, April 17, 1809, in Hoyt (ed.), *Papers of Archibald D. Murphey*, I, 27; Raleigh *Minerva*, January 18, 1810; Robert Chapman to John Haywood, March 11, 1815, in Ernest Haywood Papers.

to improve itself while providing some degree of higher education to a few dozen of the city's youth. Founded in the 1780s, the college owed much of its shaky success to the interest and exertion of leading Federalists. Throughout the period from 1800 to 1816 a majority of the school's trustees were party members, including such prominent men as Thomas and Charles Cotesworth Pinckney, Frederick and Hugh Rutledge, Thomas Rhett Smith, William Washington, Arnoldus Vanderhorst, and others.[10]

Leaders of the minority were prominent, too, in the movement to bring higher education within reach of the vast up-country population. Charles Cotesworth Pinckney in the senate and Henry William DeSaussure in the house led the 1801 legislature in founding the South Carolina College at Columbia. DeSaussure hoped the new state-supported school would surpass the College of Charleston in its offerings and be a place "where the youth of all parts of the State may be educated and a greater union of opinions produced." No doubt he hoped for a gradual lessening of hostility by the Republican up-country toward the half-Federalist coastal parishes. Federalists were well represented on the original board of trustees, although the board chose a Republican over Charles Cotesworth Pinckney as its chairman. Compensating for this rebuff, the trustees then elected a New York Federalist, Jonathan Maxcy, as the college's first president. When Maxcy died, after a fruitful fifteen-year tenure, the board asked the learned low-country Federalist Stephen Elliott to take over the office, but he declined the honor. Others contributed much hard work as trustees in these same years. It was largely through the efforts of such well-known Federalists as the two "founders" Pinckney and DeSaussure, Abraham Nott, and John and Henry Dana Ward, that South Carolina College became firmly established within a decade and a half. The ready participation of these men, chiefly residents of Charleston and vicinity, is more impressive since the college primarily served the strongly Republican area around Columbia and drew few students from Charleston until much later.[11]

10. James H. Easterby, *A History of the College of Charleston, Founded 1770* (Charleston, S.C., 1935), 260–62, lists the trustees.

11. Zahniser, *Pinckney*, 238; Daniel W. Hollis, *South Carolina College* (Columbia,

Evidence is scanty concerning Federalism and higher education in Virginia. The state's famous old college, William and Mary, was firmly Republican in its faculty and student body, and there is no hint of any significant Federalist participation in its successful career. Hampden-Sydney College, with an overwhelmingly religious orientation, had few persons associated with it whose political leanings were known. As for the University of Virginia, it began after the effective demise of the Federalist party, but Jefferson and Joseph C. Cabell must share credit for its founding with the energetic young Federalist Charles Fenton Mercer. A leader in Virginia's lower house despite his minority party label, Mercer authored the first bill to establish the university. It passed the house with heavy Federalist support in February, 1817, only to die in the senate.[12]

There is little information on the sponsorship of lower schools and academies in Virginia, but Federalists did help to found and govern several. The first board of trustees of the Staunton Academy included two locally prominent Federalists, and some also served as commissioners to superintend the building of Leesburg Academy in Loudoun County. Philip Doddridge, who later had a long career as a leader of the minority, was on the original board of Brooke Academy, one of the earliest schools in western Virginia. In 1807 the Republican-controlled Virginia legislature included Edward Carrington, a strong Richmond Federalist, among the trustees appointed to establish a female academy in that city. A decade later, the people of Richmond elected the promising young Federalist Abel Parker Upshur to serve as trustee of the new Lancastrian Institution being founded there, and to join

S.C., 1951), Vol. I of Hollis, *The University of South Carolina*, 18–19, 34–35, 40, 74; H. W. DeSaussure to John Rutledge, Jr., January 13, 1802, in Rutledge Papers, UNC; Schaper, *Sectionalism and Representation*, 405. Edwin L. Green, *A History of the University of South Carolina* (Columbia, S.C., 1916), 443–45, lists the trustees.

12. On William and Mary College, see Joseph S. Watson to David Watson, March 2, 1801, in Joseph S. Watson, "Letters from William and Mary College, 1798–1801," *Virginia Magazine of History and Biography*, XXIX (1921), 161; and Thomas L. Preston to Andrew Reid, Jr., January 7, 1802, in "Glimpses of Old College Life," *William and Mary Quarterly*, 1st ser., VIII (1899–1900), 216. Trustees of Hampden-Sydney are listed in J. B. Henneman (comp.), "Trustees of Hampden-Sydney College," *Virginia Magazine of History and Biography*, VI (1898–99), 174–81; and some trustees of Franklin and Washington colleges are in *Virginia Argus*, June 3, July 1, 1800, and Knight (ed.), *Documentary History*, III, 32. On Mercer's role in helping create the University of Virginia, see Norman K. Risjord, "The Virginia Federalists," *Journal of Southern History*, XXXIII (1967), 516–17, and Dunaway, "Charles Fenton Mercer," 10–15.

him the Richmond Common Council added three other Federalists.[13]

The encouragement of such academies by individual party members carried over into support of public education generally by Federalist legislators. The most prominent crusader for state-aided schools was Charles Fenton Mercer; indeed, he has been called "perhaps the leading Southern advocate of popular education" in these years. In January, 1816, Mercer urged the Virginia General Assembly to support a primary school in each county. This never came to a vote, but in the next session he expanded his plea to include a complete system of primary schools, academies, and the university. Struggling against heavy opposition from eastern Republicans, Mercer's education bill won wholehearted backing from his fellow Federalists, who supported it by a vote of 14 to 2. Enough house Republicans joined the small Federalist bloc to pass the bill, but it died in the heavily Republican senate. Two more years elapsed before the legislature finally approved state support for education, and again the Federalists, almost to a man, were in favor, while Republicans were evenly split.[14]

North Carolina's Federalists, despite their disappointing experiences with the state university, also were striving to improve schooling on the lower level. The Raleigh *Minerva*, the leading voice of state Federalism, urged more learning for the young as an aid in forming an American national character. Several letters appeared in the same newspaper, presumably from Federalist subscribers, on the importance of wider as well as better education in the state. On a more concrete level, the *Minerva* gave strong editorial support to local academies in Fayetteville and Raleigh. The *Minerva*'s editor, William Boylan, contributed financially to build a "female department" at the academy, and former Federalist congressman John Steele helped subscribe funds to begin an academy at Salisbury. Several prominent party members, including former senator Samuel Johnston, Congressman William Gaston, and a pair of influential Federalist legislators,

13. Joseph A. Waddell, *Annals of Augusta County, Virginia from 1726–1871* (Rev. ed.; Staunton, S. C., 1902), 203; *Alexandria Gazette*, January 21, 1800; Alfred J. Morrison, *The Beginnings of Public Education in Virginia, 1776–1860: A Study of Secondary Schools in Relation to the State Literary Fund* (Richmond, Va., 1917), 129; *Virginia Argus*, January 20, 1807; *Virginia Patriot*, July 3, 1816.

14. Welter, *Popular Education*, 32; *Virginia House Journal*, 1816, p.214; Risjord, "Virginia Federalists," 516–17; Knight (ed.), *Documentary History*, II, 550–63.

served as commissioners or trustees of academies in the three eastern towns of Halifax, Newbern, and Edenton.[15]

These scattered examples of participation in local schools can be no more than hints of the party's general concern. How deeply its members were involved in improving education in counties throughout the state is impossible to know. Nor can one say whether North Carolina Federalists were more active in these local endeavors than were Republican leaders. The only clue to statewide party opinions on secondary education is a senate vote in 1808 on the question of establishing an academy in Chatham County. The proposal failed, a majority of each party rejecting it, but nearly half the Federalist senators were favorable and only one-sixth of the Republicans were. If this single roll call is any indication—and it should not be taken to mean very much by itself—then Federalists were the party more favorable to improving local education in North Carolina, just as they were more friendly to the university.[16]

In South Carolina the extent of Federalist participation in local academies remains unknown. Very possibly it was substantial, for the party took a leading role in securing legislative support for a statewide system of public education. Although newspaper columns reveal no wide public demand for primary school financing, in 1811 South Carolina became the first southern state to pass a public education law providing monetary support for schools in every parish and district. The author of this pathbreaking law was Stephen Elliott, the same Federalist leader who was later asked to preside over South Carolina College. His bill had the energetic support of the Federalist *Charleston Courier*. No sooner was the school system established than it came under fire from Republicans who thought the state could ill afford the expense of educating its children during the costly War of 1812. In the legislative sessions of 1812 and 1813, the handful of Federalists stood unanimously against the repealing effort, and it was

15. Raleigh *Minerva*, February 17, 1806, April 16, 1807; "Philmathes," *ibid*., December 10, 1807; lists of subscribers to build the female department of the Raleigh Academy, dated February, 1807, in William Jeffreys Papers, NCDAH; Steele to John Brown, March 20, 1807, in Wagstaff (ed.), *Papers of John Steele*, II, 495. Trustees and commissioners for various academies are in *North-Carolina Journal*, September 27,1802, January 12, 1807; *Edenton Gazette*, September 8, 1809, November 5, 1811; Newbern *Carolina Federal Republican*, May 15, 1813.

16. *North Carolina Senate Journal*, 1808, p.29.

chiefly their supporting votes that saved the school law from destruction.[17] Clearly, South Carolina's early interest in education owed much to the activity of the small Federalist minority.

In Georgia, as one might expect, the scarcity of Federalists insured that their part in educational progress would be minimal. There were so few of the minority in the legislature that roll call analysis on education bills is impractical. However, William J. Hobby, editor of the Federalist newspaper in Augusta, was among the founders of an academy in that town in 1800; and in the same county, Thomas Glascock, a revolutionary general and Federalist candidate for elector in 1796, served as trustee of the Richmond Academy until his death in 1804. Otherwise, there is no clear indication of Federalist concern for popular education in this heavily Republican state.[18]

Leaving Georgia aside, Federalists could take considerable pride in their aid to universities, academies, and public education in the South. Among the founders of three of the four state universities were Mercer in Virginia, Davie in North Carolina, and Pinckney and DeSaussure in South Carolina. Federalists authored the only two legislative attempts to secure public financing for lower education—Mercer's comprehensive Virginia measure in 1817 and Stephen Elliott's 1811 public school law in South Carolina. In the legislatures of Virginia and both Carolinas, the average Federalist member was more friendly (or less hostile) to education than the average Republican on most roll call votes. While the evidence is sparse, it nearly all points to the conclusion that southern Federalists were probably more interested in fostering education at all levels than were their Republican contemporaries.

17. J. Perrin Anderson, "Public Education in Ante-Bellum South Carolina," *South Carolina Historical Association Proceedings, III* (1933), 4; Hollis, *South Carolina College*, I, 74; *Charleston Courier*, December 13, 1811, and "Philpatris," February 8, 1813; *South Carolina House Journal*, 1812, p.133; 1813 pp. 110–11. In 1813 Republicans were evenly divided and Federalists were 6–0 against repeal. Nita K. Pyburn, "The Public School System of Charleston Before 1860," *South Carolina Historical and Genealogical Magazine*, LXI (1960), 86–98, gives a brief account of the school system erected under this 1811 law.

18. *Augusta Herald*, June 25, 1800; *Augusta Chronicle*, December 22, 1804; Knight (ed.), *Documentary History*, II, 503. Elbert W. G. Boogher, *Secondary Education in Georgia, 1732–1858* (Philadelphia, Pa., 1933), list academies founded between 1800 and 1816 but gives no information on trustees. Outside two or three counties, it would be almost impossible to identify Federalists among them.

Chapter 23 FEDERALISTS AND BANKING

As COMMERCIAL-MINDED men and, more broadly, as advocates of southern economic growth, Federalist party leaders could hardly ignore the need for an adequate banking system. The South needed a supply of money larger than that provided by gold and silver alone. In 1800, banknote circulation was very limited outside the major southern ports, and the lack of specie severely cramped business operations. Yet banking involved politics as well as economics, and southern Federalists usually supported only those banks which they dominated or believed were nonpartisan in operation. They were quite cool toward any bank that they suspected of being subject to partisan Republican control and toward new banks that might compete with an existing Federalist-run institution.

This subordination of economics to political considerations is obvious in the radically altered attitude of many Federalists toward the Bank of the United States. The first bank was the creation of Hamilton himself and retained during its life the loyal support of Federalists everywhere. Prominent party members helped operate the bank's three southern offices by holding a number of seats on the local boards of directors in Norfolk and Savannah, and an actual majority of seats at the Charleston branch. One of the very few southerners to serve as a national bank director was the Richmond Federalist James McClurg. Whenever the bank was at issue in southern legislative debates, Federalists defended it, most notably in fighting to prevent state taxes on the national bank's notes. When antibank men in Congress opposed the bank's recharter in 1810 and 1811, southern Federalists unanimously voted to extend its life, and a North Carolina congressman gave one of the major probank speeches in the House. The southern party press did its part too in supporting recharter and roundly scored Republicans for the bank's death.[1]

After the first bank expired, southern Federalists continued to profess, as William Gaston did, that a national bank would be "eminently beneficial to the Country and useful to the government." They were not backward in pointing up the evils of unrestricted loans and note circulation by the state banks, which now had no overseer to rein in their excesses.[2] When the sad experience of wartime years finally convinced the Republican majority that another national bank was essential, one might have expected the Federalists to be well satisfied at this conversion of the unbelievers. Instead, the small crew of southern Federalists in Congress voted almost unanimously against the Second Bank of the United States.[3]

Once the bank was in operation, many Federalists reversed themselves again, putting aside their hostility and working to obtain a share in its operation. As early as April, 1816, the *Virginia Patriot* noted with pleasure some talk in Washington that the party might find itself in control of the bank's board of directors. Meetings at Norfolk and Richmond, which had prominent Federalist participation, asked for branches in those towns. So well had some forgotten their recent opposition to the bank that the *Augusta Herald* could gloat over the new charter as a vindication of long-standing Federalist policy: "Thus

1. Savannah *Columbian Museum*, January 25, 1806. Lists of directors for the Southern branches were often published in the newspapers: Savannah *Columbian Museum*, June 25, 1802; *South-Carolina State-Gazette*, February 21, 1800; *Norfolk Gazette*, February 15, 1805, and others. For the Federalist defense of the First Bank, see Chapter 9, herein.

2. William Gaston's circular to constituents, in *Virginia Patriot*, June 22, 1814; *Augusta Herald*, September 14, 1815.

3. John Stanly to Gaston, November 11, 1814, in William Gaston Papers; Samuel Hopkins to John Cropper, November 6, 1814, in John Cropper Papers; and see Chapter 13, herein.

do those who were heretofore opposed to the Federal Administration endeavor to walk in their footsteps, and thus do they continue to furnish testimony upon testimony, to the necessity, propriety and wisdom of those measures against which they formerly declaimed."[4]

The same confusing mixture of banks and politics appeared on the state level as well. This was especially true in Virginia, where the complex history of banking after 1800 was seldom pleasing to the Federalist minority. At the beginning of the century Federalists either controlled or had a large voice in the only two banks operating in Virginia, but neither proved to be a permanent institution. The Norfolk branch office of the Bank of the United States, established in 1799, was secure from Republican interference but died with the expiration of the parent charter in 1811. If its dealings were typical of other banks at that time, then its main service was providing the Federalist-leaning merchants of Norfolk and vicinity with short-term commercial credit. The Bank of Alexandria, situated in the District of Columbia on Virginia's side of the Potomac River, provided a similar service in that area.

Although located outside of the state, Alexandria was the chief market town for northern Virginia; its merchants were generally Federalists, and many of them lived in the counties around the city. The bank's Virginia charter was due to expire in 1800 unless renewed, and since the legislature had already defeated one attempt at extension the year before, prospects were not good. When the assembly convened at Richmond in December, the bank's friends presented a petition for recharter, lobbied the delegates energetically, and argued for an entire day on the floor of the house. However, there were fewer Federalists in this legislature than in the last, and even though some Republicans who had opposed the bank in 1799 now voted for it, the effort to renew failed by two votes.[5] This left the northern Virginia region without a financial institution of its own.

4. *Virginia Patriot*, April 20, November 5, 1815; Norfolk *American Beacon*, November 12, 1816; *Augusta Herald*, April 18, 1816.

5. The forty-two Federalist members were almost unanimous in favor of the charter, with only one defecting; but Republicans were more than two to one against. Thomas Swann to Charles Simms, December 26, 1800, January 9, 1801, both in Charles Simms Papers; *Alexandria Advertiser*, January 26, 1801, and "An Alexandrian," January 22, 1801; *Virginia House Journal*, 1800, p. 60; Joseph S. Davis, *Essays in the Earlier History of American Corporations* (2 vols.; Cambridge, Mass., 1917), II, 78–80.

For more than a decade the assembly refused to allow the benefits of banking to the Federalist counties along the Potomac. In January, 1805, legislators prohibited the circulation inside Virginia of notes issued by the Bank of the Potowmac, located in the District of Columbia. This law passed the senate by only nine to eight with all four Federalists voting in the negative; two of them, Francis Peyton from northern Virginia and Philip Doddridge from the west, were so disgusted that they entered an official protest in the senate journal. Free circulation of the Potowmac notes, they said, was essential to "trade and agriculture, in those parts of the state, where the Bank of Virginia and its branches cannot be resorted to."

In the same session, the lower house crushed a Federalist bill to set up a new bank in Fairfax County near Alexandria. The minority party supported the motion by a three-to-one margin, but Republicans opposed it by the same ratio. A year later, the house again denied a bank to the northern counties, defeating a Federalist plan to give the Bank of the Potowmac authority to operate in Virginia. This time the Republican majority was divided. Some wanted to quash the bill at once by postponing it until after final adjournment, but others were willing to listen to debate on the subject. United almost to a man, the Federalist delegates fought off the threat of postponement but lost their attempt to pass the bill itself, and the counties around Alexandria still remained without adequate banking services.[6]

Even as the legislature turned down requests for a bank in the north, it was approving a much bigger project for a statewide Bank of Virginia. The bank was to have official support, because the state of Virginia itself would purchase one-third of the stock. This would give the state a large voice in management since the state treasurer, under legislative direction, would vote this huge block of shares as a unit. Such a prospect disturbed the moneyed Federalists at Richmond. Their great objection to the state bank, as Chief Justice John Marshall explained to his brother, was a fear that it would be a political rather than a monetary institution, entirely under state control.[7]

6. *Virginia House Journal*, 1804, p. 109; 1805, p. 65; *Virginia Senate Journal*, 1804, p. 68; Thomas Jones letter in *Virginia Gazette*, May 11, 1805.

7. John Marshall to James Marshall, February 2, 1804, photostat in John Marshall Papers.

Most of the party had no such fears; when the state bank charter came before the assembly in January, 1803, it had warm Federalist endorsement, including support from two of the most prominent newspapers. The bill sailed through the lower house, with Federalist members providing almost the entire margin of victory. A hostile senate killed the bank, but even there Federalists voted three to one for it. Next year the probank forces won their battle, obtaining with little difficulty a charter for the Bank of Virginia, which would have headquarters in Richmond and branches in Norfolk, Petersburg, and Fredericksburg. When the public was invited to purchase stock, the offering was oversubscribed, to loud Federalist cheers. Those who had misgivings about the possible intrusion of politics into the bank must have been soothed by the first election of officers, in which two prominent Republican directors supported a young Federalist against one of their own party for the position of first teller.[8]

Within a few months, this pleasant picture suddenly vanished as Republicans dropped their conciliatory attitude and injected strict partisanship into the Bank of Virginia's affairs. The 1804 legislature set out to Republicanize the bank with a thoroughness that alarmed and disgusted Federalists. A small minority in the assembly, they could only sit and watch as Republicans instructed the treasurer to vote the state's bank shares in a partisan fashion. He was to cast ballots for ten Republican directors at Richmond, Norfolk, and Petersburg, and for nine Republicans at the Fredericksburg branch. After a long and spirited discussion the majority caucus agreed to this resolution, and it passed the house with ease. Some disconsolate Federalists either joined in the overwhelming vote of 124 to 14 or refused to vote at all. The senate quickly concurred, giving 14 votes for the instruction and only 6, including all 4 Federalist votes, against. One of

8. *Virginia Gazette* editorial, reprinted in Martinsburg *Berkeley & Jefferson Intelligencer,* February 11, 1803. In the house, Federalists recorded 23 yeas and 4 nays; Republicans were in favor by only 66–62; *Virginia House Journal,* 1802, p. 60; *Virginia Senate Journal,* January 25, 1802. In 1803, approval of the charter was apparently an easy business in the house, for there was no roll call vote. See *Virginia Gazette,* May 2, 1804, and "A Federalist," September 8, 1804, on the bank's auspicious start. Comments about heavy Federalist opposition to the bank, in Larkin Smith to Littleton W. Tazewell, August 11, 1804, in Littleton Tazewell Papers, VSL; and Charles E. Wynes, "Banking in Virginia, 1789–1820," *Essays in History,* IV (1957), 40, are erroneous.

the helpless minority poured out his distress to a constituent: "What will such political intolerance end in? Is it possible that the considerate members of the community can approve of such measures? If *Federalism* is such a great political sin . . . they had better at once enact a Law to make Federalism a disqualification from every office of honor profit & trust under the Common Wealth."[9]

The attempt to control the election of bank directors was entirely successful. At each branch the board was divided precisely as the legislature intended: ten Republicans and three Federalists at Norfolk and Petersburg, ten Republicans and four Federalists at Richmond, and nine Republicans and four Federalists in Fredericksburg. Altogether, only fourteen of the fifty-three directors, or about one-fourth, were members of the minority party. In succeeding years Federalist influence diminished still more, and by 1811, only seven of the thirty-five directors whose politics could be identified were Federalists.[10]

Excluded from any large part in the Bank of Virginia's affairs, Federalists lost interest in the entire subject of banks. Republicans were quite satisfied with their permanent dominance in the company, and for many years they, too, ceased to make banking a political issue. Not until January, 1811, did the subject again occupy legislative attention, and even then there was little interest outside the assembly chambers. At issue was the renewed demand for bank facilities in the northwest, which was not served by any of the Bank of Virginia's branches. Federalists were strong in these neglected counties, and they badly wanted a bank there that would be less subject to political control by the Republican state government. With surprising ease, considering the previous disappointments of the Alexandria and Potowmac banks, the house agreed to charter two local banks west of the Blue Ridge, at Lynchburg and Winchester. A comparison of the vote by parties shows that Federalist delegates were far more favorable to-

9. Richard Drummond Bayly to Cropper, January 6, 1805, in John Cropper Papers; *Norfolk Gazette*, January 9, May 8, 1805; *Virginia House Journal*, 1804, p. 69; *Virginia Senate Journal*, 1804, pp. 44–45. For a Republican report of this episode, see Robert Saunders to Joseph Prentis, Jr., January 2, 1805, in Prentis Transcripts, UVa, and William Munford to John Preston, January 10, 1805, in William Campbell Preston Papers, LC.

10. Ammon, "Richmond Junto," 401–402. Lists of directors appeared every February in the *Virginia Argus* and other papers.

ward each bank than Republicans were. However, house approval was in vain, for the senate quietly shelved both bills without a record vote.[11]

Nevertheless, the problem would not disappear, and the legislature again had to consider the bank issue in December, 1811. This time the proposal was for a new statewide institution similar to the Bank of Virginia. Its home was to be in Richmond and its offices in various towns, including neglected Lynchburg and Winchester. This bill would, in a roundabout way, give the western towns the banking privileges Federalists had sought the previous year; but instead of praising the endeavor, the party was now firmly opposed to it. Federalists worried that the Farmers' Bank of Virginia, as the new company would be called, was simply a copy of the existing Bank of Virginia and would contain all its repugnant features. Federalists in the house of delegates opposed the Farmers' Bank on two key votes. They objected almost unanimously to giving the state the same participation in the new company as it had in the Bank of Virginia; only one Federalist broke ranks to join Republicans in attaching this clause to the bill. On the final motion to approve the charter, Federalists were more than three to one in the negative, and Republicans were just as strongly in favor. Thus did the politics, not the economics, of banking guide Federalist thinking on the subject.[12]

Once the new bank seemed sure of approval, party attitudes began to change, and in the senate two of the three Federalist members voted for the bank. As soon as the bill became law the editor of the *Norfolk Gazette*, whose town would receive a branch, urged citizens to buy stock in the Farmers' Bank to benefit both themselves and the community. A few months later "A Stockholder" wrote to express pleasure that "as far as this Bank has progressed, party spirit seems not to have exercised its mischievous influence." Indeed, Federalists had at least their fair share in running the new company; in 1816 three or more of the five Norfolk directors, and three of the six at Richmond, were members of the party. No complaints about the Farmers' Bank

11. Federalist delegates were 24–10 in favor of a Lynchburg bank and 21–10 in favor of a Winchester bank; Republicans approved Lynchburg by 78–51 but were evenly divided on the Winchester request: *Virginia House Journal*, 1810, pp. 79, 85.

12. *Martinsburg Gazette*, March 6, 1812; *Virginia House Journal*, 1811, pp. 96, 102; Wynes, "Banking in Virginia," 41–42.

operations or about any intrusion of Republican politics into its affairs ever appeared in the party press or in the correspondence of Federalist leaders.[13]

The successful nonpartisan operation of the Farmers' Bank did not wholly satisfy Federalists because their area of greatest political strength, the upper Potomac, was still without a bank of its own. In the entire west the only chartered banking facilities were the Farmer's branches at Lynchburg and Winchester. The east, by contrast, had branches of each statewide bank at Richmond, Norfolk, Petersburg, and Fredericksburg, for a total of eight. There were a few private unchartered banks in the west, but the legislature required all state taxes to be paid either in notes of the two statewide banks or in specie, both of which were scarce west of the Blue Ridge. Even worse, in February, 1816, the assembly overrode Federalist objections and passed a stringent law to prohibit all circulation of private banknotes.[14]

This uncomfortable situation led the grand jury of Federalist Jefferson County to protest. In strong terms the jury criticized the refusal to accept notes of the private western banks for taxes and demanded that the legislature charter more banks in the northwest. The chief Federalist newspaper, the *Virginia Patriot*, deplored the "rude language" of the protest but agreed that the Potomac counties needed some relief. Reinforcing the grand jury, a citizens' petition from Jefferson County asked the assembly to incorporate a bank there or else require the Bank of Virginia to set up a local branch. Another petition from the same county specifically requested a charter for the "Farmers', Mechanics', and Merchants' Bank," either as a branch of one of the statewide institutions or separately. From Hampshire, also a predominantly Federalist county, the president and stockholders of the Bank of the South Branch of the Potowmac, a private unchartered company, asked to be "admitted as a Branch of the Bank of Virginia, or Farmers' Bank of Virginia, or, if that cannot be obtained, to be incorporated as an independent Bank."[15]

13. *Virginia Senate Journal,* 1811, p. 63; *Norfolk Gazette*, April 15, 1812, and "A Stockholder," July 27, 1812; *Virginia Patriot*, January 6, 1816 (list of directors) and "A Stockholder," April 7, May 1, 1816.

14. *Virginia House Journal,* 1815, p. 192. Federalists were 16–3 against the bill; Republicans voted 91–15 for it.

15. *Virginia Patriot*, April 27, 1816; *Virginia House Journal*, 1815, pp. 23, 32, 34.

Responding to the desires of his fellow partisans, the Federalist leader in the lower house, Charles Fenton Mercer, persuaded the delegates to form a committee headed by himself to consider the western protests. In early January, 1816, Mercer reported the committee's conclusions—that more competition in banking would help prevent abuses by the existing banks; and that the local private banks were all beneficial to the state and should be given charters. The real question, Mercer said, was whether western Virginia would be forced to use depreciated paper money issued by out-of-state banks or be allowed to use notes from Virginia banks, which the state could regulate and tax. The fruit of this report, a bill "to establish sundry Banks within this Commonwealth," received hearty Federalist endorsement, but Republicans from eastern Virginia killed it by a substantial margin.[16]

So long as their own northwestern counties were denied an adequate supply of banking capital, Virginia Federalists retaliated by refusing any favors for the eastern Republican planters or the eastern-dominated statewide banks. In early 1814, while Republican delegates were advocating abolition of the state's stamp tax on banknotes, Federalists insisted on keeping it. In December of the same year, a group of easterners requested a charter for the Real Estate Bank of Virginia, which could extend more credit to planters than the existing banks run primarily for merchants. Although Republicans divided evenly on the bill, Federalists were 28–5 against, providing the margin of defeat.[17] The issue of specie payments provoked another show of Federalist unity and hostility toward the statewide banks. During the war years, banks in Virginia refused to redeem their notes for hard money in order to keep enough specie on hand to continue doing business.

Once the war ended, there was a broad public demand for resumption of specie payments, and the 1816 legislature debated whether to force banks to start redeeming their notes again by the middle of 1817. Friends of the Bank of Virginia and the Farmers' Bank tried to push this mandatory date back to January, 1818, but Federalists stubbornly

16. *Virginia House Journal*, 1815, p. 160; Federalists supported the bill by 22–8 but Republicans were 93–33 against. The actual vote was on a motion to postpone the measure until April and thus kill it. Mercer's report is on pp. 97–99.

17. *Virginia House Journal*, 1813, p. 162; 1814, p. 128.

voted 24–2 against accommodating them. Half the Federalist members even wanted to speed up the resumption of specie payments to February, 1817, much to the two banks' discomfort.

Just when it seemed that the whole question of banking in Virginia was dissolving into partisan ill feeling, the conflict was suddenly resolved. Republican opposition to chartering new western banks had faded since early 1816, and a bill to carry out the Mercer committee's recommendations now passed by the slim margin of two votes. Federalists, dividing 21–6 in favor, more than offset the negative Republican vote, and the west had its banks. Thereafter, a period of relative calm ensued.[18]

Like her neighbor Virginia, North Carolina also found the bank problem intruding into politics. There were no banks at all in that state until 1804, and for at least another half-dozen years the amount of banking capital was insufficient. The needs of trade had to be met by other means; but these were all unsatisfactory because specie was scarce, out-of-state banknotes were not always accepted, and the state's own paper money from Confederation days was worn, torn, and suspect. The need for bank facilities finally became too apparent to ignore. In 1804, with little opposition, the legislature chartered the Bank of Newbern in the state's largest town and the Bank of Cape-Fear in Wilmington, its greatest port. Both institutions were well located for carrying out the major function of banks at that time—aiding commerce by granting short-term credit to merchants.[19]

Economically, the banks prospered from the start and, politically, they were not so partisan as the statewide Bank of Virginia. The merchant community in the two port towns and in Fayetteville, where the Cape Fear bank had a branch, was mainly Federalist and so were the banks' stockholders and directors. Still, Republicans were not excluded and the stockholders chose their directors without regard to political opinions. Nevertheless, some Republican politicians disliked Federalist dominance over the two companies and believed a state

18. *Virginia House Journal*, 1816, pp. 71, 74, 133.

19. Beecher Flanagan, "A History of State Banking in North Carolina to 1866" (Ph.D. dissertation, George Peabody University, 1935), 22–28; Davis R. Dewey, *State Banking Before the Civil War* (Washington, D.C., 1910), 18.

bank might give more scope to their own party's monied men. There were other objections to the Newbern and Cape Fear banks. Situated in the southeast, they did not adequately serve either the northwestern tobacco counties or the trading centers of the state's agricultural interior. They also imprudently issued too many paper notes, which therefore depreciated and were not well accepted by businessmen in Virginia or even by some inside North Carolina.[20]

The first attempt to establish a competing bank came less than a year after the Newbern and Cape Fear institutions began operating. Sectional and party desires, and the example of Virginia in setting up her statewide system in 1804, led some Republican and backcountry members of the 1805 legislature to become enthusiastic about a state bank. Yet the partisan line was not firmly drawn; a few leading Federalists fought the bank but could not sway a majority, even in their own party. A motion in the upper house to impede the state bank's operations by refusing to allow its notes to be received for tax payments attracted only five Federalist senators, while eleven supported the bank's position. On the final vote to charter the new bank, Federalists approved by a three-to-two margin in the house and by two-to-one in the senate. Republican members were much more strongly in favor, but at least the majority of Federalist legislators was willing to allow a state bank to compete with the two controlled by their own party.[21]

Mere legislative approval could not, however, bring a state bank to life; stockholders had to be convinced to put up the necessary capital. This the bank could not do, partly because the financial community in the Fayetteville, Wilmington, and Newbern areas had an interest in preserving the monopoly of the existing banks. The northeastern

20. Gilpatrick, *Jeffersonian Democracy,* 149–51; Flanagan, "State Banking," 27–28; Stephen Cabarrus to Duncan Cameron, November 23, 1806; in Cameron Family Papers; Penelope Swann to Mrs. Iredell, February 15, 1807, in James Iredell, Jr., Papers. Directors are listed yearly, usually in January, in the *Raleigh Register* and *Wilmington Gazette*. In most years there were three to five known Federalists and one or two Republicans on the Newbern bank board, and three Federalists and two Republicans among the Cape-Fear directors. The rest of the eleven directors at each bank were not politically active. A list of stockholders in the Bank of Newbern, April 25, 1815, shows fifty names, mostly of obsure persons; among them are six to ten known Federalists and only one or two Republicans: *Ernest Haywood Papers*.

21. Gilpatrick, *Jeffersonian Democracy*, 150; *North Carolina House Journal*, 1805, p. 36; *North Carolina Senate Journal*, 1805, p. 33.

trading area around Edenton, wishing a separate bank of its own, also stood aloof. Failing to sell enough shares, the state bank could not raise its required minimum capital, and the assembly repealed its charter in December, 1806. At the same time, senators from Edenton and vicinity pressed for a local bank to serve their corner of the state. They won the sympathy of a large minority of Republican members, but Federalists were roundly hostile. Since the leading hometown supporters of the bank were Republicans, Federalist opposition may partly have been a partisan reaction. Also, most Federalist senators represented counties already served by the Newbern and Cape Fear banks, and sectional loyalty may have been equally important in their veto of the Edenton proposal.[22]

The next year the two banks, still free of competition, were subjected to state supervision for the first time. The Republican state government exercised its charter right to purchase $25,000 worth of stock in each bank and to elect three directors of each. Even with this mild degree of state participation, some Republicans remained antagonistic. In 1809, casting aspersions on the honesty and usefulness of banks and bankers generally, a representative from Halifax, William Drew, proposed a 2 percent annual tax on the capital stock of the Federalist-controlled banks. At that time the Newbern shares had a par value of $200,000, and the Cape Fear bank's capital was $250,000, so that the levy would produce about $9,000 per year. Members directly interested in the banks were quick to oppose Drew's plan. William Watts Jones of Wilmington and William Gaston of Newbern, both Federalists and bank directors, denounced it in the house of commons. In the senate, eleven of the fourteen Federalists voted against the bill, but the heavy Republican majority easily prevailed. Jones, Gaston, and their colleagues made some impression on the house, which approved the tax without a record vote but cut the rate in half, to 1 percent.[23]

Friends of the southeastern banks faced an even more serious chal-

22. Gilpatrick, *Jeffersonian Democracy*, 150; Cabarrus to Duncan Cameron, November 23, 1806, in Cameron Family Papers; a Wake County legislator to his constituents, in Raleigh *Minerva*, February 2, 1807; *North Carolina Senate Journal*, 1807, p. 15.

23. Flanagan, "State Banking," 55, 88; Schauinger, *William Gaston*, 55–57; *North Carolina Senate Journal*, 1809, p. 30. Republicans were 26–14 in favor of the 2 percent tax in the senate.

lenge in 1810 when the issue of a state bank was again raised. The reasons advanced for such an institution had gained weight with the passage of time, partly because the existing banks, contrary to legislative expectations in 1804, had not acted to retire from circulation the state's ragged paper money of the 1780s. Indeed, they had added to the mass of depreciated currency by increasing their own note issues to excess. Various local cliques that wanted banking services extended outside the Cape Fear Valley were more insistent than ever after the legislature refused to charter the Edenton bank. Apparently the only hope for those commercial centers having no banks was to join in setting up a statewide corporation with numerous branches. And of course the strictly partisan Republicans grew more disgusted yearly with continued Federalist control of the old banks and would be glad to see them humbled.

The pressure for extended banking finally proved irresistible in December, 1810, when the assembly debated establishing a state bank that would withdraw the old paper money from circulation and might eventually absorb the Newbern and Cape Fear banks. Among the chief house opponents of this bill were five prominent Federalists (along with two Republicans). In their speeches the Federalists were, as one historian points out, "oddly enough, now found defending depreciated currency and shuddering at a 'moneyed aristocracy.'" Actually, they were simply defending Federalist-run banks in Federalist towns against the threat of overpowering competition from a state-controlled (and presumably Republican) bank. After hours of argument, three-fifths of the Federalists and one-third of the Republican members joined in attempting to kill the bill, but it passed the house easily without amendment. In the senate, Federalist opposition was even weaker, perhaps because all could see that the bank was obviously headed for victory.[24]

With branches to be set up in Raleigh, Edenton, Newbern, Wilmington, Tarboro, Fayetteville, and Salisbury, and an authorized capital of $1.6 million, the state bank could clearly overwhelm the two local banks if permitted to do so. Investors still had to subscribe

24. Gilpatrick, *Jeffersonian Democracy*, 152; Flanagan, "State Banking," 35–43; *North Carolina House Journal*, 1810, p. 52; *North Carolina Senate Journal*, 1809, p. 46. Federalist senators divided evenly, but Republicans were 24–10 in favor of the bank.

enough stock to give life to the venture, and the decision lay with local merchants and financiers—mostly Federalists—in the seven branch towns. In 1805 such men had withdrawn their support from a state bank and some still did so, but most fell in line with the new plan and bought enough stock to enable the bank to commence operations in 1811. In fact, so heavy was the Federalist financial stake in the bank that the first officers and directors were chiefly of that party. The original board of directors contained only four Republicans but four certain and two probable Federalists. The politics of the remaining seven members are unknown; but possibly all were Federalists, because the directors chose William Polk, one of the state's most prominent Federalists, as first president by a 13–4 margin over a Republican. The president of the branch bank at Fayetteville was Federalist William Barry Grove, while two other branch presidents were Republicans and the remaining three were not politically active.[25]

Finding that the state bank was not, as some of them had feared, merely an instrument of the Republican party, Federalists relaxed their suspicious attitude. Before 1811, on every legislative vote involving banking, Federalists had been more inclined than Republicans to protect the interests of the Newbern and Cape Fear banks and to prevent the chartering of any competing institution. Once the party leaders realized that they would enjoy at least an equal influence with Republicans in the state bank, they lost interest in protecting the two local banks. In 1811, for example, the assembly amended the state bank charter of the previous year by extending it to 1835, exempting the bank from the stock tax that the two other banks had to pay, and allowing it to retain part of the dividends due on the stock reserved for the state. This very generous bill passed both houses without a roll call and without a single complaint from Federalists, who, just one year earlier, had so vigorously fought the state bank's very existence. The party did not entirely shun the two older banks and did support their recharter, but on four of ten major votes in 1813 and 1814, Federalists were actually less inclined than Republicans to favor the banks' interests. When the original charters were extended, ene-

25. John A. Cameron to Duncan Cameron, January 7, 1811, in Cameron Family Papers; Flanagan, "State Banking," 139–40; *Norfolk Gazette*, June 26, 1811; *Raleigh Register*, June 21, 1811.

mies of the two local banks offered a number of restricting or damaging amendments. The most important of these, to require the creation of branches at six outlying towns within half a year, was proposed by a leading Federalist and received proportionally more support from his party than from Republicans.[26]

Thus the bipartisan operation of the state bank had converted most Federalists from being firm defenders of the local banks to a position of neutrality and sometimes even mild hostility. Some avid Republicans, though, were vexed at the unexpectedly heavy Federalist participation in the state bank and looked for some way to curb this trend. At least twice they sought to vote the state-owned stock as a bloc in bank elections. This was the weapon with which Virginia Republicans had reduced Federalist influence in the Bank of Virginia, and the North Carolina Jeffersonians intended to do the same. Bills to "direct how the State will vote its shares for directors of the State Bank" came before the senate in 1813 and 1814 but failed both times. As might be expected, every single Federalist opposed them, and in 1814 not even a majority of Republican senators would support the idea of injecting partisanship into bank elections.[27] Except for this unsuccessful Republican venture, North Carolina's banking history after 1810 was essentially free of party conflict.

South Carolina never did see much partisan controversy over banking, perhaps because Federalists were much less effective in local affairs there than farther north. The Bank of South Carolina (unconnected with the state) began operating in Charleston in 1792 and received a legislative charter in 1801. Like the Charleston office of the Bank of the United States, it did business chiefly with merchants in that port; but Federalists clearly ran the national branch bank, and the Bank of South Carolina was almost nonpolitical. Its directors included members of both parties, though a majority of the board was

26. Gilpatrick, *Jeffersonian Democracy*, 152; Flanagan, "State Banking," 43–44; *North Carolina House Journal*, 1813, p. 30; 1814, pp. 28–29; *North Carolina Senate Journal*, 1814, pp. 27, 34, 36.

27. *North Carolina Senate Journal*, 1813, p. 34; 1814, p. 12. In 1815 some Republicans criticized the state treasurer for voting the state's shares for at least one Federalist director: John Haywood to Duncan Cameron, December 6, 1815, in Cameron Family Papers.

not active in politics on either side, and there was never a public complaint of partisanship in the election of directors or in business operations.[28]

Party lines did form temporarily in 1802 when the assembly debated incorporating the State Bank, which would compete with the existing Charleston institutions. The proposed charter required three of the bank's fifteen directors to be legislative appointees and pledged the state to buy three-eighths of the total capital. If the assembly desired, these shares voted together might easily control the election of all the directors. Federalists were extremely cool to this plan, fearing that state participation would bring Republican politics into the new bank. Attempting to guarantee at least some turnover in what threatened to be a Republican-dominated board of directors, the Federalist legislators voted 14–1 to force one director to retire each year. Although it won some Republican backing, this mild restriction failed to pass. The minority could neither block the charter nor remove state influence from it. Republicans controlled the bank during its first years, though not in a blatant way, and in 1811 Federalists vainly resisted a plan to expand the number of state-appointed directors. Despite these occasional partisan clashes in the assembly, the Federalists never accused the State Bank's Republican directors of allowing party affiliation to influence the conduct of business.[29]

Two new banks were chartered in 1810 without controversy, but some Carolinians felt a need for still another facility. In the 1812 legislature Stephen Elliott, one of the handful of Federalist senators, introduced a bill to create the Bank of the State of South Carolina as a semipublic corporation. It would have as its initial capital all the existing assets of the state government, and it could raise an additional $600,000 on the faith of the state if necessary. All profit from operations would go into the public treasury and all state funds would be

28. J. Mauldin Lesesne, *The Bank of the State of South Carolina: A General and Political History* (Columbia, S.C., 1970), 6–9; lists of directors in *South-Carolina State-Gazette*, February 11, 12, 1800–1802, and *Charleston Courier*, February 10–15 of later years.

29. *South Carolina House Journal*, 1802, pp. 138–39; 1811, p. 168; Lesesne, *Bank of the State of South Carolina*, 9–10; lists of directors in *South-Carolina State-Gazette*, October 21, 1801, March 12, 1802, and *Charleston Courier*, March 9–15 of later years.

deposited in the bank. The legislature would directly elect the president and all twelve directors. Even with Elliott's sponsorship this proposal did not please the few Federalists in the assembly; three in the house voted against the bank and only one for it. Republicans were enthusiastic, however, and the charter had no trouble passing. An almost unanimously Republican legislature then chose Elliott as first president of the bank. He served until 1830 and according to the bank's historian was "probably the most able president" in its history. Under his supervision the total capital expanded rapidly; branches were set up in Georgetown, Columbia, and Camden; and the bank's influence spread throughout the state. Clearly, South Carolinians of both parties showed a greater desire than the citizens of Virginia or North Carolina to approach banking on economic rather than political terms.[30]

The situation in Georgia was even quieter since there were scarcely enough Federalists to concern even the most vigilant Republican. The minority did have a strong influence in the Savannah branch of the Bank of the United States, but this did not prevent the Federalist editor of the *Augusta Herald* from expressing himself several times in favor of a competing state bank as "highly beneficial to commercial men, and particularly advantageous to the planting interest." When the legislature created the Planters' Bank in 1807, the new institution seemed to operate on nonpolitical lines. Nearly all its directors were either Republicans or politically inactive, but at least two prominent Federalists served on the board at one time or another. Neither the Bank of Augusta nor the Bank of the State of Georgia, both chartered before 1815, contained any known Federalists; but at this late date there were hardly any left, even in Savannah or Augusta. The two party newspapers never raised a cry of political discrimination against any of the state's banks, showing that Federalist interest in banking participation was reasonably well satisfied.[31]

30. *South Carolina House Journal*, 1812, p. 183; *South Carolina Senate Journal*, 1812, p. 246; Lesesne, *Bank of the State of South Carolina*, Chaps. 2–3.

31. The *Augusta Herald* editorialized in favor of a bank, November 6, 1806, December 17, 1807, and November 8, 1810; lists of directors for the Planters' Bank are in Savannah *Federal Republican Advocate*, December 14, 1807; Augusta *Mirror*, January 28, 1811, January 18, 1813; Savannah *Columbian Museum*, January 13, 1812, January 6, 1814; Savannah *Republican*, January 3, 1815. Lists of directors for the Bank of Augusta

Taking all the southern states together, a clear contrast is shown between a general Federalist desire for banking capital to aid commerce, and a partisan bias against allowing Republican politicians to use banks for their own purposes. Sometimes, too, local jealousies appeared, as when Federalists wished to preserve a bank in one area by obstructing the creation of competing banks which they might otherwise be expected to favor. As in several other states in this period, it was difficult to separate partisanship from banking or any economic question.

---

are in *Augusta Herald*, June 21, 1810, December 10, 1812; Augusta *Chronicle*, December 15, 1810; Savannah *Columbian Museum*, December 9, 1811. For state bank directors, see *Athens Gazette*, December 21, 1815, and *Augusta Herald*, May 23, 1816. For general information, see Robert P. Brooks, *The Financial History of Georgia, 1732–1950* (Athens, Ga., 1952), 10–11; and Thomas P. Govan, "Banking and the Credit System in Georgia, 1810–1860," *Journal of Southern History*, IV (1938), 166–67.

Chapter 24 FEDERALISTS AND SOUTHERN ECONOMIC DEVELOPMENT

FOR members of a party whose northern wing was devoted to diversified economic development, southern Federalists had an unexpectedly mixed attitude toward the growth of commerce, manufacturing, and agriculture in their section of the country. Quite a number of individual Federalists took part in such commercial enterprises as canals, turnpikes, bridges, and river clearings. Some were active, too, in improving the condition of southern agriculture. Manufacturing, however, had political overtones as the handmaiden of a Republican foreign policy looking toward less dependence on Britain and attracted little Federalist interest. Furthermore, when called upon to vote money and other aid for economic development, Federalist legislators were governed more by local and political concerns than by a broad, unified party view of state-assisted economic progress.

The single greatest handicap to southern development in the early nineteenth century was woefully inadequate transportation. A vigorous program of internal improvements would help the whole economy, although merchants would gain more immediate benefit than others. Drawing disproportionate strength from the commercial class, southern Federalists took a deep interest, as private citizens, in fostering internal improvements. The involvement of George Washington and other northern Virginia Federalists in the Potowmac Company is well known. With their active encouragement and financial assistance, the company cleared a considerable portion of the Potomac River for navigation. The other great improvement project in early Virginia, the James River and Kanawha Company, also attracted Federalist money and talent.[1]

Carolina Federalists showed a similar concern in their own states' major canal and river projects. William R. Davie of North Carolina was the chief mover behind the Roanoke Navigation Company, chartered in 1797. Among its early directors were former senator Samuel Johnston, party editor Abraham Hodge, and other local Federalists. In South Carolina, Charles Cotesworth Pinckney was eager to promote canal building as early as the 1780s and was a director and stockholder in both of that state's major improvement efforts, the Santee and the Catawba canal companies. Numerous Federalists from Charleston and vicinity served on the board of the Santee company, and one of them, John F. Grimké, was also president of the Catawba corporation for a time. The handful of Federalists in Georgia could not have contributed much to that state's internal improvement program, but at least one party leader is on record as a strong supporter of better transportation. Judge George Walton, a signer of the Declaration of Independence and a former senator and governor, delivered a lengthy argument for good roads in a charge to the Richmond County grand jury just before the 1800 election.[2]

Local enterprises also enjoyed their share of Federalist support. At least three well-known South Carolina Federalists were directors of the Charleston Bridge Company, and others sat on the board of the

1. Corra Bacon-Foster, "Early Chapters in the Development of the Potomac Route to the West," *Records of the Columbia Historical Society*, XV (1912), 98–121.

2. Robinson, *Davie*, 294; *North-Carolina Journal*, June 4, 1807; Zahniser, *Pinckney*, 77; *Charleston Courier* lists directors of the Santee Canal Company in January of each year, from 1803; *South-Carolina State-Gazette*, March 20, 1800, has the Catawba Company's officers for that year; Davis, *Essays in Earlier History of American Corporations*, II, 123–25, 137–40, 142–48; Brunhouse, "David Ramsay," 149–50; *Augusta Herald*, September 24, 1800. Although Federalists were scarce in Georgia, they held two of the seven seats on the state's short-lived Board of Public Works in 1825–26: Fletcher M. Green, "Georgia's Board of Public Works, 1817–1826," *Georgia Historical Quarterly*, XXII (1938), 131.

Charleston Water Company. A single North Carolina congressman owned fully 25 percent of the stock in the Clubfoot and Harlow's Creek Company, and a representative from Virginia was president of the Little River Turnpike Company in that state. Virginia Federalists also contributed to an ill-fated venture to construct a road from Staunton to Richmond, and they made up one-third of the original directors of the Richmond Dock Company, formed to improve the James River around that city. The strongly partisan Richmond newspaper, the *Virginia Patriot*, heartily endorsed the dock company, asking citizens to buy stock in it. The paper also reprinted part of a pamphlet entitled "The Beneficial Effects of Good Roads in a General System of Defence" and gave its editorial support to a petition from southern Virginia asking that a road be built from Richmond to North Carolina to attract farm produce to market in the capital.[3]

Other party leaders also spoke out for internal improvements. The *Berkeley and Jefferson Intelligencer* in northwestern Virginia hoped the legislature would imitate Pennsylvania's appropriation of $200,000 for roads, at a time when the entire Virginia state budget was scarcely half a million dollars. The Raleigh *Minerva* asked North Carolina to follow Pennsylvania's example by voting public money for canals, and Federalist papers in Alexandria and Norfolk reprinted favorable congressional remarks on internal improvements. The *Courier* of Charleston badgered the South Carolina assembly to improve existing turnpikes in the interior counties and to build new ones, because the poor condition of intermediate roads caused a great part of the backcountry produce to be diverted from Charleston to Augusta. In Augusta itself the Federalist *Herald* prominently displayed an address to the legislatures of both Georgia and South Carolina on the advantages of a road from the Savannah River all the way to Kentucky and Tennessee. At a cost of about $100,000 to each state, it claimed, Augusta would be able to attract all the beef, pork, and hemp exports

3. Charleston *City Gazette*, June 12, 1810; *Charleston Courier*, April 5, 1803; *South-Carolina State-Gazette*, May 6, 1802; Clifford R. Henshaw, "North Carolina Canals Before 1860," *North Carolina Historical Review*, XXV (1948), 9; Waddell, *Annals of Augusta County*, 224; *Virginia Patriot*, January 17, February 28, June 8, 1816, October 26, December 22, 1810; Edward A. Wyatt IV, "George Keith Taylor, 1769–1815, Virginia Federalist and Humanitarian," *William and Mary Quarterly*, 2nd ser., XVI (1936), 4, 8.

from those two transmontane states and could in turn provide them with imported goods. In no time the city "would become the greatest tobacco, cotton, hemp, butter, cheese, pork, stall-fed beef, and horse market on the continent."[4]

For all these editorial effusions, when the southern states actually faced the question of public financial support for internal improvements, the Federalist response was mixed. Only the Virginia party clearly favored state aid for transportation. Virginia's Federalist legislators were primarily from the west, the region most in need of such improvement; very few were from the slave-laden eastern counties, which would pay most of the taxes to support a program of state aid and might suffer from the increased competition of western staples in the markets. In South Carolina the situation was reversed. Nearly all the Federalists who remained in the legislature after 1800 sat for Charleston or the coastal plantation parishes, which had quite adequate transportation to overseas markets for their rice and cotton. Federalists had no direct incentive to approve state assistance for the canals and roads that the Republican up-country wanted. This lack of interest is evident in legislative votes throughout the period.

North Carolina's situation lay midway between those of her neighboring states, because Federalism was not concentrated in any one section. Both the isolated mountain counties, most in need of transportation, and the rich tobacco counties, which would bear most of the tax burden, were heavily Republican. Transportation was poor nearly everywhere in North Carolina, and almost all sections stood to benefit at least partially from internal improvements. Given this complex situation, neither party was firmly on either side of the question. On this issue as on nearly every other state question, party affiliation was much less influential than sectional or other considerations in determining legislative attitudes.

Virginia's first step toward comprehensive public involvement in transportation was the appointment by the 1811 legislature of a com-

4. Martinsburg *Berkeley & Jefferson Intelligencer*, April 8, 1808; Raleigh *Minerva*, March 9, 1807; *Alexandria Advertiser*, February 27, 1806; *Norfolk Gazette*, January 4, 1813; *Charleston Courier*, March 29, April 14, November 16, 1804, December 12, 1806; "Appius," in *Augusta Herald*, February 18, 1801.

mission to study the improvement of navigation on the upper James River. The chairman was Chief Justice John Marshall, and most of the active members were Federalists. From the committee's report the Federalist legislative leader Charles Fenton Mercer (who initially had asked for the committee) drew up detailed plans for a state system of internal improvements. In December, 1812, he urged the legislature to establish a standing fund for internal improvements, beginning with the state-owned stock in the Bank of Virginia, Farmer's Bank of Virginia, James River and Kanawha Company, and Potowmac Company. Although Mercer won broad Federalist support, he was unable to pass his plan over Republican opposition. He failed again in 1814, partly because the ongoing war absorbed both legislative attention and state funds. Two years later he made a third trial and this time succeeded. A board of public works was set up to administer the internal improvements fund, and among the ten members elected, the assembly chose Mercer and one or two other Federalists.[5]

In contrast to this vigorous activity, the South Carolina Federalists were not very interested in massive state aid for transportation. As early as 1804, a bill was before the lower house to appropriate $50,000 yearly toward improving river navigation. If passed, it would have committed the state to spend something like one-fifth of its entire budget on internal improvements. Republican members endorsed the plan by 34–29, but a heavy 12–6 rejection by Federalists doomed it. Next year, a one-time appropriation of $50,000 for improving five rivers and cutting a canal was approved by a large margin, although Federalists members were tied, 7–7. These Federalist legislators, representing chiefly the coastal region, felt their constituents would pay more in taxes for internal improvements than they would gain in bene-

5. Elmer G. Dickinson, "The Influence of Sectionalism upon the History of the James River and Kanawha Company in West Virginia" (M.A. thesis, Duke University, 1946), 13; Philip M. Rice, "Internal Improvements in Virginia, 1775–1860" (Ph.D. dissertation, University of North Carolina, 1950), 122–24, 127–44; Charles Fenton Mercer to W. C. Nicholas, April 14, 1815, in Nicholas Papers, LC; *Virginia House Journal*, 1812, pp. 83–89; 1815, pp. 125, 158, 184; Columbia *Telescope*, February 27, 1816; Faulkner, *Jurisprudence of Marshall*, 25. Hodges, "Pro-Governmentalism," 324–26, and Carter Goodrich, "The Virginia System of Mixed Enterprise: A Study of State Planning of Internal Improvements," *Political Science Quarterly*, LXIV (1949), 355–87, cover the general story of Virginia's commitment to state action.

fits. This legislative attitude did not, however, diminish the commitment of a number of individual leaders to the cause of internal improvements. When the state finally established a board of public works in 1819 to oversee spending $1 million on rivers, canals, and turnpikes, two Federalists (Abraham Blanding and William R. Davie, both up-country men) were among its five members. Blanding later served as superintendent of public works for some years after 1820.[6]

North Carolina had no legislative vote on any comprehensive transportation plan, but the attitude of Federalist assemblymen may be measured by a number of individual roll calls over the years. Between 1802 and 1812 Federalist senators supported two bills for building bridges and were divided on whether to improve the navigation of the Pee Dee River. In the house, party members voted heavily for incorporating a bridge company but were against a bill "to encourage steamboats." The nearest approach to a concerted attack on North Carolina's transportation problems came in a series of roll calls in 1815 and 1816 on the question of using state money to purchase stock in several companies. These votes, involving aid to the Deep and Haw River, Roanoke, and Tar River navigation companies, and also appointing commissioners to survey certain rivers, show Federalists in most cases slightly more willing than Republicans to assist transportation. On eleven key roll calls, Federalists members cast 64 percent of their votes for state aid, while Republicans were 58 percent in favor.[7]

In general, then, Federalists were usually friendly to the idea of internal improvements, but perhaps more from considerations of local interest than from party ideology. Federalist leaders bought stock in and served as officers or directors of several important river, canal, and turnpike companies. Newspapers lent their pages to letters, editorials, and articles promoting a wide variety of transportation improvements. In the matter of actual state financial aid to such pro-

6. *South Carolina House Journal*, 1804, p. 221; 1805, p. 174; Carl L. Epting, "Inland Navigation in South Carolina and Traffic on the Columbia Canal," *South Carolina Historical Association Proceedings*, VI (1936), 21; Robinson, *Davie*, 392; Edwin L. Green, *A History of Richland County* (Columbia, S.C., 1932), 187; Carter Goodrich, *Government Promotion of American Canals and Railroads, 1800–1890* (New York, 1960), 102–103.

7. *North Carolina House Journal*, 1812, pp. 48, 60; 1815, pp. 54–55; 1816, pp. 20, 51; *North Carolina Senate Journal*, 1802, p. 31; 1811, p. 41; 1812, p. 26.

jects, the party's attitude was mixed. Virginia's extensive system of state aid was authored by a Federalist and enacted chiefly by Federalist votes, and it was designed to benefit that area of Virginia where the party was strongest. In North Carolina the minority leaders were lukewarm at best toward any state program, and in South Carolina they were actually opposed.

The party was even more cautious toward other aspects of southern economic development. Agriculture, the mainstay of the southern economy, enjoyed a period of improvement both in farming methods and in crop and livestock selection after 1800. Except in South Carolina, large planters were overwhelmingly Republican in politics, and it is hardly surprising to find that the most prominent advocates of agricultural innovation were members of that party. Still, a number of Federalists were active in this field, particularly in South Carolina, where so many party leaders derived at least a secondary income from plantations. Occasionally, Federalist newspapers also furthered the cause of agricultural revolution; the *Virginia Patriot* of Richmond even reprinted at length John Taylor's "Arator" letters, the pioneer essay in showing that state's planters how to improve their acreage. In western Virginia the Staunton *Republican Farmer* gave badly needed encouragement to the Augusta [County] Society for the Promotion of Agriculture. Leven Powell, the Federalist congressman from northern Virginia, preferred his experimental farm to politics, and in the same area two local Federalists judged an 1810 competition run by the Arlington Institution to encourage agriculture.[8]

Among North Carolina's pioneers in agriculture were a number of ardent Federalist politicians, including John Steele, Henry W. Harrington, Ebenezer Pettigrew, and William R. Davie. In the 1820s Duncan Cameron, a legislator, congressional candidate, and judge, was elected president of the state's board of agriculture. Davie, after prod-

8. Gray, *History of Agriculture*, II, Chap. 33; *Virginia Patriot*, March–May, 1811; Waddell, *Annals of Augusta County*, 224; Leven Powell to John Rutledge, Jr., January 16, 1802, in Rutledge Papers, UNC; *Alexandria Gazette*, May 3, 1810. A. J. Morrison, "Note on the Organization of Virginia Agriculture," *William and Mary Quarterly*, 1st ser., XXVI (1917–18), 169; and Charles W. Turner, "Virginia Agricultural Reform, 1815–1860," *Agricultural History*, XXVI (1952), 80–89, show some Federalist participation in other agricultural societies.

ding North Carolina's agrarians to improve their methods, moved to South Carolina, where he maintained his interest in reforming soil cultivation. He was probably an early member of the South Carolina Agricultural Society. This organization, founded in 1785, was the most active agent for agricultural progress in the entire South until at least 1815; among its founders and earliest officers were many who became well-known Carolina Federalists—Thomas and Charles Cotesworth Pinckney, Ralph Izard, Thomas Bee, and William Drayton. Another active party member who served the cause of agricultural betterment was Benjamin Huger; as a congressman in 1803 he helped create the American Board of Agriculture and was one of the eight southern members of its Committee of Correspondence.[9] The depth of Federalist participation in the "agricultural revolution" cannot be determined without a thorough analysis of many plantation and business papers. Such research is beyond the scope of this work, but judging from the examples above, Federalists were at least mildly interested in agriculture, though less so than in improving transportation.

Manufacturing, the least important but fastest growing part of the southern economy, had little attraction for Federalists. Alexander Hamilton had expounded the virtues of manufacturing and had done his utmost to foster it; and in the North, especially in New England, a number of prominent Federalists invested in factories of one kind or another. In the South, conditions were different. Population was more scattered, markets smaller, transportation more difficult, artisans scarcer, and capital less available. Besides, those most likely to buy manufactured goods—the planters—could obtain better quality products more easily from Europe, where they had frequent business dealings, lines of credit, and regular sea contacts. In addition to these hindrances, political motives deterred Federalists from manufactur-

9. Cornelius O. Cathey, *Agricultural Developments in North Carolina, 1783–1860* (Chapel Hill, N.C., 1956), 34, 45, 66, 78; Robinson, *Davie*, 385; Nanny M. Tilley, "The Journal of the Surry County Agricultural Society," *North Carolina Historical Review*, XXIV (1947), 506; Chalmers S. Murray, *This Our Land: The Story of the Agricultural Society of South Carolina* (Charleston, S.C., 1949), 28, 32, 37; Zahniser, *Pinckney*, 268; *Augusta Herald*, March 16, 1803.

ing. Many Republicans, despite Jefferson's early aversion to manufactures, loudly encouraged in newspaper campaigns and public meetings the growth of native factories. Their goal was to reduce American dependence upon imports of British finished goods and therefore ease the impact of an interruption of trade with England.

Naturally, many Federalists—attached both to commerce and to good relations with Britain—would think twice before joining projects that might contribute to the success of a despised Republican foreign policy. There was even an occasional Federalist attack upon the idea of building up manufactures at all. The Raleigh *Minerva*, for instance, cautioned in 1811 that "at least two thirds of the democratic writers urge the policy of extensive domestic manufactories, merely from a consciousness of the fatal tendency it must have on the welfare of Great Britain." Congressman John Stanly, while admitting that America ought to have factories some day, warned his constituents that the nation could not work toward that goal for many years to come. In an even more critical vein, an anonymous Virginian wrote a harsh letter to the *Alexandria Gazette* in 1810 satirizing the whole concept of America's depending on its own factories.[10]

Various party members did, however, give some assistance to the factory movement. In a series of letters appearing in the *Minerva* early in the century, Carolinians were urged to seek economic growth through cotton and iron mills, since they lacked good ports. Even later, after the desire for home manufactures became clearly associated with Jefferson's and Madison's restrictive commercial measures, the *Minerva* reported favorably on a Wake County meeting to raise money for a factory in Raleigh. Two other Federalist newspapers printed a long address by George W. P. Custis to the citizens of northern Virginia calling on them to invest in a proposed mill for turning out woolen goods. During the embargo, a statewide campaign to drum up stock subscriptions in Virginia for the new Richmond Manufacturing Company was led by a number of prominent Federalists. Others also founded some of the earliest paper mills in North Carolina and Virginia. The most notable effort toward establishing a southern pre-

10. Raleigh *Minerva*, May 10, 1811; John Stanly's letter, *ibid*., June 7, 1810; "Anti-Pax," in *Virginia Patriot*, June 26, 1810.

war factory, the South-Carolina Homespun Company, had substantial Federalist participation in its leadership.[11] No doubt there were other local efforts that aroused support from party leaders; but, clearly, manufacturing was less attractive to most Federalists than other parts of the southern economy, partly because of its association with Republican foreign policy. Here again, politics rather than a consistent economic ideology seemed to influence Federalist thought and action.

11. Raleigh *Minerva*, July 27, August 31, 1802, August 2, 1810; address of George W. P. Custis, in *Augusta Herald*, November 9, 1809. For a list of persons appointed by a Richmond meeting to draw up plans for a local factory and take stock subscriptions in several towns, see *Virginia Argus*, June 3 and 24, 1808; Dard Hunter, *Papermaking in Pioneer America* (Philadelphia, Pa., 1952), 73–75, 165; Kathleen Bruce, *Virginia Iron Manufacture in the Slave Era* (New York, 1931), 111; Diffie E. Standard and Richard W. Griffin, "The Cotton Textile Industry in Ante-Bellum North Carolina," *North Carolina Historical Review*, XXXIV (1957), 21–24; Richard W. Griffin, "An Origin of the New South: The South Carolina Homespun Company, 1807–1815," *Business History Review*, XXXV (1961), 402–15.

SIX Who Were the Southern Federalist Voters?

Chapter 25 PAST POLITICAL DIVISIONS AND PARTY AFFILIATION

THE identity of the leaders of southern Federalism after 1800 is no secret. Those who served in Congress or for long periods in the legislatures, who were candidates for high office, or who organized their states for the party's success, were of such prominence that a satisfying amount of information about them is available for the historian. It is far more difficult to discover who among the great mass of ordinary voters supported the Federalist party.

Even the number of such voters is in doubt. To estimate the size of the Federalist electorate is easiest in Virginia, where two-party presidential contests in 1800 and 1812 left a clear record of voter preference.[1] Allowing for the likelihood that no Federalist electoral tickets were available in a few counties, and assuming that discouragement and overconfidence respectively kept some Federalists and Republicans from the polls, a reasonable estimate is that from 25 to 30 percent of Virginians were willing to vote Federalist if they had the chance.

1. Official presidential figures are in the Rare Book Room, VSL. Congressional returns are in the various newspapers in April–May of odd-numbered years. The best study of party leaders is Paul Goodman, "Social Status of Party Leadership: The House of Representatives, 1797–1804," *William and Mary Quarterly*, 3rd ser., XXV (1968), 465–74.

Congressional and legislative returns support this conclusion. North Carolina, lacking any statewide popular vote, is more difficult to gauge. The fragmentary returns of congressional and presidential elections and the proportion of Federalists and Republicans in the legislature provide the only available evidence. A careful analysis yields a figure of 25 to 35 percent as the range of Federalist strength in the state, except for 1800 when the party reached nearly 45 percent.[2]

Nothing but an educated guess can be made for South Carolina. Popular returns, even for the few contested congressional elections, exist only for the Tidewater districts; and the large number of absentees in the assembly reduces the usefulness of measuring relative strength in that body. Perhaps 10 percent of the voters of South Carolina, had they had the chance to vote for a Federalist in 1808 or 1812, would have done so; and the figure might have been as high as 20 or 25 percent in 1800.[3] In Georgia, Federalists competed in statewide congressional races in 1802, 1808, and 1810, and these results must serve as the basis for estimating party popularity. Each person could vote for four candidates; the total number of ballots averaged 55,000 for each election, and the Federalist candidates polled about 3,200. Dividing the state total by four yields a minimum of 13,750 individual voters. Since some of them would not mark a full ticket, the actual number of voters may have been near 15,000. The Federalist share of this electorate would then be about 20 percent.[4] There is no way of knowing how many voted for the Federalist candidate without realizing his party affiliation, or how many Federalists did not vote for him because they were unaware that he was one of them. Making allowances on either side would put Federalist strength at 15 to 25 percent of all voters.

Even with these estimates, which vary in reliability depending

2. A nearly complete list of extant congressional and presidential returns is in the Manuscript Division, NCDAH. The Legislative Papers, NCDAH, and the newspapers provide a few additions.

3. South Carolina's popular vote for Congress and the legislature is available in the various newspapers; the Federalist *Charleston Courier* was the most thorough but sometimes omitted returns if the party did badly, and thus Republican papers must also be used.

4. Returns are in the various Georgia newspapers for October, 1802, 1808, and 1810. The main question in trying to analyze any Georgia congressional race is what percentage of the individual voters failed to vote for four candidates.

upon the state and year, there is still the problem of identifying those groups of people that were more strongly Federalist than the state averages. The party always liked to claim direct descent from the federalists of 1788 who supported the Constitution, and they branded the Republicans as merely antifederalists in disguise. The *Augusta Herald* reminded voters that the true meaning of the term *federalist* was "synonymous with *friend of the government*." Similar claims could be read during every election campaign.[5]

Historians ever since have argued about the relationship between the constitutional struggle and the first party system. On the broadest level, taking each of the states as a whole, there is actually an inverse relation between the old federalism of 1788 and the Federalist party after 1800. Georgia, which had scurried into the new Union quickly and almost unanimously, had the weakest Federalist party. South Carolina ranked second and Virginia third in ease of ratification but stood in reverse order in their degree of later Federalist strength. It was in North Carolina, which actually rejected the Constitution at one time and finally accepted it only grudgingly, that Federalists enjoyed their greatest popular support from 1800 to 1816. Such a broad view, however, is so misleading as to be worthless.

In three states there was some meaningful connection between support of the Constitution and of the Federalist party by the political leadership, and in two states the same tendency is apparent among ordinary voters as well. Looking to the political leaders of 1788, the men who composed the ratifying conventions in each state, scarcely any antifederalists became active Federalists in politics after 1800; more than 95 percent became Republicans. The antifederalist delegates either preferred outright the loose interstate ties of the Articles of Confederation or were so suspicious of the new Constitution that they would accept it only after insertion of a Bill of Rights. They feared that popular liberties, agricultural interests, and southern institutions would be in danger from a northern-dominated central government. Although reconciled to the Constitution after its adoption, they soon had reason to believe that their fears had been prophetic. Hamilton's financial program, the opposition of Federalists to the French

5. *Augusta Herald*, July 21, 1808, and numerous other party organs, for instance, *Virginia Patriot*, October 13, 1812, and *Charleston Courier*, June 29, 1803.

revolutionary struggle in Europe, and the unpopular measures of the Adams years—all brought the former antifederalist leaders to an almost total and unqualified rejection of the later Federalist party.

Even many who had supported ratification in 1788 were frightened by these later events and showed a growing distrust toward the party of Hamilton and Adams. Only about half of the old federalist leaders who continued to be active after 1800 were firm Federalists; the other half had, at some time after 1790, become Republicans. To this extent only, then, the lines drawn during the ratification struggle continued to divide political leaders from 1800 to 1816: Half of those who supported the Constitution, but virtually none of those who opposed it, had become adherents of the Federalist party, while nearly all the antifederalists and the other half of the old federalists had entered the Republican party.[6] Only in Georgia, where ratification was unanimous at the state convention, does this pattern fail. Most of the Georgia delegates who were still in politics by 1800 had become Republicans, and since there had been no antifederalist delegates, the Republican party could not draw upon them for its leadership as it did in the three more northerly states.

In two states the partial correspondence between political alignments of 1788 and the early nineteenth century existed among the common voters as well as among leaders. Table 13 displays the relationship between Federalist party strength and attitude toward the Constitution for all the states except Georgia. If the counties within each state are ranked in descending order of Federalism during 1800–1816, it is apparent that the highest counties on the Federalist scale in Virginia and South Carolina were likely to have supported the Constitution. Where Federalism was weakest after 1800, antifederalism had been strongest in 1788, especially in South Carolina, where every one of the eleven most loyal Federalist counties had chosen delegates friendly to the Constitution. Of the twenty-two most heavily Republican counties, fewer than one-fourth had supported ratification. In

6. The post-1800 political affiliation of members of ratifying conventions is based upon their voting records as legislators or congressmen, identification by other contemporary sources or, in some cases, evidence in secondary works. The force of any theory about the relationship between federalists and antifederalists, and Federalists and Republicans is weakened by the fact that most members of the conventions were either dead or inactive politically by 1800.

Virginia the disparity was not quite so great but was still apparent. Twenty of the twenty-four strongest Federalist counties had voted for the Constitution; only one-third of the strongest Republican counties had done so. Only one of the Federalist counties had been clearly antifederalist in 1788, compared to more than half the Republican counties. In North Carolina, by contrast, there was no connection between the battle over ratification and the later two-party conflict. If anything, there was a slight tendency for Republicans to fare better than Federalists in areas that had approved the Constitution. Georgia also showed no relationship between the voting patterns of 1788 and 1800–1816; every county had been pro-Constitution, yet none of them had a consistent Federalist majority after 1800.

Table 13 **Comparison of Federalist Party Strength, 1800–1816, and Vote on the Constitution, 1788–1790**

VIRGINIA

Counties Ranked by Federalist Strength	*County Vote on the Constitution, 1788*		
	In Favor	*Divided*	*Against*
Highest Quartile	20 (83%)	3 (13%)	1 (4%)
Second Quartile	12 (50%)	1 (4%)	11 (46%)
Lowest Two Quartiles	16 (33%)	5 (11%)	27 (56%)

NORTH CAROLINA

Counties Ranked by Federalist Strength	*County Vote on the Constitution, 1788*		
	In Favor	*Divided*	*Against*
Highest Quartile	5 (31%)	8 (50%)	3 (19%)
Second Quartile	4 (27%)	6 (40%)	5 (33%)
Lowest Two Quartiles	11 (35%)	12 (39%)	8 (26%)

SOUTH CAROLINA

Counties Ranked by Federalist Strength	*County Vote on the Constitution, 1788*		
	In Favor	*Divided*	*Against*
Highest Quartile	11 (100%)	0 (0%)	0 (0%)
Second Quartile	9 (82%)	1 (9%)	1 (9%)
Lowest Two Quartiles	5 (23%)	3 (14%)	14 (63%)

The most logical explanation for the lack of correlation between sentiment for the Constitution and later Federalism in North Carolina and Georgia and for the defection of many "old federalists" to the Republican party in Virginia and South Carolina is simply that the issues were different in 1788 than after 1800. The struggle over ratification involved solely the question of whether the states ought to join in a stronger union. Once decided, this point did not recur. Instead, there arose the immensely more complex issues of how the new government ought to be organized and what its attitude should be toward foreign powers. Indeed, the most divisive party issue, revolutionary France and her expansionist tendencies, did not even exist at the time the Constitution was debated. That the leaders of the Federalist party were, by and large, men who had previously worked for the Constitution did not impress voters who thought the party was subverting that document by its conduct in office.

The Federalists' unpopular measures before 1800 made Jefferson's early years of tax relief, debt reduction, and national expansion appear brighter by comparison; and most southerners were wedded securely to the Republican party by the end of Jefferson's first term. Incessant Federalist efforts to hold themselves up as the initiators and protectors of the Constitution fell upon uncaring ears. To counter such appeals, Republicans needed only to remind southerners of the armies, taxes, debts, and sedition laws of the Adams regime. In short, the question of ratification was long dead as a political issue by 1800.

Even in South Carolina and Virginia, the apparent connection indicated in Table 13 between 1788 and the post-1800 years may be misleading. There were significant regional variations within both states. In western Virginia and eastern South Carolina, Federalist counties were much more likely than Republican counties to have favored the Constitution, but this does not hold true in the other half of either state. For instance, 94 percent of the most strongly Federalist counties in western Virginia, but only 62 percent in eastern Virginia, had elected federal delegates in 1788. Or, put the other way around, of the twenty-two western counties that voted for ratification, fifteen were later friendly to the Federalist party. Twenty-six eastern counties had also supported ratification, but only five of them later became Federalist. Likewise in South Carolina, ten of the seventeen pro-Constitution districts in the low country, but only one of eight in the up-country, were inclined toward Federalism after 1800. This striking difference according to section may indicate that even in these two states there was little real connection in voters' minds between the federalism of 1788 and the later Federalist party. Perhaps the voters of western Virginia and eastern South Carolina favored the Constitution and then the Federalist party, not because they consciously associated one with the other, but because they believed each movement, in its own way, would serve the cause of their section.

Besides the ratification controversy, one other previous political dispute might have affected voter affiliation in the first party system—the division between Loyalist and patriot during the Revolution. The question of a connection between Federalism and Toryism was a touchy subject in the years before 1816; Republicans professed to see such a link, while Federalists denied it. No election could pass without its charges of Toryism, particularly in years when Federalists were publicly defending British commercial measures and complaining that their own government was too aggressive in protecting American interests. Because of the widespread, repeated Republican claims that the enemies of Jefferson and Madison were descended from the enemies of independence, Federalist spokesmen had to spend an embarrassing amount of time defending themselves. Their favorite tactic was to recite the list of prominent revolutionary leaders who later became Federalist—Washington, Adams, Hamilton, Jay, Henry, and so on. Could a political party formed and led by such men be a haven for Tories? Allied with this was an attempt to discover Republicans who had been certified enemies of the Revolution. There were few such men, but occasionally one would be found, and Federalists made the most of him.[7]

Despite what Republicans said, there is no evidence at all that former Loyalists were prominent in the leadership of southern Federalism. On the other hand, it is logical to expect that many ordinary Loyalists might have become rank-and-file members of the Federalist

7. Examples of the Federalist defense against the charge of Toryism are in *Augusta Herald*, August 15, 1805, and *Charleston Courier*, October 20, 1808.

party. A voter who had been attached to England during the Revolution would see the Republican party treating Britain as a dangerous enemy after 1800 and condemning its government almost without pause, whereas the Federalists excused and defended English actions. There was another reason, too, that might attract former Loyalists to the Federalist cause. In all the southern states those who had opposed the Revolution openly had suffered civil and economic disabilities, and one of the most controversial political issues after 1781 was how far and how fast to relax the wartime discrimination against Tories. In the two Carolinas, especially, prominent future Federalists took the lead in urging a rapid and easy reentry by former Loyalists into postwar life, and they came out publicly for easing the harshness of wartime laws. Some in the Loyalist community might later wish to repay with their votes a Federalist party created by men who had befriended them in the 1780s. Finally, the Loyalist concept of society and government, emphasizing a hierarchical, stable community, was much more akin to post-1800 Federalist social thought than to Republican notions of a fluid and semidemocratic society. Logic therefore points clearly toward the likelihood of a political connection between revolutionary Loyalism and later Federalism.

The evidence, however, does not bear out this conclusion. While the extent of Loyalism cannot be measured from county to county, recent studies indicate reasonably well the location of southern Loyalists in the Revolution. Tories in Virginia were limited almost entirely to the area around Norfolk and to a few other Tidewater counties but were almost wholly absent from the valley and mountain areas, which later became the home of Federalism. There were some antiwar outbreaks in the west, but the participants were merely expressing opposition to high taxes and conscription, not an actual desire for British victory. Only two places in the state, the Eastern Shore and Bedford County in the western Piedmont, exhibited both Loyalist sentiment and Federalist voting strength. Against these can be balanced other counties that produced Tory sympathizers in the Revolution but became solidly Republican after 1800, such as Middlesex, Elizabeth City, James City, and Warwick. The single most concentrated group of Loyalists resided in the port of Norfolk, which was later a Federalist town—but no more so than some western cities that knew nothing of Toryism.[8]

In North Carolina there is slightly more reason for thinking that Tory sentiment may have inclined some people to become Federalists. Independence was unpopular in many places throughout the Piedmont, especially in the Scottish settlements on the upper Cape Fear, the area that was most unswerving in its Federalist politics after 1800. The three most vigorously Loyalist counties (Cumberland, Anson, and New Hanover) were all strong Federalist counties later. However, several other centers of Toryism—indicated by enlistments in the British forces, confiscations of property, and claims filed by individuals—were among the strongest Republican counties in the state after 1800. On the whole, the evidence may point to a slight association of Federalist and Loyalist sentiments, which could hardly have been a major source of party support except in one or two places.[9]

The two centers of South Carolina Loyalism were Charleston and the up-country west of the Wateree and Catawba rivers. The city of Charleston did become a Federalist stronghold, but this fact alone does not necessarily show a connection between the two political movements. A dozen low-country parishes voted more Federalist than Charleston and another dozen were more Republican, so the city's politics after 1800 were no different from many parishes that had not been dens of Toryism. In the up-country, there is even less reason to suspect a tie between Tories and Federalists. The most rabidly Loyalist area was west of the Wateree and Catawba, between those rivers and the Georgia border. Not one of these eight counties elected a single Federalist to the legislature after 1800. If Tories were still voting in large numbers, they must have been good Republicans. By contrast, the seven districts east of the river line, where Loyalism had been much less prevalent, sent twenty-seven Federalist legisla-

8. Isaac S. Harrel, *Loyalism in Virginia: Chapters in the Economic History of the Revolution* (Durham, N.C., 1926), 33–35, 39–40, 50–54, 60–62; Peter M. Mitchell, "Loyalist Property and the Revolution in Virginia" (Ph.D. dissertation, University of Colorado, 1965), appendix; Wallace Brown, *The King's Friends: The Composition and Motives of the American Loyalist Claimants* (Providence, R.I., 1965), 331–32.

9. Robert O. DeMond, *The Loyalists in North Carolina During the Revolution* (Durham, N.C., 1940), 49–50, Appendix B; Brown, *King's Friends*, 335–36.

tors to the lower house and several more to the state senate.[10] The situation in Georgia is much more difficult to judge because the British armies occupied so large a portion of the state that many men assumed the role of Loyalist from sheer self-protection rather than from conviction. Also, measurements of Federalist strength are far less precise than in other states. In general, the most recent studies do not show any relationship at all between political leanings in 1775–1781 and 1800–1816.[11]

Altogether, the search for some connection between Loyalism and Federalism in the South cannot yield any very satisfying result. Even the extent of Tory strength itself is impossible to measure with confidence, and population shifts after 1780, especially from migration into the South Carolina backcountry and Georgia, further cloud the investigation. Logic certainly provides reason enough to explain a tie between Tory and Federalist, if only the evidence indicated that such a relationship existed. On the whole, however, Federalist propagandists were correct in denying that their party had its roots in the opposition to independence.

In exploring how the first party system may have been shaped by previous political alignments, one should not overlook the sectional rivalry within the southern states. Sectionalism was certainly a powerful force in state politics, as shown by any study of legislative votes from the colonial era onward. However, intrastate geography had no consistent effect upon party divisions in the years after 1800. Federalists were not a coastal-based party throughout the South, nor were they always a vehicle for expressing the political frustrations of the underrepresented west. The situation differed greatly from state to state. In Virginia the party's strength was beyond the Blue Ridge, which marked the dividing line between low and up-country. More than half of all Federalist legislators from 1800 through 1816 resided west of the Blue Ridge; during these years Federalists won almost a third of western elections to the house of delegates but only a tenth of the elections in the east. Congressional results tell the same story; ex-

10. Robert W. Barnwell, Jr., "Loyalism in South Carolina, 1765–1785" (Ph.D. dissertation, Duke University, 1941), 29–31, 94, 130–35; Brown, *King's Friends*, 340.

11. Kenneth Coleman, *The American Revolution in Georgia, 1763–1789* (Athens, Ga., 1958), 71–72; Robert G. Mitchell, "Loyalist Georgia" (Ph.D. dissertation, Tulane University, 1964), 78–94, 282–83; Brown, *King's Friends*, 343–44.

cept for the Eastern Shore and Loudoun-Fairfax districts, every Federalist who sat in the national House of Representatives was chosen by western voters.

South Carolina and Georgia showed just the opposite pattern. The Federalist party in South Carolina was the preserve of Charleston merchants and coastal planters and had little existence beyond the plantation parishes. Nine of every ten Federalists in the South Carolina legislature came from the coastal districts of Beaufort, Charleston, or Georgetown. In these low-country areas the party won almost a third of the legislative elections, compared with only 5 percent in the up-country. Only the gross overrepresentation of the coastal white population kept Federalism from being an utterly insignificant force in South Carolina.

Georgia's Federalists were too few to cause more than a ripple on the surface of that state's political life, but the congressional elections of 1802, 1808, and 1810, in which Federalist candidates ran, show the party's votes distributed in a clear geographical pattern. Of the six coastal counties, four were in the most heavily Federalist quartile of all Georgia counties. Also in the top quartile were three of the eight Savannah River counties and only one of the twenty interior counties, most of which were still in the frontier stage of settlement. The average Federalist share of the popular vote in the three elections was 15 percent on the coast, 9 percent along the Savannah River, and only 6 percent on the frontier.[12] While this comparison is not so striking as the sectional division in South Carolina, it does show that the strength of Federalist sentiment varied considerably among Georgia's three regions.

As for North Carolina, sectionalism had nothing whatever to do with her political parties. Issues that arrayed west against east came annually before the legislature and the voters, but they did not follow party lines. The most consistently Federalist area in the state, the Fayetteville congressional district, sat squarely across the sectional dividing line. In the General Assembly after 1800, Federalists filled 32 percent of eastern and 31 percent of western seats, showing no abnormal strength or weakness in either section. Besides the Fayetteville

12. These percentages refer to the *total* number of votes cast (each voter could support up to four candidates), not to the number of individual voters.

seat, the two districts that Federalist congressmen won most often were Salisbury and Newbern—one in the western Piedmont and one on the Atlantic coast. If these state-by-state legislative and congressional comparisons are a fair guide to the distribution of Federalists within the South, it is evident that the party's base of strength was not constant throughout the region. The Virginia Federalists were most comfortable in the western half of that state; in South Carolina and Georgia, eastern voters were more friendly than western; and in North Carolina there was no sectional partisanship at all.

Chapter 26 ECONOMIC STATUS AND PARTY AFFILIATION

THE influence of economic status on party affiliation has produced continuing discussion among historians of the early American party systems. Some have seen divisions of wealth and class paralleling those of party, while others have stressed the tug of ethnic-religious loyalty or the impact of demographic changes.[1] Whatever may have been true elsewhere, the pattern of Federalist strength in the South from 1800 to 1816 did not closely follow lines of economic class or occupation. Only one economic area, the towns, gave consistent support to the party, and no group or area consistently opposed Federalism in all four states.[2]

1. The prime economic interpretation of the first party system is Charles A. Beard, *Economic Origins of Jeffersonian Democracy* (2nd ed.; New York, 1952). Dauer, *Adams Federalists*, presents a more refined economic view, especially in Chaps. 1, 2, 17. Among recent works, Fischer, *Revolution of American Conservatism*, 201–26, makes the broadest suggestions for a many-sided basis for voter allegiance, including ethnic background, religion, and rate of population growth. Buel, *Securing the Revolution*, carries this suggestion further by stressing a basic partisan difference in attitude toward life and society, derived from underlying differences in demography; see especially Chap. 4.

2. Population figures for towns are in John Melish, *A Geographical Description of the United States, with the Contiguous British and Spanish Possessions, Intended as an Accompaniment to Melish's Map of These Countries* (2nd ed.; Philadelphia, Pa., 1816), 95–121, and in the censuses of 1800 and 1810; U.S. Census Office, *Return of the Whole Number of Persons Within the Several Districts of the United States, According to "An Act*

Even though towns were generally more strongly Federalist than the countryside, not all followed this pattern. Measurements of party strength are not easily found for units other than counties, but there is enough indirect evidence to form a general conclusion. In Virginia, where the large towns of Richmond and Norfolk voted separately from their counties, it is possible to make a direct comparison of Federalist influence in these two centers with Federalist influence in Virginia as a whole. In 1800 the Adams presidential ticket carried 50 percent of the votes in Richmond and Norfolk combined, but only 23 percent in the whole state. In 1808 the combined anti-Madison vote for Pinckney and Monroe was also 50 percent in the two towns, compared with 21 percent for all of Virginia. Four years later, however, the Federalist urban advantage had disappeared; the ticket of Rufus King and William R. Davie polled only 24 percent in Richmond and Norfolk, against 27 percent in the state. For the smaller towns, all three elections show a higher level of Federalist popularity in counties containing a town of over 1,000 population than in the remainder of the state.[3] These urban-influenced counties cast the following vote for Federalist and opposition tickets:

1800: 34% Federalist; rest of state 21% Federalist
1808: 32% opposition; rest of state 20% opposition
1812: 45% Federalist; rest of state 24% Federalist.

In North Carolina there was also a clear gradation of Federalist strength, which was highest in the towns, lower in the town-oriented counties, and lowest in the rural remainder of the state. The seven borough towns, which sent their own representatives to the lower house of the assembly, accounted for 11 percent of all the Federalists

Providing for the Second Census or Enumeration of the Inhabitants of the United States," Passed February the Twenty Eighth, One Thousand Eight Hundred (Washington, D.C., 1801, and *Aggregate Amount of Each Description of Persons Within the United States of America, and the Territories Thereof, Agreeably to Actual Enumeration Made According to Law, in Year, 1810* (Washington, D.C., 1811).

3. Excluding Richmond and Norfolk, these counties and their towns are Augusta (Staunton), Berkeley (Martinsburg), Caroline (Port Royal), Dinwiddie (Petersburg), Frederick (Winchester), Spottsylvania (Fredericksburg), and the City of Williamsburg.

ever chosen to that body, but for only 3 percent of all the Republicans.[4] Over the period from 1800 through 1816 the members of the state house divided in the following proportions:

Borough Towns: 62% Federalist members, 38% Republicans
Their Counties: 31% Federalist members, 69% Republicans
Rest of State: 26% Federalist members, 74% Republicans.

South Carolina had but one city of consequence, Charleston, and four other towns of over 1,000 persons: Georgetown, Beaufort, Columbia, and Camden. As in other states, these "urban" places showed a greater degree of Federalism than did the countryside. Charleston, of course, was the residence or place of business of many Federalist leaders and was the one district in the state with a semipermanent party organization. From 1800 through 1816, identifiable Federalists held the office of intendant for nine years and Republicans for only five years; and the average Federalist share of the popular vote for Congress in Charleston was 43 percent, though it did not exceed 10 percent in the rest of the state. Legislative elections showed a similar contrast; in the seventeen-year period, Federalists held 30 percent of the state house seats in Charleston, 30 percent in the four districts dominated by the lesser towns,[5] and only 13 percent in the remainder of South Carolina.

Georgia's two major towns, Savannah and Augusta, were also centers of the small remnant of Federalist influence existing in that state. Since the party had almost no one in the legislature and put up candidates for Congress only three times, any reliable estimate of Federalist popular support is extremely difficult to reach. However, in the three congressional contests about 11 percent of the votes in Chatham and Richmond counties was cast for the Federalist candidates (compared with only 6 percent in the rest of the state). Federalists also dominated the city government in Savannah for some years after

4. The borough towns were Wilmington, Newbern, Edenton, Halifax, Fayetteville, Hillsborough, and Salisbury; their counties were New Hanover, Craven, Chowan, Halifax, Cumberland, Orange, and Rowan.

5. These districts were Kershaw (Camden), Richland (Columbia), Prince George's Winyaw (Georgetown), and St. Helena's (Beaufort).

1800 and occasionally elected their legislative nominees in the two counties.[6]

All this is not to say that towns were uniformly Federalist, for wide variations existed according to size and location. Except for the 1812 election in Virginia, the largest towns in each state (Richmond, Norfolk, Newbern, Wilmington, Charleston, Savannah, and Augusta) were always more strongly Federalist than their states as a whole. Among the counties containing smaller towns with populations over 1,000, there was no such regularity. In Virginia the eastern urban counties were no less Republican than the surrounding rural areas; only the western small towns seemed inclined to Federalism. Of the North Carolina towns, Salisbury voted Federalist, but Edenton and Hillsborough were Republican. In South Carolina, Richland County, dominated by Columbia, never elected a Federalist to the assembly, although St. Helena's Parish (Beaufort) often did. In Georgia the two counties containing towns of about 1,000 population were at least as heavily Republican as the whole state. Still, despite these exceptions and variations, it was usually true that a southern town or town-dominated county was likely to have a higher proportion of Federalists than an entirely rural county.

In the urban environment, if one may call towns of a few hundred families urban, resided two general classes of voters. One included the "lower" occupations, generally referred to as the mechanics. These men, ranging from unskilled common laborers to skilled craftsmen, were, according to nearly unanimous testimony, firmly Republican. Federalists admitted it and Republicans bragged of it.[7] One reason for the attachment of workingmen to the Jeffersonian cause was that some of them were immigrants, and Federalists made no secret of their disgust with the "foreign wretches" who were shifting the balance of urban politics against the party of Washington.[8] Mechanics may also have been favorably disposed toward the French revolution-

6. *Alexandria Gazette*, November 15, 1802; Savannah *Public Intelligencer*, October 9, 1807; Savannah *Columbian Museum*, September 16, October 10, 1811; Fischer, *Revolution of American Conservatism*, 407.

7. Savannah *Southern Patriot*, October 6, 1806; Newbern *True Republican*, August 2, 1810; *Virginia Patriot*, March 24, 1812; *Charleston Courier*, May 4, 1803.

8. Savannah *American Patriot*, June 5, 1812; "Camillus," in *Virginia Patriot*, June 28, July 2, 1811; *North-Carolina Journal*, September 7, 1801; *Charleston Courier*, March 10, 1803.

ary ideas of liberty and equality and therefore toward the Republican party, whose leaders were said to be friends of France.

The voting pattern of the other large class of townspeople was quite different. Since the towns as a group were more heavily Federalist than the countryside, and since the mechanics in the towns were heavily Republican, then the remainder of town voters must have been largely Federalist. These would be the classic Hamiltonians—the merchants; shipowners; financiers; and their professional allies, the lawyers, clerics, tutors, and doctors. For several reasons this group, which was a small minority in the total southern population but often able to dominate city politics, was Federalist.

Men in these occupations first became attracted during the 1780s to the philosophy which later became part of Federalism. They shared a belief that a strong federal government could enhance the value of continental and state bonds, make interstate commercial transactions easier, win for American trade a stronger position abroad, preserve order at home, and defend the nation against its enemies. Hamilton's financial program, holding out benefits to the same commercial-financial-professional group, could only weld it closer to the emerging Federalist party. Once formed, these political loyalties were not easily broken. They were reinforced by the constant exchange of ideas between southerners and their mercantile and financial contacts in the major northern cities, where the Federalist party was vigorous well after 1800. Also, owning shares in the Bank of the United States or experiencing the benefits of its credit and currency facilities might attract the southern business class to Federalism. The bank was preeminently a Federalist institution, and the men who enjoyed its use naturally rallied to the party that created and defended it.

When the European wars began to influence American politics in the mid-1790s, these businessmen and their associates had yet another reason to support the Federalist party. Their overseas economic ties were chiefly with Britain, where lawyers, doctors, and clergymen were often trained or had associates. The whole fabric of American urban culture—legal, social, economic, and political—was primarily English in origin, a fact of great importance to men of cosmopolitan education and business ties. When France threatened British prosperity and independence, many southern businessmen reacted with a feeling of sympathy toward Britain, an emotion they shared with the Federalist party generally. Republicans, increasingly identified by Anglophiles as the pro-French party, would have little attraction for these men.

In the towns the commercial and financial class had an importance disproportionate to its small size, for from it came most of the leaders of southern Federalism. Yet this urban group, no matter how heavily committed to the party, could provide it with only a small number of actual voters. The South was more than 90 percent rural and agricultural, and it was in the countryside that most Federalist votes were cast. There the relationship between economics and politics begins to blur; no consistent association can be found between Federalism and rural wealth. The two are rather closely related in South Carolina but less so in Georgia, and no apparent connection seems to exist between economic status and party politics in rural North Carolina or Virginia.

The wealth of South Carolina, in the form of slaves and fertile land, was concentrated in a coastal strip comprising the Beaufort, Charleston, and Georgetown districts. In these rich plantation parishes Federalist political opinions were much more apparent than in the poorer up-country. The coastal planters were not predominantly Federalist, but more of them than of common farmers voted for the party. The tendency for plantation parishes to be relatively kinder to Federalism was well marked. During the entire period from 1800 through 1816, twenty-one of South Carolina's forty-four election districts refused to send even one Federalist to the state legislature. Only one of these twenty-one was in the richest one-fourth of the state's districts, and only six were among the richest half.[9] Of the thirteen election districts with fewest slaves, ten were among those which never elected a Federalist.

At the opposite extreme, all but one of the eleven most heavily Federalist districts ranked in the richest half of districts, and six were in the richest fourth. Expressed another way, the eleven districts paying the highest tax per white citizen and containing more than two slaves for every white person elected 122 Federalists and 269 Repub-

9. Rank according to wealth is based on state tax per white capita for each district or parish; the amounts for 1808–1809 are in the *Charleston Courier*, June 25, 1809.

licans to the state house; the eleven districts paying the least tax per white person elected 530 Republicans and just 8 Federalists. An examination of the per capita state tax rate merely confirms the conclusion. The eleven strongest Federalist districts paid an average tax in 1808 of $5.16 per white person; the twenty-two strongest Republican districts paid only $0.23 per person. These comparisons do not indicate an absolute association between planters and Federalists, or a total antagonism toward the party by poorer farmers; but there was a much greater likelihood that a Federalist candidate would be elected from a wealthy district than from a poor one.

Analysis of Georgia is hindered by the dearth of Federalist candidates, but in the three statewide congressional races, Federalists performed somewhat better in the richer, plantation-dominated Tidewater counties than in the poorer upland areas. The contrast would have been greater except that the 1808 candidate, John M. Dooly, was himself an up-country man and attracted many votes from his home region because of personal popularity. The other two nominees, Matthew McAllister in 1802 and John Elliott in 1810, ran best in the plantation counties along the lower Savannah River and the Atlantic coast. To do so, they obviously had to gain the votes of the local planter elite. This picture of the Federalist party in Georgia does not correspond to that previously sketched by historians of the state. According to the earlier view, Federalist strength was supposedly drawn from the up-country frontier, while the backbone of the Republican party was formed by the wealthy class dominating the lower part of the state.[10] However, the statewide congressional vote indicates that wealth and Federalism were to some degree partners, not enemies, in nineteenth-century Georgia.

Six of the nine counties most generous to Federalists were in the richest half of all counties and only three were in the poorest half; in addition, these nine most heavily Federalist counties included four of the seven that were more than 50 percent Negro.[11] In the counties where Federalists received almost no votes, there were fewer Negroes and less wealth. Only three of these seventeen strongest Republican

10. E. Merton Coulter, *Georgia: A Short History* (Chapel Hill, N.C., 1960), 239–41.

11. Value of land, lots, slaves, and buildings for each county, as assessed for the direct tax of 1813, is in Warden, *Statistical, Political, and Historical Account*.

counties were in the highest quartile ranked by wealth. Altogether, thirty-four counties voted in one or more of the three congressional contests, and ten of these contained more than $500 worth of property per white person. In the ten rich counties (all plantation or urban areas) the Federalists averaged 12 percent of the votes for Congress, but in the eleven poorest counties (each with less than $225 worth of property per person) they mustered less than 8 percent. Taking the average of the three elections, white people in the strongest Federalist counties each owned $524 worth of land, slaves, and buildings, while whites in the weakest Federalist counties owned only $241 each. This shows no absolute correlation between riches and a Federalist outlook in politics, but it does at least indicate that wealthy planters were more sympathetic to the party than were poorer white farmers.

In the two more northerly states, where most southern Federalists lived, the relationship of economics to politics was radically different. There was no connection whatever between slave-laden plantations and Federalism; if anything, the party was sometimes more warmly received in the poorer areas. North Carolina Republicans, for example, drew most of their leadership from the tobacco plantation counties along the Virginia border and from the region of the Albemarle and Pamlico Sounds, but the poorer frontier counties in the mountains were also heavily Republican. Both the richest and the poorest, and the oldest and the newest sections of the state were hostile to Federalism.[12]

Suffrage requirements in North Carolina afford a check on this analysis. All taxpayers (meaning all adult white males, since there was a poll tax) could vote for members of the house of commons, but only fifty-acre freeholders could choose state senators. If there was an economic basis to politics, those owning fifty acres or more should have voted differently from persons holding little or no land, and there should have been a significant difference in party strength between the house (elected by everyone) and the senate (elected by the richer two-thirds of voters). In fact, there was no such difference over the long term; the proportion of Federalists in the senate from 1800 through

12. Rank according to wealth is based on the average levy per white capita for the direct tax of 1800; the amount of tax per county is in the *Raleigh Register*, October 15, 1801.

1816 was neither higher nor lower than the percentage in the house.[13]

The small difference that does exist between economic groups suggests that Federalism in North Carolina may have been associated, though only very slightly, with a lack of property. Only six of the strong Federalist counties were among the richer half of the state's counties; nine fell in the poorer half. Of the strongest Republican counties, seventeen were in the richer half and only twelve in the poorer half. Ranking all the counties by quartiles according to Federalist strength and taking the average tax per white person in each quartile reveals virtually no party distinction on the basis of wealth. Whites in the most heavily Federalist counties paid, on the average, fifty cents in the direct tax of 1800; whites in the most heavily Republican counties paid fifty-seven cents each. These figures show that economic status had little or nothing to do with political affilation in rural North Carolina.

In the largest of the southern states, Virginia, there was also no substantial economic explanation for party alignments. A few of the rich tobacco plantation counties elected an occasional Federalist to the house of delegates, but on the whole this prosperous Piedmont area was solidly Republican. Some of the worn-out Tidewater counties, formerly growing tobacco but now declining into corn production, were also friendly to Federalists. Most, however, were heavily Republican, as were the influential planters who still guided politics there. Many of the mountainous frontier counties west of the Blue Ridge voted heavily Federalist, but the equally poor counties of remote southwestern Virginia utterly rejected the party. In the Shenandoah Valley, which was fertile but lacking in slaves and plantations, there was strong two-party competition.

Each region and economic level was split, with a small tendency for Federalist areas to be slightly poorer than Republican ones. This becomes apparent in ranking the counties by political affiliation and then by wealth. Twenty-four counties stood in the most heavily Federalist quartile, and of these, two were in the wealthiest and thirteen

13. Richard P. McCormick uses the differences in suffrage requirements to reach the same conclusion about North Carolina in the next political generation in "Suffrage Classes and Party Alignments: A Study in Voter Behavior," *Mississippi Valley Historical Review*, XLVI (1959), 397–410.

were in the poorest quartiles.[14] Of the most heavily Republican counties, fifteen were in the wealthiest one-fourth of all counties and only seven were in the poorest. A comparison of the voting histories of counties with the average state tax payment per white person in 1810 reinforces this conclusion. The Federalist counties paid thirty-two cents in per capita taxes and the Republican counties paid seventy-three cents. This is a clear if limited indication that poorer areas were more likely than rich counties to vote for Federalists.

Although the political pattern of agricultural counties varied widely from state to state, as Table 14 and the foregoing discussion show, nowhere were small farmers or rich planters as friendly to the Federalist party as townsmen were. The lords of the manor did, obviously, have certain interests in common with the commercial class. Their staple crops (cotton, tobacco, and rice) needed reliable transportation to distant markets in the North or abroad and competent agents to supervise shipment and sale. Until the crops were finally sold and proceeds remitted, the planters could usually exist only on credit, and for this they again looked to the merchants and financiers. Like these two urban groups, many planters had correspondents in the northern cities of Philadelphia, New York, and Boston, where the leading houses that handled southern staples were often vigorously Federalist. As men of some standing in their rural communities, the planters may also have found something to praise in the Federalists' proclamation that theirs was the party of "order and regular government."

Yet powerful forces were also at work pulling the inhabitants of southern manor houses toward the Republican party. Not the least among these may have been the pleasure of seeing men of their own class leading that party. The outstanding Republicans—Jefferson, Madison, and Monroe—were all planters; so were most of the prominent state figures (Giles, Randolph, Macon, Charles Pinckney, William Alston, James Jackson, John Milledge, among others). With such men the southern planter could sympathize, confident that to whatever extent political issues affected their individual economic situa-

14. Figures are based upon state taxes per white capita; the tax for each county is in the *Virginia Argus*, January 5, 1811.

Table 14 **Federalist Strength, 1800–1816, and Per Capita Wealth**

Counties Ranked by Federalist Strength	Counties Ranked by Per Capita Wealth: First Quartile	Second Quartile	Third Quartile	Fourth Quartile
GEORGIA				
First Quartile	5 (63%)	1 (12%)	1 (12%)	1 (12%)
Second Quartile	0 (0%)	2 (25%)	4 (50%)	2 (25%)
Lowest Two Quartiles	3 (19%)	5 (31%)	3 (19%)	5 (31%)
SOUTH CAROLINA				
First Quartile	6 (60%)	3 (30%)	1 (10%)	0 (0%)
Second Quartile	4 (36%)	2 (18%)	4 (36%)	1 (9%)
Lowest Two Quartiles	1 (5%)	5 (23%)	6 (27%)	10 (45%)
NORTH CAROLINA				
First Quartile	1 (7%)	5 (33%)	5 (33%)	4 (27%)
Second Quartile	3 (20%)	3 (20%)	6 (40%)	3 (20%)
Lowest Two Quartiles	10 (34%)	7 (24%)	4 (14%)	8 (28%)
VIRGINIA				
First Quartile	2 (8%)	2 (8%)	7 (29%)	13 (54%)
Second Quartile	7 (29%)	7 (29%)	6 (25%)	4 (17%)
Lowest Two Quartiles	15 (31%)	16 (33%)	11 (22%)	7 (14%)

tions, the Republican leaders had the plantation owner's interests at heart. The national Federalist leaders, by contrast, were northern men who placed commerce and finance above agriculture. Adams, Hamilton, Pickering, King, Bayard, and their like, might easily represent interests opposed to those of the planters; at least, they would not instinctively view political issues through a planter's eyes. On the state level in the South many Federalist politicians could boast of landed estates, but they were matched at least man-for-man by nonplanters.

Reinforcing this kinship of interest with Republican leadership was a strong economic grievance against the Federalist administration of John Adams. The direct tax levied during the French crisis lay heaviest upon the South, for three-fifths of all slaves were included in each state's taxable population. Within the southern states the direct tax was apportioned according to the value of slaves, land, and town improvements. Obviously the plantation owners, with their many Negroes, vast fertile acreage, and large houses, would pay considerably more than merchants and others whose wealth was in securities or stock-in-trade. Here was an apparent direct discrimination against planters by the Federalist taxmakers.

As for the small farmers, who were a great majority of the electorate in every state, it is difficult to find rational economic motives for their votes. Many were subsistence farmers, whose marketable surplus of produce was quite small and who lived on the very fringe of the money economy. Perhaps they would sell enough to buy salt, tools, and whatever clothing they did not make, but the balance between satisfaction and disaster in their lives did not rest, as it did with the planters, upon the sale of a large quantity of staples in some distant foreign market. Policies of the government in relation to foreign commerce had great importance to the planter and the urban business class, but to the small farmer they were largely theoretical. The only way in which the national government could affect the subsistence farmer economically was to tax him, and the direct tax of Adams' last years was probably as unpopular with these citizens as it was with the wealthy.

Undoubtedly many of the poor farmers rarely saw one newspaper a month, if that; they must have received most of their information on public affairs from more prosperous neighbors at the tavern, church, militia muster, court, or market. Perhaps they did not even form an opinion of candidates until polling day, when they might observe the eager aspirants in person or simply follow the lead of some respected and influential man in the county. This would help account for the uneven pattern of party loyalty in the South, where one county could lean toward the Federalists while its neighbor, apparently exactly like it in all visible characteristics, could be heavily Republican. If the handful of men who made up a county's political, economic, and social elite made known their party preference, numbers of their poorer neighbors might have hastened to follow this lead. Thus the party chosen by a few leading men, perhaps for quite personal reasons having nothing to do with economics or rational evaluation of policies, could become the choice of a majority of voters in a county. Because of different education, family background, or personal experience, another small group of men only a few miles away might support the opposite party and sweep the ordinary voters of their county with them. Something of this nature must be, in part at least, responsible for the wide variation in party preference of small farmers in different southern states. Certainly the candidates of the time assumed that this was the case, because they eagerly sought open endorsement by the elite of a county, expecting that each great man could carry his "interest" with him.

In summary, there was no consistent relationship between economics and party politics in these four states, except in the towns. The upper class of merchants, financiers, and professional men in the urban environment was much more tolerant of Federalism than the general population in each state. Likewise, mechanics appear to have been overwhelmingly Republican, although not necessarily more so than the entire state. In the vast rural electorate, only two states showed a positive association of Federalism and property, whereas in North Carolina and Virginia there was a slight tendency for wealthy areas to be more Republican and for poorer counties to vote Federalist. It is important, however, to bear in mind that these are relative measures only, and that in every state a clear majority of every economic group except the urban business class supported the Republican party after 1800.

Chapter 27 DEMOGRAPHIC PATTERNS AND PARTY AFFILIATION

IN THE preceding two chapters we have examined pre-1800 political patterns and economic differences to discover clues that might explain the voting behavior of southern counties after 1800. There are also several noneconomic factors that might affect a person's outlook toward society in general and politics in particular. Age, rate of population growth, religion, and national origin can all be measured (with differing degrees of reliability) and compared with county voting patterns in the early national period.

Scholars are increasingly using a generational approach to the study of age groups in history and have in several cases broken new ground in understanding how individuals' religious, political, and social attitudes have been shaped in their maturing years.[1] The study of generations in the early Republic, however, is hindered by the scarcity of census information. Adult white males—the voting population—are broken into only three categories in the 1810 census: ages 16–26, 26–45, and over 45. Assuming that half of the 16–26-year age group

1. Few students of early national history have used the "generational" approach, but one good example is Stanley Elkins and Eric McKitrick, "The Founding Fathers: Young Men of the Revolution," *Political Science Quarterly*, LXXXI (1961), 181–216. The concept is also central to Fischer, *Revolution of American Conservatism*.

was 21 or older, the voting population was divided into a young, a middle-aged, and an older generation, containing 24 percent, 47 percent, and 29 percent of adults respectively.

There are two ways of approaching the influence of age upon political outlook. One is to use a rigid chronological assumption that older people are more conservative in their attitudes than the young. Another is to ask what significant events may have helped to shape people's minds in the formative period of adolescence and young adulthood. David H. Fischer has used the first approach in studying Federalist political leaders (chiefly in New England and the middle states) after 1800. He found older men retreating in disgust from the leveling tendencies of the age, while younger Federalists tried to adjust their party's outlook to new realities. As discussed in Chapter 18 herein, the Fischer thesis does not apply well to southern Federalist leaders.

There is, however, the possibility that among the general electorate, age may have affected partisan alignments. If one considers the Federalists to be the conservative party of the times, it is easy enough to calculate the average age of white male adults and determine whether Federalist counties were "older" than Republican areas. This proves to be the case in three of the four southern states, although the differences are so small as to be almost insignificant. In Virginia, voters in Federalist counties were a half year older than Republicans, and in North Carolina and Georgia they were a full year older. South Carolina reversed the pattern, with Republican areas averaging three-fourths of a year older than Federalist districts.

One may go beyond the chronological assumption and refine the investigation by asking what the political climate was when each of these generations matured. Assuming that young men's social and political values were chiefly formed in their late teens, the youngest generation would have become politically aware between about 1800 and 1805. This was Jefferson's idyllic first term, when the Republican party was rapidly increasing its popularity through abolition of internal taxes, the purchase of Louisiana, and other appealing measures. The political climate to which southern youths were exposed was very favorable to the formation of a Republican political allegiance.

The middle generation, aged 26 to 45 in 1810, would have grown to political awareness from about 1781 to 1800, years of crisis and the creation of a national government. This generation was always in the shadow of Washington (as leader of the successful war for independence, organizer of a stronger Union, head of the young nation, and defender against the French in 1798). Members of this Washington generation might have felt kindly disposed toward the political party that claimed him as its patron saint.

Finally, the older generation (most of them between 45 and 60 years of age in 1810) would have reached political awareness in the years of resistance and Revolution, from about 1765 to 1780. The constant theme of politics in this period was fear and suspicion of governmental authority, as American leaders drifted toward armed rebellion against the supposed menace of tyranny. To such a generation, the Federalist war measures of 1798–1800 might have resembled too much the British "repression" in the prerevolutionary years. Men who were willing to find a deliberate conspiracy by government against liberty in the 1770s might well suspect another in the late 1790s. It would be reasonable to expect this age group to be less inclined toward Federalism than the middle-aged men.

Generational analysis thus provides a logical reason to think that both young and old men should favor Republicanism and the middle generation should favor Federalism. Unfortunately, the available evidence does not support the theory. Only in South Carolina does one find Federalist districts having a higher than average proportion of middle-aged voters and a lower than average share of young and old men. In Georgia, there is also a very slight tendency in this direction, but North Carolina and Virginia show just the opposite of the predicted result. The accompanying table summarizes the figures.

Some historians have proposed to explain the geography of party affiliation in these years by differences in the rate of population growth. Federalists, according to this view, owed part of their dour attitude about politics and their fear of the future to the fact that they lived chiefly in stagnant or even declining areas of the country. Counties whose white population was dropping or increasing very slowly obviously could expect little share in the future growth of the American nation. Their greatness was in the past, and every year of westward expansion or urbanization only reduced the weight of these backwater

Table 15 **Testing the Generational Theory Against the 1810 Census**

State	*Do Federalist Counties Have Few Young Men?*	*Do Federalist Counties Have More Middle-Aged Men?*	*Do Federalist Counties Have Few Old Men?*
Va.	NO (+0.3%)*	NO (−3.2%)	NO (+3.2%)
N.C.	YES (−0.3%)	NO (−1.3%)	NO (+2.0%)
S.C.	YES (−2.9%)	YES (+9.3%)	YES (−5.8%)
Ga.	YES (−4.5%)	YES (+0.8%)	NO (+2.2%)

* Percentages refer to the differences between the proportion of each generation in Federalist counties compared to Republican counties.

counties on the national scale. No wonder they looked backward to a more stable society and decried the hustle and change of the present. Republicans, on the other hand, welcomed the future and did not encourage the static social institutions of the past, in part simply because they lived in expanding, vigorous parts of the country.[2]

However well this idea may fit the political patterns of the North, it does not much correspond to reality in the southern states. South Carolina is the only obvious confirmation of the stagnation-versus-growth theory, since the shrinking remnant of that state's Federalist party took shelter in the coastal plantation parishes, which were actually losing white population over the years. The most heavily Republican area, the backcountry, was growing faster than anywhere else in the state. The same was true, though not so starkly, for Georgia. Counties that voted most readily for Federalist candidates were along the coast and the Savannah River or in the older northern counties. After 1800 they grew much more slowly than the almost completely Republican counties of the middle Georgia frontier, where settlers poured into the recently opened Creek cession.

The great bulk of southern Federalists, however, lived in North Carolina and Virginia, and in these two states the situation was quite different. Virginia's western counties, where Federalists were numerous, grew steadily after 1800 while the east marked time. Many eastern counties, their tobacco lands worn out, actually lost population as

2. Fischer, *Revolution of American Conservatism*, 215–17, and to a lesser extent, Buel, *Securing the Revolution*, 81–90, view the rate of population growth as an important factor in party alignments.

planters migrated farther west in search of better soil. In the two decades of 1800–1820, the average Federalist county in Virginia gained population at nearly three times the rate of the average Republican county. Because party lines in North Carolina had little to do with intrastate sectionalism, neither the Federalists nor their opponents were concentrated in fast- or slow-growing counties. The most rapidly expanding part of the state was the mountainous west; the declining area, as in Virginia, was the slave-laden tobacco region to the east. Both groups of counties were heavily Republican, and Federalists were strongest on the central coast and in the southern Piedmont, regions of neither spectacular population growth nor decline. Table 16 shows the relationship between population and politics for each state. Obviously Federalist voting is not consistently associated with declining or stagnant geographical regions in the South.

Table 16 **Median Percentage Change in White Population, 1800–1820, for Federalist and Republican Counties**

	Virginia	*North Carolina*	*South Carolina*	*Georgia*
Federalist Counties	+13%	+26%	−9%	+26%
Republican Counties	+5%	+25%	+23%	+44%

Religion as a determining force in political behavior has also drawn the attention of historians of every period from colonial days to the twentieth century. Some students of the first party system have sought to show a connection between religious and political affiliation, particularly in some northern states where religion was a salient issue. The question of Congregational disestablishment agitated the politics of Massachusetts, Connecticut, and New Hampshire, aligning the bulk of Federalists against a coalition of Republicans and some dissenting Federalists. The Congregational and other clergy took an active part in election campaigns and preached from the pulpit on issues of the day.[3] There was a much less direct connection between church and party in the middle states, and in the South there was al-

3. See especially William A. Robinson, *Jeffersonian Democracy in New England* (New Haven, Conn., 1916); Richard J. Purcell, *Connecticut in Transition, 1775–1818* (Washington, D.C., 1918); Charles B. Kinney, Jr., *Church and State: The Struggle for Separation in New Hampshire, 1630–1900* (New York, 1955); and William Gribbin, *The Churches Militant: The War of 1812 and American Religion* (New Haven, Conn., 1973).

most none. Southern church life was dominated by the strength of the Great Revival, which swept eastward over the Alleghenies and quickened the pace of religion in the coastal region after 1800. The most recent historian of this influential movement has made a thorough search for direct partisanship among the clergy and religious organizations but has found none.[4]

Nevertheless, there were subsidiary ways in which religion affected the first party system. One of the chief Federalist arguments against Jefferson and the Republicans generally was that they were enemies of Christianity. Throughout the first few years of the new century, Federalists repeatedly warned the southern public of the danger of an irreligious administration. Jefferson's partiality toward the French Revolution, the consideration he showed Thomas Paine, the comments he wrote in *Notes on Virginia*—all were trumpeted as evidence of an anti-Christian attitude. An article on "Mr. Jefferson's Impiety" was widely published in the Federalist press in 1803, leading one western Virginia Republican to fear that it "will do hurt to the Republican Interest, if not refuted. ⅞ of the people on this side of the Mountains . . . are professors of Religion" who would think ill of the president if they were swayed by the Federalist charges. The editor of the *Augusta Herald* carried on the same attack in Georgia, saying that "there are at this moment in these United States, a great number of open and avowed Deists . . . who style themselves *Democrats* and *Republicans*, and who are supported and paid by men in high office . . . for the very purpose of bringing christians and christianity into contempt and disrepute, and, if possible, to root out entirely a belief in christianity from amongst us."[5]

The impact of such charges was reduced by two influences working in favor of the Republicans. The Great Revival, though not in any way a partisan movement, did help take the edge off complaints about Jefferson's anti-Christian attitude. Federalists had predicted dire days for religion if the Republicans won control of the national government; instead, southern religion was thriving as never before. Church membership soared as revival meetings produced new converts by

4. John B. Boles, *The Great Revival, 1787–1805: The Origins of the Southern Evangelical Mind* (Lexington, Ky., 1972), Chap. 11.

5. *Virginia Gazette*, October 27, 1802; *Charleston Courier*, April 5, 1803, December 4, 1806; William McKinley to James Madison, May 14, 1804, in Madison Papers, LC; *Augusta Herald*, October 26, 1803.

the thousands. The years of greatest vigor and most rapid growth in the history of southern Christianity coincided with the first years of Republican rule in Washington. In the face of this evidence, Federalists were not likely to convince many voters that religion was unsafe in a nation ruled by Republicans.

Moreover, the Baptist church, largest in membership and probably strongest in missionary activity, had a special reason to favor the Republican cause. Baptists had led the fight for religious freedom in Virginia before 1800, and they had found in Jefferson and Madison strong allies for disestablishment. The religious issue had been an important one in Virginia politics, and although it was essentially settled before the rise of national parties, Baptists long remembered who their friends had been. In an extremely unusual action for a southern church group, the Appomattox Association of Baptists in Virginia passed an official resolution praising Jefferson's administration. A similar feeling may have existed among Baptists in other states, because the Virginia crusade for toleration was widely followed throughout the South.[6]

There was another way, too, in which religion and politics might have been related. An individual's religious affiliation and his political party membership might both be independent variables reflecting his basic outlook on life and society. Federalists, for instance, held an elitist and rather gloomy view of human nature and wished for a stable, hierarchical society in which each class of men had bonds of obligation to other classes and to the common good. The same feeling was often prominent in the social thinking (*not* necessarily the theological dogma) of conservative churches such as the Presbyterian, Lutheran, German Reformed, and, to some extent, the Episcopal and pacifist denominations. Conversely, the Republican beliefs in equality of treatment, hostility to institutional repression of man's independent nature, and the possibility of reforming and improving human society were also expressed by the more democratic churches, especially the Baptists.

In spite of these possible relationships between religion and party loyalty, this question has been investigated very little in the South. Indeed, the paucity of sound evidence on the distribution of church

6. Maude H. Woodfin, "Contemporary Opinion in Virginia of Thomas Jefferson," in Avery Craven (ed.), *Essays in Honor of William E. Dodd* (Chicago, 1935), 75, 80, 81.

membership rules out any firm conclusions. Fortunately, however, the particular pattern of southern social history after 1815 allows the use, with much caution, of statistics from a later generation. The census of 1850 tabulated by county the number of church "accommodations" (i.e., seats in church buildings) for every major denomination.[7] Normally, evidence this far removed from the period under study would be virtually worthless, but this is not so for the South Atlantic states. Unlike the Northeast, the 1840s and 1850s brought no rush of foreign immigration into these states; and unlike the West, no massive internal influx of population altered the residential patterns of 1815. In fact, areas of strength for each major Protestant denomination are virtually the same in 1850 as they were in the 1790s.

Even so, one should attempt only the most general and tentative conclusions when applying religious statistics of 1850 to the political alignments of 1800–1815. This caution is especially necessary because the census did not count actual membership in churches but only the total seating capacity of church buildings. A county might have had a number of Presbyterians, for instance, but no Presbyterian church yet erected. Or there might have been a huge Baptist church built in anticipation of future growth or to serve neighboring areas, which far exceeded the needs of the actual number of Baptist communicants. Therefore, statistics for any single county cannot be used with safety, and it is necessary to compare groups of counties to help cancel aberrations and inaccuracies.

As Table 17 shows, there was often a distinct connection between party and religion, but it was not always the same from state to state. Everywhere but Georgia, Republican counties had far more Baptists than Federalist counties (70 percent more in North Carolina, 85 percent more in Virginia, and 95 percent more in South Carolina). In every state but South Carolina, Federalist counties contained many more Presbyterians than did Republican counties—nearly twice as many in Virginia and Georgia, and four times as many in North Carolina. In all four states Methodists were distributed evenly among the counties. In the smaller denominations the picture varies considerably. In Virginia, but not elsewhere, the pacifist sects (Quakers, Mennonites, Moravians, Dunkers), as well as the Lutheran and German

7. U.S. Census Office, *The Seventh Census of the United States: 1850* (Washington, D.C., 1853). Religious statistics are at the end of each state's section in the volume.

Table 17 **Religion and Party Affiliation: Distribution of Church Accommodations (1850 Census) in Federalist and Republican Counties**

Voting Pattern of Counties	*Baptist*	*Methodist*	*Presbyterian*	*Episcopal*	*Pacifists*	*German*
	*Division of Total Church Seats by Denomination**					
			VIRGINIA			
Federalist	19%	42%	20%	9%	5%	4%
Republican	36%	37%	11%	10%	1%	3%
			NORTH CAROLINA			
Federalist	27%	38%	17%	4%	3%	11%
Republican	46%	41%	4%	3%	4%	1%
			SOUTH CAROLINA			
Federalist	20%	32%	14%	26%	0%	2%
Republican	39%	38%	16%	1%	0%	4%
			GEORGIA			
Federalist	47%	40%	7%	2%	0%	4%
Republican	46%	41%	4%	3%	4%	1%

**Pacifists* = Quakers, Moravians, Mennonites, Dunkers; *German* = German Reformed and Lutheran.

Reformed churches, were very heavily concentrated in Federalist counties.

Religion often overlaps with national origin, and the presence of conflicting national and linguistic groups can sometimes explain much in American politics. In recent years many historians have reassessed the pattern of politics in various places and periods, putting new emphasis on the clash of ethnic groups and their cultural outlooks rather than on economic class. David H. Fischer, John A. Munroe, and Rudolph and Margaret Pasler, among other students of the Jeffersonian era, have suggested an investigation into the relationship of national origin and party affiliation.

Even though nearly all the southern white population in the early nineteenth century was British, there were significant cleavages of nationality. The English proper (including the Welsh) made up only about two-thirds of the population, the remainder being divided among Scots, Scotch-Irish, southern Irish, Germans, and a few miscellaneous groups. In some counties the non-English nationalities together made up a majority. These divisions of origin were often important in *state* politics, but whether they influenced *party* politics is much more difficult to determine.

The chief barrier to such an analysis is the absence of reliable answers to the two most basic questions: How many of each nationality were there and how were these people distributed? The early censuses contain no official statistics on national origin, and impressionistic evidence such as travelers' accounts is far too vague to be of much help. Early in this century, the Census Bureau did attempt, in its volume *A Century of Population Growth*, to tabulate the nationality of heads of families from the 1790 census; but this was done simply by casting the surnames into various national groups. No account was taken of the fact that many names had already been Anglicized by 1790 or that some important names might be shared by two or more nationalities. The result was a census estimate that placed the English share of the white population far too high.

The best work on early nationality groups is the American Council of Learned Societies' lengthy study, published as part of the American Historical Association *Annual Report* for 1931. Essentially, their method was to compare the percentage of persons having, say, distinctively Scotch-Irish names in an American locality with the percentage having such names in northern Ireland. If 10 percent of the people in Ulster and 1 percent of the people in an American locality bore these distinctive names, then the population of the American place was assumed to be one-tenth (or 10 percent) Scotch-Irish in origin. Of course, care was taken to choose names that were unlikely to have been Anglicized in large numbers or held by members of another nationality. The same procedure was followed for Scots, southern Irish, and Germans.[8] While yielding acceptable results for a large unit such as a state, which had many thousands of heads of families,

8. American Council of Learned Societies, "Report of Committee on Linguistic and National Stocks in the Population of the United States," American Historical Association *Annual Report for 1931* (Washington, D.C., 1932), 103–441. A good recent study of ethnicity and politics is Owen S. Ireland, "The Ethnic-Religious Dimensions of Pennsylvania Politics, 1778–1779," *William and Mary Quarterly*, 3rd ser., XXX (1973), 423–48.

this method is considerably less reliable when used for counties. The presence of a single name-holder might make a difference of several percentage points in a county's population distribution. Therefore, discussion must concentrate on groups of counties only—the most heavily Federalist counties in a state and the most heavily Republican counties. Even so, no great reliance can be placed on the nationality estimates, and the conclusions reached here must be considered tentative only.

In each of the southern states the pattern of settlement produced a similar distribution of national groups. The English, first to arrive in great numbers, were dominant everywhere along the coast and usually into the Piedmont as well. The various non-English nationalities —Scots, Scotch-Irish, Germans, and Irish—arrived much later and entered the South, not directly from the coast, but indirectly by way of Pennsylvania. Beginning in the early eighteenth century, especially after the 1740s, these new peoples swarmed down the valley of Virginia and spread into the entire western area of the Carolinas and Georgia. A huge colony of Scots also settled in the upper Cape Fear Valley in North Carolina's eastern Piedmont.

This particular pattern of nationalities complicates the problem of analysis. The minority stocks happened to live in the western sections of their states and in areas that were rather poor economically and had few slaves. There is no satisfactory way to disentangle these influences from the nationality question. Suppose one discovered that Scottish and Scotch-Irish areas leaned strongly toward one political party, what exactly would be proved? Were these counties behaving in this way because they were western counties reacting in a sectional way, or because they were poor counties reacting from economic motives? Ideally, one should be able to compare the behavior of western Scottish counties with the behavior of western non-Scottish counties, and do the same with poor Scottish counties and poor non-Scottish counties. Such an analysis would isolate the influence of nationality and make for much more reliable conclusions. Unfortunately, the statistics on national origin are simply not accurate enough to allow this, as has been explained earlier. Furthermore, that information is from the 1790 census and cannot be applied with confidence to a period two decades later.

There are two reasons why one might expect the minority nationalities to have behaved differently from the English majority in the Jeffersonian years, and both are rooted in the previous history of the South. During the Revolution, many Scots and Scotch-Irish were Tories. The lists of estates seized, members of Tory regiments, and Loyalists receiving compensation from the British government are heavy with Scottish and Scotch-Irish names. Given the ferocity of the Revolution in the South—in many places it was a brutal civil war—it is not surprising that these two national groups would come under blanket suspicion. The problem was especially acute in North Carolina, whose upper Cape Fear counties were the strongest Tory bastion in the entire South. The rebel majority imposed much discriminatory legislation on Loyalists, and not all of it was removed at war's end. When the question of harsh or lenient treatment of these people arose in the 1780s, several future Federalist leaders (William R. Davie, James Iredell, Samuel Johnston) were prominent in seeking to ameliorate the anti-Loyalist measures. The work of these men in restoring former Tories to a position of equality in postwar North Carolina may well have been remembered with gratitude in the close-knit Scottish and Scotch-Irish communities along the upper Cape Fear.

Generally, all these minorities suffered a history of discrimination and often contempt from the English-dominated society in the southern colonies. Everywhere the Scottish and Scotch-Irish Presbyterians and the German Lutheran and Reformed congregations had to fight the Anglican establishment regarding religion. The western areas of each colony, where these new nationalities chiefly settled, were denied a fair share of political participation and sometimes even law enforcement. There is little doubt that the eastern Englishmen viewed these newcomers, with their different language, religion, and culture, as hardly the equals of old-stock colonists. Thus sectional hostilities within the southern states from the 1780s on were largely based on ethnic differences. Facing such treatment by the dominant political group in each state, the minority nationalities naturally would react by giving their support to the local opposition group—the Federalist party.

Perhaps these explanations are logical, but they do not quite fit the available evidence. In North Carolina alone there is a clear and well-marked preference of ethnic minorities for the Federalist cause. As Table 18 shows, the average Federalist county in that state had twice as many Scots, Scotch-Irish, Irish, and Germans as the typical Republican county. In fact, the Federalist areas were more than 40 percent non-English in their national origin, whereas the Republican counties were four-fifths English. Very possibly the Tory connection explains much of this sharp division between ethnic groups. Outside this one state, however, there is no consistent tendency for any nationality to favor one party over the other, except that Germans everywhere were more likely to live in Federalist counties than in Republican ones. Scots in Georgia were particularly attracted to Federalism, it seems, while Scotch-Irish areas in both Georgia and South Carolina were more inclined toward Republicanism than the average county. There is little to support the view that minority nationalities throughout the South were markedly Federalist in their voting.

Table 18 **Division of Population in Federalist and Republican Counties According to National Origin, 1790**

	Percentage of White Population:				
	English	*Scottish*	*Scotch-Irish*	*Irish*	*German*
		VIRGINIA*			
Federalist counties	66%	11%	7%	6%	10%
Republican counties	70%	11%	6%	6%	7%
		NORTH CAROLINA			
Federalist counties	59%	21%	8%	7%	5%
Republican counties	80%	10%	4%	4%	2%
		SOUTH CAROLINA			
Federalist counties	72%	16%	6%	3%	3%
Republican counties	66%	15%	12%	5%	2%
		GEORGIA*			
Federalist counties	56%	23%	6%	4%	11%
Republican counties	66%	12%	12%	3%	7%

*For Virginia, state censuses of 1780s are used, and many counties are missing; for Georgia, federal census of 1820 is used.

No single influence, therefore, whether it originated in past political history, geography, economics, or demography, explains the pattern of southern Federalism. The party drew its voting support from different groups of people in each state. There was, in fact, only one thing common to Federalists everywhere—the fear of France. Disgust with the unsettling, radical ideas of the French Revolution and its bloody massacres; anger at the revolutionary government's attempt to spread its doctrine through Europe by force of arms and through America by agents such as Genet; abhorrence of Napoleonic tyranny; suspicion that many Republicans were infatuated with France—all these feelings animated Federalists in the South. They desired to maintain a deferential society and to live in an orderly world; French ideas and ambition threatened this. They revered organized religion as a pillar of social order and morality; the French attacked or scorned religion. They believed in government by men of talents, respectability, and economic standing; the French spread "equality and fraternity" at bayonet point. Simply put, France threatened the creed of many southern Federalist voters, whatever their station in life, their geographic residence, or their political and ethnic ancestry.

There is no evidence, of course, that the ordinary citizen, alone on his farm, shared this conservative philosophy of society and responded to it in his voting. However, this outlook, coupled with the fear that French arms or influence might destroy the existing system, is apparent in the letters of nearly every southern Federalist who wrote on politics at all. Furthermore, party newspapers year after year were full of editorials, letters, articles, speeches, and other warnings against just such a French threat. Since it was from the newspapers, either directly or secondhand, that the isolated rural majority received its impressions of the outside world, this constant refrain must have had its effect. Federalist campaign propaganda in congressional elections and in the presidential contests of 1800, 1808, and 1812 also dwelt upon the same theme: France threatened America's traditional religious and social institutions, and the Republicans were the pro-French party; therefore, all who wished to preserve the American system should vote Federalist.

It is very often deceptive to think that the common voter paid any attention to such partisan arguments; political scientists have shown repeatedly that matters entirely apart from ideology usually determine most people's votes. At this period in American history, though, most of the other influences were absent. There had not been much time for the development of traditional party loyalties by 1800, since the parties themselves had existed less than a decade. It was therefore impossible to inherit party loyalty from past generations, as millions of voters do in the twentieth century. Personal impressions of candidates, too, were hard to form because, except on the legislative level, voters seldom heard or saw the contenders. Also, there were practically no impartial newspapers, and it is very unlikely that a Federalist who could afford one of the weekly journals would subscribe to one published by a Republican editor. Unless a man had access to newspapers of both parties or made a practice of riding long miles to seek out Republican friends for discussions, he might have lived this entire period after 1800 receiving all his news of the nation and the world through a strongly Federalist filter. He would read year after year that the French desired universal rule, that the Republicans were unreasonably inclined toward Napoleon and hated England, and that if the administration were not ousted, it would chain America to Bonaparte's prison. In the course of a week or a month he might pass this "information" on to many who were not fortunate enough to receive a newspaper, and if his neighbors held him in any esteem, they might follow his lead on election day.

This can only be speculation, but it might well be that Federalism in the South after 1800 was based primarily on a fear of France, circulated and perpetuated by such verbal distribution as that described above. It is clear that the pattern of Federalist support throughout the region cannot be explained by a continuation of the political lines formed in the Revolution and in the constitutional struggle of 1788–1789, an economic division between wealthy planter and small farmer, sectional rivalry within the states, ethnic background, or religious belief. It is also a fact that, when the political furor over domestic issues was at its height, from 1801 through about 1806, the Federalists suffered a precipitate decline in public support and party effort in the South. This was also the period in which foreign affairs, especially relations with France and England, were quietest. In the years just before 1800, when France was the chief concern of American politics and statecraft, the Federalist party was at its peak of southern popularity. After 1806, the French again began to seem dangerous, and Federalism gained at the polls, reaching a secondary peak during the War of 1812, when the fear of being tied to the French kite was again widespread. No sooner did Napoleon fall in 1815 than the party began its final decline to extinction. It was not the end of the American war with England, but the end of the long European war and the removal of France as a possible danger to America that foretold the disintegration of the Federalist party in the South.

Maps Showing Party Alignment by County

ABBREVIATIONS:

CC	: Charles City
Char	: Charlotte
Cumb	: Cumberland
Fluv	: Fluvanna
Glou	: Gloucester
IofW	: Isle of Wight
JC	: James City
K&Q	: King and Queen
KG	: King George
KW	: King William
Lune	: Lunenberg
Mid	: Middlesex
NK	: New Kent
Nott	: Nottoway
Pow	: Powhatan
PE	: Prince Edward
PG	: Prince George
PW	: Prince William
Rich	: Richmond [county]
Spot	: Spotsylvania
War	: Warwick

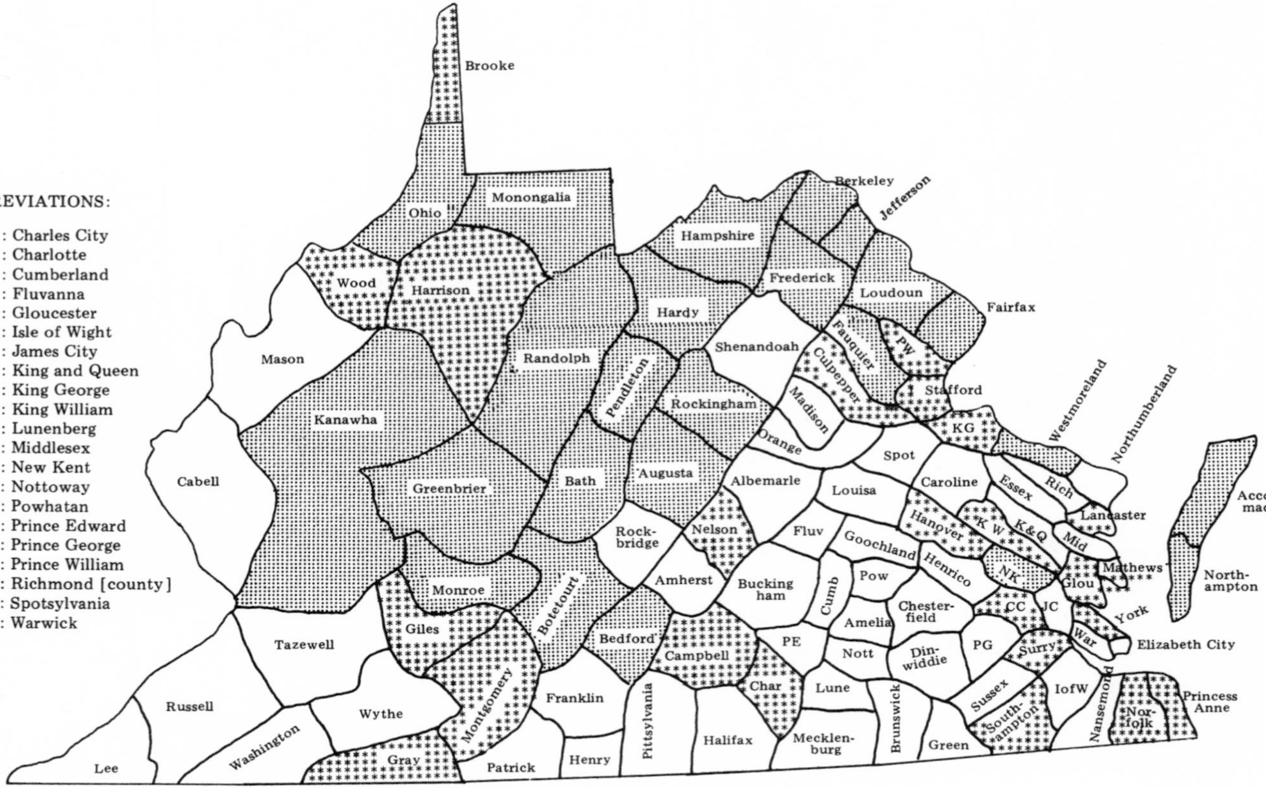

COUNTIES RANKED BY FEDERALIST STRENGTH, 1800-1816

First Quartile — Second Quartile — Lowest Two Quartiles

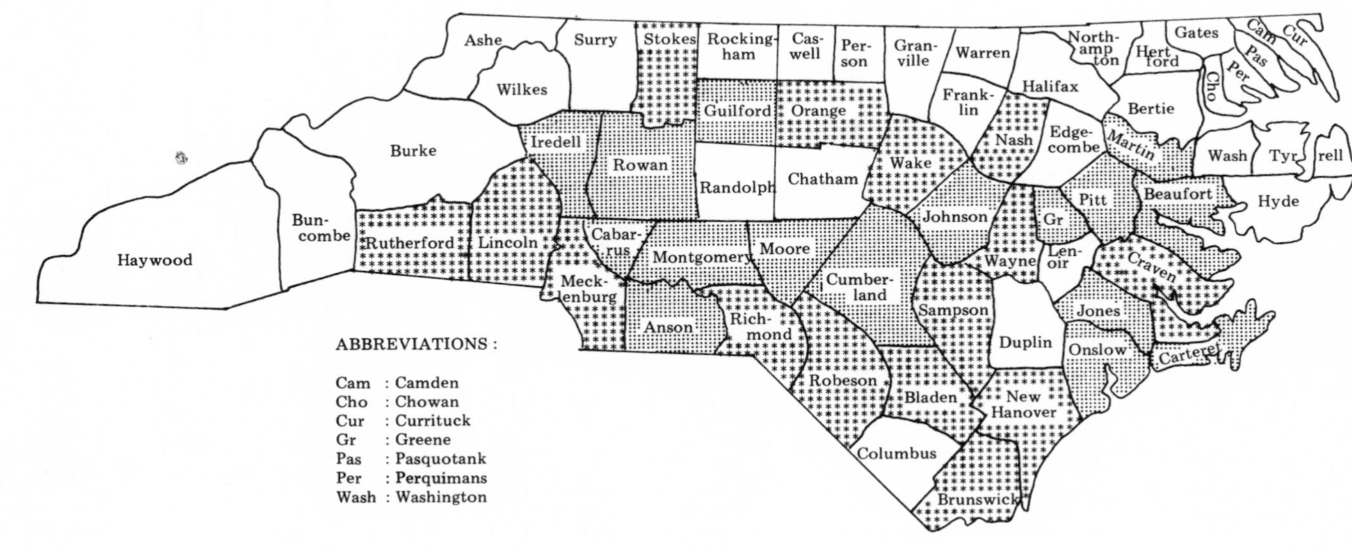

COUNTIES RANKED BY FEDERALIST STRENGTH, 1800-1816

ABBREVIATIONS:

Bal : Baldwin
Gr : Greene
Han : Hancock
Jack : Jackson
Jeff : Jefferson
Ogle : Oglethorpe
Put : Putnam
Ran : Randolph
War : Warren
Wash : Washington
Wilk : Wilkinson

COUNTIES RANKED BY FEDERALIST STRENGTH, 1800-1816

First Quartile   Second Quartile   Lowest Two Quartiles

BIBLIOGRAPHY

PRIMARY SOURCES

Unpublished Manuscript Collections

Duke University, Durham, North Carolina

- Ambler-Brown
- David Campbell
- Dandridge
- H. W. DeSaussure
- James Iredell, Jr.
- Joseph Jones
- Munford-Ellis

Georgia Historical Society, Savannah

- Philip Box Letterbook
- Mulford

Historical Society of Pennsylvania, Philadelphia

- Dreer Collection
- Gratz

Houghton Library, Harvard University, Cambridge, Massachusetts

- Loring Andrews
- Joseph Dennie
- John Rutledge, Jr.
- Simes Collection

Library of Congress, Washington, D.C.

- Breckinridge Family
- Alexander Hamilton
- Robert Goodloe Harper
- Thomas Jefferson

James Madison
John Marshall
James Monroe
Wilson Cary Nicholas
Pinckney Family
Leven Powell
William Campbell Preston
John Randolph
Charles Simms
Thomas Sumter

Massachusetts Historical Society, Boston

Coolidge Collection
Harrison Gray Otis
Timothy Pickering
Theodore Sedgwick

New-York Historical Society, New York

Rufus King

New York Public Library, New York

James Madison
Miscellaneous
James Monroe
William Patterson Transcripts

North Carolina Department of Archives and History, Raleigh

Wood Jones Hamlin
Hayes Collection
Legislative Papers
William Jeffreys
Charles E. Johnson
Charles Pettigrew
William Polk
Montfort Stokes

University of Georgia, Athens

Abraham Baldwin
Shaler Hillyer Letterbook

Southern Historical Collection, University of North Carolina, Chapel Hill

Walter Alves
Arnold-Screven
Hutchins G. Burton
Cameron Family
Davie
William Gaston
Joseph D. Hamilton
Ernest Haywood
Archibald Henderson Collection
William Johnson
Calvin Jones
Lenoir Family

Norwood
George W. Polk
John Randolph
John Rutledge
John Steele
Nicholas P. Trist
James Webb

South Caroliniana Library, University of South Carolina, Columbia

Robert Anderson
Robert Brown
H. W. DeSaussure
Peter Freneau
C. C. Pinckney
John Rutledge

Alderman Library, University of Virginia, Charlottesville

Breckinridge
Breckinridge-Watts
Joseph Bryan
W. W. Burrows
Cabell Deposit
Carr-Cary
Edgehill-Randolph
Gwathmey Collection
Charles Hamilton Autographs
Harry Heth
James McDowell
Wilson Cary Nicholas
Prentis Family Letterbooks
Prentis Transcripts
John Randolph of Roanoke
Stratton Letter
Creed Taylor
Watson

Virginia Historical Society, Richmond

John Cropper

Virginia State Library, Richmond

Littleton W. Tazewell
William Wirt

Yale University Library, New Haven, Connecticut

Morse Family

Published Manuscript Collections

Battle, Kemp P., ed. *Letters of Nathaniel Macon, John Steele, and William Barry Grove*. Chapel Hill: University of North Carolina Press, 1902.

Brunhouse, Robert L., ed. *David Ramsay, 1749–1815: Selections from His Writings*. Philadelphia: American Philosophical Society, 1965.

"Correspondence of Col. Leven Powell, M.C., Relating to the Election of 1800." *The John P. Branch Historical Papers of Randolph-Macon College*, I (1901), 54–63.

Cross, Jack L. "John Marshall on the French Revolution and on American Politics." *William and Mary Quarterly*, Third Series, XII (1955), 631–49.

Flournoy, H. W., ed. *Calendar of Virginia State Papers*. 11 volumes. Richmond: Commonwealth of Virginia, 1875–1893.

"Glimpses of Old College Life." *William and Mary Quarterly*, First Series, VIII (1899–1900), 153–60.

Hamilton, J. G. deRoulhac, ed. *The Papers of Thomas Ruffin*. 4 volumes. Raleigh, N.C.: Edwards & Broughton, 1918–20.

———, ed. *William R. Davie: A Memoir, Followed by His Letters, with Notes by Kemp P. Battle*. Chapel Hill: University of North Carolina Press, 1907.

Hamilton, John C., ed. *The Works of Alexander Hamilton*. 7 volumes. New York: J. F. Trow, 1850–51.

Hartridge, Walter C., ed. *Letters of Robert Mackay to His Wife*. Athens: University of Georgia Press, 1949.

Haynes, George H., ed. "Letters of Samuel Taggart." *Proceedings of the American Antiquarian Society*, New Series, XXXIII (1923), 113–226, 297–438.

Heaney, Howell J., ed. "The Letters of Bushrod Washington (1762–1829) in the Hampton L. Carson Collection of the Free Library of Philadelphia." *American Journal of Legal History*, II (1958), 161–71.

Hooker, Edward. "Diary of Edward Hooker." *American Historical Association Annual Report for 1896*, I, (1897), 842–929.

Hopkins, James F., ed. *The Papers of Henry Clay*. 5 volumes to date. Lexington: University of Kentucky Press, 1959–.

Hoyt, William H., ed. *The Papers of Archibald D. Murphey*. 2 volumes. Raleigh, N.C.: E. M. Uzzell, 1914.

Keith, Alice B. and William H. Masterson, eds. *The Papers of John Gray Blount*. 3 volumes to date. Raleigh, N.C.: Department of Archives and History, 1952–.

King, Charles R., ed. *The Life and Correspondence of Rufus King*. 6 volumes. New York: G. P. Putnam's Sons, 1894–1900.

"Letters of John Taylor of Caroline County, of Virginia." *The John P. Branch Historical Papers of Randolph-Macon College*, II (1908), 253–353.

"Letters to David Watson." *Virginia Magazine of History and Biography*, XXIX (1921), 257–86.

"The Leven Powell Correspondence." *The John P. Branch Historical Papers of Randolph-Macon College*, III (1903), 217–53.

Lodge, Henry Cabot. *The Life and Letters of George Cabot*. Boston: Little Brown, 1877.

McPherson, Elizabeth G., ed. "Unpublished Letters from North Carolinians to Jefferson." *North Carolina Historical Review*, XII (1935), 252–83, 354–80.

Mason, Jonathan. *Extracts from a Diary Kept by the Hon. Jonathan Mason of a Journey from Boston to Savannah in the Year 1804*. Cambridge, Mass.: John Wilson & Son, 1885.

Morison, Samuel Eliot. *The Life and Letters of Harrison Gray Otis, Federalist, 1765–1848*. 2 volumes. Boston: Houghton Mifflin, 1913.

Salley, Harriet M., ed. *Correspondence (1785–1818) of John Milledge, Governor of Georgia, 1802–1806*. Columbia, S.C.: State Commercial Printing, 1949.

Steiner, Bernard C. *The Life and Correspondence of James McHenry: Secretary of War Under Washington and Adams*. Cleveland, Ohio: Burrows Brothers, 1907.

Thayer, Theodore, ed. "Nathaniel Pendleton's 'Short Account of the Sea Coast of Georgia with Respect to Agriculture, Shipbuilding, Navigation, and the Timber Trade.'" *Georgia Historical Quarterly*, XLI (1957), 70–81.

Tilley, Nanny M. "The Journal of the Surry County Agricultural Society." *North Carolina Historical Review*, XXIV (1947), 494–531.
Turlington, S. Baily, ed. "Letters from Old Trunks." *Virginia Magazine of History and Biography*, XLV (1937), 40–45.
Von Briesen, Martha, ed. *The Letters of Elijah Fletcher*. Charlottesville: University Press of Virginia, 1965.
Wagstaff, H. M., ed. *The Harrington Letters*. Chapel Hill: University of North Carolina Press, 1914.
———, ed. *The Harris Letters*. Chapel Hill: University of North Carolina Press, 1916.
———, ed. *The Papers of John Steele*. 2 volumes. Raleigh, N.C.: Edwards & Broughton, 1924.
Watson, Joseph Shelton. "Letters from William and Mary College, 1789–1801." *Virginia Magazine of History and Biography*, XXIX (1921), 130–79.
Wyllie, John C. "Observations Made During a Short Residence in Virginia." *Virginia Magazine of History and Biography*, LXXVI (1968), 387–414.

Contemporary Pamphlets

Lenoir, William. *To the Citizens of the Twelfth Election District of the State of North Carolina*. Fort Defiance, N.C., 1806.
Simons, James. *A Rallying Point, for All True Friends to Their Country*. Charleston, S.C., 1800.
Smith, Thomas Rhett. *An Oration Delivered in Saint Michael's Church the Fifth of July, 1802*. Charleston, S.C., 1802.
Stanly, John. *Letter to His Constituents*. Washington, D.C., 1802.
———. *To the Electors of the Counties of Johnston, Wayne, Green, Lenoir, Jones, Craven, and Carteret*. n.d.
A True Republican Federalist. *Animadversions on James Holland's Strictures on General Joseph Dickson's Circular Letter of the First of May, 1800*. Lincolnton, N.C., 1800.

Newspapers

District of Columbia

Alexandria Advertiser
Alexandria *Columbian Mirror*
Alexandria Gazette

Georgia

Athens Gazette
Athens *Georgia Express*
Augusta Chronicle
Augusta Herald
Augusta *Mirror of the Times*
Louisville Gazette
Milledgeville *Georgia Argus*
Milledgeville *Georgia Journal*
Savannah *American Patriot*
Savannah *Columbian Museum & Savannah Advertiser*
Savannah *Federal Republican Advocate*
Savannah *Georgia Gazette*
Savannah *Georgia Republican*
Savannah *Public Intelligencer*

Savannah *Republican*
Savannah *Southern Patriot*
Sparta *Farmer's Gazette*
Washington *Monitor*

North Carolina

Edenton Gazette
Halifax *North-Carolina Journal*
Newbern *Carolina Federal Republican*
Newbern Gazette
Newbern Herald
New Bern *True Republican*
Raleigh *Minerva*
Raleigh *North-Carolina Minerva*
Raleigh Register
Raleigh *Star*
Salisbury *North-Carolina Mercury & Salisbury Advertiser*
Wilmington Gazette

South Carolina

Charleston *Carolina Weekly Messenger*
Charleston *Carolina Gazette*
Charleston *City Gazette*
Charleston Courier
Charleston *Investigator*
Charleston *South-Carolina State-Gazette*
Charleston *Southern Patriot*
Charleston *Times*
Columbia *Telescope*
Georgetown Gazette
Pendleton *Miller's Weekly Messenger*

Virginia

Abingdon *Political Prospect*
Charlestown *Farmer's Repository*
Fincastle Weekly Advertiser
Fredericksburg *Courier*
Fredericksburg *Virginia Herald*
Leesburg *Genius of Liberty*
Leesburg *True American*
Leesburg *Washingtonian*
Lexington *Rockbridge Repository*
Lexington *Virginia Telegraphe*
Lynchburg Press
Martinsburg *Berkeley & Jefferson Intelligencer*
Martinsburg Gazette
Morgantown *Monongalia Gazette*
Morgantown *Monongalia Spectator*
Norfolk *American Beacon*
Norfolk *Commercial Register*
Norfolk Gazette and Publick Ledger

Petersburg Daily Courier
Petersburg Intelligencer
Petersburg *Republican*
Richmond *Enquirer*
Richmond *Examiner*
Richmond *Virginia Argus*
Richmond *Virginia Federalist*
Richmond *Virginia Gazette*
Richmond *Virginia Patriot*
Staunton *Candid Review*
Staunton Eagle
Staunton *People's Friend*
Staunton *Political Censor*
Staunton *Republican Farmer*
Winchester *Centinel*
Winchester *Gazette*
Winchester *Philanthropist*

Other Primary Sources

Bezanson, Anne, *et al. Wholesale Prices in Philadelphia, 1784–1861*. Philadelphia: Pennsylvania University Press, 1936.

Biographical Directory of the American Congress, 1774–1961. Washington, D.C.: Government Printing Office, 1961.

Brigham, Clarence S. *History and Bibliography of American Newspapers, 1690–1820*. 2 volumes. Worcester, Mass.: American Antiquarian Society, 1947.

Burnham, W. Dean. *Presidential Ballots, 1836–1892*. Baltimore, Md.: Johns Hopkins Press, 1955.

Cole, Arthur H. *Wholesale Commodity Prices in the United States, 1700–1861*. Cambridge, Mass.: Harvard University Press, 1938.

Debates and Proceedings of the Congress of the United States, 1789–1824. 42 volumes. Washington, D.C.: Gales and Seaton, 1834–56.

Drayton, John. *A View of South-Carolina, As Respects Her Natural and Civil Concerns*. Charleston, S.C.: W. P. Young, 1802.

Georgia Official and Statistical Register, 1971–1972. Atlanta: State of Georgia, 1972.

Knight, Edgar W., ed. *A Documentary History of Education in the South Before 1860*. 5 volumes. Chapel Hill: University of North Carolina Press, 1949–53.

Melish, John. *A Geographical Description of the United States, with the Contiguous British and Spanish Possessions, Intended as an Accompaniment to Melish's Map of These Countries*. Philadelphia: T. H. Palmer, 1816.

Mills, Robert. *Statistics of South Carolina, Including a View of Its Natural, Civil, and Military History, General and Particular*. Charleston, S.C.: Hurlbut and Lloyd, 1826.

North Carolina House Journal, 1800–16.

North Carolina Senate Journal, 1800–16.

Paullin, Charles O. *Atlas of the Historical Geography of the United States*. Washington, D.C.: Carnegie Institution, 1932.

Reynolds, Emily B. and Joan R. Faunt, comps. *Biographical Directory of the Senate of the State of South Carolina, 1776–1964*. Columbia: South Carolina Archives Department, 1964.

South Carolina House Journal, 1800–16.

South Carolina Senate Journal, 1800–16.

U.S. Bureau of the Census. *Historical Statistics of the United States: Colonial Times to 1957*. Washington, D.C.: Government Printing Office, 1960.

U.S. Census Office. *Aggregate Amount of Each Description of Persons Within the United States of America, and the Territories Thereof, Agreeably to Actual Enumeration Made According to Law, in Year, 1810*. Washington, D.C., 1811.

———. *Return of the Whole Number of Persons Within the Several Districts of the United States, According to "An Act Providing for the Second Census or Enumeration of the Inhabitants of the United States," Passed February the Twenty Eighth, One Thousand Eight Hundred*. Washington, D.C., 1801.

———. *The Seventh Census of the United States: 1850*. Washington, D.C.: Robert Armstrong, 1853.

Virginia House Journal, 1800–16.

Virginia Senate Journal, 1800–16.

Waddell, Joseph A. *Annals of Augusta County, Virginia from 1726–1871*. Rev. ed. Staunton, Va.: C. R. Caldwell, 1902.

Warden, D. B. *A Statistical, Political, and Historical Account of the United States of North America*. 2 volumes. Edinburgh, Scotland: A. Constable, 1819.

SECONDARY SOURCES

Books

Abernethy, Thomas P. *The Burr Conspiracy*. New York: Oxford University Press, 1954.

———. *The South in the New Nation, 1789–1819*. Vol. IV of 10 vols., in Wendell Holmes Stephenson and E. Merton Coulter, eds., *A History of the South*. Baton Rouge: Louisiana State University Press, 1961.

Adams, Henry. *History of the United States of America During the Administrations of Thomas Jefferson and James Madison*. 9 volumes. New York: Charles Scribner's Sons, 1889–91.

Alden, John Richard. *The First South*. Baton Rouge: Louisiana State University Press, 1961.

———. *The South in the Revolution, 1763–1789*. Vol. III of 10 vols., in Wendell Holmes Stephenson and E. Merton Coulter, eds., *A History of the South*. Baton Rouge: Louisiana State University Press, 1957.

Ambler, Charles H. *Sectionalism in Virginia from 1776 to 1861*. Chicago: University of Chicago Press, 1910.

———. *Thomas Ritchie: A Study in Virginia Politics*. Richmond, Va.: Bell Book and Stationery, 1913.

Ammon, Harry. *The Genet Mission*. New York: W. W. Norton, 1973.

———. *James Monroe: The Quest for National Identity*. New York: McGraw-Hill, 1971.

Anderson, Lee F., *et al*. *Legislative Roll-Call Analysis*. Evanston, Ill.: Northwestern University Press, 1966.

Aronson, Sidney H. *Status and Kinship in the Higher Civil Service: Standards of Selection in the Administrations of John Adams, Thomas Jefferson, and Andrew Jackson*. Cambridge, Mass.: Harvard University Press, 1964.

Balinky, Alexander. *Albert Gallatin: Fiscal Theories and Policies*. New Brunswick, N.J.: Rutgers University Press, 1958.

Banner, James M., Jr. *To the Hartford Convention: The Federalists and the Origins of Party Politics in Massachusetts, 1789–1815*. New York: Alfred A. Knopf, 1970.

Battle, Kemp P. *History of the University of North Carolina*. 2 volumes. Raleigh, N.C.: Edwards and Broughton, 1907–12.

Beard, Charles A. *Economic Origins of Jeffersonian Democracy*. New York: Macmillan, 1952.

Beeman, Richard R. *The Old Dominion and the New Nation, 1788–1801*. Lexington: University of Kentucky Press, 1972.

Bemis, Samuel F. *Jay's Treaty: A Study in Commerce and Diplomacy*. New York: Macmillan, 1923.

Bernhard, Winfred E. A. *Fisher Ames: Federalist and Statesman, 1758–1808*. Chapel Hill: University of North Carolina Press, 1965.

Beveridge, Albert J. *The Life of John Marshall*. 4 volumes. Boston: Houghton Mifflin, 1916–19.

Boles, John B. *The Great Revival, 1787–1805: The Origins of the Southern Evangelical Mind*. Lexington: University of Kentucky Press, 1972.

Bonner, James C. *A History of Georgia Agriculture, 1732–1860*. Athens: University of Georgia Press, 1964.

Boogher, Elbert W. G. *Secondary Education in Georgia, 1732–1858*. Philadelphia: University of Pennsylvania Press, 1933.

Bowman, Albert H. *The Struggle for Neutrality: Franco-American Diplomacy During the Federalist Era*. Knoxville: University of Tennessee Press, 1974.

Brant, Irving. *James Madison: Secretary of State, 1800–1809*. Indianapolis, In.: Bobbs-Merrill, 1953.

Brooks, Robert P. *The Financial History of Georgia, 1732–1950*. Athens: University of Georgia Press, 1952.

Brown, Everett S. *The Constitutional History of the Louisiana Purchase, 1803–1812*. Berkeley: University of California Press, 1920.

Brown, Ralph H. *Mirror for Americans: A Likeness of the Eastern Seaboard, 1810*. New York: American Geographical Society, 1943.

Brown, Wallace. *The King's Friends: The Composition and Motives of the American Loyalist Claimants*. Providence, R.I.: Brown University Press, 1965.

Bruce, Kathleen. *Virginia Iron Manufacture in the Slave Era*. New York: Appleton-Century, 1931.

Buel, Richard, Jr. *Securing the Revolution: Ideology in American Politics, 1789–1815*. Ithaca, N.Y.: Cornell University Press, 1972.

Cathey, Cornelius O. *Agricultural Developments in North Carolina, 1783–1860*. Chapel Hill: University of North Carolina Press, 1956.

Charles, Joseph. *The Origins of the American Party System: Three Essays*. Williamsburg, Va.: Institute of Early American History and Culture, 1956.

Clark, Thomas D., ed. *The Expanding South, 1750–1825: The Ohio Valley and Cotton Frontier*. Vol. II of 3 vols., in *Travels in the Old South: A Bibliography*. Norman: University of Oklahoma Press, 1956.

Clauder, Anna C. *American Commerce as Affected by the Wars of the French Revolution and Napoleon, 1793–1812*. Philadelphia: University of Pennsylvania Press, 1932.

Cole, Donald B. *Jacksonian Democracy in New Hampshire, 1800–1851*. Cambridge, Mass.: Harvard University Press, 1970.

Coleman, Kenneth. *The American Revolution in Georgia, 1763–1789*. Athens: University of Georgia Press, 1958.

Combs, Jerald A. *The Jay Treaty: Political Battleground of the Founding Fathers*. Berkeley and Los Angeles: University of California Press, 1970.

Coulter, E. Merton. *Georgia: A Short History*. Rev. ed. Chapel Hill: University of North Carolina Press, 1960.

Cox, Isaac J. *The West Florida Controversy, 1798–1813: A Study in American Diplomacy*. Baltimore, Md.: Johns Hopkins Press, 1918.

Crittenden, Charles Christopher. *The Commerce of North Carolina, 1763–1789*. New Haven, Conn.: Yale University Press, 1936.

Cunningham, Noble E., Jr. *The Jeffersonian Republicans: The Formation of Party Organization, 1789–1801*. Chapel Hill: University of North Carolina Press, 1957.

———. *The Jeffersonian Republicans in Power: Party Operations, 1801–1809*. Chapel Hill: University of North Carolina Press, 1963.

Dauer, Manning J. *The Adams Federalists*. Baltimore, Md.: Johns Hopkins Press, 1953.

Davis, Joseph S. *Essays in the Earlier History of American Corporations*. 2 volumes. Cambridge, Mass.: Harvard University Press, 1917.

Davis, Richard B. *Intellectual Life of Jefferson's Virginia, 1790–1830*. Chapel Hill: University of North Carolina Press, 1964.

DeConde, Alexander. *Entangling Alliance: Politics and Diplomacy Under George Washington*. Durham, N.C.: Duke University Press, 1958.

———. *The Quasi-War: The Politics and Diplomacy of the Undeclared War with France, 1797–1801*. New York: Scribner's, 1966.

DeMond, Robert O. *The Loyalists in North Carolina During the Revolution*. Durham, N.C.: Duke University Press, 1940.

Dewey, Davis R. *State Banking Before the Civil War*. Washington, D.C.: Government Printing Office, 1910.

Douglass, Elisha P. *Rebels and Democrats: The Struggle for Equal Political Rights and Majority Rule During the American Revolution*. Chapel Hill: University of North Carolina Press, 1955.

Easterby, James H. *A History of the College of Charleston, Founded 1770*. Charleston, S.C.: College of Charleston, 1935.

Elliott, Robert N., Jr. *The Raleigh Register, 1799–1863*. Chapel Hill: University of North Carolina Press, 1955.

Ellis, Richard E. *The Jeffersonian Crisis: Courts and Politics in the Young Republic*. New York: Oxford University Press, 1971.

Faulkner, Robert K. *The Jurisprudence of John Marshall*. Princeton, N.J.: Princeton University Press, 1968.

Faust, Albert B. *The German Element in the United States*. 2 volumes. Boston: Houghton Mifflin, 1909.

Fischer, David H. *The Revolution of American Conservatism: The Federalist Party in the Age of Jeffersonian Democracy*. New York: Harper & Row, 1965.

Flanders, Ralph B. *Plantation Slavery in Georgia*. Chapel Hill: University of North Carolina Press, 1933.

Foster, William O. *James Jackson: Duellist and Militant Statesman, 1757–1806*. Athens: University of Georgia Press, 1960.

Fox, Dixon Ryan. *The Decline of Aristocracy in the Politics of New York, 1801–1840*. New York: Columbia University Press, 1919.

Gilpatrick, Delbert H. *Jeffersonian Democracy in North Carolina, 1789–1816*. New York: Columbia University Press, 1931.

Goodman, Paul. *The Democratic-Republicans of Massachusetts: Politics in a Young Republic*. Cambridge, Mass.: Harvard University Press, 1964.

Goodrich, Carter. *Government Promotion of American Canals and Railroads, 1800–1860*. New York: Columbia University Press, 1960.

Gray, Lewis C. *History of Agriculture in the Southern United States to 1860*. 2 volumes. Washington, D.C.: Carnegie Institution, 1933.

Green, Edwin L. *A History of Richland County*. Columbia: University of South Carolina Press, 1932.

———. *A History of the University of South Carolina*. Columbia, S.C.: State Company, 1916.

Green, Fletcher M. *Constitutional Development in the South Atlantic States, 1776–1860: A Study in the Evolution of Democracy*. Chapel Hill: University of North Carolina Press, 1930.

Gribbin, William. *The Churches Militant: The War of 1812 and American Religion*. New Haven, Conn.: Yale University Press, 1973.

Griffith, Louis T. and John E. Talmadge. *Georgia Journalism, 1763–1950*. Athens: University of Georgia Press, 1951.

Hamilton, Milton W. *The Country Printer: New York State, 1785–1830*. New York: Columbia University Press, 1936.

Hammond, Bray. *Banks and Politics in America: From the Revolution to the Civil War*. Princeton, N.J.: Princeton University Press, 1957.

Harrel, Isaac S. *Loyalism in Virginia: Chapters in the Economic History of the Revolution*. Durham, N.C.: Duke University Press, 1926.

Hatcher, William B. *Edward Livingston: Jeffersonian Republican and Jacksonian Democrat*. Baton Rouge: Louisiana State University Press, 1940.

Henderson, Dwight F. *Courts for a New Nation*. Washington, D.C.: Public Affairs Press, 1971.

Henderson, H. James. *Party Politics in the Continental Congress*. New York: McGraw-Hill, 1974.

Henry, Howell M. *The Police Contrôl of the Slave in South Carolina*. Nashville, Tenn.: Vanderbilt University Press, 1914.

Higginbotham, Sanford W. *The Keystone in the Democratic Arch: Pennsylvania Politics, 1800–1816*. Harrisburg: Pennsylvania Historical and Museum Commission, 1952.

Hoffman, William S. *Andrew Jackson and North Carolina Politics*. Chapel Hill: University of North Carolina Press, 1958.

Hofstadter, Richard. *The Idea of a Party System: The Rise of Legitimate Opposition in the United States, 1780–1840*. Berkeley and Los Angeles: University of California Press, 1969.

Hollis, Daniel W. *South Carolina College*. Vol. I of 2 vols., in *The University of South Carolina*. Columbia: University of South Carolina Press, 1951.

Horsman, Reginald. *The Causes of the War of 1812*. Philadelphia: University of Pennsylvania Press, 1962.

Hunter, Dard. *Papermaking in Pioneer America*. Philadelphia: University of Pennsylvania Press, 1952.

Irwin, Ray W. *The Diplomatic Relations of the United States with the Barbary Powers, 1776–1816*. Chapel Hill: University of North Carolina Press, 1931.

Jensen, Merrill. *The New Nation: A History of the United States During the Confederation, 1781–1789*. New York: Alfred A. Knopf, 1950.

Johnson, Guion G. *Ante-Bellum North Carolina: A Social History*. Chapel Hill: University of North Carolina Press, 1937.

Jordan, Winthrop D. *White Over Black: American Attitudes Toward the Negro, 1550–1812*. Chapel Hill: University of North Carolina Press, 1968.

Kerber, Linda K. *The Federalists in Dissent*. Ithaca, N.Y.: Cornell University Press, 1970.

Key, V. O. *Southern Politics in State and Nation*. New York: Alfred A. Knopf, 1949.

King, William L. *The Newspaper Press of Charleston, South Carolina*. Charleston, S.C.: E. Perry, 1872.

Kinney, Charles B., Jr. *Church and State: The Struggle for Separation in New Hampshire,*

1630–1900. New York: Columbia University Press, 1955.
Kurtz, Stephen G. *The Administration of John Adams: The Collapse of Federalism, 1795–1800*. Philadelphia: University of Pennsylvania Press, 1957.
Lefler, Hugh T. and Albert R. Newsome. *North Carolina: The History of a Southern State*. Rev. ed. Chapel Hill: University of North Carolina Press, 1963.
Lesesne, J. Mauldin. *The Bank of the State of South Carolina: A General and Political History*. Columbia: University of South Carolina Press, 1970.
Leyburn, James G. *The Scotch-Irish: A Social History*. Chapel Hill: University of North Carolina Press, 1962.
Livermore, Shaw. *The Twilight of Federalism: The Disintegration of the Federalist Party, 1815–1830*. Princeton, N.J.: Princeton University Press, 1962.
Lyon, William H. *The Pioneer Editor in Missouri, 1808–1860*. Columbia: University of Missouri Press, 1965.
Magrath, C. Peter. *Yazoo: Law and Politics in the New Republic: The Case of Fletcher v. Peck*. Providence, R.I.: Brown University Press, 1966.
Main, Jackson Turner. *The Antifederalists: Critics of the Constitution, 1781–1788*. Chapel Hill: University of North Carolina Press, 1961.
———. *Political Parties Before the Constitution*. Chapel Hill: University of North Carolina Press, 1973.
———. *The Social Structure of Revolutionary America*. Princeton: Princeton University Press, 1965.
———. *The Sovereign States, 1775–1783*. New York: Franklin Watts, 1973.
Malone, Dumas. *Jefferson the President: First Term, 1801–1805*. Boston: Little Brown, 1970.
———. *Jefferson the President: Second Term, 1805–1809*. Boston: Little Brown, 1974.
Manross, William W. *The Episcopal Church in the United States, 1800–1840: A Study in Church Life*. New York: Columbia University Press, 1938.
McColley, Robert. *Slavery and Jeffersonian Virginia*. Urbana: University of Illinois Press, 1964.
McDonald, Forrest. *We the People: The Economic Origins of the Constitution*. Chicago: University of Chicago Press, 1958.
Meyer, Duane G. *Highland Scots of North Carolina*. Chapel Hill: University of North Carolina Press, 1961.
Morrison, Alfred J. *The Beginnings of Public Education in Virginia 1776–1860: A Study of Secondary Schools in Relation to the State Literary Fund*. Richmond: State Board of Education, 1917.
Munroe, John A. *Federalist Delaware, 1775–1815*. New Brunswick, N.J.: Rutgers University Press, 1954.
Murray, Chalmers S. *This Our Land: The Story of the Agricultural Society of South Carolina*. Charleston: Carolina Art Association, 1949.
Murray, Paul. *The Whig Party in Georgia, 1825–1853*. Chapel Hill: University of North Carolina Press, 1948.
Nettels, Curtis P. *The Emergence of a National Economy, 1775–1815*. New York: Holt, Rinehart & Winston, 1962.
Nevins, Allan. *The American States During and After the Revolution, 1775–1789*. New York: Macmillan, 1924.
Newsome, Albert R. *The Presidential Election of 1824 in North Carolina*. Chapel Hill: University of North Carolina Press, 1939.
O'Neall, John B., *Biographical Sketches of the Bench and Bar of South Carolina*. 2 volumes. Charleston, S.C.: S. G. Courtenay, 1859.

Orr, Dorothy. *A History of Education in Georgia*. Chapel Hill: University of North Carolina Press, 1950.
Pasler, Rudolph J. and Margaret C. Pasler. *The New Jersey Federalists*. Rutherford, N.J.: Fairleigh Dickinson University Press, 1975.
Perkins, Bradford. *Prologue to War: England and the United States, 1805–1812*. Berkeley and Los Angeles: University of California Press, 1961.
Phillips, Ulrich B. *American Negro Slavery*. New York: Appleton and Company, 1918.
———. *Georgia and State Rights*. Washington, D.C.: Government Printing Office, 1902.
Porter, Albert O. *County Government in Virginia: A Legislative History, 1607–1904*. New York: Columbia University Press, 1947.
Prince, Carl E. *New Jersey's Jeffersonian Republicans: The Genesis of an Early Party Machine, 1789–1817*. Chapel Hill: University of North Carolina Press, 1967.
Purcell, Richard J. *Connecticut in Transition: 1775–1818*. Rev. ed. Middletown, Conn.: Wesleyan University Press, 1963.
Quincy, Edmund. *Life of Josiah Quincy of Massachusetts*. Boston: Ticknor & Fields, 1867.
Rice, Madeleine H. *American Catholic Opinion in the Slavery Controversy*. New York: Columbia University Press, 1944.
Rice, Otis K. *The Allegheny Frontier: West Virginia Beginnings, 1730–1830*. Lexington: University of Kentucky Press, 1970.
Rice, Stuart. *Quantitative Methods in Politics*. New York: F. S. Crofts, 1928.
Risjord, Norman K. *The Old Republicans: Southern Conservatism in the Age of Jefferson*. New York: Columbia University Press, 1965.
Robert, Joseph C. *The Tobacco Kingdom: Plantation, Market, and Factory in Virginia and North Carolina, 1800–1860*. Durham, N.C.: Duke University Press, 1938.
Robinson, Blackwell P. *William R. Davie*. Chapel Hill: University of North Carolina Press, 1957.
Robinson, William A. *Jeffersonian Democracy in New England*. New Haven, Conn.: Yale University Press 1916.
Rogers, George C. *Evolution of a Federalist: William Loughton Smith of Charleston, 1758–1812*. Columbia: University of South Carolina Press, 1962.
Rose, Lisle A. *Prologue to Democracy: The Federalists in the South, 1789–1800*. Lexington: University of Kentucky Press, 1968.
Rutland, Robert A. *The Ordeal of the Constitution: The Antifederalists and the Ratification Struggle of 1787–1788*. Norman: University of Oklahoma Press, 1966.
Schaper, William A. *Sectionalism and Representation in South Carolina*. Washington, D.C.: American Historical Association, 1901.
Schauinger, Joseph H. *William Gaston, Carolinian*. Milwaukee, Wis.: Bruce Publishing Company, 1949.
Sears, Louis M. *Jefferson and the Embargo*. Durham, N.C.: Duke University Press, 1927.
Singer, Charles G. *South Carolina in the Confederation*. Philadelphia: University of Pennsylvania Press, 1941.
Smith, James Morton. *Freedom's Fetters: The Alien and Sedition Laws and American Civil Liberties*. Ithaca, N.Y.: Cornell University Press, 1956.
Stampp, Kenneth M. *The Peculiar Institution: Slavery in the Ante-Bellum South*. New York: Alfred A. Knopf, 1956.
Stewart, Donald H. *The Opposition Press of the Federalist Period*. Albany: State University of New York Press, 1969.
Strickland, Reba C. *Religion and the State in Georgia in the Eighteenth Century*. New York: Columbia University Press, 1939.
Sydnor, Charles S. *The Development of Southern Sectionalism, 1819–1848*. Baton Rouge:

Louisiana State University Press, 1948.
———. *Gentlemen Freeholders: Political Practices in Washington's Virginia*. Chapel Hill: University of North Carolina Press, 1952.
Taylor, Rosser H. *Ante-Bellum South Carolina: A Social and Cultural History*. Chapel Hill: University of North Carolina Press, 1942.
———. *Slaveholding in North Carolina: An Economic View*. Chapel Hill: University of North Carolina Press, 1926.
Thompson, Ernest Trice. *Presbyterians in the South*, Vol. I of 3 vols. *1607–1861*. Richmond, Va.: John Knox Press, 1963.
Trenholme, Louise Irby. *The Ratification of the Federal Constitution in North Carolina*. New York: Columbia University Press, 1932.
Van Doren, Carl. *The Great Rehearsal* New York: Viking Press, 1948.
Varg, Paul A. *Foreign Policies of the Founding Fathers*. East Lansing: Michigan State University Press, 1963.
Wallace, David Duncan. *The Historical Background of Religion in South Carolina*. n.p., n.d. [1917].
Walters, Raymond, Jr. *Albert Gallatin: Jeffersonian Financier and Diplomat*. New York: Macmillan, 1957.
Ware, Ethel K. *A Constitutional History of Georgia*. New York: Columbia University Press, 1947.
Warren, Charles. *The Supreme Court in United States History*. 2 volumes. Rev. ed. Boston: Little, Brown, 1947.
Welter, Rush. *Popular Education and Democratic Thought in America*. New York: Columbia University Press, 1962.
Whitaker, Arthur P. *The Mississippi Question, 1795–1803: A Study in Trade, Politics, and Diplomacy*. New York: Appleton-Century, 1934.
White, Leonard D. *The Federalists: A Study in Administrative History, 1789–1801*. New York: Macmillan, 1948.
Williamson, Chilton. *American Suffrage: From Property to Democracy, 1760–1860*. Princeton, N.J.: Princeton University Press, 1960.
Wolfe, John Harold. *Jeffersonian Democracy in South Carolina*. Chapel Hill: University of North Carolina Press, 1940.
Wust, Klaus G. *The Virginia Germans*. Charlottesville: University Press of Virginia, 1969.
Zahniser, Marvin R. *Charles Cotesworth Pinckney: Founding Father*. Chapel Hill: University of North Carolina Press, 1967.

Articles and Essays

Abbot, William W. "The Structure of Politics in Georgia, 1782—1789." *William and Mary Quarterly*, Third Series, XIV (1957), 47—65.
American Council of Learned Societies. "Report of Committee on Linguistic and National Stocks in the Population of the United States." *Annual Report for 1931*. Washington, D.C.: American Historical Association, 1932.
Ammon, Harry. "James Monroe and the Election of 1808 in Virginia." *William and Mary Quarterly*, Third Series, XX (1963), 33–56.
———. "The Richmond Junto, 1800–1824." *Virginia Magazine of History and Biography*, LXI (1953), 395–418.
Anderson, J. Perrin. "Public Education in Ante-Bellum South Carolina." *South Carolina Historical Association Proceedings*, III (1933), 3–11.
Arena, C. Richard. "Philadelphia-Mississippi Valley Trade and the Deposit Closure of 1802." *Pennsylvania History*, XXX (1963), 28–45.

Bacon-Foster, Corra. "Early Chapters in the Development of the Potomac Route to the West." *Records of the Columbia Historical Society*, XV (1912), 96–322.

Bacot, D. Huger. "The South Carolina Up Country at the End of the Eighteenth Century." *American Historical Review*, XXVIII (1928), 682–98.

Bertier de Sauvigny, Guillaume de. "The American Press and the Fall of Napoleon in 1814." *Proceedings of the American Philosophical Society*, XCVIII (1954), 337–76.

Boyd, William K. "Currency and Banking in North Carolina, 1790–1836." *Trinity College Historical Society Papers*, X (1914), 52–86.

Carter, Edward C., II. "A 'Wild Irishman' Under Every Federalist's Bed: Naturalization in Philadelphia, 1789–1806." *Pennsylvania Magazine of History and Biography*, XCIV (1970), 331–46.

Cometti, Elizabeth. "John Rutledge, Jr., Federalist." *Journal of Southern History*, XIII (1947), 186–219.

Cowan, George S., Jr. "Chief Justice John Rutledge and the Jay Treaty." *South Carolina Historical Magazine*, LXII (1961), 10–23.

Crane, Wilder, Jr. "A Caveat on Roll-Call Studies of Party Voting." *Midwest Journal of Political Science*, IV (1960), 237–49.

Daniels, G. W. "American Cotton Trade with Liverpool Under the Embargo and Non-Intercourse Acts." *American Historical Review*, XXI (1916), 276–87.

East, Robert A. "Economic Development and New England Federalism, 1803–1814." *New England Quarterly*, X (1937), 430–66.

Egan, Clifford L. "The United States, France, and West Florida, 1803–1807." *Florida Historical Quarterly*, XLVII (1969), 227–52.

Elkins, Stanley and Eric McKitrick. "The Founding Fathers: Young Men of the Revolution." *Political Science Quarterly*, LXXXI (1961), 181–216.

Epting, Carl L. "Inland Navigation in South Carolina and Traffic on the Columbia River." *South Carolina Historical Association Proceedings*, VI (1936), 18–28.

Farnham, Thomas J. "The Virginia Amendments of 1795: An Episode in the Opposition to Jay's Treaty." *Virginia Magazine of History and Biography*, LXXV (1967), 75–88.

Faulkner, Robert K. "John Marshall and the Burr Trial." *Journal of American History*, LIII (1966), 247–58.

Ferguson, Eugene S. "Mr. Jefferson's Dry Docks." *American Neptune*, XI (1951), 108–15.

Galpin, W. Freeman. "The American Grain Trade Under the Embargo of 1808." *Journal of Economic and Business History*, II (1929), 71–100.

Goodman, Paul. "Social Status of Party Leadership: The House of Representatives, 1797–1804." *William and Mary Quarterly*, Third Series, XXV (1968), 465–74.

Goodrich, Carter. "The Virginia System of Mixed Enterprise: A Study of State Planning of Internal Improvements." *Political Science Quarterly*, LXIV (1949), 355–87.

Govan, Thomas P. "Banking and the Credit System in Georgia, 1810–1860." *Journal of Southern History*, IV (1938), 164–84.

———. "John M. Berrien and the Administration of Andrew Jackson." *Journal of Southern History*, V (1939), 447–67.

Green, Fletcher M. "Georgia's Board of Public Works, 1817–1826." *Georgia Historical Quarterly*, XXII (1938), 117–37.

Griffin, Richard W. "An Origin of the New South: The South Carolina Homespun Company, 1807–1815." *Business History Review*, XXXV (1961), 402–15.

Grumm, John G. "The Means of Measuring Conflict and Cohesion in the Legislature." *Southwestern Social Science Quarterly*, LXIV (1964), 377–88.

Haller, Mark H. "The Rise of the Jackson Party in Maryland, 1820–1829." *Journal of Southern History*, XXVIII (1962), 307–26.

Harrison, Joseph H., Jr. "Oligarchs and Democrats: The Richmond Junto." *Virginia Magazine of History and Biography*, LXXVIII (1970), 184–98.

Hatzenbuehler, Ronald L. "Party Unity and the Vote for War in the House of Representatives, 1812." *William and Mary Quarterly*, Third Series, XXIX (1972), 367–90.

Heaton, Herbert. "Non-Importation, 1807–1812." *Journal of Economic History*, I (1941), 178–98.

Henderson, Archibald. "A Federalist of the Old School." *North Carolina Booklet*, XVII (1917), 3–38.

Henderson, Elizabeth K. "The Attack on the Judiciary in Pennsylvania, 1800–1810." *Pennsylvania Magazine of History and Biography*, LXI (1937), 113–36.

Henderson, H. James. "Quantitative Approaches to Party Formation in the United States Congress: A Comment." *William and Mary Quarterly*, Third Series, XXX (1973), 307–24.

Henneman, J. B. "Trustees of Hampden-Sydney College." *Virginia Magazine of History and Biography*, VI (1898–99), 174–84.

Henshaw, Clifford R. "North Carolina Canals Before 1860." *North Carolina Historical Review*, XXV (1948), 1–56.

Hodges, Wiley E. "Pro-Governmentalism in Virginia, 1789–1836: A Pragmatic Liberal Pattern in the Political Heritage." *Journal of Politics*, XXV (1963), 333–60.

Howe, John R., Jr. "Republican Thought and the Polical Violence of the 1790's." *American Quarterly*, XIX (1967), 147–65.

Ireland, Owen S. "The Ethnic-Religious Dimensions of Pennsylvania Politics, 1778–1779." *William and Mary Quarterly*, Third Series, XXX (1973), 423–48.

Kaminski, John P. "Controversy Amid Consensus: The Adoption of the Federal Constitution in Georgia." *Georgia Historical Quarterly*, LVIII (1974), 244–61.

Knudson, Jerry W. "Newspaper Reaction to the Louisiana Purchase: 'This New, Immense, Unbounded World.'" *Missouri Historical Review*, LXIII (1969), 182–213.

———. "The Rage Around Tom Paine: Newspaper Reaction to His Homecoming in 1802." *New-York Historical Society Quarterly*, LIII (1969), 34–63.

Lambert, Robert S. "The Confiscation of Loyalist Property in Georgia, 1782–1786." *William and Mary Quarterly*, Third Series, XX (1963), 80–94.

Latimer, Margaret K. "South Carolina: A Protagonist of the War of 1812." *American Historical Review*, LXI (1956), 914–29.

Lemmon, Sarah M. "Dissent in North Carolina During the War of 1812." *North Carolina Historical Review*, LXIX (1972), 108–18.

Lerche, Charles O., Jr. "Jefferson and the Election of 1800: A Case Study in the Political Smear." *William and Mary Quarterly*, Third Series, V (1948), 467–91.

Lillich, Richard B. "The Chase Impeachment." *American Journal of Legal History*, IV (1960), 49–72.

Lycan, Gilbert L. "Alexander Hamilton and the North Carolina Federalists." *North Carolina Historical Review*, XXV (1948), 442–65.

Main, Jackson Turner. "Sections and Politics in Virginia, 1781–1787." *William and Mary Quarterly*, Third Series, XII (1955), 96–112.

McCormick, Richard P. "Party Formation in New Jersey in the Jackson Era." *Proceedings of the New Jersey Historical Society*, LXXXIII (1965), 161–73.

———. "Suffrage Classes and Party Alignments: A Study in Voter Behavior." *Mississippi Valley Historical Review*, XLVI (1959), 397–410.

McFarland, Daniel W. "North Carolina Newspapers, Editors, and Journalistic Politics, 1815–1835." *North Carolina Historical Review*, XXX (1953), 376–414.

Morgan, William G. "The Congressional Nominating Caucuses of 1816: The Struggle

Against the Virginia Dynasty." *Virginia Magazine of History and Biography*, LXXX (1972), 461–75.

Morison, Samuel Eliot. "The First National Nominating Convention." *American Historical Review*, XVII (1912), 744–65.

Morrison, A. J. "Note on the Organization of Virginia Agriculture." *William and Mary Quarterly*, First Series, XXVI (1917–18), 169–73.

Murdock, John S. "The First National Nominating Convention." *American Historical Review*, I (1896), 680–84.

Padover, Saul K. "The Political Ideas of John Marshall." *Social Research*, XXVI (1959), 47–70.

Pancake, John S. "'The Invisibles:' A Chapter in the Opposition to President Madison." *Journal of Southern History*, XXI (1955), 17–37.

Perry, Percival. "The Naval-Stores Industry in the Old South, 1790–1860." *Journal of Southern History*, XXXIV (1968), 509–26.

Pfifer, Edward W. "Money, Banking, and Burke County in the Ante-Bellum Era." *North Carolina Historical Review*, XXXVII (1960), 22–37.

Phillips, Ulrich B. "The South Carolina Federalists." *American Historical Review*, XIV (1909), 529–43, 731–43.

Pole, J. R. "Representation and Authority in Virginia from the Revolution to Reform." *Journal of Southern History*, XXIV (1958), 16–50.

Pool, William C. "An Economic Interpretation of the Ratification of the Federal Constitution in North Carolina." *North Carolina Historical Review*, XXVII (1950), 119–41, 289–313, 437–61.

Preyer, Norris W. "Southern Support of the Tariff of 1816: A Reappraisal." *Journal of Southern History*, XXV (1959), 306–22.

Prince, Carl E. "The Passing of the Aristocracy: Jefferson's Removal of the Federalists, 1801–1805." *Journal of American History*, LVII (1970), 563–75.

Pyburn, Nita K. "The Public School System of Charleston Before 1860." *South Carolina Historical Magazine*, LXI (1960), 86–98.

Rice, Otis K. "West Virginia Printers and Their Work, 1790–1830." *West Virginia History*, XIV (1953), 197–338.

Richards, Leonard L. "John Adams and the Moderate Federalists: The Cape Fear as a Test Case." *North Carolina Historical Review*, XLIII (1966), 14–30.

Risjord, Norman K. "How the 'Common Man' Voted in Jefferson's Virginia," in John B. Boles, ed., *America: The Middle Period; Essays in Honor of Bernard Mayo*. Charlottesville: University Press of Virginia, 1973, pp. 36–64.

———. "The Virginia Federalists." *Journal of Southern History*, XXXIII (1967), 486–517.

———. "Virginians and the Constitution: A Multivariant Analysis." *William and Mary Quarterly*, Third Series, XXXI (1974), 613–32.

Risjord, Norman K. and Gordon DenBoer. "The Evolution of Political Parties in Virginia, 1782–1800." *Journal of American History*, LX (1974), 961–84.

Roll, Charles W. "We, Some of the People: Apportionment in the Thirteen State Conventions Ratifying the Constitution." *Journal of American History*, LVI (1969), 21–40.

Scanlon, James E. "A Sudden Conceit: Jefferson and the Louisiana Government Bill of 1804." *Louisiana History*, IX (1968), 139–62.

Sellers, Charles G. "Who Were the Southern Whigs?" *American Historical Review*, LIX (1954), 335–46.

Smith, C. Jay, Jr. "John Macpherson Berrien," in Horace Montgomery, ed. *Georgians in Profile: Historical Essays in Honor of Ellis Merton Coulter*. Athens: University of Georgia Press, 1958, pp. 168–191.

Standard, Diffie and Richard W. Griffin. "The Cotton Textile Industry in Ante-Bellum North Carolina." *North Carolina Historical Review*, XXXIV (1957), 15–35.

Steel, Anthony. "Impressment in the Monroe-Pinkney Negotiation, 1806–1807." *American Historical Review*, LVII (1952), 352–69.

Talmadge, John E. "Georgia's Federalist Press and the War of 1812." *Journal of Southern History*, XIX (1953), 488–500.

Thomas, Robert E. "The Virginia Convention of 1788: A Criticism of Beard's *An Economic Interpretation of the Constitution*." *Journal of Southern History*, XIX (1953), 63–72.

Thornton, Mary Lindsay. "Public Printing in North Carolina, 1749–1815." *North Carolina Historical Review*, XXI (1944), 181–202.

Turlington, S. Baily. "Richmond During the War of 1812: The Vigilance Committee." *Virginia Magazine of History and Biography*, VII (1900), 225–41.

Turner, Charles W. "Virginia Agricultural Reform, 1815–1860." *Agricultural History*, XXVI (1952), 80–89.

Turner, Kathryn. "Federalist Policy and the Judiciary Act of 1801." *William and Mary Quarterly*, Third Series, XXII (1965), 3–32.

Turner, Lynn W. "The Impeachment of John Pickering." *American Historical Review*, LIV (1946), 485–507.

Upton, Anthony F. "The Road to Power in Virginia in the Early Nineteenth Century." *Virginia Magazine of History and Biography*, LXII (1954), 259–80.

Vinson, John Chalmers. "Electioneering in the South, 1800–1840." *Georgia Review*, X (1956), 265–73.

Walters, Raymond, Jr. "The Origins of the Second Bank of the United States." *Journal of Political Economy*, LIII (1945), 115–31.

Wehtje, Myron F. "The Congressional Elections of 1799 in Virginia." *West Virginia History*, XXIX (1968), 251–73.

———. "Opposition in Virginia to the War of 1812." *Virginia Magazine of History and Biography*, LXXVIII (1970), 65–86.

Williams, Max R. "The Foundations of the Whig Party in North Carolina." *North Carolina Historical Review*, XLVII (1970), 115–29.

Woodfin, Maude H. "Contemporary Opinion in Virginia of Thomas Jefferson," in Avery Craven, ed. *Essays in Honor of William E. Dodd*. Chicago: University of Chicago Press, 1935, pp. 30–85.

Wyatt, Edward A., IV. "George Keith Taylor, 1769–1815, Virginia Federalist and Humanitarian." *William and Mary Quarterly*, Second Series, XVI (1936), 1–18.

Wynes, Charles E. "Banking in Virginia, 1789–1820." *Essays in History*, IV (1957), 35–50.

Dissertations and Theses

Abbot, William W., III. "The Structure of Politics in Georgia, 1782–1789." M.A. thesis, Duke University, 1950.

Allen, Carlos Richard, Jr. "The Great Revival in Virginia, 1783–1812." M.A. thesis, University of Virginia, 1948.

Ammon, Harry. "The Republican Party in Virginia, 1789 to 1824." Ph.D. dissertation, University of Virginia, 1948.

Averitt, Jack N. "The Democratic Party in Georgia, 1824–1837." Ph.D. dissertation, University of North Carolina, 1957.

Bachelder, Horace L. "The Presidential Election of 1824 in Virginia." M.A. thesis, Duke University, 1942.

Barber, William DeArmond. "The West in National Politics: 1784–1804." Ph.D. dissertation, University of Wisconsin, 1961.
Barlow, William R. "Congress During the War of 1812." Ph.D. dissertation, Ohio State University, 1961.
Barnwell, Robert W., Jr. "Loyalism in South Carolina, 1765–1785." Ph.D. dissertation, Duke University, 1941.
Brownsword, Alan W. "Connecticut Political Patterns, 1817–1828." Ph.D. dissertation, University of Wisconsin, 1962.
Cubbison, Mary Paige. "The Virginia Antifederalists: A Summary View, September 1786–May 1788." M.A. thesis, Duke University, 1961.
DesChamps, Margaret B. "The Presbyterian Church in the South Atlantic States, 1801–1861." Ph.D. dissertation, Emory University, 1952.
Dickinson, Elmer G. "The Influence of Sectionalism upon the History of the James River and Kanawha Company in West Virginia." M.A. thesis, Duke University, 1946.
Dunaway, Wayland F. "Charles Fenton Mercer." M.A. thesis, University of Chicago, 1917.
Dunson, Linton R., Jr. "Early Manifestations of Anti-Nationalism in Georgia, 1787–1838." Ph.D. dissertation, University of Virginia, 1969.
Egan, Clifford L. "Franco-American Relations, 1803–1814." Ph.D. dissertation, University of Colorado, 1969.
Flanagan, Beecher. "A History of State Banking in North Carolina to 1866." Ph.D. dissertation, George Peabody University, 1935.
Fritz, Harry W. "The Collapse of Party: President, Congress, and the Decline of Party Action, 1807–1817." Ph.D. dissertation, Washington University of St. Louis, 1971.
Gaines, Edwin. "Outrageous Encounter: The Chesapeake-Leopard Affair of 1807." Ph.D. dissertation, University of Virginia, 1960.
Hatzenbuehler, Ronald L. "Foreign Policy Voting in the United States Congress, 1808–1812." Ph.D. dissertation, Kent State University, 1972.
Hickey, Donald Robert. "The Federalists and the War of 1812." Ph.D. dissertation, University of Illinois, 1972.
Hood, Fred J. "Presbyterianism and the New American Nation, 1783–1826: A Case Study of Religion and National Life." Ph.D. dissertation, Princeton University, 1968.
Koesy, Sheldon F. "Continuity and Change in North Carolina, 1775–1789." Ph.D. dissertation, Duke University, 1963.
Kuehl, John W. "The Quest for Identity in an Age of Insecurity: The XYZ Affair and American Nationalism." Ph.D. dissertation, University of Wisconsin, 1968.
Kuroda, Tadahisa. "The County Court System of Virginia From the Revolution to the Civil War." Ph.D. dissertation, Columbia University, 1969.
Lacy, Alexander B., Jr. "Jefferson and Congress: Congressional Methods and Politics, 1801–1809." Ph.D. dissertation, University of Virginia, 1964.
Lamplugh, George R. "Politics on the Periphery: Factions and Parties in Georgia, 1776–1806." Ph.D. dissertation, Emory University, 1973.
Lander, Ernest McPherson. "Manufacturing in Ante-Bellum South Carolina." Ph.D. dissertation, University of North Carolina, 1950.
Lowery, Charles D. "James Barbour, A Politician and Planter of Ante-Bellum Virginia." Ph.D. dissertation, University of Virginia, 1966.
MacPhee, Donald A. "The *Tertium Quid* Movement: A Study in Political Insurgency." Ph.D. dissertation, University of California at Berkeley, 1959.

McCarrell, David K. "The Formation of the Jeffersonian Party in Virginia." Ph.D. dissertation, Duke University, 1937.

McFarland, Daniel M. "Rip Van Winkle: Political Evolution in North Carolina, 1815–1835." Ph.D. dissertation, University of Pennsylvania, 1954.

Mendenhall, Marjorie S. "A History of Agriculture in South Carolina, 1790–1860: An Economic and Social Study." Ph.D. dissertation, University of North Carolina, 1940.

Mitchell, Peter M. "Loyalist Property and the Revolution in Virginia." Ph.D. dissertation, University of Colorado, 1965.

Mitchell, Robert G. "Loyalist Georgia." Ph.D. dissertation, Tulane University, 1964.

Moore, William G. "Economic Coercion as a Policy of the United States, 1794–1805." Ph.D. dissertation, University of Alabama, 1960.

Morgan, William G. "Presidential Nominations in the Federal Era, 1788–1826." Ph.D. dissertation, University of Southern California, 1969.

Nance, Joseph M. "The Attitude of New England Toward Western Expansion, 1800–1850." Ph.D. dissertation, University of Texas, 1941.

Nielsen, George R. "The Indispensable Institution: The Congressional Party During the Era of Good Feelings." Ph.D. dissertation, University of Iowa, 1968.

Ohline, Howard H. "Politics and Slavery: The Issue of Slavery in National Politics, 1787–1815." Ph.D. dissertation, University of Missouri, 1969.

Rice, Philip M. "Internal Improvements in Virginia, 1775–1860." Ph.D. dissertation, University of North Carolina, 1950.

Rich, Myra L. "The Experimental Years: Virginia, 1781–1789." Ph.D. dissertation, Yale University, 1966.

Russo, David L. "The Southern Republicans and American Political Nationalism, 1815–1825." Ph.D. dissertation, Yale University, 1966.

Stamps, Norman L. "Political Parties in Connecticut, 1789–1819." Ph.D. dissertation, Yale University, 1950.

Starr, Raymond G. "The Conservative Revolution: South Carolina Public Affairs, 1775–1790." Ph.D. dissertation, University of Texas, 1964.

Sutton, Robert P. "The Virginia Constitutional Convention of 1829–30: A Profile Analysis of Late-Jeffersonian Virginia." Ph.D. dissertation, University of Virginia, 1967.

Townshend, Leah. "Baptists in South Carolina." Ph.D. dissertation, University of South Carolina, 1929.

Turhollow, Anthony F. "The Struggle for the Recharter of the First Bank of the United States: A Study in Early American Politics." Ph.D. dissertation, University of California at Berkeley, 1955.

Ulmer, Shirley Sidney. "The South Carolina Delegates to the Constitutional Convention of 1787: An Analytical Study." Ph.D. dissertation, Duke University, 1956.

Upton, Anthony Frederick. "Political Structure of Virginia, 1790–1830." M.A. thesis, Duke University, 1953.

Wagner, Edward J., II. "State-Federal Relations During the War of 1812." Ph.D. dissertation, Ohio State University, 1963.

White, Patrick C. T. "Anglo-American Relations from 1803 to 1815." Ph.D. dissertation, University of Minnesota, 1954.

Whitehurst, George William. "The Commerce of Virginia, 1789–1815." M.A. thesis, University of Virginia, 1951.

Wild, Philip F. "South Carolina Politics: 1816–1833." Ph.D. dissertation, University of Pennsylvania, 1949.

INDEX

A

Accomac County, Va., 145
Adams, John: in 1796 election, 13, 235, 248, 252; policies of, 14–15, 17, 46–47, 51–53, 65, 385–86; in 1800 election, 17–27, 29–32, 80, 107, 215, 259, 263; support for, 87, 108, 237, 368, 376; mentioned, 3, 43, 63, 66–69, 81–82, 115–16, 141, 147, 153, 202, 222, 247, 249, 253, 287, 310, 366, 369
Adams, John Quincy, 191–94
Age: of Federalist leaders, 274; and party affiliation, 388–90
Agriculture, 5, 140, 356–58
Albemarle-Pamlico region, N.C., 216, 382
Alexander, Evan, 232
Alexander, Nathaniel, 219, 232
Alexandria, D.C., 5, 200, 334–35
Alien and Sedition Acts, 15, 20, 30, 36–37, 87, 91, 247, 255
Allegheny Mountains, 145, 258, 392
Alston, William, 384
Alves, Gavin, 326
Alves, Walter, 21
Ames, Fisher, 18
Amherst County, Va., 209–10
Andrews, Loring, 283–84
Anson County, N.C., 371
Antifederalists, 9–10, 365–66
Apportionment, 151, 204, 209–11, 224, 226–28, 235, 244–46
Arator. *See* Taylor, John, of Caroline
Army, 20, 45, 87, 127, 135, 183–88
Articles of Confederation, 8–9, 365
Assumption Bill, 235
Augusta, Ga.: economy of, 5, 348, 352; politics in, 27, 77*n*, 249–51, 258, 271, 273, 377–78; mentioned, 252, 254, 331
Augusta County, Va., 145–46, 267, 356
Augusta Herald: on domestic politics, 104–105, 120, 169–70, 251, 365; on foreign affairs, 127, 170; in state affairs, 255–56, 273; on economics, 333–34, 348, 352–53; mentioned, 249, 253, 280, 291
Austin, William, 24, 263

B

Baltimore *Federal Republican*, 156
Baltimore massacre, 156–57
Bank of the United States: First, 10, 36, 116–18, 237, 332–33, 348, 379; Second, 183–90, 332–34
Barbary War, 69–71
Baring Brothers, 64
Barnwell district, S.C., 239
Bayard, James A., 385
Beaufort, S.C., 31, 242, 373, 377–80
Bedford County, Va., 370
Bedinger, Henry, 154
Bee, Thomas, 357

Berceau incident, 63–65, 74
Berkeley and Jefferson Intelligencer, 317, 352
Berkeley County, Va., 176, 266–67
Berlin and Milan decrees, 129–30, 156
Berrien, John Macpherson, 90, 104, 181, 192–94, 254–55, 322
Beverly, Carter, 162
Bill of Rights, 9–10, 365
Blackledge, William, 133
Blanding, Abraham, 355
Blount, John Gray, 26
Blount, William, 26
Blue Ridge Mountains, 166–67, 200–203, 209–10, 213, 301–302, 372
Bonus Bill, 184
Botetourt County, Va., 176, 265–67
Boylan, Abraham H., 179
Boylan, William: as party organizer, 249–50, 269, 291; as editor, 280–82, 287–89. *See also* Raleigh *Minerva*
Breckinridge, James, 73, 127, 167, 176, 265–66
Britain: and American foreign policy, 12–13, 76–78, 379–80; and France, 60, 130–31, 164; in American politics, 68, 123, 132, 370; Federalists and, 72–73, 88, 124–26, 128–29, 136–37, 162; and American commerce, 73, 75–76, 96, 123–24, 127–29, 156; in War of 1812, pp. 140, 168; mentioned, 146
Browne, Peter, 150
Buncombe County, N.C., 288
Burr, Aaron, 32–35, 81, 110–14, 250
Butler, Pierce, 236

C

Cabell, Joseph C., 328
Cadore letter, 130–31
Caldwell, Elias B., 260
Calhoun, John C., 183–84, 188, 190
Callender, James T., 66–67, 81
Camden, S.C., 348, 377
Cameron, Duncan, 90, 118, 149, 222, 231, 270, 356
Cameron, John A., 149, 182
Campbell, S.L., 116
Canada, invasion of, 136, 140, 158–61, 168, 171, 174
Cape Fear Valley, 30, 216–18, 371, 398–99
Carnes, Thomas P., 252, 254–55
Carolina Federal Republican, 117, 133, 148, 165, 179
Carolina Weekly Messenger, 97, 284
Carrington, Edward, 112, 328
Catawba River, 371
Census data, 395
Century of Population Growth, 397
Charleston, S.C.: economy of, 5, 53, 96, 123, 332, 346–47, 351–53; politics of, 19, 31, 76–77, 89, 124, 142, 159–60, 242–43, 283–85, 371, 373, 377–78, 380; elections in, 26–27, 83, 85, 102, 105, 152–53, 165, 168–69, 175, 236–38, 271–72; mentioned, 18, 50, 74, 246, 258, 275, 291, 326–27
Charleston *City Gazette*, 152
Charleston Courier: on foreign affairs, 58, 60, 71, 73, 78, 122–23; on domestic politics, 65, 102, 115, 118, 144, 152, 165, 272; in War of 1812, pp. 155–56, 162, 169, 170; history of, 283–84, 290–91; on social issues, 309, 312, 315, 330; on economic policy, 352; mentioned, 74–75, 271
Chase, Samuel, impeachment of, 50–51
Chatham County, Ga., 249–51, 377
Chatham County, N.C., 330
Chesapeake Bay, 159
Chesapeake affair, 76–78, 125
Chesterfield district, S.C., 239
Chisholm v. *Georgia*, 248
Christ Church Parish, S.C., 238
Civil liberties, 15, 122, 156–57, 174
Civil service, 43–47, 118
Clark, John, 252–53
Clarke County, Ga., 252
Clarksburg, Va., 77*n*
Clay, Henry, 183–84, 188, 190–93
Clayton, Augustin S., 193, 252
Clinton, DeWitt, 141–46, 148–53, 178–79, 216, 269
Clinton, George, 62–63, 97–98, 260
Coleman, William, 283
Coleraine, treaty of, 248
Colhoun, John, 49
Colston, Edward, 176, 182, 184, 186, 189
Columbia, S.C., 5, 31, 77*n*, 142, 242, 327, 348, 377–78
Commerce: in South, 5, 56, 334–35, 341,

350; French interference with, 14, 53, 71–72, 136; and European war, 68, 74–75, 121, 126–29, 136, 146, 178, 379–80; Spanish interference with, 70; and embargo, 96, 107–108, 134; British interference with, 123–24, 164, 174; and Macon's Bill, 126–27; Federalists and, 146, 249, 332, 379–80
Congress: elects president, 34–35; and Judiciary Act, 35, 47–49; investigates Adams administration, 46–47; and impeachments, 49–51; and Louisiana, 61; and embargo, 78; and James Wilkinson, 113–15; and First Bank of United States, 117–18; and Jackson affair, 125–26; and War of 1812, pp. 127–28, 131, 134–37, 141–42; and Seamen's Bill, 158; and postwar nationalism, 183–89, 333; Federalist unity in, 362
Conservatism, 8–9, 11–12, 22
Constitutions, state, 8, 181, 209–11, 228
Constitutions, U.S.: ratification of, 9–10, 247, 365–69; Federalists and, 55, 308–309; Twelfth Amendment to, 61–63, 67; mentioned, 199, 200, 214
Corbin, Francis, 99–100, 160
County courts, 200–201
Coxe, Tench, 65
Crafts, William, 175, 192
Craig, John, 176
Craven County, N.C., 149
Crawford, William H., 177–78, 191–93
Culpepper, John, 78, 86, 121, 166, 176, 180
Cumberland County, N.C., 149, 371
Custis, George W. P., 358

D

Darlington district, S.C., 239
Davie, William R.: career of, 17, 26, 85, 89, 216, 221; on domestic politics, 34, 36, 39, 58, 399; on War of 1812, pp. 137–40, 162; in 1812 election, 146–47, 261, 376; in education, 322, 324; in economic development, 351, 355–57; mentioned, 172, 260, 331
Davies, Joseph, 143
Davis, Augustine, 157. See also *Virginia Gazette; Virginia Patriot*
Debt, national, 20, 87, 156, 183
DeKalb, Baron, 312
Democracy, 8, 194–95, 307–10
Demography and politics, 4, 211–12, 217–18, 279, 388–401
DeSaussure, Henry William: career of, 44, 90, 259, 261, 273, 283; on suffrage, 311; in education, 327; mentioned, 331
Detroit, Mich., 140
Dickens, Samuel, 175–76, 186
District of Columbia, 317
Doddridge, Philip, 328, 335
Dooly, John M., 104–105, 132, 192–93, 252, 254, 381
Drayton, William, 193, 357
Drew, William, 343

E

Eastern Shore, Va., 24, 29, 85, 133, 145–47, 167, 171, 176, 200–203, 258, 265–67, 291, 370–72
Economy: southern, 5–6, 58; as political issue, 20, 87–88, 134; effect of embargo on, 95–96, 107, 121–22, 219–20
Economics and party alignment, 22, 55, 217–18, 238, 375–87
Edenton, N.C., 5, 123, 330, 343–44, 378
Edenton Gazette, 123, 285
Edgefield district, S.C., 242
Electioneering, 7, 258
Election laws and procedures: in South, 7*n*, 23–28, 263, 279; in Virginia, 30, 84, 98–99, 144, 147–48, 202–203, 263–64; U.S., 61–63; in North Carolina, 101, 148–51, 216, 224–25, 268; in South Carolina, 102, 151–52; in Georgia, 250. *See also* Apportionment; Redistricting; Voting
Elections, congressional: in 1796–97, p. 13; in 1798–99, pp. 14, 247; in 1800–01, pp. 28–29, 80–81; in 1802–03, pp. 81–83, 251; in 1804–05, pp. 83–85; in 1806–07, p. 86; in 1808–09, pp. 94, 104–106, 216, 251–52; in 1810–11, pp. 131–33, 252; in 1812–13, pp. 165–67, 216; in 1814–15, pp. 168–73; in 1816–17, pp. 175–77; after 1817, p. 180
Elections, gubernatorial, 206*n*, 208, 218–21, 254
Elections, legislative: in South, 13, 80, 168, 175–77, 275; in Virginia, 24, 28,

287; in North Carolina, 149–51, 215–18; in South Carolina, 238–39; in Georgia, 250–52
Elections, presidential: of 1796, pp. 13, 248, 252; of 1800, pp. 16–35, 80, 215, 222–23, 376; of 1804, pp. 62–63, 83–84; of 1808, pp. 97–104, 260; of 1812, pp. 139–53, 260–61, 264, 376; of 1816, pp. 177–78; of 1824, pp. 191–93; of 1828, pp. 193–94
Elections, U.S. Senate, 206*n*, 221, 239, 254
Elizabeth City County, Va., 370
Elliott, John, 132, 181, 192, 251, 381
Elliott, Stephen, 327, 330–31, 347–48
Embargo Act of 1807, pp. 78, 95–96, 107, 121–22, 219–20, 260
Embargo of 1812, p. 135
Erskine, David M., 122–25, 128
Evans, Thomas, 24–25, 44, 89, 291
Exposition of Crawfordites, 178
Eyre, John, 171

F

Fairfax County, Va., 335
Farmers and planters in politics, 6*n*, 384–86
Fayetteville, N.C.: economy of, 5, 342, 344; politics in, 30, 77*n*, 84–86, 105, 132, 150, 166, 172, 180, 270–71, 373
Federalists in 1788, pp. 10, 13, 365–66
Federal population, 226, 385–86
Finance, public: in states, 8, 228–29; Federalist criticism of, 63–65, 67, 115–16; in War of 1812, pp. 137, 140, 156, 160–61; mentioned, 15, 122
Fischer, David H., 273–75, 389, 396
Florida, 70–71, 116, 183–84, 188–89
Foreign affairs and party politics, 12–13, 74, 90–91, 190, 379–80, 402
France: Federalists and, 14, 17, 21, 68, 71–74, 91, 97, 121, 128–29, 137, 146, 162–64, 221, 313, 401; and United States, 53, 56–60, 68, 72–73, 96, 116, 127, 131, 136
Franklin County, Ga., 252
Frederick County, Va., 155
Fredericksburg, Va., 77*n*. 336–39
French crisis, 14, 36, 53, 68, 86, 90, 108, 140–41, 215, 235, 247
French Revolution, 11–12, 365–66, 378–79, 393, 401
Fries Rebellion, 22
Fritz, Harry, 262
Frontier, 249, 307
Funding, 10

G

Gabriel Conspiracy, 319
Gales, Joseph. See *Raleigh Register*
Gallatin, Albert, 64–66, 116–17, 135, 137
Gaston, William: career of, 101, 132–33, 142, 166, 176, 182, 192, 223, 259, 262; on War of 1812, pp. 135, 161, 163, 174, 185, 333, 343; on postwar nationalism, 182, 184–85, 187; on banking, 185, 333, 343; on education, 322, 329
Genet, Edmond, 12, 90, 401
Geography, 3–4
Georgetown, S.C., 31, 83, 168–69, 348, 373, 377, 380
Georgia: elections in, 27–30, 81, 104–105, 132, 153, 165, 169–70, 175, 181, 192; Federalist strength in, 89–90, 181, 249–55, 364, 366, 373, 377–78, 381–82, 390–91, 400; party organization in, 249–50, 258, 271, 273; education in, 331; economic development in, 348, 351–53
Germans, 4, 397
Ghent, Treaty of, 170, 174
Gibbons, Thomas, 16, 253
Giles, William B., 125–26, 128, 199, 384
Glascock, Thomas, 251, 331
Glasgow, James, 26
Goode, Samuel, 37
Grand juries, 149, 177, 339, 351
Great Revival, 3, 392–94
Greenbrier County, Va., 204
Greene County, Ga., 252
Greenville district, S.C., 239
Griffin, Thomas, 59, 171, 265
Grimké, John F., 90, 351
Grove, William Barry, 16, 43, 47, 57, 163, 322, 345
Gunboats, 115–16
Gunn, James, 16, 27, 34, 38, 247

H

Habersham, Joseph, 89, 253
Halifax, N.C., 5, 34, 85, 150, 172, 218, 330, 343
Halifax County, Va., 100
Hall, Allmand, 282

Hamilton, Alexander: economic program of, 10–12, 91, 117, 237, 248, 332, 357; in 1800, pp. 17, 19, 27, 33; killed, 110; as party organizer, 260; mentioned, 3, 13, 17, 108, 112, 141, 183–86, 188–89, 215, 235, 365, 369, 379, 385
Hampshire County, Va., 136, 266, 339
Hanover County, Va., 267
Harper, Robert Goodloe, 37
Harrington, Henry W., 356
Harrison County, Va., 209–10
Hartford Convention, 160–62, 177
Hassell, William, 282–83
Henderson, Archibald: on domestic politics, 33, 35–36, 47–48, 109; career of, 142, 268–69; on courts, 231; and education, 323
Henry, Patrick, 10, 369
Hertford County, N.C., 231
Heth, William, 45
Hillsborough, N.C., 5, 101, 175, 218, 378
Hobby, William J., 250–53. *See also* Savannah *Columbia Museum*
Hodge, Abraham, 45, 282, 287, 351
Hopkins, John, 142–43
Huger, Benjamin: on domestic politics, 27, 36–37, 52–53, 62; career of, 83–84, 168–69, 175, 181, 240, 242, 246, 357; on postwar nationalism, 182–84, 186–87; on slavery, 314–15
Huger, Daniel Elliott, 193

I

Ideology, 37–38, 307–13, 321–22, 401–403
Immigration, 311–13, 378
Impeachment, 49–51
Impressment, 73, 136, 158, 164, 174
Index of cohesion, 300–301
Internal improvements, 183–84, 190, 300, 350–56
Iredell, James, Jr., 182, 193, 221–22
Iredell, James, Sr., 399
Irish, 4, 397
Izard, Ralph, 357

J

Jackson, Andrew, 183, 186–94, 264
Jackson, Francis James, 125–26, 128
Jackson, James, 248, 252–56, 384
Jackson, John G., 133, 167, 176
Jacobinism, 71, 164, 307, 312, 321
James City County, Va., 370
James River, Va., 354
Jay, John, 143, 369
Jay Treaty, 12–13, 91, 108, 235, 237, 248
Jefferson, Thomas: in 1796 election, 13, 235; in 1800 election, 17, 19, 23–35; Federalist attacks on, 18–22, 53, 63–67, 74, 115–16, 208, 312–13, 393; and patronage, 38, 43–46, 55, 118, 253; and domestic policy, 51, 62–63, 108, 110–15, 312–13; and foreign policy, 56–61, 69–71, 74–75, 78; popularity of, 81–82, 87–88, 237, 368; and Republican schisms, 98, 119–20; in 1808 election, 100; and embargo, 121–22; mentioned, 51, 68, 79–80, 90–91, 97, 120, 123, 130, 133, 146, 159, 163, 178–79, 184, 189, 199, 218–19, 222, 242, 249, 259, 287, 289, 307, 328, 346, 358, 369, 378, 384, 389, 393, 399
Jefferson County, Va., 266, 339
Johnston, James, 251
Johnston, Samuel, 89, 222, 322, 329, 351, 399
Jones, James, 249
Jones, John Paul, 212
Jones, Meriwether, 286–87
Jones, Seaborn, 250
Judiciary, state: Federalists in, 32, 207, 222, 240, 253–55; reform of, 209, 211–14, 219, 226, 229–32
Judiciary Act of 1801, pp. 35–37, 47–49, 55

K

Kanawha County, Va., 209–10
Kennedy, William, 166, 269
Kershaw district, S.C., 239
King, Rufus: in 1808 election, 98–101, 260; in 1812 election, 143, 146–47, 153, 202–203, 261, 376; in 1816 election, 177; mentioned, 385
King, William R., 132

L

Leadership, political, 273–74, 278, 322, 380, 384
Leander, 73

Lee, Henry, 16, 33, 36, 97, 146, 156
Legislatures, state: party politics in, 60, 203–208, 218–26, 239–42, 254–55, 286–303, 323–26, 334–46; and education, 323–31; and banking, 334–48; and internal improvements, 353–56. *See also* Elections
Leipzig, battle of, 163
Lewis, Joseph, Jr.: on domestic politics, 59, 78, 113, 315; on foreign affairs, 78, 127, 237; career of, 85–86, 133, 167, 171, 176
Lewis, Thomas, Jr., 59, 83
Lexington, Va., 5
Liberty County, Ga., 251
Lincoln County, Ga., 252
Livingston, Edward, 66–67
Livingston, Robert, 60
Loudoun County, Va., 34, 85, 133, 145, 167, 171, 208, 264, 328, 373
Louisiana Government Bill, 60–61, 67
Louisiana Purchase, 56–60, 67, 87
Lowndes, James, 272
Lowndes, Thomas: on domestic politics, 50, 53, 88, 314–15; career of, 83–85, 105, 240, 272
Loyalism, 369–72, 399–400
Lunenburg County, Va., 25
Lynchburg, Va., 337–39

M

McAllister, Matthew, 81, 254, 381
McBryde, Archibald, 117, 126, 131, 135, 142
McClurg, James, 333
McHenry, James, 23
McKay, James I., 182, 193
McMillan, Alexander, 176
McNeill, Archibald, 180
Macon, Nathaniel, 127, 173, 191, 259, 384
Macon's Bill, 126–27
Madison, James: and foreign affairs, 70, 121–24, 130–31, 134; in 1808 election, 97–103, 107, 202–203; Federalists and, 114–16, 123–25; and Republican schisms, 119–20; in 1812 election, 141–48, 151–53; in War of 1812, pp. 160–61; mentioned, 97, 120, 124, 128, 133, 146, 149–50, 162–63, 167, 176–77, 199, 237, 261, 358, 369, 384
Mangum, Willie P., 182, 192, 194
Manufacturing, 5–6, 186, 357–59
Marlborough district, S.C., 239
Marshall, John: career of, 16, 18, 28, 49, 143; on politics, 30, 34, 36, 38, 48, 99, 136, 139; in Burr trial, 111–13; and economic development, 335, 354; mentioned, 113, 146, 199
Martinsburg, Va., 5
Mass meetings, 76–77, 99–100, 155, 266–68, 270–71, 333
Maxcy, Jonathan, 327
Mazzei, Philip, 21–22
Mercer, Charles Fenton: career of, 145–46, 176, 180, 208; on Treaty of Ghent, 170; and postwar nationalism, 182–85, 189; and education, 328–29, 331; and economic development, 340–41, 354
Middlesex County, Va., 370
Military preparedness, 127–28, 134–35, 159–60, 215
Militia, 78, 118, 127, 135, 207, 240, 320
Milledge, John, 384
Monongalia Spectator, 182
Monroe, James: in diplomacy, 60, 75; in 1808 election, 97–103, 107, 144, 260, 263, 376; Federalists and, 144, 180, 208, 263; in 1816 election, 177–78; mentioned, 76, 182, 191, 384
Monroe County, Va., 209–10
Monroe-Pinkney Treaty, 75
Moore, Alfred, 182
Moscow, retreat from, 163
Munroe, John A., 396
Murphey, Archibald, 269

N

Napoleon Bonaparte: and Louisiana, 57–60; Federalist fear of, 71, 111, 121, 128–29, 136–37, 155–56, 160–64, 307; and American commerce, 71–73, 122, 129–31; and Florida, 71, 116; mentioned, 17, 68, 73–77, 97, 178–79, 309, 401–402
Nash, Frederick, 231
Nationalism, postwar, 183–89, 190–91
National origin: and religion, 4–5, 396; and politics, 30, 217, 396–400; and Loyalism, 371, 399
Naturalization Act, 313

Navy, 15, 45, 53, 78, 115–16, 127–28, 135, 159–60, 183
Neutrality Proclamation, 90
Newbern, N.C.: economy of, 5, 341–45; politics in, 25, 30, 77*n*, 132–33, 150, 166, 172, 176, 217, 221, 302, 374, 378; mentioned, 117, 135, 280, 330
Newbern *Herald*, 133
New England, 154–55, 161–62
New Hanover County, N.C., 371
New Haven letter, 44
New Kent County, Va., 77*n*
New Orleans, 56–59
New York, 18, 146
New York, N.Y., Federalist conventions in, 97–98, 142–43, 260
New York, Treaty of, 248
Noel, John Y., 254
Nonimportation Act, 75–76
Nonintercourse Act, 122, 126–27
Norfolk, Va.: economy of, 5, 96, 332–39; politics in, 29, 77*n*, 124, 200, 207, 258, 267, 370, 376, 378
Norfolk Gazette: on foreign affairs, 76–78, 122, 124, 156; on gunboats, 115–16; history of, 179–80, 285; on banking, 338
North Carolina: elections in, 25–30, 82–85, 100–101, 104–106, 132–33, 144, 148–51, 165–66, 172–76, 192–93, 270–71; Federalist strength in, 89–90, 181–82, 215–23, 364, 367–68, 371, 376–78, 381–83, 390–92, 399–400; party organization in, 166, 258, 268–71; public printing in, 287–90; slavery in, 316–19; education in, 322–26, 329–30; banking in, 341–46; economic development in, 351–59; ratification of Constitution in, 367; Loyalism in, 371, 399; sectionalism in, 373–74
North-Carolina Journal, 45, 229, 282, 315
North Carolina Minerva, 33–34, 38, 140
Northampton County, Va., 145
Northern Neck, 30, 176
Northwest in War of 1812, p. 140
Notes on Virginia, 393
Nott, Abraham, 37, 90, 181, 240, 327
Nottoway County, Va., 157

O

Orange County, N.C., 21, 77*n*, 149
Orange district, S.C., 239
Orders in Council, 123–24, 130, 140, 146, 156, 158
Otis, Harrison Gray, 23
Owen, James, 189

P

Pace and Nicholson, 286
Paine, Thomas, 65–67, 81, 393
Panic of 1819, p. 185
Parker, Josiah, 37
Partisanship: in legislatures, 8, 204–206, 218–26, 239–40, 253–55, 292–303; on national issues, 43–49, 55, 62–63, 184–86, 189–90, 262; in banking, 184–86, 332–49; and press, 277–83, 291; in education, 323–27, 330–31; in economic policy, 350, 354, 357–58
Party organization: national, 18, 22–23, 83, 97–98, 101, 141–43, 177, 191, 249, 259–62, 273, 279; in South, 23, 88–89, 257–59, 262, 275, 302; and press, 23, 179, 279–84; in Virginia, 23–24, 99–100, 106, 143–47, 167, 171, 191–92, 201–202, 209, 261–67; in North Carolina, 25, 29, 101, 133, 166, 219–20, 226, 268–71; in South Carolina, 26–27, 102, 152, 165, 271–73; in Georgia, 27, 249–50, 252, 255, 273
Pasler, Rudolph and Margaret, 396
Patronage: national, 39, 43–47, 55, 89–90, 118, 141, 179–82; state, 181–82, 205–206, 223, 236–40, 253–54; and press, 283, 286–90
Peace Ticket, N.C., 269
Pearson, Joseph: and Wilkinson, 114; on foreign affairs, 126, 131; career of, 132, 142–43, 166, 259; on War of 1812, pp. 137–38, 161; on tax reform, 233
Pensacola, Fla., 189
People's ticket, N.C., 193
Perry, Oliver Hazard, 159
Personal influence in politics, 83, 172, 201–202, 236–37, 252–55, 386–87
Petersburg, Va., 5, 76–77, 96, 336–39
Pettigrew, Ebenezer, 356
Peyton, Francis, 335
Philadelphia (ship), 69
Philadelphia convention of 1787, p. 9
Philo-Laos. *See* Randolph, John

Phocion. *See* Smith, William Loughton
Pickering, John, 49–50
Pickering, Timothy, 23, 385
Piedmont, 30, 147, 166, 200–201, 216, 370, 383, 398
Pinckney, Charles, 31, 236, 239, 384
Pinckney, Charles Cotesworth: in 1800 election, 16–18, 22–23, 27, 32, 34, 80, 259, 263; in 1804 election, 83; in 1808 election, 98–103, 107, 260, 264, 376; in 1812 election, 142–43; in state politics, 239, 273; in education, 327; in economic development, 351, 357; mentioned, 14, 30, 260, 331
Pinckney, Thomas, 16, 18, 27, 118, 327, 357
Pindall, James, 186
Pinkney, William, 75–76
Political parties, development of, 10–13
Polk, William, 89, 118, 192–93, 220, 269, 322, 345
Powell, Leven, 33, 35, 356
Press: and public opinion, 6, 278–79; in elections, 22, 84, 99, 142, 148–49, 178; in party organization, 23, 262–63, 267–68, 271, 279; distrust of, 37; strength of, 179, 275; in state politics, 209, 226–31, 241, 249, 255; and economic development, 352–53, 356
Prices, 87–88, 123, 134
Property, Federalists and, 311, 318
Public opinion: press and, 6–7, 277–79, 386–87; Federalists and, 67, 226–27, 236, 256, 261; on political issues, 68–69, 108, 210, 324
Pulaski, Casimir, 312
Purviance, Samuel D., 58–59
Putnam, General Rufus, 45

Q

Quasi-Federalists, 14
Quasi war. *See* French crisis

R

Raleigh, N.C., 150, 192, 220, 269, 280–82, 344
Raleigh *Minerva*: on domestic politics, 25, 38, 60, 63, 105–106, 116–17, 119; on foreign affairs, 75, 135, 155; in state politics, 148–49, 229, 231, 269, 302; on social issues, 309, 313, 329; on economic development, 352, 358. *See also* Boylan, William
Raleigh Register, 149, 281–82, 287–90
Raleigh *Star*, 150, 289–90
Randolph, John, 70, 110, 113–14, 119, 139, 171, 199, 208, 384
Read, Jacob, 16, 118, 273
Redistricting, 203–204, 225–26, 240–42
Religion: in South, 3–5, 396; as political issue, 21, 65–66, 392; and party alignment, 217, 307, 392–96; and society, 394; Federalists and, 401; mentioned, 67
Republican party: and foreign affairs, 12–13, 60, 68, 74, 76, 131; and federalists of 1788, p. 13; strength of, 18, 108–109, 378–79; on Washington, 37; on Twelfth Amendment, 61–63; and public finance, 63–65; in Virginia, 98–100, 199, 203, 208–11; and Burr trial, 112–13; and banking, 117–18, 342, 346–48; and patronage, 118; schisms in, 119–20, 208, 270–71; and War of 1812, pp. 134–35, 141–42, 159–60; in North Carolina, 148–50; and postwar nationalism, 186, 190; organization of, 258–59, 263, 275, 302; and public printing, 286–90; and education, 322–31; and economic development, 354, 358; Baptists and, 394
Rhetoric, Federalist, 22, 54, 67, 81–82
Rice, Stuart Arthur, 300
Richland district, S.C., 378
Richmond, Va.: economy of, 5, 96, 333–39, 352, 358; politics in, 24, 28–29, 77*n*, 99–100, 106, 111–12, 124, 200, 258, 267, 376, 378; mentioned, 142, 157, 263, 328–29
Richmond County, Ga., 249–51, 355, 377
Rockbridge County, Va., 105, 155
Rockingham County, N.C., 173
Roll call analysis, 292–95, 299–301
Rowan County, N.C., 227–28
Rutledge, Frederick, 327
Rutledge, Hugh, 327
Rutledge, John, Jr.: career of, 16, 18, 83, 97–98, 239–40, 242, 259–62, 291; on domestic politics, 20, 33, 44; on foreign

affairs, 59, 72–73, 77; in 1812 election, 142, 153, 165, 272
Rutledge, John, Sr., 237

S

St. Matthew's Parish, S.C., 239
St. Michael's Parish, S.C., 238
St. Thomas and St. Denis Parish, S.C., 237
Salisbury, N.C.: economy of, 5, 344; politics in, 30, 132, 166, 225, 270–71, 374, 378; mentioned, 33, 106, 268, 329
Savannah, Ga.: economy of, 5, 53, 332, 348; politics in, 27, 77*n*, 157, 169–70, 249–50, 253, 258, 271, 273, 377–78; mentioned, 16, 45, 104, 137
Savannah *American Patriot*, 137
Savannah *Columbian Museum*, 57, 179, 249, 273, 331, 255–56, 280, 282
Savannah River, 255, 352, 373, 381, 391
Schley, William, 193
Scotch-Irish, 4, 397
Scots, 4, 217, 397
Seamen's bill, 158
Sectionalism: in South, 190, 311, 318, 368–69, 372–74; in Virginia, 209–14; in North Carolina, 216, 226–28; in South Carolina, 237–39, 244–45; in Georgia, 252–55; in legislatures, 301–302; and banking, 342–43; and economic development, 350, 353–56
Shenandoah Valley, 30, 34, 145, 167, 171, 208, 212, 258, 301, 383, 398
Simons, James, 89
Slavery, 299, 313–20
Slocumb, Jesse, 176
Smith, Major, of Virginia, 265
Smith, Robert, 119
Smith, Thomas Rhett, 85, 169, 327
Smith, William Loughton, 74, 272
Social structure and politics, 6, 8–9, 152, 238, 243–44, 378–89, 384–85
Society, Federalist view of, 308–10, 318–19, 321–22, 394, 401
South Carolina: elections in, 18–19, 26–27, 29–31, 83–85, 101–105, 132, 151–53, 165, 168–69, 175, 192, 272; party organization in, 26, 102, 165, 271–73; Federalist strength in, 89–90, 181, 235–40, 364–68, 371–73, 377–81, 390–91, 400; sectionalism in, 237–39, 244–45, 373; suffrage in, 311; education in, 326–27, 330–31; banking in, 346–48; economic development in, 351–59; Loyalism in, 371–72
South-Carolina State-Gazette, 33–34, 283
Spain, relations with, 56, 59, 69–71, 113–14, 188–89
Specie payments, resumption of, 340
Stanford, Richard, 173, 175, 269
Stanly, John: on domestic politics, 52–53, 117; on foreign affairs, 126, 135; career of, 142, 182, 192–93, 221, 290, 358
States, admission of, 183–84
Staunton, Va.: economy of, 5, 352; politics in, 77*n*, 133; Federalist conventions in, 99–100, 144–47, 264; mentioned, 129, 328
Staunton *Political Censor*, 313
Staunton *Republican Farmer*, 145, 356
Steele, John: on domestic politics, 34, 58, 91, 106; career of, 89, 223; on state issues, 230–31, 233; and education, 329; and agriculture, 356
Stephens, William, 66, 253
Stephenson, James, 59, 127, 139, 266
Stokes, Montfort, 232
Stratton, John, 82
Swoope, Jacob, 125–26, 131

T

Taliaferro, Benjamin, 249
Tarboro, N.C., 344
Tariff, protective, 183, 186–87, 190, 237
Tate, Magnus, 171, 176, 266
Taxation: state, 8, 212, 226, 232–34, 300; in 1800 election, 15, 20; direct tax, 15, 26, 87, 183–84, 187, 385–86; internal taxes, 51–53; in War of 1812, pp. 135, 140, 156, 174
Taylor, Allen, 208
Taylor, John, of Caroline, 147, 356
Taylor, John Louis, 322
Taylor, Robert B., 118, 207, 267
Tidewater, 3, 30, 147, 200–201, 364, 370, 381–83
Toryism. *See* Loyalism
Towns: economy of, 5, 96, 124; Federalists in, 30, 199–200, 249

Tripoli. *See* Barbary War
Turner, James, 232

U

Upshur, Abel Parker, 328

V

Van Alen, Peter L., 254
Vanderhorst, Arnoldus, 327
Virginia: party organization in, 23–24, 99–100, 144–46, 258, 263–67; elections in, 23–25, 28–30, 83, 85–86, 98–100, 103–104, 106, 133, 143–48, 166–67, 170–72, 176–77, 191–93, 263–64, 267; Federalist strength in, 89–90, 181, 200–207, 363, 367–70, 372–73, 376–78, 383–84, 390–92; public printing in, 286–87; suffrage in, 311; slavery in, 316–19; education in, 327–28; banking in, 334–41; economic development in, 351–59; Loyalism in, 370–71; sectionalism in, 372–73
Virginia and Kentucky Resolutions, 247
Virginia Federalist, 20
Virginia Gazette: on domestic politics, 66, 83–84, 99, 123; on foreign affairs, 72, 78
Virginia Patriot: on foreign affairs, 129, 159, 161; on domestic politics, 177–78, 205; problems of, 285–86; on immigration bill, 311; on banking, 333, 339; on economic development, 352, 356
Voting: methods of, 7, 83*n*, 200; qualifications for, 7, 152, 242–44, 311, 382

W

Wake County, N.C., 358
Walton, George, 254, 351
Ward, Henry Dana, 327
Ward, John, 240, 296, 327
War Hawks, 135, 137
War of 1812: as political issue, 139–42, 159–60, 165, 168, 173, 216; Federalist attitude toward, 154–56
Warren Junto, 222
Warwick County, Va., 370
Washington, Bushrod, 142–43
Washington, George: presidency of, 12–13; as Federalist campaign issue, 20–22, 65, 82, 102; Federalist veneration of, 37–38; and internal improvements, 351; mentioned, 63, 66–67, 69, 77, 81, 87, 98, 115–17, 123, 183, 199, 249, 287, 310, 369, 390
Washington, William, 327
Washington (D.C.) *Federalist*, 260
Wateree River, 371
Welter, Rush, 321
Westmoreland County, Va., 77*n*
Whig party, 194–95
Whiskey Rebellion, 22, 66
White, Francis, 266
Wickham, John, 112
Wilkes County, Ga., 252
Wilkinson, James, 110, 113–15, 208
Williams, Benjamin, 216, 218–20
Williamsburg, Va., 34, 157
Wilmington, N.C., 5, 30, 76–77, 108*n*, 341–44, 378
Wilmington Gazette, 116, 149, 159, 179, 282–83
Winchester, Va., 337–39
Wohlhopter, Philip, 179
Wright, Joshua G., 231

X

XYZ Affair, 14, 90

Y

Yazoo land frauds, 248